Gary Govich

CAREER CRIMINAL
The Code of The Streets

10th Anniversary Edition

CAREER CRIMINAL

THE CODE OF THE STREETS

EDITED BY MELISSA OGG
COVER DESIGN BY ORIGINAL BOOK COVER DESIGNS

In Memory Of

John Vanden Huevel

FOREWORD

BY JOE MENSCH

I heard about this eccentric Russian neighborhood with a sordid criminal past. The stories sounded almost comical cartoonish even. Finally, I had to go see it for myself. So I took the Q Train to the southern edge of Brooklyn, arriving at the last stop, Brighton Beach.

Walking down the long two-story staircase that led onto the street I started to feel an ominous almost imposing presence.

I navigated my way through narrow streets under the overhead L train. The air was thick with smoke coming up from the manhole covers and Cyrillic signs hung on all the shops. Russian pop songs blared from a steady of passing cars.

That was an eerie darkness that loomed over the entire place. I couldn't make out what it was, like there was some sinister to this place buried right beneath the surface.

I took a side street and as I passed through dated architecture on the close together apartment houses, old blue-haired ladies in fake fur and heavy makeup gossiped on lawn chairs. I finally arrived at Tatiana restaurant on the boardwalk sat down and ordered some pierogis.

A group of young guys wearing track suits and bright neck medallions sat down near me. In Russian, they ordered a magnum of vodka, which arrived in a big brass bucket, filled with ice. No food, just the bottle. They sat there for a while, not saying much.

Soon the magnum was empty.

One look at these young men, mostly in their twenties, and you could tell that they weren't your ordinary nine-fivers.

I continued to eat and within a few more moments 3 or 4 older men in European suits, John Gotti types wearing neckties and gold watches, walked up the steps and onto the boardwalk.

In passing, they caught the attention of one of the young men beside me. Their pace slowed. One of the hardened youngsters, the one nearest my position stood up from his seat. At this point the tension was thick enough for me to know that at any moment I could be looking at violence or possibly worse.

As the Gotti look-alikes slowed their walk down even further, their contemptuous stare never left that of the young Russians who finally mumbled something and sat back down.

Finally, with the men out of frame, in unison, one of the track suit younger men lifted his glass and barked out a few Russian words, the rest if the young men repeated the same set of words, and in unison, they all drank deeply from their glasses.

I got the check.

Walking back to the subway, I couldn't help but think back to the stories that just a few hours ago sounded like exaggerated make-believe might in fact some validity.

I went home, typed in "Russian Mafia Brighton Beach," and ordered the first ten books that popped up. They all looked like journalistic accounts of police proceedings. I didn't look too closely, just hit "purchase." The books all arrived in the same box a few days later. One of them had a striking cover, a white graphic of a man's face and under it, two hands holding pistols. The title was Career Criminal: My Life In The Russian Mafia Until The Day I Died. By Gary "Gunz" Govich.

I decided to start there.

Turns out, this was not journalism, but a memoir. A rough-edged, self-published, confessional account of a guy who had started with nothing, pulled himself up through the Russian underworld and lived to tell the tale.

It was bombastic and vainglorious but underneath it all was a deep sense of regret and tragedy.

I should mention at this point that I was looking for a subject for my first movie, which I knew had to be a crime drama. And about halfway through I knew. You know how you just know something and nothing or nobody would be able to convince you that what you know... you don't really know. It was was one of those kinds of "I know."

The book revealed a fresh angle on gangsters themselves: white collar criminals, trained on the streets and now situated in Wall Street offices.

I finished the book in two days and set about finding the author.

Since it was self-published, there were no official channels. I dug around online and found an interview with the author conducted by another author, Thomas Drinkard, for his blog. I wrote to Mr. Drinkard, expressing my interest in making a movie and asked for Mr. Govich's contact info.

Mr. Drinkard did the exact same thing I would have done. He refused. He insisted that it wasn't his place to reveal someone's personal information. Moreover, he pointed out, I had no credentials except a short film.

I wrote back, this time I was determined to get at Mr.Govich. I had to make this man understand that *"I knew."* My goal wasn't to invade the privacy of a hardened gangster. I needed to make this movie, *my movie*. I nattered on for pages about my vision for the film, he either shared in my vision, or he understood that I wasn't going away.

Finally, he relented.

I sat down and wrote a short screenplay, ten pages long, adapted from a scene in the book. Then I wrote a long letter, introducing myself and explaining my intentions for the film. I emailed the letter, the screenplay, and a link to my short film, to Mr. Govich.

A week went by with no reply. Then:

Ok...

You got me to read it.... That's more than I can say for most of the people that have contacted me. I enjoyed your short film, Not bad work.....but are you really ready for something like this. Think about the ramifications for yourself and your family...before we even talk further I want you to think long and hard about taking on a project like this. This is no fairy tale... I carry a firearm with me at all times, I live in a place where that is ordinary... You live in a place where only the bad guys get to carry.

I enjoyed your adaptation as well.

I might be interested | Ask yourself if YOU really are.

Let me pray on it a few days.

GG

And that's how all this shit got started.

Enjoy the 10th Anniversary edition of Career Criminal.

- Joe

P.S. Making this son of a bitch wasn't a walk in the park. It took four years, and numerous setbacks. Putting together the right cast, production teams... and in the end the real issue is money. Pulling a few million dollars from out of the ether requires sacrifice, commitment, and a level of determination that is equivalent to that of climbing to the peak of mount Everest. But I knew that this was going to happen as soon as I put that book down. I tell you this not to pat myself on the back. Nothing worthwhile ever comes easy. Anything is possible in this world. And when you know, don't ever let anyone tell you otherwise. My sincere hope is that you enjoy the adaptation as much I enjoyed making it for you. Thank you for believing in all of us and allowing us your very important moments to share in our passion.

From the movie "Payback" 2021 — 2ofaKind.

CONTENTS

PART 1

ОДЕССА МАМА

✳✳✳

PROFESSIONAL BAD GUY

Ima teach you a couple of things
   How a gangster thinks
   How a hustler slings
   How a Russian drinks
   How we pull them strings
   Push them things
   Buy them minks
   Cha-cha-cha-ching
   -Anonymous

THE BIG SCORE.
   You know what I'm talking about.
   The final score, the heist, that one shiest that puts you over the top — *That last swindle that enables you to go legit and leave The-Life forever.*

It's different for everyone.
The amount that is.

For the small-time conman-criminal, it could be a few hundred thousand or perhaps a million. For the true professional, I'm talking about someone who's risen above and beyond the call of streets—*for him*, it's more than the cream. It goes beyond stacks of green paper with pictures of presidents that's dead.

That man needs legendary status.
He needs his name to rings bells from Brighton to Tokyo.

A WISE MAN ONCE DECODED IT FOR ME;
The money—it's just a *piece* of it.
It's success we covet.
Money comes with success — and Power.
And the freedom to do whatever-the-fuck you want.
Whenever you want to do it.

IT'S QUITE INTOXICATING, THE EMBRACE OF SUCCESS.
It fills you better than a Peter Luger 14oz porterhouse.
It's sexier than an AM Vanquish.
It compels people of influence into its orbit
Women *compromise themselves just to be in its presence.*
There's an aura that surrounds you once you've achieved that level of respect and notoriety.

HERE'S THE THING.
When you do great things, the whole street knows about it, and you're a player—*a shot-caller*—a force to be taken seriously.

In turn, people of substance are drawn to you.
Substantial people are drawn to individuals of substance.
Birds of a feather ...

You can always count on high-status people, palling around with high-ranking members of the underworld. That's provided they're masters of their trade and have achieved the same level of notoriety in the dark as their successful counterparts achieved in the light.

Musicians—*especially*—Love the dark allure of the world below. They sing about how properly they sling and how strong their "gangsta" is.

Truth be told.
Most of 'em tremble at the sight of a 4|5 automatic.

It's always been entertaining to watch these so-called gangster-rappers prance around—*dressed up like circus clowns*—acting like "people" outta fear them. In reality, these are the same cowards who cry like children when faced with the prospect of getting a taste of the violence they preach.

Don't get it twisted; some are the truth. But, of course, there are exceptions to every rule. For the most part these rappers are soft like a Twinkie filling. They write songs about a lifestyle they've only lived through fantasy. If they choose, they won't put themselves in compromising positions. Why else would they leave the hood after they get a taste of the paper.

ME | I come up under a different code.
I'm talkin' bout cockback-squeeze-reload.
++||— *Not some stories told* —

THE WINTER OF '99.

My *brigada* rented a three-hundred-foot yacht out of Sheepshead Bay to commemorate the 25th birthday of the younger brother to an Italian "friend" of ours. There was plenty of alcohol, stash and sleazy woman allocated for the event.

The only thing missing was entertainment.

A younger associate, Fred "Lover," suggested we hire some rappers for the affair. My *brigada* fancied rap music. It was a close depiction of the daily grind of life | *For us, anyway.*

I DIALED MY ASSISTANT LUCY.

An attractive twenty-two-year-old female with straight, jet-black hair, dark complexion and a real pretty mouth. At 5'1- 110 pounds, she was a catch for any young gangster.

Lucy dressed like a supermodel.
She could afford it — I paid her handsomely.

Her only flaw was a pair of freaky looking googly eyes. They only got that way when she was stressed or when she had business with the white-lady.

A Rattlesnake ++||— She was *ColdasIce* —

She'd just as soon laugh with you as she'd poke you with her jigger — She loved the lifestyle more than most men I knew.

Because of her petite figure and sexy demeanor, even the most ruthless of the brotherhood underestimated her.

Slavic criminals truly consider women the weaker sex.

Americans have it backwards | It isn't the man who thinks with his small head. In European culture, it's the woman, thinking with her "sweet-spot".

What harm could a woman cause?
Especially a 110-pound one.

Those who thought like that never met the black 3|8 Taurus she carried in her purse, or the Gerber easy-open installed in her stocking.

I TOLD LUCY TO CONTACT THE AGENT FOR A HIGHLY ADMIRED GROUP OF rappers. At the time they were top of the charts.

It's fairly easy to book an appearance by any act you want to see. The only requirement being that you bring the cream. Any one of your favorite movie stars or performers will appear at your son's Bar-Mitzvah for the right price.

Don't believe me —|— Go ask Justin Timberlake.

In ten minutes, Lucy hit me back on the cell—*she had the agent on hold for me*—fifteen minutes later, I booked the act for 12,000$. Lucy told the rappers about the event and the "people" attending. The group seized the opportunity to socialize with the crux of the New York underworld.

PARTY NIGHT.

As primary host and benefactor, I arrived early to ensure all went according to plan. Unsurprisingly, most of the females and all the alcohol and narcotics were right where they needed to be.

I grabbed a bottle of Georgi and sparked a Cohiba.

The boat was looking real clean.

About two hours later, twenty-eight of us would be out in the open ocean enjoying the fruits of our thug-life. After the guests arrived, the rappers showed up in their signature Suburban 1500's. Rims spinning and flossing-grills. We set sail for what promised to be a memorable evening.

The passengers read like a who's-who of the mob.

From soldier to crime boss to captain, Russians and Italians alike gathered to enjoy a fine time, get lifted, fuck sleazy woman and hash out the next criminal venture. We got about three miles from shore and the music kicked the party into full-tilt.

The rappers had a grand time. They knew what they were getting into. They brought their own entourage, dope and sleazy women.

2AM, A SMALL COMMOTION BROKE OUT ON THE DECK.

By that time, I was feeling right — For me, that usually involved at least a half-gallon of Georgi and large baggie of fishscale.

Stumbling and numb from GeorgiVodka and cocaine, I staggered to the center of the ruckus. I discovered one of my soldiers, Roma, getting tossed around by a few of the rappers.

Roma was new to the game.
We hadn't even given him a nickname.

He was an ordinary youngblood I'd met during one of my drunken adventures, who'd spared me the fate of being blasted in the face with a very large-caliber weapon. I felt like I owed him.

I decided to share my way of life with him.

Unfortunately, he was still soft around the edges.

It appeared Roma had approached one of the rappers to tell him that he sounded much better on his record than in person. Here were these bulky black gentlemen pushing around little 5'6, 160-pound Roma.

I WAS DRESSED IN A DARK BLACK ARMANI COSTUME.

I got it on Delancey from a Russian named Shnuroyk (Shoelace). He owned a shop and owed me some paper. It was probably a fake, but it intimidated real enough.

September in Brooklyn gets chilly, on the ocean it's about fifteen to thirty degrees colder. I was bundled up in a black full-length wool overcoat — Jerry Albania and Sammy Movemaker saw me throw off my coat and reach into the back of my pants.

They knew it was showtime.

JERRY ALBANIA WAS 5'9 AND 230 POUNDS.

A heavy-set fellow with thick black wavy hair, dark haunting eyes, and a fair complexion. Jerry was about as heartless as they came—*he never tried to hide his mean side*—He dressed, acted, and carried himself like the genuine article. Jerry was Albanian hence the name "Albania" that he wore for his *kliytchka* (nickname).

++||— Albanians are a merciless lot —

They'll kill you for a buffalo nickel and enjoy a gyro while your body rots. A while back, my superiors had me tutor Jerry on the nuances of criminal life. It was immediately obvious that he had a great deal of talent and a true love of the trade.

He worked hard to realize the knowledge I gifted him.

Once his education was complete he far surpassed any expectations I'd had for him. Jerry put together quite a crew of his own and was no force to be trifled with. The name he established on the street was fast to rival even my own. But he never forgot the bond we developed those eighteen months we spent together.

Jerry Albania was no criminal mastermind, but he was far more than your ordinary trigger man — I knew Jerry had my back on any move I made.

SAMMY MOVEMAKER WAS A JOKER.

A shameless cocaine addict and generally unreliable — He stood

6'1 at 170 pounds, more tracks than chinamen commissioned for the Union Pacific could lay in a year's time ran up both of his forearms into the veiny areas of his neck.

He was the cousin of a godfather.

In fact, he was the first cousin blood relation of my employer.

Sammy liked to be called "Movemaker" because he fancied himself a top criminal. He had somehow con(vinced) himself that he was balls2THEwall making power moves, you know, writing huge tickets for chop-stock, flipping birds of coke, slangin' and hustling like grown folk do. We mockingly called him "MoveFaker" Sammy wasn't making moves | He was *faking them*.

After my success training Jerry, his cousin entrusted me to make a proper lawbreaker out of Sammy—*My best efforts proved worthless*. He just didn't have the Jacobs to exist on the streets.

What he had *was a godfather for a cousin*.

That earned him some points with the crew.

I kept him around, hoping he'd someday prove himself worthy of being in the company he kept.

Back to the boat:

Roma was taking quite the beating. By the time I got over to the action, he was on the floor being kicked by two entertainers. There were about sixteen in their group, most of them stood around just laughing at how bad Roma was getting beat.

Jerry snatched one of their bigger associates and backhanded him before throwing him off the boat.

Sammy squared off with two savage looking rappers.

A few soldiers who saw the fracas moved towards the hot-zone. We couldn't allow those sideshows to trample one of our own. The dope must've made them delusional. They must've forgotten where they were.

I DIDN'T HESITATE TO PULL ACE FROM THE BACK OF MY PANTS.

He was always at the ready.

Every single person on the cruise had been frisked before being allowed entry. This included the artists, who surprisingly didn't come with any firearms. After all, a bunch of drunken criminals in the middle of the ocean, each carrying a small arsenal could only result in mishap | *This was supposed to be a Birthday not a Deathday.*

There were only two blasters allowed on this vessel
Mine was one of them.

Ace | Was a black 9mm Browning BDM with a high capacity magazine. With one in the hole, he was able to resolve fourteen potential problems — I preferred Browning because of their small grips.

I racked the slide and installed a slug in the chamber, then fired a round in the air for effect. Two more band members were already overboard. After hearing the gunshot one of those two jumped. The other was thrown by Mark "La-Onda" a tall lanky fellow who kept close with Movefaker—*Unlike Faker*—Mark was to be taken a bit more seriously.

I pointed Ace at the most menacing of the group.

He'd starred in a couple picture shows and was by far the most venerated. By that time, reality sank in for the musicians, and they were willing to do just about whatever to spare their lives.

I told them all to jump.

They gawked at me, as though they'd collectively just choked on chicken bones.

THE BROTHER OF THE FELLOW WHOSE PARTY IT WAS A NAMELESS MAN.

A gentleman I like to refer to as "George" pulled out the other blaster. He was a made man in the Gambino crime family.

Short and stocky with tattoos covering his left arm, he'd been on the lam for more than two years, dodging a murder beef the feds were trying to dress him in. He fired a shot in the water to alert them to the fact that if they were to move back towards the boat | That would be the very last move they made in this world.

I grabbed the ass end of my burner.

Quickly running up on "12-Chains" I busted him square across the cheek. Purple blood spurt out the side and ran down his face.

Gripped in fear.
He smelled like urine.

"The man told you jump. Now get the fuck in the water," Jerry exclaimed. OneXOne — They jumped overboard.

Some of the oldtimers burst into laughter.

It was pitch-darkness at our distance from shore.

We had the attendants lower two of the four small rowboats they kept on the yacht in case of emergency—*Way I figured*—for the group freezing in the ocean—that would be such an occasion.

THE GAMBINO BUTTON-MAN EMPTIED HIS CLIP INTO THE OCEAN.

I could make out a faint grin on his chapped lips.

He was higher than Buzz Aldrin on his Apollo11 moon mission. Someone yelled, "Brooklyn's that way," and I relaxed a bit.

Everyone was still laughing.

I reunited with my bottle of Georgi, almost empty, I took the last swig then sat down next to Roma. Still clutching Ace, I wrapped my arm around Roma.

THAT INCIDENT WAS ONE OF ONLY THREE TIMES WHERE I DREW MY PISTOL AND DEATH DIDN'T COME TO COLLECT.

Why not murder those fools then grind them up for shark food right then and there? That would have been the more desirable course of action.

Disrespect one of our associates and face the penalty.
— ✳ — *This was* OUR CREED — ✳ —

There should've been corpses floating that cold September eve. It was the perfect place to do it, in the middle of the ocean where gunfire goes unheard and chopped up limbs and torsos would be unlikely to survive the sharks long enough to float onto some beach weeks or months later. Sure, and while we're at it let's just snuff out the staff on the boat too.

Right... and Slick Willy smoked —||— But he *never* inhaled.

This is the real world and you can't just kill anyone you want to. *Well, you can,* but most likely you'd end up in prison or death row.

Those were high-profile people paddling back to shore.

There, too, was the fact that their whereabouts were known by more than one outside party, such as the agent who booked the gig, not to mention the boat full of civilians who were quite shaken—for them, dock couldn't come fast enough.

We'd struck them harder than they struck us.

Their humiliation was far worse than ours.

And what of the cold as steel gangsta rappers? Those same ones who pissed themselves and were quick to run for their lives.

What of their retaliation? Surely it would come hard and swift.

IT WAS NO SECRET WHERE TO FIND US.

Right there in good old Brighton Beach, sipping warm vodka from porcelain teacups. That was a quarrel they did not need.

It was one they knew they could never win.

> Beat us with a bat and we come back with jiggers.
> Stick us with a knife and we bring the heaters.
> Plug *one of us* | And you'd better murder *us all*.

We were the authentic spectacle.

The fact they left with their lives intact, no bones broken, or a limb missing — was miracle enough.

* * *

ON THE DAY I WAS BORN.

The nurses *didn't* all gather round to gaze at the wide wonder at the boy they had found. The head nurse *didn't* speak up and say leave this one alone. There certainly wasn't a six-shooter wrapped around my hip when I came out the womb.

Mama breast fed me, I was coddled and nurtured to love life and treat others with respect and kindness.

When I was four years old, I looked at Mr. Rodgers, he was my hero. I was just like every other American kid out there.

We all are † Until we're not.

Fast forward ten years and the world has a way of reimagining your dreams into someone else's nightmares.

++||— CRIME BECAME MY CAREER —
I considered myself a craftsman | a True Professional.

Everybody has a craft.

Clean or dirty, safe or dangerous — We all have a part to play in the enigma of our world.

A professional is a person who earns money practicing their craft. Having labored many years and becoming experienced in a particular skill, you learn the gradations and eventually reach the title of master.

Every tradesman needs a tool.
A carpenter needs his hammer.
An electrician needs his cutters.
A brain surgeon needs his scalpel.
A poker player needs a deck of cards.
The same way a smuggler needs corrupt customs officials.

You just can't work without tools.

The dedicated *master* professional requires the finest tools money can buy—*the purpose is two-fold*—They're not only a finer quality, allowing for better performance, but they act as a status quo for all to recognize them as experts of their art.

PICTURE THIS:

You've been experiencing chest pains for over a month | You suspect it may be your heart. Your coworkers recommend a cardiologist so you go ahead and schedule an appointment.

Upon entering his cabinet, the doctor arrives wearing coffee-stained scrubs, equipped with what looks to be a thirty-year-old stethoscope that's practically falling to ruins. His office comes across old and uncared for. The certifications that hang on his wall are dusty and wrinkled. Would you still trust that man to make the proper diagnosis? *No need to answer that.* That quack of a doctor wouldn't have the right tools for the job, or at least he wouldn't appear to.

And in modern day America | Appearance *means everything.*

A criminal has tools as well.
Those tools — Fear, Deception, and Treachery.

A professional criminal is a chameleon.
They can be anything—*they can become anyone*—Provided that identity churns out a profit.

Through experience I've concluded that most people have a propensity for crime, even if only in small ways. We either do it for the thrill or because it makes us feel better than the rest.

There is the rare exception of an honest man in this dishonest world — Such a man or woman has obviously found it necessary to go into reclusion. I've heard of sightings of this elusive creature, but until I see them with my own eyes—*like the Sasquatch*—they will remain something of a myth.

If we're all criminals:
Then the overwhelming majority of us are amateurs.

While the layman sees an opportunity and decides to take it, the professional criminal is able to *create* opportunities.

This individual not only actively searches for a crime to commit, the professional criminal assembles teams of similar people and generates situations in which crime can be safely perpetrated in a controlled environment for maximum profit.

SO HOW DO YOU JOIN A CRIMINAL SOCIETY SUCH AS THE *MAFIYA*?

Can an Italian male just walk out his apartment into the street and say—"*I think I'll become a mobster today*"—go get himself a pinstripe suit, a gold pinky ring and a .38special then stroll into

Sparks Steakhouse, sit down with the *Paiyzons'*[1] and order a cup of cappuccino | He could, *but it wouldn't make him a mobster.*

In fact, Ginzo Anthony, you know, the mook with meat-hook fingers, would escort him to the dumpster and physically persuade him to never return.

In the same respect.

A Russian youngblood can't put on a velour warm-up and platinum Rolex then prance into Café Arbat, have a seat amongst the *Bratva*[2] and sip warm vodka from a white porcelain teacup.

If one could muster up the courage to do this—*I would praise his efforts*—Although I imagine the outcome would involve becoming severely intoxicated, losing said Rolex along with any and all portable wealth | And perhaps even his life.

The *Mafiya*||Mafia is not only an exclusive brotherhood.
It's a multi-billion-dollar business.
You can't just prance into something like that.

* * *

IMAGINE JOE NOBODY.

Picture him casually walking into the board room of Superior Energy during their quarterly earnings meeting, pulling up a chair, picking up a dossier than putting his feet up on the conference table and proclaiming himself the new VP of Kanuter valves—The Harvard-tie wearing blue-bloods would shit themselves a pumpkin.

Captains of business such as these hire from within. It's the old boys club and to become a member you've got to be plugged in.

For those who believe there's no such thing as the *Mafiya*:

I would be more than happy to sell you your own fast lane on the Belt Parkway, you know, so you can avoid the rush hour commute.

The *Mafiya*||Mafia is like cancer of the dick | Its gonna hit you hardest in places where it hurts the most.

You think to yourself "That's not a thing, *That can't be real.*"
By the time you figure it out | It's already 2Late

Organized crime has been steadily growing in power since its inception in the 1920s. Italian Organized crime doesn't operate in the open anymore. Former mayor Rudy made sure of that. It lost much of its power, being replaced by the more contemporary and versatile Russian Mob, which has expanded its business interests into territory undreamed of by the Italians. Italians and the Russians have been working together—from the jump off.

Joining the *mafiya.*

It's just like joining like any Fortune 500 conglomerate.
You've got to have the proper credentials and there needs to be an open position. The latter happens often, seeing as how mobsters are devoted to killing one another, getting thrown in prison for RICO charges or for just plain stupidity. There is a position in organized crime for all sorts of talent.

From the Street-Thug to the sophisticated Con-Man.
From the Accountant to the Assassin | *Everyone's invited.*

If you fancy yourself StoneCold||Steve.
Go right now and get straight to Thuggin.

Go do you some DIRT.
Do you some proper JackMoves.
Get you a few JumpOuts.
Slang you a few nice rocks.
Chop you up a few good stocks.

Show the street that your G goes hard, and you will discover for yourself — There is no need to seek out the *mafiya* to become a member. If organized crime deems you an earner[3], you can count on a summons being issued by one if not multiple crime families.

These people have their hands in every dirty till in the city.

If you qualify and are deemed trustworthy, An interview will be scheduled for you to begin work as a professional bad guy under the blanket of a criminal brotherhood (AKA the *mafiya*||mafia).

FEAR IS THE PRIMARY TOOL OF THE *MAFIYA*.

It's how they maintain their vast criminal enterprise.

For the *mafiya*—fear greases the wheel.

Fear is much stronger than love—it lasts much longer.

Love fades and contempt takes its place.

Fear lingers and brings forth other emotions, like doubt.

Fear encourages procrastination and cowardice.

Besides | *You always hurt the ones you love.*

Most are too afraid to hurt the ones they fear.

For control purposes | Distrust and envy are used internally as well.

Distrust is stronger than trust

Envy is stronger than adoration, respect or admiration.

It's this fear the organized criminal element preys on.

It's the high-school-bully principle applied to adult life. A bully picks on the runt of the litter, because he knows that runt can't hurt him back. If the day comes that the runt does hurt the bully, even if in a minute way, the bully will leave him alone and move on to someone weaker. After all | There are plenty of other kids who won't hit back.

* * *

I WAS SIXTEEN YEARS-OLD.

When first exposed to Russian organized crime.
Since then, I've been a thief, con-artist and enforcer of policy.

Ultimately—*A Murderer.*

From the ages of sixteen to twenty-nine, crime paid my bills.
I achieved the reputation of key earner and created some of the most lucrative money-making schemes in Russian *mafiya* history.
I put together one of the most infamous *brigadas* to ever walk the streets of Brighton Beach and reached the rank of "Bratan" (captain) in perhaps one of the most notorious criminal organizations in modern history.

I'm not patting myself on the back | *It's just fact.*

I've had occasion recently, to ponder my reasoning for leading this lifestyle—*initially it was for the money*—But as time passed and my influence grew, it became obvious I was remarkably skilled at what I did. Then it became about the acclaim and appreciation of my peers. Much later, I did what I did because I couldn't do anything else. It was how I put the shoes on my feet.

And my feet were used to Ferragamo's.

It was the pursuit of my next pair of 800$ Italian loafers that led me to Salt Lake City.

I WAS AFTER THAT NEXT BIG SCORE.
For me — It would be the final one.

I'd been there more than a half-dozen times, procuring items, hauling them back to Brooklyn for a 1000% profit. It was a no-lose situation —||— Lay out $10,000 and bring home 100 rocks.
It was a hazardous proposition.
But for me, just walking out my Brooklyn condo was a hazard.

That particular felony was very sophisticated and not for your conventional villain. It usually took two or three months to complete. 90,000$ for three months work sounds about right.

SLC had been a reservoir of revenue for me.

Whenever my resources were running light, I'd just take a little road trip and come back flush. In the past, 100,000$ usually made right my financial situation.

That trip would be unique.
I would invest 100,000$ and come off with 1MM$.
Of course it would take bit longer.
My estimate was 5to6 months.

FOUR MONTHS INTO THE TRIP.

Everything was going according to plan, in fact things were progressing quite nicely. I anticipated making my return ahead of schedule.

I rented an apartment and purchased a silver '03 Ford F-150 pickup with a covered bed. The vehicle was for transporting the package home. The apartment was an important part of the deception involved in procuring said package — It's peculiar how a collage of dope, vodka and a sleazy woman can foil even the best-laid plans.

SEPTEMBER 2004, A BLURRY HAZE OF VICODIN AND ABSOLUT.

Go ahead and add about an ounce of crystal methamphetamine spread out over the course of a week and a woman with 36 triple D's prepared to do whatever it takes to part you from your meth + money.

A pretty complex equation with only one outcome ||25-LIFE||

. . .

I FULLY RECALL DISCHARGING BOTH OF MY WEAPONS.

Then the beating I took from the arresting officers. The judge's words still ring clear in my mind: "Bail is denied." It wasn't the first time I'd faced a long stint in the clink. It also wasn't the first time I was held without bail.

That time was different, and I knew it.

They were holding me by the dick so hard—I could feel greasy lawman donut-eating fingers twisting up my short+curlies.

The certainty of my situation assaulted my innards. I could still hear Tamara begging me not to take the trip to SLC again. Fuckin cunt — *How did she know.*

I put on the orange suit and was escorted, in shackles binding my arms to my feet, across the street from the courthouse to 701 Baker Street. It was apparent the deputies at the jail had advance notification of my arrival — *They didn't like Out-of-Towners.* Particularly ones who emptied two clips at the laws.

I was processed into a tank on the seventh floor.

It was called the gladiator tank. Everyone there had a bull's-eye on their jumpsuit. We were all violent criminals.

I still felt the crystal and the seven-day bender that helped lead me there. GeorgiVodka and a few Xanax always helped ease the pain of a bender like that one | *I would be hard-pressed to find either item in that setting.*

HAVING IMAGINED MYSELF GETTING KNIFED IN THE BACK BY AN ICEPICK.

I dropped to my knees in a fit of panic.

Crystal will bring about both auditory and visual hallucinations after three straight days of consumption. In light of recent stress— *brought about by facing life in prison*—I was experiencing one of those promised side effects. I wobbled, my eyes shook and rolled inside my

20

head | I fancied it was all a bad dream and passed out right there on the jailhouse floor.

I DON'T REMEMBER BEING BROUGHT INTO PROTECTIVE CUSTODY.

it was a solitary, 6X9 cell with a hard metal bed and a combination toilet|water fountain. The bruises on my back and legs came from the deputies picking me up and moving me there.

I was stripped naked and the air conditioning had been left on the 'frozen felon' setting—I got up off the floor—it'd been three days since my arrest and the drugs still flowed through my system. *Fifteen solid years of consistent drug and alcohol use* | It don't go away in a few hours.

One of my contacts was gone and my vision impaired. I took out the other one and threw it into the metal toilet.

++||— Quite the pickle I was in —

THE FLAP ON THE BOTTOM OF THE DOOR OPENED

Instantly a plastic tray shoved into the cell.

Fried fish with a side of wet corn was on the menu.

Toilet water would serve as a condiment.

I flung the tray across the cell than screamed and smashed my fists against the door. I was left there, alone, for almost a day | A day in which I didn't stop screaming.

FINALLY THE DOOR OPENED.

I was naked and foaming at the mouth.

I felt like an animal and was ready to fight my way out.

Three deputies rushed inside, attempting to subdue me. I lunged at the largest — a 6'2 heavyset black male and bit his neck.

The other two pounced on me

++||— I TASTED BLOOD AND LAUGHED —
Five more deputies beat me until I passed out.

I woke up strapped down to a gurney in what looked like a medical wing. An older, pretty nurse dressed in blue scrubs stood over me with a needle and a bottle of clear white liquid.

I was hurt bad and passing in and out of consciousness.

"This will calm you down," she whispered.

Finally — *Some Dope* —

I relaxed a little, in anticipation of my medicine.

The withdrawals were unbearable.

The euphoria of the drugs took immediately and offered temporary relief from my predicament. Eight deputies stood by, ready to wheel my gurney to the elevator once the meds kicked in and I was calm. I asked them where they were taking me.

His reply — *A right-hook to the chin.*

The dope in my bloodstream numbed the pain.

When the elevator stopped, I was taken through a long white corridor, and the gurney came to a stop at a cell in the basement of the facility. Everything was white; the walls, the cells and even the nurse that greeted me wore white scrubs under a white doctor's robe.

Medical equipment was scattered throughout the wing.

This cell appeared reinforced and better constructed. One of the deputies smiled and said to me: "Welcome to your new home".

They undid the bracers and allowed me to stand up. They knew that dope was keeping my behavior in check but were more than prepared to dish out another beating if the situation arose.

Another deputy threw down a clear plastic trash bag with my orange jumpsuit inside. I reached for the bag and was knocked to the floor with an overhead right, another shove, and I was inside the 4X6 room ++||— The heavy white door was already closing behind me —

There was a small showerhead towards the back of the cell and a grated hole in the middle of the floor. *I assumed that hole would be my toilet.*

The cell reeked of anguish.

A rancid smell consisting of vomit, excrement and Lysol mixed with mop water. I felt the suffering that had taken place in that room, and the drugs began to fade | Five days into my incarceration and I hadn't eaten a thing. The air was brick cold — *I was still naked.*

I smashed on the tiny window until it caught the attention of a fat black deputy—a sloppy, dark-skinned ashy fellow with a scruffy unshaven bloated face and a dirty uniform half tucked out of his pants. I begged for a drink and my jumpsuit

He cackled | *Callous to my state of affairs.*

I battered on the door so hard the skin on my hands cut open from the pressure.

++||— *No one came —*

I JUST WASN'T CAPABLE OF DOING IT.

The pain of withdrawal from dope and alcohol consumed me.

I balled up like a baby and cried myself to sleep.

WHEN I AWOKE MY HANDS WERE BLOODY AND SWOLLEN.
Inside the white rubber cell was a cup of water, a brown paper bag and the pants from my Orange County-issued jumpsuit. The bag contained a 10oz milk, a Ziplock with a bit of cereal and a banana — I drank the milk, still wincing at the sight of food.

I put on the pants and felt some modest sense of relief.

I lived a tough life .
A life full of broken promises.
Shattered dreams, many regrets and plenty of death.
++||— I pondered on that —

At twenty-nine years old.
I'd done what most are unable to do in a lifetime.
I made and spent millions.
I loved to the fullest.

I loved Judi and I cried again.
Knowing I would never again feel her warm shoulder.
I had lived so that I denied myself nothing.
I lived however I'd wanted to.
My entire life.

Now | I no longer wanted to live.

I WAS GOING DIRECTLY TO HELL.

How could there be any kind of redemption for a man who traded his integrity for a few Rolex wristclocks and a Lexus GS 400.

I removed my pants, moved towards the hole in the middle of the room and squatted to make a shit — It would be my very last one.

I REFLECTED ON A LIFE SENTENCE FOLLOWED BY AN ETERNITY IN HELL.

I'd always been great at cheating and cutting corners. I knew what to do next almost on impulse.

Your humble friend and narrator *would have to Snuff It.*

I would rob the state of Utah of their little life sentence.
Go straight down and get to doin my eternity in hell.

Give Satan his little eternity bit.
Then get right back to it.

♚LIKE A MOTHERFUKIN SOLDIER♚

I got on my knees and said my final prayer to God.
I bid goodbye to those most important to me | *Embracing My Fate.*

Searching the door for hinges — I found a U-shaped latch that would work just fine. Making a noose from the pants was relatively easy work.

I tied the noose around the door and leaned forward.
As the air escape my lungs | I THOUGHT OF TIMES THAT WEREN'T SO COLD.
When all my dreams were still wrapped in tinsel.

THIS WAS IT | Not quite how I imagined it would be.

Ну что ж, Господа и Дамы.
Time to say goodbye to the bad guy.

Gary *"Gunny"* Govich
++|♜|— **Triple G** —|♜|++
THE BADDEST GUY YOU EVER GONNA SEE.

1.
2.
3.

COMIN FROM WHERE I'M FROM

Sometimes it get rough
Sometimes it get hard
Sometimes you gotta fight the pain
Sometimes you gotta walk to work
Sometimes you gotta do a little dirt
Comin from where I'm from
-Anthony Hamilton

I'm not from Russia — I'm from Odessa (ah-dhey-sa).
Now, *I know what you're thinking.*
How can I be a Russian mobster if I'm not even from Russia?
Being a Russian G is a lot like being a Cowboy.

It's an attitude.

Odessa, located in the southwest Ukraine, was a former satellite of the USSR, and Russian was—*and still is*—the primary language of the nationals.

. . .

ODESSA.

She's unlike any other satellite in the former Soviet Bloc. It's perhaps Russia's largest port of call. Which makes it a paradise for smugglers and criminals — *You need to get goods into or out of the country?* You do it through Odessa's docks.

Odessa has developed a thriving black market since communism came to the Ukraine in 1917 | Odessa is infamous for harboring the most notorious and immoral characters on the continent.

THERE IS AN OLD RUSSIAN SAYING, *"Одесса Мама"*.

When a criminal from Odessa pulls off a noteworthy act. A proper piece of villainy, one for which he receives acclaim.

His likely reply — "Одесса Мама." (Odessa is my mother).

That's how deeply imbedded crime is into the psyche of most of Odessa's citizenry ++|| — *It's the way of life in Odessa* —

I've used the expression | *More times than a few.*

When you're a certified criminal operating in Odessa.

The community grants you the title of **"Uhrk"** (ooh-rh-k). Whenever I hear that word I always think of an Orc. Just like the Orcs from *The Lord of the Rings*, these are ugly creatures. And I don't mean in appearances only. Uhrki (plural of Uhrk) are many. They often travel in bands, seeking their next act of delinquency. They're not bashful of violence, if required.

It's man's nature to want more than what he already has.

I present to you a system, where everyone is "supposed" to be equal — A system in which no man is permitted to have more than the next. This was the main factor in the collapse of the USSR. Man won't accept equality | He looks to surpass his peers.

It's human nature.

A system where an engineer gets paid the same as the trash man. That's a system that can't ever work. This very principle has allowed Odessa to flourish as the black-market capital of Russia.

MY PATERNAL GRANDFATHER MIKHAIL MAHNIGOVICH WAS A CRIMINAL operating in Odessa's underworld — He earned the respect of the country's best villains.

Among the Uhrki he was a considered a hero.

Mikhail stood six-foot one, prison tattoos covered his muscular physique. He wasn't an educated man, but what he lacked in intelligence he made up for with charismatic brutality.

My best estimates place his birth somewhere around 1905.

I never bothered to learn the exact date.

Mikhail's first major criminal act took place during the great famine of 1921. He assembled a small group of young Uhrki who hijacked a train full of rice and bread headed for the capital. Mikhail directed the train into town and unloaded the food to the townsfolk, who were becoming extinct from starvation —|— *The provisions fed them for months.*

TWO GOVERNMENT MEN WERE KILLED IN THE PROCESS.

The authorities arrived to search for their cargo, and the whereabouts of the murdered men. Back then—*Communist Russia of old*—a slight like that warranted a very special death, probably involving days or weeks of torture. The villagers wouldn't dime-out my Pappy's whereabouts.

KGB were called in to smoke the crew out of hiding.

"Comrade Commissar" threatened to execute five people every day the perpetrators remained secreted.

A week passed—*thirty-five innocents were executed*—still, the townsfolk wouldn't knock on my grandfather or his crew. They understood that although thirty-five may have perished, the food saved the lives of thousands.

On the sixth day Police had a lead — They were tipped off. The perpetrators were holed up in the basement of a retail food store. Authorities found two bodies. Both stabbed multiple times, and a small portion of the stolen food.

One of the corpses was the store manager. The other, a known rapist and suspected ChoMo.

The store manager—*an informer for the KGB*—was despised by the locals. He knew when the train was due in town. It would have been easy to assume that his plan was to sell the stolen merchandise at his place of business.

The other, well, was a rapist who liked to diddle children. Criminal was one thing, but in the Russian underworld rapists and Pedofiles were looked upon as lower than dopefiends. Times may have changed, but hatred for rapists still remains the same even today. Mikhail offered the citizenry another act of kindness by killing these two scoundrels. For both the people and the laws justice had been rendered.

Old Pappy sure was a shysty one.

For the next twenty years, things went relatively well for my grandfather. Pappy married and had three children, two boys and girl. He remained a criminal by trade and amassed a small bit of wealth for his family.

卍 THEN THE NAZIS CAME 卍

Mikhail Mahnigovich was Jewish, his wife and children, Jews as well. When the Nazi Blitzkrieg came through town, Odessa was unprepared—*how could they have been*—comrade Stalin had only recently purged all the top generals.

Hitler's despised both Russian and Jew alike.

Slavic folk (Russians) and full-blood Jewish, 1/2Jew, 1/4Jew, 1/64 part Jew, any and every Jew or Slav was considered Untermensch (sub-human).

I present to you, *my Pappy*, Mikhail Mahnigovich: Both Russian and Jew | There was an extraordinary brand of hatred reserved for such a creature. My grandfather, aware that neither he nor his family could be saved from impending doom, went into hiding.

They hid inside a barn for almost a month.

When the neighbors heard there were Jews hiding locally, they alerted the Romanian patrols. Russians hated Jews almost as much as the Nazis. There was a bit of flawed logic behind this.

Firstly, at the time, Jews held almost all the wealth in Odessa. People were jealous, and most Russians felt the Nazis only attacked them to kill their Jews. The villagers were quick to give up their Jewish neighbors, so long as the Nazis left them alone.

Unfortunately — Nazi hate does not discriminate.

Sparing villagers from digging their own mass graves then queuing up every living soul in the town, woman and children first, for a turn with the machine gunner —卐— NOPE — *That was not on the daily nazi roster of 'things-to-do'.*

WHEN MY GRANDFATHER WAS CAPTURED, NAZI SS *"DEATHS HEAD"* UNIT shot his wife and beat his children to death right in from of him.

The only thing that saved him was his size.

Nazi villains needed workers in the camps — At six-foot-one and almost three-hundred pounds, Mikhail would do quite nicely.

He was packed into a cattle car — DESTINATION AUSCHWITZ.
In Auschwitz | Surviving longer than six months was a miracle.

Mikhail spent a little over three years there.

His new career | Carrying tubs of boiling hot iron-ore—*still in liquid form*—to opposite ends of the camp. As he sprinted, the ore would splash up on his skin. If the ore was too dry before he reached his destination. Nazis brutes were set to shoot him in the head and find someone better suited for the job.

THE AWFULNESS HE MUST HAVE SEEN.
I just cannot begin to fathom it.

The man that entered the camp at almost three-hundred pounds was gone forever. When allied forced liberated the camp — He weighed less than one-hundred and ten pounds.

By the time the Red Army arrived at Auschwitz, they found the camp empty. In an attempt to cover their war crimes, heavily armed SS forced over sixty-thousand prisoners out of the camp and into a long march in sub-zero temperatures.

Pappy lost three toes on that death march.

FINALLY LIBERATED, PAPPY MADE HIS RETURN TO ODESSA.
Stop1 | The home of the man who had betrayed his family.

He done business with this "comrade" in the past and on at least one occasion, they met at Pappy's *datcha*[1] to celebrate their children's birthdays.

Two a.m. | Mikhail entered the man's house undetected.
Two of his most loyal soldiers were with him.

They grabbed the "comrade". Mikhail woke up his wife and son.
MY Pappy beat them to death while he watched.

> *His eyes were gouged out.*
> *His tongue cut in half.*
> *His fingers broken.*
> —||Eye4Eye||—
> Such was the law of the land.
> He would have to live with that pain for the rest of his life.

THEY BURNED DOWN HIS HOUSE AND LEFT HIM TO HIS FATE.

My grandfather remarried a few years later, and on a warm day in March 1946, they had their only child—*my father,* Boris Mahnigovich.

GRISHA (GREE-SHA) KLEZMIR, WAS BORN IN ODESSA AROUND 1910.
He was my maternal grandfather, on my mother's side.
I don't know much more about him.
He died long before I was born.
I only know these facts: At Five feet and five inches approximately one hundred-fifty pounds, he was neither tall nor muscular.

Age nineteen, he joined the Soviet army. In Communist Russia, service was mandatory—there were very few exceptions. Men became soldiers, women—clerks or medical personnel. In peacetime, under Soviet law, only a two-year term was required.

Grisha chose the armed forces as his career.

> *He quickly gained ranks in Stalin's army.*

MAJOR GRISHA COMMANDED TEN-TANK DIVISIONS.

He fought the Germans fiercely during the Nazi occupation.

Grisha wasn't a commander who sat inside a tent and dished out orders ++||—*He carried an automatic*— Throughout the course of WW2, Major Grisha was personally responsible for twenty-seven confirmed Nazi kills. When the Nazis reached Moscow, he was promoted to general and privy to counsels with Stalin himself.

For his fearless acts of courage:

For his unwavering service to the Soviet state, Grisha was granted admission to the Communist party and awarded the post of Supreme-Soviet Police Secretary.

My grandfather Grisha understood that black market trade was an integral part of Odessa's culture and although he frowned upon it but he always acted fairly. Grisha was a man of great character and high moral standards—*an uncompromising man*—who stood for truth and loved by all as a war hero and patriot.

During a Nazi air raid Grisha lost his wife and daughter.

With the war finally over, he returned home to Odessa to find a new bride and start over. September 1947 Grisha married a local woman, Klara. In the first few days of January 1952 Klara gave birth to my mother, Stella Klezmir.

WHEN RUSSIA BEGAN INVASIONS INTO AFGHANISTAN:

Grisha was very outspoken against the war.

His hero status and position of authority in the Communist party made him someone to be listened to. Grisha realized that speaking against policy was probably not his best course of action — *He stood on his laurels and spoke his mind.*

In the former USSR.
Speaking your mind made you a traitor.

Some of Grisha's party associates alerted him that KGB operatives were on the way to arrest him for treason | Torture him into signing a confession then Execute him.

Grisha Klezmir would not die a traitor. He donned his full military uniform, complete with his decorations for valor —*then hung himself in the dining room of his waterfront home* — My mother was the first person to discover him.

She and my grandmother had to cut him down.

WHICH BRING US TO MY FATHER.

My father — Boris, was a bit of a bad boy in his youth.

Being the son of an infamous underworld figure had its pluses, but Boris was uninterested in the black-market lifestyle.

Music was my father's calling.

Age sixteen | He moved to Kiev to escape the pressures of joining the family business. Music isn't a very lucrative business in any country. My father quickly found himself with a rumbling stomach and no pot to piss in. At seventeen Boris committed his first crime. It was the simple act of stealing bread from a local nightclub where he couldn't book a gig | He got caught.

Dad was never any good at being a crook.

Boris was thrown in jail, awaiting trial, a quick conviction, and the five to ten years of hard labor which seemed imminent.

· · ·

PAPPY USED HIS CONNECTIONS AND SOME CONTRABAND TO GET THE charges dismissed under the condition that Boris would return home and give it up—his dream of being a professional guitar player.

My father was and still is a very stubborn man, when he sets his mind to something he won't let it go | *Ever.*

He agreed to the deal, returned to Odessa and became more involved in the family business—he never gave up on the guitar.

At age nineteen, dad was pinched in a black-market sting.

Several criminals were arrested, tried and sentenced to either prison or hard labor. Local crime was getting out of control.

The government demanded fallguys.
They needed to make examples.
Dad was stuck inside a textbook case of wrong place||wrong time.

Mikhail again used his influence, but prison time, *this time*, was unavoidable. For Pappy, prison was an accepted risk | *Part of the game.*
++||— My Pappy spent over fifteen years in Russian gulag's —

EVEN LOCKED DOWN, PAPPY USED HIS CONNECTIONS TO SMUGGLE GOODS and bribe guards to secure a much more comfortable stay.

Some of his crimes, by American standards, would warrant life sentences. He never did more than four years a stint.

My father, he wasn't made from the same dough.

Sentenced to eight months in one of Odessa's prison facilities, Pappy made sure that my father's brief stay in the "Zone"[2] was a fairly painless one.

Around the time of my father's incarceration.
The Soviet Union sent their first troops into Afghanistan.

AFGHANISTAN WAS VIETNAM ++||— *THE RUSSIAN VERSION* —
An un-winnable war funded with the lives of an entire generation of youth. Americans knew of the Russian deployment and sent aid to the Afghani "freedom fighters."

Aid in the form of US currency, training for the rebel forces and weapons, such as truckloads of stinger missiles — A heat seeking shoulder operated Brutus which required no training to operate. Stingers worked exceptionally well on Russian choppers and tanks.

Inside the Afghan Mountains—*theUSofAmerica*—even went ahead and built vast underground compounds complete with niceties like plumbing and ice-cold air-conditioning | *Among those trained in guerrilla tactics was a long-bearded pajama-wearer* named Osama Bin Laden.

Pappy was a man of great resource and many connections.

People in the upper ranks of government were his clientele. Pappy used his influences, to keep my father out from the Soviet armed forces. He pulled whatever strings he needed to secure my father a medical pardon.

When Boris came home from prison.

He was surprised to discover that people had begun to appreciate his music. There's something to be said for the bad boy musician.

Woman love him — Men admire him.

Boris had street cred | He'd been to prison.
++||— He sang from experience —

Boris formed a band with Misha Gulko as lead vocalist.

They played in restaurants and nightclubs and earned a reputation for pleasing the crowd. Boris' band toured the country for almost six years, during which time his popularity grew exponentially. By age twenty-eight, dad cut three studio albums and Misha-G *would later become one of the most prominent Russian musicians in the country.*

During an unscheduled show.

At a café in his hometown of Odessa, Boris was challenged to a wager by the band members. The wager | Bedding down with a woman who every man in the band wanted to lay.

Proper drunk on cheap vodka straight.
Dad accepted without hesitation.

Misha-G, the lead singer, had been romancing the woman for three months, and she had resisted his sexual advances. Boris would have three weeks in which to consummate with her. If successful, he gets the entire pot—*two-thousand rubles*—considering most Russians earned three-hundred rubles a month.

That was long money

The female, A big fan of the band and the politically motivated music that had become their staple was a recent medical school graduate — Her name was Stella Klezmir.

An unlikely couple.
The drunk guitarist — Son of a criminal and an educated doctor with a war hero dad —||— *Whoever said love was blind...*

My father won the bet.

From what they've told me, my parents fell in love the moment they met. Their courtship was pretty short, seeing as how mom became pregnant a few weeks into the relationship.

A few months and they were married.

Pappy got them into government-subsidized apartment on Academic Pavlov, right across the street from the university where mom received her medical degree.

BY RUSSIAN STANDARDS, MY PARENTS HAD IT ALL.

A summer home, plenty of jewels, a late-model automobile. They were always dining out and entertaining company.

My mother earned a wage from the state AND received gifts. As gifts that were customarily given to doctors for their service.

Doctors earned the same paycheck the hospital janitor did.

What would motivate a professional to attend four years of medical school on top of the college was required? People who did it strictly for the humanitarian aspect were few and far between.

In the former Soviet Union.

If ever you found yourself Busted-up, throwd-off, or simply feeling that medical assistance was required, you'd better come with paper money or something of value to give to the doctor on duty. If you were just regular Joey Communist with less than nothing to offer then fine, go get to waiting in the ER. Until you either bleed to death *or hell freezes over.*

Whichever one come first.

On the other hand, if you brought some rubles or a few loaves of bread, almost magically, you skip the line and receive the best medical care in the antiquated hospital of your choice.

The whole system was corrupt from the inside out.

From the directors of the hospitals down to clerks; all were guilty of accepting "gifts."

It was a harsh reality.

So was 25-life in some rotten prison in SLC Utah.

It was the system that was in place.

You could either work with it *or get right to getting* FukT.

MARCH 20, 1975.

After a twenty-hour labor in which Stella almost died, my parents had their first child. A son they named Grisha Mahnigovich. My first name was a tribute to my grandfather Grisha — *Mom insisted on that.*

* * *

THE MINUTE I COULD WALK I WAS A TROUBLEMAKER.

From sticking other kids' hands in electrical sockets, to locking out the whole kindergarten class while I ate everyone's lunch, there was no bit of mischief I wasn't accomplished at.

Back then, it was cute.

People would smile and pat me on the head.

I wish I could remember more of the fatherland.

Unfortunately, all I have is what relatives have told me. Too many years of dope and warm vodka straight morphed my early childhood memories into a thick fog.

I do have snippets of recollection.

I remember the ocean | We lived a few blocks from the Black Sea, and I recall the ocean in all its beauty. I recall my nanny, Olga, an elderly, loving lady, and the fish stew she made for me.

I was four years old, when dad decided that we needed to pack our bags and get to gettin. The Russian public in general had this concept that America was the Promised Land—*a place where dreams were manufactured right from the dream factory*—and Willy Wonka himself walked around handing out free bars of chocolate candy.

DAD THOUGHT HIS FAMILY WOULD HAVE A BETTER LIFE IN AMERICA.

After all, *his wife was a doctor*. From the rumors he'd heard, American doctors made millions and drove Mercedes Benz sedans.

There was also the issue of the war in Afghanistan.

Young Russian bodies were coming home by the caravan. The ones who survived returned invalids and paraplegics. Nobody knew when the war would end — It could last twenty more years. If the current mortality rate was any indication, Russia would soon have to lower the minimum age for mandatory military service to seventeen just to keep pace. There was already gossip of new legislation in the works for this possibility.

Boris wanted his only son to have no part of it.

Now for the kicker | Boris was Jewish.
That makes me a half-Jew.

Russians are fiercely antisemitic.

If you were a Jew in the former USSR, on your passport under "nationality," it wouldn't say "Russian" — It would say "Jewish."

Antisemitism was deep imbedded in the minds of the Russian citizenry. Jews were their own nationality and had no rights under the Communist regime. So someone like me—*a half-Jew*—would have to serve my mandatory tour in the armed forces and, if fortunate enough to survive whatever nastiness was in store for me, would come home to absolutely no rights or claims to citizenship

I'd probably end up taking over my grandfather's business.

A questionable future.
Prison and death, strong possibilities.

WANTING TO LEAVE COMMUNIST RUSSIA WAS ALL FINE AND WELL;

Physically leaving the country, that was where you might run into a few setbacks. Obtaining a visa for a simple vacation outside the Soviet Bloc was a long and arduous process — Emigrating to a free society was about as easy as finding whiskey in a churchhouse.

Why would you want to leave a perfectly euphoric society where everything belongs to the people and everyone is equal? That just didn't make much sense to the comrades running the show.

Besides, people just weren't allowed to come and go as they pleased | There was that old iron curtain business.

So how did a *good* communist depart for foreign shores?

The answer here is simple — *They didn't.*

Russia allowed people to emigrate, and while these people may have been communists, they were far from good. The USSR had a policy of allowing only criminals to leave the country.

Convicted criminals were given permission to emigrate to any place they wanted. Russia didn't want such vermin infesting their cities and terrorizing their communities.

During the wave of emigration that began in the 1960s and ending in 1979 — More than ninety percent of people leaving the former Soviet Union were convicted felons of the worst sort.

Russian policy was to keep the good intellectual types and donate the villains to any place that would take them.

Ethnics like Jews and gypsies were allowed passage as well.

It just so happened that most of the convicts leaving in droves were of Jewish descent. There was no place for these non-citizens in Russia's perfect world. There's a trick to giving all your murderers, thieves, and rapists to your enemy.

Don't tell them they're criminals.

When Comrade Commissar approved their walking papers and sent them over to the embassy to get their temporary green card, they all claimed political asylum. They didn't tell the clerk they were leaving because they were tired of doing time in the "Zone" for committing criminal acts. No country would take them if that were the case.

Their stories were the same.

They'd been persecuted for their political views on communism and the socialist state. America took the bulk of these "political refugees" because we were no friend to communism and our policy at the time was "any enemy of Marx is a friend of ours."

Both my father and Pappy were Jews and convicts.

STELLA DIDN'T SHARE BORIS' ENTHUSIASM.

The only thing Stella knew of America, she'd heard from the Soviet propaganda machine. She didn't know the language, choosing to study German instead of English at the institute. Mostly she feared leaving her home and starting over in an unfamiliar place.

Neither Pappy nor his wife Betsy had any interest in leaving.

They had a wonderful apartment, plenty of food, and a thriving business. The biggest advocate against leaving Odessa was Klara, my grandmother on my mother's side. She was a wonderful lady, full of love and generosity. She didn't want to leave the grave of her beloved husband Grisha.

In 1978 the family finally gave in.
They did it for me — For my future.

My family was able to reserve a seat on one of the last planes to leave for America. They obtained their exit papers and a temporary visa to Italy. From there — The big-bird to New York.

Oh yeah, I forgot to mention one tidbit of information.

When you leave Communist Russia, you can't take anything with you — *All your property must be turned over to the state.*
If you leave your communist homeland under the pretense of political refuge, what you're basically saying is that you don't want anything communism has to offer | So you won't be needing anything you may have acquired during your stay in the country.

Hell, it was never even yours to begin with.

Everything belongs to the people (*e.g.* the few KGB agents who confiscate your money, jewelry and anything else of portable value, then split it up amongst themselves and their handlers).

My family gave up everything they had.

Anybody caught attempting to smuggle jewelry or other valuable items was sentenced to harsh prison terms. With the window cracked and a few rays of sunlight finally able to shine down, they weren't taking any chances. They were allowed to take five small suitcases on the airplane, one for every passenger.

In exchange for their valuables, they were given five-hundred American dollars and had their Russian citizenships was revoked forever | *Everyone's, except for mine.*

. . .

WE SPENT A FEW COMFORTABLE MONTHS IN ITALY.

My family arrived at the customs terminal of John F. Kennedy Airport on August 11, 1979.

When we reached the immigration office, the clerk looked at our passports then he raised an eyebrow at my father. He looked again at the passports. "What's your name ... Manygoshits?" he asked laughingly and smiled a friendly smile at me. "I'm gonna do you folks a favor and change this for you. Trust me, you'll thank me later," he stated. With a wink he handed me my temporary papers and I became Gary Govich.

At the age of four and my life in America began.

None of us spoke a lick of English.

We relied solely on the charities of various Jewish organizations such as NYANA for help with housing and food.

We spent a month in a transit camp until we were able to secure a small apartment on Kings Highway in Brooklyn. It was a roach-infested rat-hole, one-bedroom flat in a four-story building with no elevator. Mom, Dad, Pappy, and my grandmother Klara struggled to cram into that tiny space.

Money was in short supply.

Nobody in my family knew anything about a fuckin' thing.

We were in a strange land and no one spoke the language. Everyone was terrified and questioning their next move. I can imagine the frustration and self-doubt that plagued my father.

Shortly after the move both my mom and dad started English classes at night and looking for work. My mother looked in the medical field and my father looked for anything he could get to support the family.

. . .

THE JEWISH CENTER ON KINGS HIGHWAY.

Scheduled an interview at the local labor hall downtown for my father to meet with one of their counselors to assess his skills and capabilities. When dad sat down and the fellow asked him questions, his reply was a blank stare.

Boris didn't understand a word 'ol boy was saying.

He did speak a little English, his only two words "pipe" and "chair. Boris did the smart thing. He said "pipe." Repeatedly. Whenever questioned, he simply replied ... "pipe."

The counselor soon got the gist, Boris must be a plumber.

He was handed a small slip of paper and instructed to report to the address penciled on it at six a.m. sharp the following day. The place was a machine shop—they fitted pipes for commercial use in the oil field.

Dad took three trains to get to his new job.

Dad knew fitting pipes, the same way a soccer coach knows throwing baseballs. Still, The old man had to provide for a family of five. He swallowed his pride and began work that day as a machinist. It would remain his trade for the next twenty-three years.

Things went different for my mother.

She was under the impression, once she became fluent in English, a sweetheart doctor job would be waiting for her at the hospital of her choice.

For the next three months she studied English | All day long.

After completing her course—*she picked up a paper*—and got to looking for doctor work. Stella put on her business suit, and reported to an interview at a Jewish hospital that one of the charity organizations scheduled for her.

What she found was heartbreaking.

The United States would not recognize a medical degree from a communist country. If she wanted to doctor in America, she would have to attend medical school ++||— *One More Again* —

Unprepared for the adversity and devastated.

Stella lost all hope. She committed to a puzzle factory in a local hospital for a month to recover from the breakdown.

With mom in the hospital, my father working twelve-hour days, I was left under the supervision of my grandparents. Over sixty—they were able to collect social security.

* * *

WHEN MY MOTHER CAME HOME FROM THE HOSPITAL.

She was prepared to do anything to support the family.

Stella found work as a home attendant cleaning up after old folk.

Pappy and Betsy moved, into their own apartment, a few miles away. My parents would leave for work before the sunrise. I stayed home with Klara. They bickered nightly about my father's persistence to move to this America | *Where they slaved for peanuts.*

Dad was forced to find a second job.

He purchased a guitar and began playing gigs in small Russian nightclubs on Brighton Beach. His drinking got much worse. But he was never violent with my mother or me.

How could he be.
He was never around.

IN 1981 MOM WAS OFFERED EMPLOYMENT AT A *YESHIVA*.
She was to be the cleaning lady. I was to attend at a fraction of the cost if she took the job.

THE AMERICAN DREAM — *from Doctor to cleaning lady.*

* * *

I KEPT TO MYSELF MY FIRST YEAR AS AN AMERICAN.
I didn't know a word of English and found it difficult to communicate with other children.

At five, I began my first year of education.

I skipped kindergarten—*I was a bright child with a thirst for knowledge*—I wasn't much like the other Jewish kids. They had nice clothes and expensive packed lunches. I wore the same rags every day and my mom cleaned their toilets. The staff often told me how lucky I was to even be able to attend | The kids made fun of me.

I was determined to excel in my studies.

I was the top student in every class, always coming up with new ways to stand out. I hated not knowing the language, *so I stopped talking.*

I didn't speak Russian with my family anymore.
I just didn't speak anything.

For almost three years, I kept my mouth shut.
I guess that bit of quiet time had an impact on me
Because for the rest of my life || *I never kept silent again.*

At nine years-old,. I was a bit chubby, I dressed funny, and had nothing to offer other kids ||— *I had no friends* —||

. . .

For my ninth birthday, my parents decided to buy me a bicycle.

It was a used bike but in pretty good shape.

I didn't know how to ride it, so with training wheels, my grandmother supervising, I was allowed to ride in the park. We lived right next to a public playground. It was a well-kept, pretty place considering it was in the slums and right at heart of the Italian ghetto.

A rainy Sunday, and I wanted to ride my bike.
Hard rain | My grandmother didn't want to take me to the park.

I went anyway.

I rode the half mile to the park as the sky cleared.

Near the entrance, there were a few handball courts where some of the neighborhood kids hung out. There were three of them there, and as I rode by, one motioned me over to them. It was the first time anyone from the neighborhood wanted to talk to me.

We were that strange Russian family.
Everyone whispered about us when we passed by them.

This was the Cold-War early 1980s. There were less than three hundred thousand Russians in the whole of New York City. In a city of fifteen million people—*that's not very many.*

I rode over to them.

Two were around my age, the third looked older.

The one who called me over was named Joe, he lived in a large house right next to my apartment.

I got off the bike and let it sit on its training wheels.

Without saying a word, The oldest of the three grabbed my bike while Joe and the other kids started smashing on me.

I didn't know what to do.

I started to scream.

I fell to the ground, and as they kicked, Joe hollered; "Fuckin Russian. Get the fuck out of our neighborhood".

I lay there on that pavement for a long while.

I thought of what I might have done to provoke them. I thought about the humiliation I'd suffered at the hands of my neighbor. I thought about having my property taken from me, only because I was too weak to stop it from happening.

I FELT LIKE A COWARD.

It made me feel sick from inside out.

I SPOKE TO GOD FOR THE FIRST TIME IN MY LIFE.
How could He allow innocent people to suffer?
There, on the wet concrete, I had what most would call a moment of clarity. At the age of nine, it became apparent to me that there were two types of people in this world:

THE TAKERS AND THE TAKEN-FROM.

I swore I would never allow myself to be taken from again.
I swore to God HimSelf that from that day forward that I would never let fear drive me to a coward again. When I stood, I felt a new inner strength | A new determination I couldn't explain.

I HID IN THE BATHROOM UNTIL MY FATHER CAME HOME THAT NIGHT.
Klara made *borscht*[3] and potatoes with garlic.
I lied and told my parents I'd been jumped in the park by some

kids I'd never seen before and that they stole my bike.

They scolded me for taking the bike out without permission and sent me to my bedroom to study. My parents were upset and wanted to call the cops. Klara reminded them of the police in Odessa and what a complaint like this would mean in their homeland.

They didn't need the attention.

It was just something that happened. We would have to accept that it happened—and *that it might happen again.*

My new resolve would not permit me to do the same.

THE FOLLOWING SATURDAY.

I saw Joe straightening his garage. Joe was shorter than me, and he was real wiry. He was a popular kid and usually had plenty of friends over.

That day, he was alone.

As I walked by, I saw a thin smirk form on his small lips and felt adrenaline well up inside of me. I picked up a large stone, about the size of a softball, that chipped off the curb. It was triangle-shaped and had a sharp edge. There was no hesitation, I ran up on Joe and cracked the blunt edge of the rock on the top of his head.

As he fell to the floor | Beautiful purple Blood poured from his scalp.

His mother burst from the house and chased me away.

I RAN DOWN THE BLOCK ONTO THE MAIN AVENUE.

It felt like I could run forever.

I felt that soft delight only revenge can bring.

I wandered a bit, content with myself and numb to the world, then walked the long way home, completely around the block, so I wouldn't pass Joe's house again.

OPENING MY DOOR, THE FIRST FIGURE I SAW WAS PAPPY.

He grabbed my hand and pulled me into the kitchen where we shared our family dinners. Both my parents were waiting for me, *they were shouting.* They threatened a beating when I refused to explain. Pappy whispered something to my father. Boris took down another cup of vodka and waved his hand.

My grandfather took me into the other room.

Pappy told me that Joe was seriously hurt, and his father had been up to the house, threatening to call the police. He sat me down on the bed beside him and asked again for my explanation.

I always felt a special kind of closeness with Pappy.
It was a bond I didn't share with anyone else in the family.

I know he felt it too.

I told Pappy why I'd done it.
He suspected my stolen bike to be the reason.

PAPPY OFFERED ME MY FIRST PIECE OF WISDOM THAT DAY.

"You know Gary" he said, "even a dog can fight. Sure, a dog has plenty of courage. But it's our wits that make us men," he finished, got up, patted me on the head then walked out the room and told my parents that Joe and his friends had stolen my bike.

My father demanded I go to Joe's house to apologize for beating up the little thief.

The idea did not sit well with me.

"He stole my bike and *I'm* the one who should be sorry?" I shouted. Pappy's nodded, indicated that apologizing would be the right thing to do. I agreed and went to Joe's house with both my father and Pappy at my side.

His mother answered and let us inside.

Joe was holding an ice-pack on his head. His father spoke for him, "Our son told us about the bicycle. We apologize for him," he said. The father nudged Joe — *He finally apologized* | We shook hands.

They promised the bike would be returned.

WALKING OUT OF JOE'S HOME — PAPPY PUT HIS HAND ON MY SHOULDER.

++||— *I felt like a champion* —

I NEVER DID GET THAT BIKE BACK, THOUGH.

1.
2.
3.

EVERYTHING COUNTS...... IN LARGE AMOUNTS

The grabbing hands
  Grab all they can
  All for themselves
  After all
  It's a competitive world
  And everything counts...... in large amounts
  Everything || Everything
  Everything Counts-In Large Amounts
-Depeche Mode

THINGS WERE PRETTY NORMAL FOR THE NEXT FEW YEARS.
  "Normal" as in the other kids left me the fuck alone.

Two years passed.

Another Russian family moved into my neighborhood.
  I had a new friend to spend time with. A shy fellow named Vladimir (Vlad). He attended public school and I only got to see him a few hours a day and on weekends.

Still, it was nice having someone to talk with.

I DID EXTREMELY WELL IN MY STUDIES.

It was Hebrew school, so we spent half the day doing typical school work, the other half learning religion and how to speak Hebrew. I enjoyed all my classes and soon became one of the top students in the school.

I spoke Hebrew so well the instructors felt I was on track to become a Rabbi[1]. The thought of their son someday becoming a distinguished man especially excited my family.

Unfortunately, I was a pretender;

A functional illiterate — reading but not understanding the Hebrew Scriptures. I learned to speed-read and had the teachers and my parents fooled. I didn't care much for Hebrew, but it pleased everyone and made them all treat me better.

I DREAMED OF BECOMING A BASEBALLER.

I was a fan of the New York Yankees.

I looked at their games on a black&white television my father salvaged from atop a large heap of trash bags.

Even at age eleven, I never had any misconceptions of the world or how it worked. If I couldn't become a baseball player (maybe the Yankees didn't like Russians) then I'd be an architect.

I loved to build model kits and always had a knack for detail.

I WAS ELEVEN WHEN BETSY, PAPPY'S WIFE DIED OF STROKE.

Hers would be the first of many funeral services I'd have to attend.

. . .

At thirteen, we moved into a better apartment.

My father gave up playing the guitar — He sacrificed his passion for a more practical moonlighting gig. Driving a limousine.

Our new home was a condominium on the seventh floor of a midsized apartment complex. To keep up the mortgage my mother needed to work a job that paid more money. When denied a raise at the *yeshiva,* she was forced to quit. I was consequently enrolled in public school. I excitedly looked forward to leaving the *yeshiva.*

Vlad and I met on the Sunday before our move.
We declared ourselves *foreverfriends* and swore we'd meet again.

I was enrolled in a fine school a half-mile from my home in what was then a predominantly Italian area. The shock of my first day of public school made me lightheaded.

If there was ever an odd man out | It was Me.

Everyone stared at me and whispered as I walked by.
Nobody tried to provoke any fights with me. I was so strange to the other kids, they just wanted to avoid me.
In the cafeteria | *I was an island.*

Towards the end of the year I made a new friend — Adam C.

Tall for his age, he had long blonde hippie-hair, soft blue eyes, and a sharp nose that pointed upward. He transferred from Beverly Hills and touted the California tan, expensive clothes, and what seemed to be a fanbase consisting of every girl in the school.

They followed him and giggled.

He immediately became the most popular kid in the entire world.
On a Friday, during lunch, Adam sat down next to me. I was usually the nerd with his own table. That day was no different.

Adam told me about himself and invited me to his house to "kick it" after school. At the time I didn't know what to think about these peculiar events. Later, after getting to know Adam, it became apparent that he was a compassionate person who had simply felt bad for me.

WE WALKED TO HIS MANSION.

It was in one of the wealthiest areas in Brooklyn.

He confided in me that his parents had divorced, that his father had recently won custody of him.

WE ENTERED THE HOUSE THROUGH THE GARAGE.

Inside | A RED FERRARI COUPE.

"My brother, High, must be home," Adam said.

There was a thick metal bar, about three feet high, sticking out the ground at the entrance of the garage. I stared at it wondering what it was used for. "That's there so the thieves can't tow truck it out the garage like the last one." Adam laughed.

We walked through the house, and through many rooms lined with luxurious artwork and photos of his father and brother with celebrities. I was particularly impressed with the ones of Arnold Schwarzenegger and Sylvester Stallone.

He directed me to the basement.

DJ equipment was positioned in the rear.

There were countless milk crates filled with records.

Adam produced a small metal tin from under one of his leather sofas, then pulled out a sack of grass and some EZ wider papers. He broke it up on a glass top table then started twisting.

He slid into the cushions and relaxed — In moments Adam was taking a deep pull on the lit joint.

. . .

57

I NEVER HAD ANY INTENTION TO SMOKE GREEN DOPE.

I'd seen all the "this is your brain on drugs" commercials, you know, the ones where the guy puts the egg—*your brain*—in the pan, and it fries. Familiar Fear and Adrenaline rushed into my innards.

There he was, the most accepted youth, living the life I dreamed of, and offering me something I knew was wrong.

Perhaps I was wrong about the stuff.

Perhaps I was wrong about all of it.

I accepted and inhaled deeply letting out the smoke with an abrasive cough. Adam smiled. "First time?" I didn't answer.

That very first high is beyond explanation.
It was a concentration of an inner calm previously unknown.
I felt free of physical bonds.

When he turned on the music | *I almost cried.*

We sat for almost two hours, laughing and listening to music. He told me he would help me fit in with some of the other kids. Adam loaned me a few of his shirts and gave me ten bucks for a taxi home.

At the end of the school year Adam was invited to a party.

I went with him and I tasted vodka for the first time.

Many people think Alcoholism Is genetic. Coming from a long history of alcoholism | I tend to Agree.

I was an alcoholic the very first drink I took.
It made me courageous and powerful.

It gave me a sense of belonging.
A *Peaceful Feeling* | *That everything would be fine if I just kept on drinking.*

* * *

THAT SUMMER BREAK, I DECIDED I NEEDED A JOB.

At such a young age, I didn't have many options.

My mother suggested I deliver newspaper.

I picked up a *Daily News* then called the number in the classifieds for a job as a delivery boy. Within a few days I received my first shipment of papers and was assigned a small route, covering about two miles of area near my home. I woke up at dawn to carry the papers from house to house in a shopping cart. Every day, especially on Sunday, I was left with anywhere from 25-100 extra copies.

My instructions were clear; tear off the cover of any unused copies and return them to the route master (the guy who collected the money). I soon realized, I could make an additional forty dollars a week selling the extra papers under the L train tracks.

It was against policy but I didn't care, so long as I could make extra coin. On rainy days I wouldn't deliver the paper at all — I just went under the L and sold everything I had for face value.

IT WAS JUST A SUMMER JOB. WHEN SCHOOL RESUMED — I QUIT.

My replacement was a pretty sixteen-year-old female who seemed sweet. I took her around to all the stops showing her the fastest ways to get the job done.

On my last day | *I shared my secret with her.*
I took her with me under the L and we sold every paper we had.

That week when I met the route master informed me that the girl I'd trusted had told him what I'd been doing. He demanded I turn all pilfer over to him immediately or first my parents would be told then law enforcement would be involved.

I didn't tell him that the same girl, so fast to sell me out, was a partner in the crime | I knew what a rat was.

Pappy schooled me early on; if I were to get caught in a criminal act, I should *never* talk to any authority figure about it. Under no circumstance should I betray anyone else involved.

I WENT HOME AND GOT ALL THE MONEY I SAVED (STOLE) THAT SUMMER.
It was almost five-hundred dollars | *I gave all of it up.*

DURING MY FIRST BIT INSIDE THE CLINK.
I had incident to reflect back on the situation.

I knew exactly what he did with the money. He had himself a good laugh at my stupidity and put that paper right in his back pocket, probably even sharing some with his girl informant.

People are People.
Some things can always be counted on.
I got shook down | Plain and Simple.

WHEN I TOLD PAPPY WHAT HAPPENED, HE JUST SMILED.
I was insulted by his cheerful reaction to a situation where I had just lost my entire summer savings.

"You're done getting a free ride, Gary. From now on, lessons cost you. Be man enough to accept the loss and learn some more wisdom," he whispered in Russian. "*Never share your plans with a stranger.*" He laughed.

MY NEXT JOB — AT A COMIC BOOK SHOP WAS TWO BLOCKS FROM HOME.
When I first entered the store, it was still under construction, panels of sheetrock and debris scattered about both of its rooms.

The owner, James V., was a hulk of a man | The kind you expect to be breaking bones for the neighborhood shylock.

James had dark brown slick hair that was long in the back.

60

Attached to his massive head were sideburns that would make even Elvis blush. He stood around six foot and must have weighed no less than three hundred and fifty stomach-bulging pounds — He looked like a portly Frankenstein monster without the neck plugs.

I LATER FOUND JAMES TO BE ONE OF THE GENTLEST|KINDEST MEN I WOULD EVER HAVE THE PRIVILEGE TO KNOW.

JAMES V. TOOK A LIKING TO ME AS SOON AS WE MET.

He offered me a job on the spot — James planned to open the store at five-thirty a.m. Collectors could stop in for a cup of coffee on their way to work.

Waking up at five a.m. was no joy for me.

I would stumble around like a zombie until I could pinch some of my father's vodka from bottles he kept under the sink. I replaced what I took with water.

The comic book industry was booming.
The store did exceptionally well.

James trusted me enough to use the register and stock the back room — By that time I'd become skilled in the nuances of the buyer|seller relationship.

— ||— MANIPULATION CAME NATURALLY FOR ME —||—

I was convinced those mooks would buy pruned dogshit if it had some kind of collectible value. I took advantage of every unsuspecting pigeon who entered the store—*however that looked like.*

Charging more than retail value for something they purchased or offering to pay grossly under market for something they brought in to sell. James didn't agree with my methods and on more than one occasion, stepped in and ruined my deals.

ALTHOUGH JAMES V. WAS AN UNINTELLIGENT MAN, HE WAS OF VIRTUOUS character maintaining a moral compass that highlighted integrity.

JAMES' CONCERNS SPOKE TO HIS HONOR.
It was something he always kept clean.

INTELLIGENCE AND WISDOM RARELY SHARE AN AFFILIATION.

The first is acquired with ease.
It's available to any and all.
It can be purchased, sold | Even stolen.
It's a volatile substance | *Never holding for long any tangent or definition.*
It's value is, at best, inconsistent.

—|| ♟ ||— WISDOM CAN ONLY BE EARNED —|| ♟ ||—
It's never traded in currency.

If ever granted opportunity to acquire some:
Make certain | Place it right close to your essence.
Its qualities are *Extremely fragile.*
Always keep it on the ready.
Knaves and scoundrels will come to filch it.

++||— It must be protected —

Take heed my words.
Take from me this if anything at all.

When cared for and applied properly.
WISDOM | Will become your Most Valuable Treasure.

JAMES DROPPED OUT OF SCHOOL AT TWELVE.

He worked for over twenty years in the meat department of a large grocery chain, eventually making supervisor and retiring with a small pension. He collected comic books since childhood as a hobby and kept a very extensive collection worth upwards of 50,000$.

James invested his life savings into that comic shop.

One day when I was low on money, I came to work and, almost naturally, opened the register, took out a twenty, and put it in my pocket.

ALARMS DIDN'T GO OFF.
Sirens didn't flash.
Nothing Exploded.

I was just twenty bucks richer.

I COULD HAVE ASKED JAMES FOR AN ADVANCE.
I don't know why I stole that money.

All I knew was that stealing it didn't bother me nearly as much as it should have.

* * *

I GRADUATED INTERMEDIATE SCHOOL WITH HONORS.

I'd been accepted to some of the top high schools in the city but opted to stay close to home so I could work at the comic store.

Adam was headed for out of town prep-school.

We agreed to stay in touch.

He left me an ounce of tress and his brother's number in case I needed more.

BUSINESS AT THE STORE COULDN'T HAVE BEEN BETTER.
Collecting was reaching its peak. Issues grew in price daily. James hired an Asian named Kenny. He took over my cleaning responsibilities. I was left to deal exclusively with the clientele.

Kenny was a no older than fourteen and extremely sharp for his age — *I was wary of him moving in on my job.*

One of our best customers, a fella named John owned the flower shop across the street | One day John just stopped buying comics.

It was the strangest thing.

He would come in and look around, but he wouldn't buy anything. When I inquired about his lack of patronage, he told me his wife put restrictions on his spending. He said comic books were the cause of many arguments, and he just had enough.

It sounded believable.

Until I caught him throwing signals to Kenny.
One thing I have a talent for is seeing the obvious.
I cornered John and asked him what the gestures meant. He shrugged it off and told me I was seeing things.

Please | *Don't piss down my back and tell me it's raining.*

That night, I waited for Kenny to go to the head and searched his school bag. Like Carl Lewis at the 84 Olympics, *he was caught.*

When Kenny came out of the bathroom, an unexpected fist to the chin greeted him. It knocked little Kenny to the ground, and I proceeded to smash on him with violent blows to his temple.

As fast as he could, James pulled me off the almost unconscious Kenny, demanding to know the cause of the wrangle. I pointed to the bag on the floor, so full of loot it was barely able to close.

James was noticeably hurt by what I'd shown him.

He took Kenny into the bathroom and helped clean up his face. James took money from the till and handed Kenny his pay before asking him to leave.

I asked James why he would pay a thief his wages after he was caught stealing. "What's right is right. If I didn't pay him the money he rightfully earned, that would make me no less a thief than he was," he replied. After that incident, John began buying new releases again.

TWO WEEKS LATER.

John called in an order of about two-hundred dollars and asked to have them delivered to his shop across the street. He congratulated me on the job I'd done smelling out his deal with Kenny.

He offered me a similar arrangement.

It was a pretty lucrative deal in which he would pay half the cover price of every new issue I stole and almost 60% of the book value of any classic. Realizing there was, in fact, a bounty to be made. I rationalized that James wouldn't miss the small of amount of shrink.

++||— I agreed —

OVER THE NEXT THREE MONTHS.

I saved over 6,000$ in cash as a result of my arrangement with

John the florist—*since I was stealing for John*—I figured stealing a little for myself was icing on the cake. I estimated my personal collection worth upwards of 4,000$. I hid the money in a hole I cut in the mattress of my futon, bought expensive clothes from boutiques on the avenue where I worked, and sometimes took cabs to eat at exclusive restaurants.

I acquired a taste for the charmed life.

Business at the comic shop wasn't suffering and I was happier than an Englishman at tea-time.

HIGH SCHOOL WAS RIGHT ACROSS FROM THE SLUM.
It was more than four miles from my home. I took three busses to get there. Right across from my school were the bricks[2] — A vast urban wasteland (ninety-six buildings covering six blocks) that spanned nearly three miles. Within were some of the most loathsome lawbreakers this side of the Mason-Dixon Line.

ONCE INSIDE | You were in the concrete jungle.
It was survival of the fittest.
In the jungle, weak lambs were devoured by the lion.
In the jungle | *Only the powerful survived.*

YOU COULD ALMOST SMELL THE SUFFERING THAT FILLED UP THE PLACE.
Most of the students at my school lived inside the bricks. The other unfortunates were youths with grades under par.
Then there was me | I'd chosen a small bit of coin over a proper education. I didn't realize I'd made the wrong choice until I was faced with its consequences.

We all have choices to make.
Some of us get tricked along the way.
++||— Stupid is a choice too —

I put on my best game-face and walked through the doors.

The school was a dilapidated old building—grayish|white paint flaked from the walls. At the door was a small security post and directly inside was a large lunchroom. The worn basketball court was to the right. Taking a left turn, you'd find some small offices where staff practiced their trade. There were many exits scattered throughout that first floor. The very back exit led to an old football|baseball field. In back of the field was an intermediate school with a small yard and playground then another small school for the mentally handicapped.

There were few, if any, Russians at that high school.

By the second week, I'd made a lifelong friend.

His name was RJ.

He was an Irish youngblood with dirty-blonde hair, a pale, freckly complexion and a prickly nose. RJ stood five-foot eight and was an average build for someone his age and size. We met while he passed a note to a girl using me as the messenger.

After class, we decided to stop and enjoy a few drinks at the middle school's playground. RJ laughed when I pulled out the fifth of vodka I had concealed in my backpack. I offered him a swig, he replied by producing his own pint of blackberry brandy.

I hadn't kept in touch with Adam.

But I sure enough saw his brother High — He sold me some of the best tress I've ever seen even to this day. I dug in the pocket of my designer jeans and pulled out a crumpled joint. After taking a few fast pulls, I leaned back on the concrete staircase we'd camped on and passed the joint to RJ.

. . .

I<small>T WAS LESS THAN THREE MONTHS INTO THE SCHOOL YEAR.</small>

I was sitting on over 9000$ in cash and the same in collectibles.

I stashed about 40 new releases into my bag for John the florist and walked to the corner store to purchase a pack of Marlboro squares, a habit I picked up from RJ.

Through the window, I could James standing at the counter with my bag in his hand as I walked back into the store. I'de left my bag open and on his way to the head he scoped the comic's inside.

I tried to lie.

James knew better.

He was stunned. There wasn't much he could do to keep himself from crying. Watching him shed tears as a direct result of my actions was not pleasant for me. I cared about James and never intended to hurt him.

Fuck it | The vodka took over and I just screamed on him. My job at the comic shop had outlived its value. It was time to move on.

I packed up my personal items I kept there and never returned.

As I walked home.
It felt like I left a small part of myself behind me.

I<small> VISITED </small>P<small>APPY AT HIS HOME.</small>

I had been to see him a few times since his Betsy passed.

On each occasion his health dwindled—*he loved vodka*—He was slowly drinking himself to death.

Mikhail lived in a small worn-down apartment building located next to the cemetery where his wife was buried. The walls of the building were a dull green and heavily faded due to many years of neglect. His third-floor apartment was a small one-bedroom flat scarcely fitted with second-hand furnishing. An old short-wave radio blurted out the news in Russian.

Pappy was always pleased to see me.

That day he was especially pleased to see the half gallon of vodka I produced from a black plastic bag I carried. Obtaining alcohol in a town like New York, it's easier than finding an egg in a henhouse.

When you're good friends with Ben (Franklin), you can get a hold of just about anything. Sideways store owners will cart you weapons-grade plutonium if you provide the correct denominations.

Pappy smiled as I sat at the battered aluminum table.

He quickly joined me, producing two tall drinking glasses and poured vodka, quickly filling both glasses to the rim. In one chug he swiftly disposed of the liquid in his glass, looking toward me to do the same. I took a swig, drinking about a quarter of it. Pappy complained about his living arrangements, wishing he'd moved to Brighton with the rest of the Russian community.

The once lifeless and decrepit Brighton Beach, was bustling with splendor in those days. Many of the Russian criminals who made their way to Brooklyn had, by then, begun setting up shop. Russian entrepreneurs started to take over Brighton Beach, (which would soon be known as Little Odessa). They had already set into motion the most lucrative criminal ventures in American history.

Pappy had never been so destitute in his life.

He couldn't even afford a vehicle | He felt lonely and abandoned.

I told Pappy I had plenty of money and would buy him any car he wanted—*that was the motive for my visit*—I sought his counsel in helping me deal with the moral implication of what I'd done to my former employer, as well as helping me determine what I should do with my money. By then, he was on his third tall glass of vodka, and demanded I finish mine before he commented.

I tilted back a tiny chair he found in some junk pile then took down the vodka, finally beginning to feel its soothing effects | I told him I was sitting on close to 10,000$ in cash, nearly the same in valuables. Then I revealed my affection for my former employer and how I felt sick at myself for betraying him.

My grandfather stood and poured me another tall glass. He offered me a sour tomato to take the edge off the vodka.

PAPPY PULLED HIS CHAIR UP NEXT TO MINE.

He put his oversized arm around my shoulder and offered me his wisdom. "Feel no pity for this man, James," he whispered. "A fool and his money are lucky to even find each other at all. More so, it's the responsibility of much smarter, more dubious men to part them," he finished.

As for The Money.

Pappy told me it would find a use for itself given the right amount of time. "Remember, money comes to money. Hold it tightly until an opportunity to multiply it arises. No need to look, just don't spend the money and more will come to you," he knowingly stated.

"Comic books are childish and have no place in a world of men," Pappy stated. He instructed me to sell my comic book collection and turn it into a more liquid asset.

They were no longer any use to me.
I didn't even want to look at them.

I REACHED INSIDE THE POCKET OF MY BLUE JEANS.

Inside, a sizable knot of bills wrapped in a rubber band — 1000$ I had specifically prepared for this encounter. I placed it on the table near the almost half-empty bottle of vodka and called myself a cab.

I didn't have to tell him to not tell my parents:
He knew they could never understand.

We spent the rest of our time together in silence.

WHEN THE CAB SOUNDED ITS HORN — I GOT UP TO LEAVE.
Pappy put his right hand on my shoulder to stop me.
He handed me my cup | *Almost empty.*

"Make sure to finish what you start, Gary," he exclaimed, sharply staring at me. "Or someone will always be willing to do it for you. What's yours is yours. Let someone take it once and everyone will think it's alright to take from you," he finished.

I swallowed the substance, already dizzy from its effects, then I staggered down the hallway.

"One more thing," Pappy whispered as he walked towards me. "This path you have chosen. It's a dangerous one. Walk careful this road, Gary. I have witnessed many good men die along its path. You will see things ordinary eyes were never meant to, and you'll have to do things you may one day come to regret. Eventually you will come to a point where the ground behind you will crumble and there will be no turning back. Be ready, be ready for anything. BE READY FOR EVERYTHING," he concluded.

HIS GRIM COLD STARE FRIGHTENED ME.

As I rode the cab back to my parent's home,
PAPPY'S WORDS SPUN ROUND MY HEAD LIKE A CAROUSEL.

Soon EVERYTHING WOULD CHANGE.

❻❻❻ I WAS ON A ONEWAY RIDE | STRAIGHT DOWN TO HELL **❻❻❻**
BEELZEBUB HIMSELF WOULD BE WAITING THERE TO SCORE ME A LOOSE.

— ψ — AND GIVE ME A WARM WELCOME HOME — ψ —

_____

1.
2.

THE FRENCH TEACHER

If I only knew the answer
  Or I thought we had a chance
  Or I could stop this
  Then I would stop this thing from spreading like a cancer
-Martin Gore

++||— MANKIND —
  What a predictable lot we are.
  WE EAT—SHIT—SLEEP—FUCK AND FIGHT
  —|— JUST LIKE ANIMALS —|—

SO, WHAT SETS US APART FROM THE WILD ANIMALS IN THE JUNGLE?
   Some would have you believe that it's our soul that disconnects us from the creatures roaming the landscape in search of a prey for their next meal—*The Soul*—they say, is that special grant from God which allows us to feel. The soul manufactures emotions such as compassion and love. It's these emotions that produce our conscience.

You know, that so small voice that instructs us on what's right and what's wrong || *The good and the bad.*

I LIVE IN A WORLD WHERE I CAN'T BUY INTO THIS THEORY.
I say to you now — People walk this earth who are soulless.

I've encountered such creatures.

Plans for a soul were not included in their blueprints. The capacity to feel has only one solitary receptor ++||— *Greed* —

Emotions such as empathy, compassion, and mercy are as foreign to them as sand is to an Eskimo.

WHAT MADE MAN UNIQUE WAS OUR ABILITY TO CREATE.
Our ability to invent and innovate. It was this ability to make something out of nothing that gave mankind dominion over the world and everything in it.

We threw all that out the window when we started building indoor shopping malls with three-hundred-dollar jeans and PlayStation consoles inside the shops.

MODERN SOCIETY IS GOVERNED TWO PRINCIPLES:

++||— MORE AND BETTER —

Last time I checked, animals don't need to fill their caves, holes, or hovels with piles of useless shit and shiny trinkets.

I have yet to meet a man who wouldn't trade his Honda for a BMW if given the opportunity. *Why is that ?* Both automobiles provide transport from point A to point B.

Fact is | Society deems the BMW a better vehicle.

Unfortunately in today's world.
The more you are worth the better you are treated.

In a civilization such as this, it makes sense to acquire more of the things that are considered better. These days it seems like everything we do is so we can have more of this or better than that.

Sadly, the More You Have — the Better You Are.
We are "the Human Race"
And after all ++||— The object of any race is to win —

Only through experience have I learned that winning is measured in dollars and cents.

People quarrel over one of three things.
MONEY — SEX — RELIGION

We want more money, better sex, and most have committed to a God *who we expect* to be **Better** at giving **More**.

Whenever feelings are hurt, negative words are exchanged, or violence is involved, one, or all, of these elements can be found to be the root of the problem. Every dispute in human history has been based on these factors. They have been the motive behind every crime man has perpetrated upon his fellows and they have sparked wars where millions have perished.

EVERY NIGHT.

My parents would argue over more money and a better life. The bickering became particularly frenzied when my uncle, Misha (Mee-Sha), decided to make an appearance at our home.

Misha was my father's half-brother
Pappy's bastard son.

75

In Odessa, Misha's career was that of a full-time shoemaker and part-time smuggler. He specialized in bringing contraband American films into the country. This was a highly rewarding enterprise. One in which he was able to squirrel away quite a bit of coin. Misha used this money and Pappy's connections to buy his tickets to the Promised Land.

THE ONE THING YOU COULD NEVER CALL MISHA WAS HANDSOME.

He was five-foot three and weighed nearly two-hundred pounds. He boasted a giant bald patch on top of his saucer-shaped head.

My uncle Misha had absolutely no skills whatsoever.

He refused to learn a trade and was fast to backhand his wife for even the slightest cross expression. The entire extent of his English vocabulary were the following two words | *Fuck* and *You*.

He took the job of waiter in a Russian *banya*[1] located near the Brighton Beach area. He often came to our home to borrow money, blubber about his many health problems, get my father drunk on ghastly amounts of vodka, or possibly all the above.

My mother detested Misha.

She considered him a louse and a wife-beater.

America was just as hard for Misha and his family as it was for ours | That is until he got connected with the Gasoliners.

THE GASOLINERS WERE A BAND OF LEGENDARY RUSSIAN CRIMINALS.

The earliest Russian organized criminal activity dates back to this crew. In the small ten-year span of their operations, the Gasoliners accumulated over a billion dollars in ill-gotten gains.

The Gasoliners, were composed of Russian|Jew immigrants, mostly from Odessa, who gained entry into the US in the mid to late

70s. They came to America with little or no money and quickly got right down to it. *Immediately*, they set up illegal gambling parlors and brothels in the Brighton Beach area.

At the time Brighton was mostly populated by blacks and Puerto Ricans. Drugs and violence transformed this once magnificent seashore wonderland into a ghetto wasteland. The shops were decrepit, in a state of disarray, and the streets were overrun with crime and reeked of sin.

THROUGH THE USE OF STRONG-ARM TACTICS.

Russians took hold and began putting the blocks to locals.

First, they initiated a program of cooperation — *If you can call it that*. What they really did | Meander into the drug and whore houses and notified the owners|operators they had new partners.

++||— *If there were any problems* — Nikolai and his and two half-brothers BaseBall and BaT would be happy to play their smash hit, "2TheNutSack".

Pretty much, after that: Everything sorted out quickly.

The local thuggery were accomplished lawbreakers but were also no match for the military training and sheer ruthlessness that the Russian *émigrés* demonstrated. The Russians were fresh from fighting a war in the Middle East. Salty and battle ready, they showed no mercy for those who stood in their path.

AFTER ALMOST A YEAR OF VICIOUS TURF WARS; THEIR RIVALS SUBMITTED

The blacks and Puerto Ricans were slowly pushed out their own district, only to be replaced with Russian pilgrims of all varieties. The new colonizers opened up businesses, then more Russians came.

The more Russians that came.
The more business thrived.

The original criminal element, then just a small but highly organized group, applied extortion to the locals and just about anyone else they could. Between the drugs, gambling, prostitution and extortion, the small group that initially moved into Brighton had themselves a sweet little hustle.

ITALIAN ORGANIZED CRIME WAS AT THE HEIGHT OF ITS POWER.

Captains from well-known crime families sent ambassadors to Brighton to claim their slice of the pie. The Russians were callous and unforgiving, and they were in no way stupid.

At the time, the Russians had neither the manpower nor the resources their predecessors did. Realizing that war with the Italians would prove catastrophic, they choose collaboration as a practical means of establishing a power base and securing assets. In the pioneering years of Russian organized crime, Russians kicked up more than half of their earning to their Italian superiors.

In the years that followed—the tables would slowly turn and the Russian *Mafiya* would be the one calling the shots.

What the Italians lacked was vision.

Their conventional rackets, although effective, were no match for the ingenuity and foresight of a people who lived under a system of oppression for thousands of years.

The mitigating factor, the major difference between the Italians and the Russians | *Creativity.*

The old guard was set in its ways.

Italians only understood that X+Y = Z.

++||— *Russians smash anything to get to Z* — For the Russian criminal, it didn't matter what had to be destroyed as long as Z was the end result.

. . .

IT ALL STARTED WITH GASOLINE.

It goes like this: A few of the Russian criminals—*thirteen in total,* deduced that they needed to launder their graft.

A small gas station on the corner of Coney Island and Brighton Beach Avenue would suffice. At the time, gasoline was a cash business, hardly anyone had a credit card, especially the immigrants who populated the area. The owners could claim bogus sales to clean up some of their dirty money. Unexpectedly, the gas station began to turn a profit.

A legal profit.

This astounded the group. They had no intention of ever earning a nickel selling gasoline. Recognizing that there was money to be made in gasoline, they had an Epiphany. *What if ?* They were to hijack one of the trucks that delivered the gas? They could sell the gas at their station and make a fortune. Just one heist would make their other operations seem like monopoly money.

The plan worked so well, they repeated the process.

They not only sold the gasoline at their station, they dismantled the trucks and sold the parts to local chop-shops, and in some cases shipped the truck in its entirety back to the fatherland.

Each successful heist produced millions in profit.

The next step | Buy up more gas stations to facilitate the fuel they'd stolen, but selling the stolen gas wasn't enough for them. They began adding water to the gasoline to maximize their profit. The Gasoliners never paid a penny in taxes on any of the gas sold.

They were making money three ways:

Selling stolen petrol, watering down stolen petrol, *and*, refusing to pay Uncle Sam taxes on the petrol they stole.

The Gasoliners used these Wild West tactics until the drivers themselves got tired of losing cargo and started riding with US marshals and outfitting trucks with tracking devices. The first applications of GPS can be accredited to these very events.

It just came too late.

The wealth from this gasoline scam was used to clean up and revitalize the Brighton Beach area. The one-time criminals were business owners, buying up restaurants, nightclubs, clothing shops and countless other establishments across the greater New York area. Their shops and restaurants are some of the most glamorous in the world and stand as reminders of their criminal achievements.

The Gasoliners eventually became victims of their own greed, murdering one another to claim a larger share of the fortune.

Those who survived had the government to face.

You don't steal enough petrol to fuel Bangkok without tripping the alarm. The United States government, aware of their operation, demanded convictions.

Whoever was left eventually completed prison terms ranging from seven to fourteen years. In many cases, prison was safer than the mercy of their partners. Don't get twisted, The Gasoliners never abandoned their criminal roots. The very few who remain, continue to practice their illicit operations.

Men like my uncle Misha proved to be very useful.

Misha was the son of a recognized villain from the old school. Everyone knew Pappy *as a stand-up, no-nonsense killer* — Because of it, my uncle was allowed entry into the restricted brotherhood of the

Gasoliners. The *banya* Misha was waitering was run by one of their junior associates.

AFTER A FEW WEEKS WORKING WITH THE GASOLINERS.

Misha stopped at our home to return all the money he'd borrowed. After Misha and my father finished a liter of Absolut, I joined then for a walk outside where Misha showcased his new, white-on-grey Mercedes 500SEL.

His wife waited in the car, nursing a swollen lip.

For more than an hour, Misha attempted to (con)vince my father to join him on the next score. Involvement even at the smallest of levels meant hundreds of thousands for the family

MY FATHER KNEW MANY OF THE ORIGINAL THIRTEEN GASOLINERS.

In Russia, he was close with at least two of them.

In fact, he had been approached by one of their people some time before Misha had come around flossing his bling.

"We didn't leave Russia to continue to live like criminals. What kind of example would you be setting for our son?" Stella exclaimed.

They argued for more than six months, until my father finally crumbled. The topic was never mentioned again.

Secretly | I dreamed of being part of the gasoline crew.
I would sit in class and drift into deep fantasy.

I BECAME ONE OF THE HIGHWAYMEN.
Mercilessly leaping from a car and intimidating the truck driver.
Sometimes shooting him dead.
Only content at the sight of the drivers blood.
Pooling atop the hot asphalt of the highway.

Most days I thought very little of my father.
I was losing all respect for the working man.

It was at RJ's house, during the opening scene of *Goodfellas*, I first heard Henry Hill declare: "For as long as I can remember. I've always wanted to be a gangster." His magnetic words entered by way of my ears they quickly crept throughout my system easily locating their final target deep inside my still soft heart.

It was glorious, the gangster life.

They had it all | Money, cars, striking women clawing at one another for a small chance to worship these men of power.

Men who demanded respect.
These men didn't ask.
++||— *They Took* —

I contemplated why they would kill each other and concluded that there were probably some murders, but for the most part, just theatrics placed into the film to shock folks into steering clear of crime — *I thought about really having to murder another person.*

HALLOWEEN, MY FRESHMAN YEAR OF HIGH SCHOOL.
It was a very cold twilight, at around seven p.m.
I was in need of some squares, so I walked out the rear of my parent's condo to the corner bodega. The streets were already littered with broken eggs, shaving cream, and toilet paper. Those "bombings" had become the Halloween ritual of the Brooklyn youth.

It was a strange time for Brooklyn.

Dinkins had been our mayor for nearly a year, and crime was steadily on the rise. He was New York's first black mayor and I can say, with great certainty, that mayoring, wasn't at the forefront of his agenda | Lawlessness and chaos became the norm.

THE MOON WAS FULL.

Children dressed in costumes giddily strolled by.

Something fell from the sky AND with a crack, shattered at my feet. Egg yolk and shells splattered my yellow Timberland work boots. I looked up at the sky to investigate and another egg nearly missed my head. Then I was pummeled with more than a dozen eggs.

Looking up again, in the twilight, I was briefly able to discern the outline of a human form perched atop the roof of a nearby apartment complex.

I entered the building, quickly I ran up the seven flights of stairs.

Panting, I reached the door to the rooftop and noticed a disabled security device. I opened the door only to be greeted with another egg, which barely missed my head.

This was the first time I'd ventured onto the roof of the condo. I saw the Manhattan skyline in the distance and was overwhelmed by the lights of the Twin Towers and the blinking light on top the Empire State.

Four male figures approached me.

THE FIRST INTRODUCED HIMSELF AS LOUIE C.

He put out his hand for me to shake. As he shook my hand with his right, with his left he slammed an egg to the top of my head.

The others burst into laughter. I found humor in the situation and decided to join in with them. We all stood there laughing and enjoying the moment.

The other three introduced themselves.

Terry D. — Lenny R. — and Sandy N.

Over the next twelve years, *we would become the Best|Worst of friends*. In the years to follow — Three of them would die — One would unsuccessfully try to murder me on two separate occasions.

Lou C. was Italian.

He lived above a pork-store on the avenue a few blocks from my home, was known as Louie *Batz*². He was the leader of the small crew.

Louie was thin and tall, about five-foot nine.

His blonde hair, grey eyes, and prominent features leant him a rugged handsomeness. His face was covered in craters from a bad spell of chicken-pox he suffered as a child. They didn't take away from his confident demeanor or his gallant features.

Lou spoke in a muted tone through a series of mumbles; it made him hard to understand. Still, he had a manner that made people want to draw close to him. He was true to his name and *about as crazy as they get* —Lou Batz was the type of guy who pulls his dick out, puts it on the table and demands you do the same | So he could see whose is bigger.

Lou dated a sweet little gal named Annie.

—|— She was totally devoted to him —|—

His mother made the finest meatballs I have ever tasted in my life.

LOU MET TERRY D. IN ELEMENTARY SCHOOL.

Terry lived on the other side of my parent's apartment building. He was a trendy hipster who fancied himself a badass hoodlum. Terry was only a few inched taller than me but weighed about as much as a sheet of loose-leaf paper.

He styled himself after Johnny Depp.

Nowadays, someone like Terry, would be known as a metrosexual but back then—he was sexy and strange. His father, Big-Terry was an exhausted heroin addict and gambler.

I often waited outside Terry's apartment door for hours on end while he prettied himself up with hairspray and eye-makeup. When he finally opened his door, the sweet stench of opium would fill the hallway. I got along with Terry exceptionally well.

LENNY R. WAS A COMEDIAN.

He'd make us double up whenever he started in with his funny voices and imitations. He was about thirty pounds overweight but still a real pretty boy. Lenny had those feminine features that make men look sweet and appealing. I thought he was a half-a-fag when he came around with his manicured fingernails.

Lenny came from money. His father was a scientist who invented something meaningful, like the smokeless ashtray or something of great significance. He used to live in the neighborhood.

I liked Lenny, he was always in a good mood and had something funny to say about everything.

We all became instant friends.

The last semester of my freshman year I took French as my foreign language. I needed to learn French about the same way as Beethoven needed a power drill. I took it because I had to and figured I might as well get it over with.

I slept through most of the classes.

Every so often, I would take a bathroom break and sip on A quart of Georgi. Towards the middle of the semester the instructor requested my presence after class.

I was particularly drunk that day.

The teacher, an older well-mannered woman named Mrs. Baitcher, reminded me of my grandmother Klara and seemed to care a lot about her students. Mrs. Baitcher informed me she could smell the liquor on my breath and told me she wanted to read my palm.

She instantly began tracing the lines on my hand.

After thoroughly probing my right hand she looked up at me solemnly. "I think you should know what I'm about to tell you, Gary," she said pausing to gauge my reaction, "I'm a gypsy and come from a long line of prophets. I've been feeling your impression since you came into my class, I had to see for myself" she finished.

I was too inebriated to care.

"You have a break in your lifeline. This means that you will have a difficult choice to make. It will not only shape your entire life. It will greatly influence the lives of the people around you. It's very rare to have such a break. In every case that I've seen, the choice has been between good and evil | Only very exceptional people are given a choice. For most, life is predetermined.

Know this, whatever you choose, you will be great and command much power. Choose wisely. People's lives will depend on you," she stated.

I nodded, pulled my hand away and left class.

We parted, I was left thinking she might be 4bits short of a nickel. But I was drunk, so it was hard to give a shit.

Once sober | Her words crept into my mushy membranes then straight into my nucleus — *A few drinks later,* I decided to forget the incident.

* * *

SHORTLY AFTER.

High mentioned that Adam would be returning home to visit for summer recess. We contacted each other and scheduled a time to meet up.

THE WEEKEND PRIOR TO ADAM'S RETURN.

Sandy N. invited all of us to his summer home in upstate New York for the weekend.

Sandy was number6[3].

He stood a very heavyset five-foot eight, was of Italian origin and lived in one of the "normal" areas around my school. The group had been friends since grade school.

I was a newcomer | An outsider.

John, Sandy's father, was a Vietnam War veteran who went on to work a monotonous desk job. He was short and unbelievably overweight but what struck me the hardest about him were his horrible chompers. He was missing all of his molars, and the few remaining teeth he had were chipped and corroded with black residue. But aside from his many hygienic shortcomings, John was a pretty nice guy. We packed into John's suburban and the seven of us took the five-hour drive to the weekend getaway.

I brought the trees and RJ brought plenty of beverages.

John wasn't one to pay mind to our alcohol and drug abuse. He mostly slumped in his recliner. There was a troubling unease about him. His eyes glazed a greyish hue and appeared to suffer a powerful indifference.

. . .

His upstate home was a small brick structure.

There were three tiny bedrooms and a bathroom with a standup shower. The house sat on four acres of land filled with greenery and wildlife.

I'd never been to the country before.

I walked the vast expanse, exploring the unprocessed settings with great wonderment.

Saturday morning:

John produced a .38 snub-nose, a .44 Magnum, and a 30aught6. Owning a firearm within New York City limits was near impossible. New York's gun laws continue to be some of the most oppressive in the nation. The probability of a regular anybody permitted to own a firearm was slim to none | *And Slim* just Left Town.

John's war hero status was inconsequential.

The Constitution explicitly avows our right as citizens to keep and bear arms, attach as many amendments as you like—*The words are crystal clear.*

So how do you stop the American public from satisfying their desire to act upon the rights granted them not by our forefathers *but by our creator HisSelf?* You can conceal it any which way. You can take away the rights of felony offenders all day long. You can focus on the fact that non-citizens aren't covered under the blanket of our Constitution. At the end of the day | The average American wants what he was promised.

The answer here is dollars and cents.
That's what it always boils down to isn't it.

You deny public ownership of firearms by applying outrageous taxes by way of permits and fees—*New York is notorious for this behavior*—for every single weapon that's registered to you, a permit is required.Not only do you have to pay for the background check as well as the permit to possess each weapon, you're required to pay annual dues for every weapon you register. Quickly becoming a prohibitively expensive discomfort ordinary society can neither afford nor be burdened with.

Adding the fact that there are laws in place prohibiting the sale of guns within the five boroughs, it's near impossible to obtain a firearm of any sort.

John wasn't going to let a few obstacles stand in the way of his Constitutional right. To men like John | Owing a gun was just as American as Catcher's Mitts and Golden Retrievers.

He listed his upstate residence as his primary dwelling.

Since his cabin was well outside the city limits, the gun laws were much more lenient, so obtaining gun wasn't easy but it was possible.

I twisted a Philly blunt, hoping its soothing smoke would ease my extremities. Lou Batz was already setting up targets when I was handed the .38 Smith.

In every picture show I've ever seen, the guns were illuminated.
SOVEREIGN OBJECTS OF INFLUENCE.
✝ Dangerous and Sexy ✝

I HELD THE WEAPON UP WITH MY RIGHT HAND.

My aim was directed at one of the bottles affixed at a distance of about thirty meters. When I squeezed the trigger and heard its astonishing roar—the blaster's recoil launched my arm into the air.

Terrified, I dropped the revolver onto the grass beneath me.

Sandy stood nearby and erupted into a gut-busting laugh.

He retrieved the revolver then clutched it with his right hand, with his left he cupped the bottom of the weapon, allowing the fingers of his left to touch the back of his right palm then pointing both of his thumbs forward. "This is how you hold a gun. Don't believe what they show you in the movies. You can't hold a gun with one hand and expect to control it. The recoil will toss your hand back, like it just did." He smirked.

I RETOOK THE SMOKER AND HELD IT LIKE HE HAD SHOWN
It felt satisfying | Now rightly comfortable in my hands.

"It's just an extension of your arm, Gary," he stated. Sandy stood behind and held my forearms as I affixed my aim. He directed me to line up the sights. *I tensed up when preparing to pull the trigger.* Sandy whacked my forearm, demanding I loosen up my wrist. "Let the pistol control your movement or your wrist can snap from the pressure," he warned.

* * *

Squeezing on the trigger | I felt the blaster spit out its parcel.

+ THE BOTTLE I HAD MARKED SHATTERED INTO DEBRIS +
MY NOSTRILS FILLED WITH THE SMELL OF BRIMSTONE AND CHALK.
Its fragrance imbued me with impressions of supremacy.

IT WAS A FEELING OF UNLIMITED CONTROL
♙ *No Limitations* ♙
THE POWER TO SWAY OPINION.
POWER ENOUGH TO PERSUADE THE INCONVINCIBLE.
THE POWER TO GRANT PARDONS AND DESIGNATE MISFORTUNE
ONTO THOSE REQUIRED TO PERISH.

IT EXEMPTED ME FROM CONSEQUENCES.
—|Ψ|— | IT MADE ME COMMANDER | —|Ψ|—

* * *

THE FOLLOWING SATURDAY, ADAM AND I REUNITED.

The thought of seeing Adam filled me with great joy. He was he was my friend when no one else wanted to be, and I loved him for that.

We would meet at a movie theater, on the corner of Kings Highway and Coney Island Avenue. That side of Kings Highway was a busy shopping district filled with expensive shops and bustling with life. The theatre — *RKO Kingsway*, was a tiny place with small screens (which in the following years would close and be replaced by an indoor flea-market).

IT WAS A BRISK DAY IN THE BEGINNINGS OF JUNE.

The breeze was quite uncommon for that time of year.

Adam arrived in a crisp BMW 325i convertible, with aftermarket BBS honeycomb wheels.

We hardly paid attention to the film, caring only for each other's company and chatting about our past year. When the show finished, we retired to Adam's mansion to sip on some beverages and get our lungs right. I followed Adam into the kitchen, where he pulled out a pickle jar filled almost to the rim with white powder. Adam grinned, spilling some onto the marble top of the island | His father was one of the biggest drug suppliers in the state.

"It will make you feel like you never have," Adam remarked.

I participated strictly as an exercise.

My desire was the study of the effects of cocaine on the human condition. I had no intention of ever upgrading from the recreational use of marijuana+vodka. Mine was merely a venture to comprehend its nature | *Purely scientific*. What intrigued me far more than the cocaine was the reality that all the wealth around me was brought about solely from the distribution of said cocaine.

Inhaling a line, of the sticky white substance through a hundred-dollar bill that Adam rolled up tightly—I *almost immediately felt its effect*—the sharp sting in my nose was replaced by an intensely-alert feeling and a forthcoming numbness of the jaw and nasal passage.

—‖— It felt good —‖— ALMOST TOO GOOD
I felt unexpectedly sharp and potent.
It gave off a fresh style of sureness certainty and determination.

I enjoyed the feeling, but was struck harshly by the residual craving for more left behind by the first intake.

It was a reaction of ravenousness hunger.

A feeling that further use was not only necessary | IT WAS MANDATORY. The reason that it created so much wealth for those who dispensed it became obvious.

No matter how much of it you did.
There would be no end to your need for more.

ADAM WENT UPSTAIRS TO HIS ROOM.
Leaving me to mull over the implementations of such a product on a market of eager consumers. *This was something people weren't capable of putting down*, and I was privy to a direct link into the very source of it. Trading in such a commodity was something I'd have to give significant contemplation.

I twisted up a fatty and retreated to Adam's room.

The door was cracked open and I found my buddy Adam, on the floor | He was convulsing. His complexion was a bright yellowish green and a thick burbling material erupted onto his lips then wept down his chin. Seeing the tracks on his left arm leading to the needle that protruded from the crook of his elbow.

I heaved.

Adam decided that sniffing cocaine was no longer adequate. Following natural progression, Adam took a more direct approach slamming straight coke into the thin capillaries of his forearm.

I fell to my knees — Cradling Adam's head in my arms.

THAT COLD JUNE DAY THE LORD RECEIVED MY VERY BEST FRIEND.
I called his brother to tell him. Adam's family didn't take well the news of his passing ++||— *They had no one to blame but themselves* —

Terry was closest to me, I shared my grief with him.
We went to the roof in silence and watched the sun set on Gotham.

WHEN THE SCHOOL YEAR ENDED.
I was faced with the prospect of finding employment for the summer. RJ found work on one of the many fishing boats occupying Sheepshead Bay. Sandy lined up a job with a neighborhood shop. Lou would spend the summer working at a bakery owned by Annie's parents. Lenny, he didn't need a job, he was spending daddy's money.
Terry and I were left to our own devices.
I was sixteen | Terry was a year older.
We both considered ourselves too good to flip burgers but possessed no skills to warrant a better job.

Terry provided the solution.

In an obscure local newspaper, he located a posting for

telemarketing work. The posting boasted of a base pay plus commission and claimed an unlimited earnings potential. *Intrigued*, Terry placed a call and immediately we were invited for an interview.

We took the subway five stops to a shifty area of Brooklyn.

The "office" was located in the basement of a two-story residential building — We met with a tall, fast-talker who called himself Steve. His bushy unkept beard summoned imaginations of a tipple beatnik. Steve's description of the job entailed convincing technology managers to purchase computer cleaning supplies over the telephone.

NOW THIS HERE — IS QUITE THE SCAM.

Please: Allow me to explain.

You call the mo-mo some large or mid-size company put in charge of Information Systems (IT)

Prior to the current Iphone\Alexa transhumanism agenda, unrefined simpletons like your mannerless friend and uncomplicated narrator classified this discipline as Data-Processing.

You inform said mo-mo that you received the business reply card he (never) mailed from a popular computer magazine such as PC Magazine, Information Weekly, or any other recognizable industry publication. You then tell him that there was a coffee mug with our company's name and logo pictured on the reply card. He would (never) receive it with our compliments —Along with the small box of ten dozen anti-static wipes at the discounted price of 2.98$ each that he'd requested.

Before your mook has a chance to exhale.

The next set of instructions stress the urgent necessity for either a purchase order number, or definitive verbal confirmation of acceptance. If an event occurs in which mo-mo seems in any way cognizant and displays an allergy towards this particular variety of snake-oil, you immediately drop the number of wipes (jars of oil) you're forcing into his throat hole.

If objections persist, you drop again, to a modest manger's box of only a dozen wipes—*Under NoCircumstance*—can you let your mo-mo off the phone until he either buys something or he provides the name of the mo-mo afterwards, you know, the very one that has been certified by the handlers with the authority to buy.

Irony resides in the fact that there *was* never a reply card.

You fished his name out of a directory or bought it from a lead source such as Dunn and Bradstreet, Leads America, or any other organization that manufactures names of mooks who they've marked as infected with the *buy-over-the-phone* disorder.

The only people who get the coffee mug are men of audacious boldness | *Individuals such as myself.*

Now here's the kicker

These mo-mo's aren't even spending their own money. They're working off a budget allocated by their company — *This fact is crucial.*

After having received and paid for their initial purchase, a more experienced deceiver, a greasy doper not unlike Steve would call a second time. "Steve" would ask how they liked the product (in most cases they never even saw it) then would be told something along the lines of... "We here at XYZ company are performing a survey for Samsung America. We'd like to know which of the following you would find more useful; A fifty-two-inch television, an Intel notebook, or a brand-new home-theatre surround-sound system".

After mo-mo makes his choice, the salesman notifies him that the item will promptly be shipped right out to him — *Of course with our compliments* — Along with the remainder of his order for the year of only an additional twelve thousand staticide wipes | *As always,* The wipes will be provided at the discounted price of 2.98$ each.

The premise here is obvious.

The company has as much use for screen wipes as a ballerina has for steel-toed construction shoes. Our mo-mo is purchasing them for the sole purpose of caressing the promotional item.

In many cases the promo would be mailed to the buyers home rather than alerting the more ethical officers of the company.

The product itself was just a plain old hand wipe

The kind you get when they bring out your fortune cookie at the Chinese buffet. Sure, it had a picture of a computer screen on the front and said "staticide wipe," but upon closer examination, you'll find it's just a moist towel in a rubbing alcohol solution | *Hardly worth anywhere close to three bucks a package.*

This is the part where the gettin gets real good.

If the captured mo-mo actually buys the "remainder of the year's supply" he will be more than thrilled to learn that wipes aren't our only fraudulent invention.

Yep | If he was ridiculous enough to bite on the wipes, then out comes the "Hood and Housing Cleaner." In reality, nothing more than a twelve-ounce can of compressed air, available at the discount price of 29.98$ a can. A few dozen cases of this classic should satisfy any cretin's appetite for buying junk over the phone.

Intelligence dictates that, after buying some of this trash, any loser gets hip to the hustle, and at the very least slams the phone down hard if ever bothered by your persistent attempts at vending him your useless drek.

Unfortunately, intelligence or any semblance of it doesn't exist in the realm of the telephone — *There's something unexplainably mystical about this instrument* | If used correctly, the telephone can project some strange component that renders the unfortunate gudgeon attached to its transceiver captive to your every suggestion.

. . .

I AM COMPELLED TO MENTION ONE INTERESTING PIECE OF NOSTALGIA.

Some years ago | There was a mo-mo who occupied the post of DPM (Data-Processing Manager) at the Toronto Stock Exchange. He was somewhat of an important bigshit and, through many years of hard work, earned himself a position of authority in which he was able to purchase just about anything he wanted, as long it pertained to computers.

He bought the small box of ten dozen wipes, paid promptly and was subsequently called by a senior sales manager.

Thus began a cyclonic shopping-binge in which, throughout the course of two years, more than 1.2million$ worth of hooey (massive amounts of garbage) was shipped to him via airmail.

The Toronto Stock Exchange has a plethora of computers, but the reality is, *this particular mo-mo,* was a degenerate of insatiable compulsion. The freebies coupled with untrue projections of his influential ranking delivered the appropriate conduit in which he continued to amass yet unheard of quantities of the most potent snake-oil concoction found anywhere on planet earth.

It got to the point where Mr. mo-mo didn't know what to do with the shit. He'd already filled multiple store rooms.

++||— *But still he bought more —*

Eventually, he was spotted by a board member, in a vacant lot, a few miles from the facility—*shovel in hand*—he was attempting to bury some of the useless computer supplies he could not stop buying. He was consequently fired from his post and, last we heard, committed himself to a Puzzle-Factory in Vancouver.

THE TELEMARKETERS AT THIS BASEMENT SCAM SHOP WERE SOME OF THE grimiest filths I'd ever laid my young eyes on.

Every last one of those lowlifes was a drug user.

I'm talking from the main bosses straight down to the bizarre sideshows that despite their obvious failings, maintained gainful employment. They smoked more trees than a throng of horsebacked Cherokee Indians. In fact most sampled enough nose-candy to choke out the Cloverfield Monster. I was astonished to find what would in polite society be construed as the sickest brand of freak I've ever beheld call somewhat important people they'd never met and sell them the equivalent of pruned dogshit. Still, educated men in positions of authority *bought it by the bushel.*

Regardless of the setting.
Terry and I were eager to get started.

The job offered a generous draw plus a ten percent commission on anything we sold. If the tools we saw selling this waste were successful then two sharp youngbloods like ourselves should be able to make a small fortune.

THE FLOOR MANAGER, RICKY K., A YOUNG ITALIAN SAID:
"If a monkey could talk, he'd be doing this job," and decided to give us a go.

Rick was a character in his own right.

He claimed to be "connected" with the Italians and fancied himself a wiseguy. His last name sounded like *Kukurooza* which means "corn" in Russian | I called him Ricky *"Kuku"*.
I didn't know it yet, but that name would follow him perpetually.
Rick was tall and slender with a sharp chin and a hawk-like nose. His black, parted hair was always in shambles. Ricky's grey eyes protruded slightly from their sockets, probably a consequence of many years of cocaine abuse. He claimed to be in his late thirties but looked no older than twenty-three.

Rick appeared to have plenty of paper.

He pushed a late-model, tan Jaguar and covered himself in expensive fashions. He always had a witty comment and spoke more with his hands than his mouth, his movements always exaggerated.

Ricky smoked grass all day long, sniffed lines of white that would make a normal heart explode and spent more time on the phone fixing bets than he ever did pushing the junk he was supposed to be.

By the close of that first day, Ricky handed us both a script and Terry and I started slamming wipes.

We took to Telemarketing
✠ LIKE CORNFLAKES TAKE TO MILK ✠

Our first few sales were supervised by senior salesmen.

Whenever we had a mo-mo on the line, ready to purchase, we'd hand the phone to someone more experienced who would close the deal. Most of the time, the buyer couldn't tell the difference in voices, and they'd just continue where we left off. When the mo-mo did notice a change in tenor, the senior salesman would cough and complain about a cold he suffered.

The telephone in the hands of a specialist, becomes a MysteriousMechanism capable of lulling a sophisticated, worldly man into a trance-like state of bewilderment

Terry and I were awarded the telephone-names: Ted Baxter (Gary) and Bill Robinson (Terry), after the famous *Bill and Ted's Excellent Adventure.*

The reason for the telephone names is two-fold.

It's the job of a salesman to configurate a facade.

The mo-mo you're calling can't see what you look like or where you're calling from. You become everyone you have ever wanted to be, *they only have a voice.* Any talented operator is able to project the image of standing seven feet tall, himself a man of auspicious taste and unquestionable authority.

The challenge is in the ability to convince *yourself* that in fact it's the mo-mo who has been honored with this incredibly great fortune. Failure to recognize this fact would prove to be both foolhardy and catastrophic. A sense of urgency must be created where there can only be one plausible outcome | Buying useless garbage whose only value is the percentage that it pays out in commissions.

The second reason is obvious.

Our product is junk with a value that's negligible at best.
The only scenario in which knowledge of our government names might be useful would be assisting law enforcement in the impending investigation.

That very first month.

Terry and I far surpassed any expectations the senior staff may have had for us. We outsold everyone on the floor. Including Rick (he was probably too busy putting 20times[4] on the Mets).

I PRACTICED THE HARD-SELL, (AKA THE SLAM-SELL).
I'd call the buyer and get right to shoving the product firmly down his cake-hole. Whenever given the chance I would enjoy shouting insults and rudely belittling anyone with the slightest audacity to question my influence. "No" was never acceptable | Its response further fueling my contempt for any mo-mo's that couldn't force out the courage to tell me to go fuck a duck and slam the phone down hard.

TERRY HAD A SMOTHER WAY, THE SOFT-SELL (AKA THE SILENT-SELL).
Within moments he became the buyer's trusted confidant.

A man of earned wisdom celebrated for recognizing unique treasures. Already living in abundance his reward was gained by revealing his valuable mysteries.

Terry was like a soothsaying mo-mo whisperer.

For Terry, "No" was a vague possibility but never a viable option.

I periodically overheard him softly mumbling confidential insights of the most important urgency. In reality the only great secret lay in the fact that Terry was a teenage inadequate with dark-painted fingernails. His predominant concerns rooted only in smoking copious amounts of dope then squandering the remainder of his commissions on necessities such as petroleum-based hair products, munchy snacks, and the never-ending acquisition of the newest dope smoking innovations (drug paraphernalia).

We attracted different types of buyers.
Mine was impulsive | His more practical.
Obviously, the object was the same.

Once we started making a decent bit of coin, Lenny wanted to get involved. Due to our success, we were able to convince Ricky Kuku to put him on the payroll. Lenny *wasn't bad* on the phone. Never truly effective, he lacked motivation.

Terry and I both come up from poverty.
We were starving ++||— *Hungry like wolves* —
And ready to devour lambs for our share of the chow.

On top of the money I made selling wipes, I supplemented my income by selling weed to the entire sales floor. *It seemed as though there was no end to their maniacal consumption.*

The fiends frequently approached me for white.

Still reeling from Adam's death, I refused to sell the detestable powder that killed him. I cut Terry and Lenny in on my deal, making them partners. They didn't do a damn thing but collect from the profits | *I felt as though they were my brothers.* Sadly, I've always held onto an altruistic notion of true friendship. Besides, I was never the type to eat with both hands.

I got the dope from High.

It puzzled me that he continued to sell the awful toxin that killed his brother, only through incident I've concluded that *business is business and above all else*

++||— The show must go on —

Throughout the course of that summer, Terry and I would make more than seven grand each selling wipes, and a few thousand more furnishing trees to the natives.

Terry spent his money frivolously buying useless junk and trinkets. By the end of the summer he was almost flat out of busted.

—| ▢ |— THE CURSE OF THE SALESMAN —| ▢ |—

It's a well-known fact that the best salesmen are the easiest to sell. He decided not to return to school, opting to keep churning out wipes.

I HAD OTHER PLANS.

Having spent only a small portion of my money I was left with almost 23,000$ in cash.

It seemed as though the horizon of unlimited victory was well within range. Further schooling was useless, but it was a commitment I was obligated to fulfill. Pappy's words, "Always finish what you start", were still clear in my mind.

EVERY PIECE OF CURRENCY ON PLANET EARTH:
COULD IN NO WAY PREPARE ME *for the calamity of that very next year.*

Ψ — Ψ — Ψ

_____

1.
2.
3.
4.

PART 2

Down2Sell Product | NotMySoul
Comin' Up

✳✳✳

5

SOMEBODY GOT TO DIE

Somebody got to die
  If I go you gots to go
  Somebody got to die
  Let the gunshots blow
  Somebody got to die
  Nobody gots to know
  That I killed your ass in the mist | Bitch
-Christopher Wallace

RJ AND I HADN'T SEEN EACH OTHER ALL SUMMER.

He spent most of his free time that summer romancing a young female he planned on marrying.

RJ was very intelligent, we shared similar interests in literature and history. He was determined to complete college. He envisioned a scholarly life journeying to majestic places of enchantment and discovering ancient artifacts of significant importance.

I wasn't sure of a career for myself.

Whatever it might be | *The inclusion of buskets filled with green money was a certainty.*

MRS. BAITCHER DIDN'T RETURN TO TEACH FRENCH THE FOLLOWING year. In her stead, a goofy old timer who resembled Mr. Magoo.

When Magoo sounded off for attendance, I spied an attractive Russian *devotchka* seated close to the main desk. After class, she introduced herself as Lita B.

LITA WAS A STUNNER.

She stood a very slender 4'9. Her curly black hair fell neatly to her shoulders. She had the sweetest blue eyes, a rounded chin and a small button nose that pointed upwards.

A bit of small-talk later and we resolved to skip class and spend the remainder of the day getting to know one another.

We went to Lita's parent's home—*a modest two-story dwelling*— just a few short blocks from the school. It was placed near the center of a complex of semi-attached homes, very common for that part of town. *We talked for a while and made our way up to her room.*

She inserted a New-Order cassette tape into her portable stereo then turned up the volume to "Bizarre-Love-Triangle."

When she moved in to kiss me, I felt a quivering tingle in the small of my stomach, you know, the one you get right before something important is about to happen.

We kissed for hours.
For me — *It was mesmerizing.*
A single moment that felt almost dreamlike.
I could not have asked for a better first kiss.

Through the course of the next few weeks Lita and I shared many intimate moments. She wasn't only my first kiss—*she was my first everything.*

. . .

WELL, THAT'S NOT ENTIRELY TRUE.

During my employ at the collectibles shop, John the florist treated me to a blowjob from a sleazy streetwalker.

John told me he was going to take a jaunt under the 3rd Avenue train tracks to find some head. He insisted I come along.

We hopped into his van and with little difficulty located what was quite possibly the foulest Puerto Rican crackhead available.

At first, she was reluctant to assist us, deciding we were plainclothes undercovers—*she cannot be blamed for caution*—two white males in a white full-sized van could easily be mistaken for the laws. Her position seemed to change quickly once John produced a crisp ten-dollar bill.

I was uneasy after John finished and my turn was up. I knew this was very possibly the least appropriate course of action | A quick swig of vodka fixed my thinker and I was ready.

It was a despicable encounter.

Putting my hand on her head left behind an offensive film-like grease, the stench of which I was unable to wash off for days.

Once finished, she demanded twenty dollars for servicing both of us. John gave her that ten-dollar bill and about six bucks in loose change he found scattered about the vehicle.

On the ride home I raised an issue that had been confusing me.

I present to you this, my dearest reader; *a man, married with small child*, still he prowls about town requiring carnal relief of the most detestable variety | I presented this very question to John.

He furnished a response I would not be able to process for many more years. "You don't pay them to fuck you, Gary. *You pay them to leave.*"

* * *

THE NEXT TWO MONTHS.

I spent every bit of my free time with Lita
I was inclined to believe that I may have found love.

RJ and his girlfriend joined us most evenings on the beach, sipping drinks and appreciating the sunset.

It was a time of independence and candor.
—||— *The truest time of my life* —||—
It's always eerily tranquil nearest the thunder.

TOWARDS THE CLOSE OF A FRIGID NOVEMBER SCHOOL DAY.

Lita met me at our pizza shop.

It was conveniently located two blocks from the school. As its rightful occupants we hoisted our flag and claimed it for our fatherland. During breaks I would post up and pump sacks of trees to the local youngbloods. It provided a modest income mainly granting provision to my own hungry addiction.

One day, I entered the parlor to find my girlfriend looking jolted.

Lita was out of it, after some light coaxing, she identified a fathead — Eddie N. as the reason for her discomfort. You see, Eddie had repeatedly made sexual advances toward Lita, which she ignored. Instead of accepting Lita'a disinterest, he doused her in profanity, labeled her a "whore" and a "slut." Of course, she was also "too ugly to fuck anyway." Eddie didn't deal well with rejection.

I told her I'd sort it out and walked her home.

A THREATENING IRISHMAN.

At twenty, Eddie was perhaps the oldest senior in Brooklyn.

Frequently detained in the backseat of a blue&white, Eddie was regarded more a nuisance than a criminal.

RJ recognized him as a scrapper who participated in golden gloves competitions as a youth.

Eddie was six feet tall.

He had typical Irish characteristics; fiery red hair, green eyes, and a pale complexion full of freckles.

It was apparent that whatever amount of time he had left after inducing panic in the student body, he spent at the gym lifting the equivalent of small automobiles. Nothing pleased Eddie more than introducing beatings sufficient enough to make a man shit his pants.

Easy to find, he occupied his established bench at the rear of the cafeteria.

More angry than nervous, I approached Eddie.

He was busy jabbering with other recognized derelicts.

I courteously requested he leave my girlfriend the fuck alone.

Eddie ignored my attempts at polite conversation and when I continued to petition him, he casually stood up and backhanded me hard across the face.

AT SIX YEARS OLD | I was fitted for my first pair of eyeglasses.

Given my unusually heavy prescription and coke-bottle lenses, by the time I reached ten, folks got to calling me *Gary "Speks."*

With the hit—*my glasses flew clean off my face*—one of Eddie's acolytes stepped on them, shattering the right lens. "You got a problem? Step up," Eddie stated with a jolly tone of amusement.

Five of his confederates surrounded me. The rogue to my left gripped a shiny, sharp looking instrument which probably wouldn't feel pleasing if inserted anyplace inside my body.

"Four p.m., small schoolyard. We'll settle it then. Unless you need your ladyboys to help you," I demanded. "You got some onions calling me out. I'm gonna give you the fair-one," he stated.

By three-thirty, there must have been more than two-hundred students gathered in the intermediate schoolyard.

I looked for Lita, but she wasn't around.

I installed a full quart of Georgi | *I felt confident and powerful.*

EDDIE APPROACHED ME FROM THE REAR.

He spit out a half-laugh, half-holler. "You got grapes, fighting for a whore. Where do you think she is now? Probably out with some fool sucking his prick. That's right, you're about to get your ass beat for nothin' but a slut we used to run demos[1] on. She didn't tell you about that, did she?" He cackled and threw off his navy-blue sweater.

"I cracked you for getting loud with me inside. Call this off now. I won't think you less of a man." His spittle dotted my cheeks as he spoke. Whether Lita was guilty of whoring was irrelevant at that point | My mettle was being tested

++||— I put up my guard and readied myself —

Eddie took a boxing stance.

He covered his face with his hands, and started hopping around like Clubber Lang come up on a battle-worn Rocky Balboa.

He came in with two hard rights blows and I hit the ground fast. Thinking it finished, he turned to leave. I stood up quickly, my nose slightly swelling from the last hit. "Where you goin', Ed?" I snarled.

He curved around and came at me again.

A hard right to the nose left my head spinning, another right and I was on my knees. "You done?" he asked, his hands still in a fighter's pose | I rushed at him, finally connecting with his left cheek.

Eddie paused for a moment. It must have stung him.

He screamed and returned for a final round. I understood that he was done holding anything back. He issued five of his strongest attacks—*It was five more than I would've preferred.* I crashed to the floor and Eddie got on top of me, pounding my head relentlessly.

Before falling completely into the calm of unconsciousness, I noticed the silhouettes of two figures sprinting towards me.

Time must have passed quickly.

When I woke, the courtyard was nearly empty.
RJ and the two others I now recognized knelt to assist me.
I slowly rose to my feet, my left eye damaged and blood still liberally flowing from my nose.

—||— *I had taken quite a beating* —||—

"We got Ed off of you as fast as we could," a harsh, gravelly voice exclaimed.

He introduced himself as CONNY K.
At his flank stood LITTLE GABE, a dubious neighborhood icon.
I knew them | There wasn't *anyone* who didn't.
— ♣ — THEY WERE TF — ♣ —

BEFORE THE LATIN KINGS SLUNG A SINGLE BAG OF BLACK-TAR.
Before the Bloods or Crips ever threw up a gang sign.
There was TF (Together-Forever | True-Friends).
Headquartered in the Coney Island projects, TF was the principal gang in Brooklyn. Originally founded by Paulie Zantz[2] a Puerto Rican national. Once a small neighborhood street gang TF grew into one of the most feared syndicates in the city.
TF was a mix of Puerto Rican and Russian first-generation immigrants, ranging in age from eleven to twenty-five. Their base membership consisted of just about every neglected youngblood in the Brighton|Coney Island area. Unlike organized criminal enterprises, they followed no rules. They took whatever they wanted through force and violence.

Everyone feared TF, gang affiliation with an organization like TF meant recognition During that time, TF was at the height of its power. Their ranks numbered over 1500Strong.

Although Paulie was the official leader of TF, there were many members of affluence. A council was put in place to control daily activities. There were nine members on the TF council, all of whom were prison hardened criminals.

To sit on the council meant you were a killer.

Plain and Simple.

The gang's primary source of income was drug trafficking and distribution, but TF was involved in just about every illegal activity you could dream up. Gun running and street sales, prostitution, gambling, armed robbery, burglary, extortion through violence, kidnapping, auto theft, credit card fraud...

If the council thought stealing crates of bananas would turn a profit, all the fruit stores in the tri-state area would suffer a banana shortage.

Most of the core members sported the TF logo ink. Depending on where you wore the logo was your rank in the crew. Only council members (with a few rare exceptions) were permitted to wear the logo in places of plain sight such as their arms or neck.

The TF organization, had at one time acquired such a reputation, professional actors like Richard Greiko (*21 Jump Street, Booker*), that grew up in the neighborhood, were given honorary membership and displayed custom TF neckchains in television and magazine appearances.

CONNY (PRONOUNCED "SONNY") WASN'T HIS GIVEN NAME.

It was a handle he picked, throwing up tags[3] on the New York subway system. People rarely called him Conny.

His friends just called him " C ".

Although the temperature was on the chilly side, he intentionally wore a cutoff shirt. A prominent black and red TF logo began right above his right elbow, its flames wrapped around the sensitive inside parts of his arm and ended atop his shoulder just under the start of his neck.

Conny was around twenty years old and lived a few blocks over from my school. He was undoubtedly of Russian descent. Conny's black lubricated hair looked as though hurricane strength winds would nary affect its position. He had a perpetual twelve-o'clock shadow and his skin was a tan shade of olive | *Staring into his cold bleak eyes was like having a spear pierce your nucleus.*

C stood a tall six-one.

The muscles on his arms flexed as he put his long arm around my shoulder. When he spoke, it was in a raspy, penetrating tone, his every word slow and planned.

He scared me more than Eddie ever could've.

LITTLE GABE WAS ALREADY RELOCATING.

He entered drivers side a silver late model Grand Cherokee Jeep, parallel-parked near the yard's entrance.

Gabe was unusually short, around five-three, and wore baggy blue jeans with a zipped, black hoody that covered his features.

"Come on with us. I been wanting to holler at you," C demanded. He shot RJ a hard stare, *this was his chance to burn off.* "I'll catch you later, Gary," RJ stated, beginning to walk to the far exit.

C escorted me to the backseat of the silver SUV.

"We gonna get you cleaned up," were the last words I heard from either of them before reaching our destination.

The Jeep stopped about a quarter of a mile from the courtyard. It was the north side of the projects.

We parked head-in-angle.

C threw on a black leather jacket before we exited the vehicle. As we soundlessly walked through the maze of brick structures, Little Gabe fell to the rear and reached behind him for the silver automatic that was tucked into the backside of his pants.

My knees trembled.
I thought they were gonna do me right there.

We fast-walked in silence, reaching one of the apartment houses about forty yards inside the complex. C produced a ring of keys from his black jeans fumbled with them, finally locating the right one as Little Gabe stood guard, blaster in hand, facing street-side.

The elevator was broke, we walked up four flights of stairs.

The hallways smelled like urine.

The current setting | *A perfect example of one of those places that, as a youngling, my mother had warned me to avoid.*

WE STOOPED AT AN APARTMENT ON THE RIGHT CORNER-SIDE.

Gabe knocked on the door, I stepped in last and followed C down a narrow off-white hallway.

Inside | A giant red TF logo had been spray-painted on the wall adjacent to the hallway. There were two large brown leather sofas on each wall and a small television and stereo housed inside a black wall unit on the east corner.

The apartment was a TF safehouse (a gang-sponsored location that drugs, guns, sex and just about anything else that violates man's laws could be obtained).

A young black man, and appealing black woman were moving about. C motioned to the man and he withdrew to the small bedroom on the west side of the dwelling. The female, likely craving her next fix, followed.

I was directed to one of the couches.

Little Gabe took a seat beside me and positioned the burner on his lap, muzzle facing me. "So, Gary Speks, *we* run shit in this town. You've been a busy young hustler. what the fuck makes you think you can pump greens in one of our spots?" Conny sat in the middle of the opposite sofa. There was the slightest hint of Russian in his accent.

The knots in my stomach were wound so tight | *I felt it in my lungs.*

I didn't answer.

"I was gonna send Gabby here to point out your error," C commented. I glanced at Little Gabe. A slight grin formed on his long thin lips. "Looks like Eddie broke you up something nice, Speks."

Conny motioned to the woman, who was stumbling around the hallway. "Get him a wet towel," Conny hollered.

She jumped at the command, running to the head and turning on the water. In seconds she returned with a soiled wet towel then began wiping the blood from my face.

"You got heart, scrapping with that tank. He was in my class when I went to the school. You saw how fast he broke out when me and Gabby rolled up." Conny laughed and waved his hand for the girl to make scarce. "Check this out. I got respect for your heart. You kept coming at him like a soldier." Conny nodded his head in conclusion.

I remained silent.

"Let me see what your holding," C demanded.

I reached into the pocket of my MC jacket and pulled out an 1|8 of sticky bud. Gabe grabbed it, looked it over, and threw it across to C.

"This is pretty good." Conny nodded, inserting it into the pocket of his leather. "We're gonna let you work your little business, Speks. You work for me now. You can either buy your shit from us or keep using your own. If you keep your own, you bring twenty-five percent up here every fuckin day. This shit is pretty alright. I might wanna meet your man," Conny coldly stated. "It's like this here, whatever you do from now on. *I mean anything.* You kick me up my money," he boasted.

You know the expression:
Stuck between a Rock and a HardPlace.
The one that kind of implies that you may be Motherfucked.

Yeah, well Conny was The Rock.
Gabe | The HardPlace.
And your coerced friend and terrified narrator:
Yah, he was the one Motherfucked.

When dealing with creatures of this particular variety, not much experience is required in determining that the word "No" is interpreted as an insult whose consequences were potentially disastrous. Besides, with Little Gabe holding the chrome 4|5 auto. I had little choice.

I felt sick | This wasn't anywhere *near* part of the plan.

I nodded.

C stood and snapped his fingers.
In seconds the thug they had earlier banished to the bedroom appeared with a dated black revolver. It sported a long barrel; it's worn grip curving at the base. Seeing it reminded me of old black&white westerns full of masked heroes and pretty damsels that needed rescue.

"Take this pound," were the first words I heard Gabe say.

"I'm straight." My voice cracked from fear. "Suit yourself. Better to have the smoker and not need it than need it and not have it," Conny called out from behind me.

"Every fuckin day," I heard C shout as I walked back through the dark grey hallway and out the safehouse.

and thus it began:

I'd morphed into a dope-boy for Conny K. | A TF council member
It's just that fucking simple.
A small mistake | A short misstep.
And you're climbing out a hole that's just too deep.

I DIDN'T WANT ANY OF IT.
It felt like I'd just walked into McDonalds and ordered a taco.

I WENT BY TERRY'S.

I'd been giving him grass on the arm and he owed me some paper. This was a good time to collect.

He told me about a three-bedroom apartment he wanted to rent. It was the upstairs of a town home located in pretty part of town. The owner was a senile WW2 veteran Terry con(vinced) into renting to a couple of kids.

Terry couldn't afford the rent alone.

He'd already approached JoJo B., a young black DJ who lived close to our building. There were two blocks right under the train trestle that all the blacks were crammed into. The rest of the area was predominantly white Italian. Terry supplied JoJo with my greens, which he'd been reselling to the locals. I didn't know JoJo, but Terry assured me he was reliable. Terry insisted that I move in with him, I could live in one of the bedrooms, I told him I'd consider it.

RJ pulled a new face into the cut.

An unknown he announced as Sal F.

They stopped at my pizza shop briefly to grab some dope and

went on about their important affairs. We kept in touch but due to my new circumstances, it was no longer safe to spend much time palling around me with me.

LITTLE GABE STAYED WITH ME AT THE PIZZERIA.

One of his greatest life pleasures was smoking my grass free of charge | AllDayLong.

By seventeen, L-G was already a two-time loser with numerous drug charges and an aggravated robbery on his sheet. By law, he was considered a juvenile and other than a few short stints at Rikers, he hadn't done any real time. By no means was Little Gabe your garden variety badguy.

++||— *He always felt like he had something to prove* —

Using the most lenient of standards, his abnormally short stature and insubstantial build disqualified him from appearing physically formidable none whatever. Upon first glance one could even assume him frail and incapable of performing even basic badguy activities.

Making assumptions often proved terminal when dealing with a zealot like Gabe. He had an acute intuition when it came to disrespect or belittlement. Once he sensed the slightest contempt, Little Gabe mutated into an infuriated berserker whose bloodlust was satisfied only after inflicting biblical carnage.

GABE WAS THAT WHATEVERMAN.
Whatever you need.
Whenever you need it.
++||— Anybody you need it done to —

Forever *on the Ready*.
To push his jigger | To squeeze his trigger.

* * *

TWO DAYS BEFORE CHRISTMAS.

There was a thin coat of dirty snow on the ground.

Business was outstanding.

After giving C his skim and paying off all expenses, including gifts, I was holding close to 39,000$ in cash.

I was almost ready to purchase my first vehicle. I settled on a black Chevy Blazer a low mileage, pre-owned. The dealership agreed to have her ready on January third of the following year. It would give them time to put on the aftermarket wheels I required.

Little Gabe hadn't been around for a few days.

He'd attempted to rob a few locals near the TF safehouse in the Coney Island projects. In a coke-fueled rage, he pointed his pistol to the sky and emptied the magazine. Police collared him for unlawful possession of a firearm, and he was being held at Rikers, waiting on the judge.

I CLOSED OUT THE DAY'S TILL AT SIX P.M.

I made my way through the projects to the safehouse. Walking through those the bricks every day wasn't pleasant. Hidden villains lay scattered throughout the expanse | *They knew I was holding.*

Their glimpsers like x-ray units set to notice the smallest of defects — *Here* — Weakness could not go unchallenged.

I carried a switchblade Gabe traded me for some grass.

Once upstairs, I was surprised to see Conny sitting on one of the couches. C was hardly ever at the safehouse.

He only came by nightly to pick up his take.

I noticed his black leather shoulder-holster immediately; also the black 9mm Smith&Wesson at his side. Clear plastic surgical gloves covered his hands. He loaded a fresh magazine with hollow-tip slugs. "Never fill your magazines too high. Give the bullets room to breathe," he declared, nodding as I handed him the day's cream.

"Have a seat, Speks," he demanded.

My lips immediately dried as I sat on the sofa opposite his.

He left room in the magazine for one more slug, loaded the weapon, and effortlessly pulled back the slide, installing a round into the chamber. "I gotta do this little bit of work for Pushka. Little guy ain't around for a while. You gonna ride with me," he affirmed, never taking his eyes from the magazine he filled.

> Alex P. was one of the original thirteen Gasoliners
> He was known on the street as Pushka
> *(Poo-sh-ka | Russian slag for "pistol").*

Gasoliners no longer sullied their hands with "work." People like Pushka contracted out to individuals like Conny who had a solid street rep and were ready for the whatever. At the time I hadn't heard very much about him — One thing was for certain, you don't get a name like Pushka for baking prize-winning chocolate-chip cookies.

Conny handed me the blaster.

That little voice inside my head told me to get up and bolt, that it wasn't too late—*I hesitated before grabbing it*—C's eyes probed directly into my essence, a wrong move meant termination | I grabbed it by its handle and stood up, tucking it into my jeans.

"Let's roll," he exclaimed.

> As we walked outside into the courtyard.
> Twilight had almost passed and darkness overtook the night sky.

C handed me keys to the silver Cherokee Jeep and instructed me to drive. I had never driven before, a fact that I quickly relayed to Conny. He smiled. "Better drive careful then."

"Mama raised a Hellrazor || Major ||
Born Thuggin'
Heartless and Mean | Thuggin' at 16 on the scene,"

2PAC ROARED FROM THE SPEAKERS as Conny guided a route to Brighton Beach — Our destination was a deadbeat gambler who owed Pushka more than fifty Rocks. He was late on two weeks' vig[4] and wasn't returning phone calls. Now considered a liability, he would need to be persuaded.

Thick chunks of snow fell as we neared the train-trestle.

I reached into the pocket of my brown North-Face and pulled a quart of Georgi | It was my second of the day.
"How the fuck can you drink this shit, Speks? It takes like asshole," C stated after grabbing the bottle and untwisting the cap.
I laughed in an attempt to mask the terror that gripped my innards. My hand shook as I swallowed the rest of the bottle. The sauce instantly started to work its hypnotic effect—*it felt a little easier.*

We parked inside a lot near the entrance to the boardwalk.

Although the temperature was harsh, restaurants set up their tables outside. Russian émigrés casually dined in the cold.
We walked about three blocks into a campus of tall apartment houses then Conny stepped inside the door of a plain looking structure. The security lock to the gated door was broke open and as we strolled inside, C motioned for the stairs, I followed behind as we walked up four flights | *I was anxious and unsteady.*

We came to a worn green door.

C smiled at me before knocking hard on it.
The door creaked open, an antique Russian face stuck itself out.

"It's cold out here. Let us in before we catch ammonia," Conny said in Russian.

The decaying man had a receding hairline, typical of many aging Russian Jewish immigrants. He was a skeletal five-feet five and smelled like he hadn't bathed in days.

He opened the door wide.

The apartment was in shambles.

Russian newspapers and clothing were scattered everywhere. It reeked of mold. He led us into the small kitchen where we were greeted with an open bottle of Absolut atop a decaying wooden table.

Conny grabbed the bottle and two glasses from the cupboard.

"Where you been, Johra?" (Jh-ohh-ra {Russian for George}) C said nonchalantly as he expired the bottle, pouring vodka to the rim of both glasses, and handing one to me | Conny promptly downed the vodka.

++||— His manner changed immediately —

It was like there was a demon at the bottom of the glass and drinking the potion *had jolted open the ninth gate*. He flung the glass at the refrigerator, breaking it into shards. I became aware to the fact that we'd come there to do more than just talk.

Johra seemed unshaken by the abrupt sound of breakage.

Conny stepped right into his face. He grabbed Johra by the neck and demanded the money he owed.

Johra spoke calmly and told C that he didn't have the money to pay. Conny's reply was a right fist to his nose. It dropped Johra to the hardwood floor. "Put your gun on this loser. He moves he dies," he barked at me.

Adrenaline rushed my body.
I nervously pulled the weapon and pointed it at Johra.
He sat helpless on the floor.

C rummaged through the mess flinging magazines violently in an effort to find anything of portable value. On a small end-table underneath some newspaper pages, he located a syringe and a few empty bags of heroin. Conny's slick back hair had lost its place due to his exaggerated movements.

He pushed me aside as he picked Johra off the floor and with his right elbow held his neck to the wall. "You wanna slam that garbage instead of paying me?" C screamed as he pounded on Johra's abdomen. "Where's the fuckin money?" he continued. *Conny wasn't looking for an answer.* He just kept smashing on him. "You better give me some money," C panted.

Conny stepped back and let Johra recover his breath.

Johra picked his head up and smirked | He spit right in Conny's face then wobbled and fell, ass down. He sat on the floor, looking up at Conny. *"Go to hell,"* he shouted in Russian. Johra laughed softy as Conny wiped the spit off his face.

IN THE CONSEQUENT SECONDS | *My life changed forever.*

Conny drew the chrome pistol, a Star Industries 4|5 auto. "You first," Conny snickered before he shot twice at his face.

The first bullet missed and hit the wall.
The latter met the top of Johra's skull.
It sent bits of brain and bone into the wall behind him.
Some blood spattered on C's leather.
A few droplets hit my face.

I STOOD THERE FROZEN IN TIME.

The walls of the room began to close in on me fast.
I was afraid to move—*fuck*—I was afraid to breathe.

Conny grabbed me by the hood of my coat.

He dragged me out of the apartment, and down the stairs.

Conny grabbed my blaster and put it in his pocket.

I was lightheaded as we walked to the SUV, pausing every few steps. C pushed me along until we finally neared the vehicle. He reached into my coat pocket and grabbed the key then turned down the stereo as we pulled out slowly.

His serene composure struck my blood cold.
Conny was no longer there.

In his stead | Vasili Komaroff—*theWolfofMoscow.*
I'll never forget the absence of the look on Conny's face.

We made it to Pappy's apartment around nine p.m.

"Get rid of this," Conny remarked, dropping the chrome heater on my lap. *It was still warm.* "I'll be by tomorrow morning at nine. You're gonna ride with me until the Gabby gets home. Find someone to work your weed spot," he instructed then reached into his pocket and handed me a rolled-up knot of money.

"*Dahvaye,*[5] Speks," he finished.

I left the car in hazy bewilderment.
⊨ I expected the nightmare to end at any time ⊨

Closing in on the Pappy's apartment door I could hear the static buzz of short-wave radio advertising the Odessa restaurant.

Pappy looked terrible. He knew something was off. *It was Johra's dried blood on my face that gave me away.*

Hastily, he pulled me inside.

Pappy sat me down on the metal chair closest to his living room.

There was a full glass of vodka on the table. He handed me the liquid, I drank the whole thing down, then took the chrome gun from my pocket and placed it on the table. Pappy stared at the pistol and quickly back at me. "Who was killed?" he asked.

After relaying the events, *I put my hands over my face and cried*

Pappy picked up the 4|5 auto. He removed the magazine, then cocked back the slide, releasing the shell in the chamber. He dropped the five hollow-tips into my cup of Stolichnaya then went into the commode to get me some wet towels.

I was still crying when he returned.

He sat down and drank more vodka and I continued to cry for what felt like days. By the end of his bottle, I ran out of tears and resorted to sobs. Pappy slapped me clear across the face and handed me a wet white towel. I used it to wipe the tears and the blood from my face.

"I waited until you were out of tears. Never cry again. That man wasn't family, he was nobody. You did him a favor tonight. He knew exactly what would happen when he spit on that man," Pappy remarked. "I'm gonna tell you something, son. Every man dies... not every man really lives. For a brief moment he was alive. For those last seconds, his life was worth more than the thousands he owed. He was worth more than the sum of all the mistakes he'd ever made. I am happy for him, Gary | He died like a man."

He paused, then swigged from his cup.

"Remember this always. It's better to die like a man than to live like a coward. He died with dignity, a*nd dignity is every man's right*," Pappy exclaimed.

He removed the slide from the pistol, exposing the barrel, the guide rod, and the recoil spring, then laid them all on the table.

Pappy left to the kitchen and returned with some Ziplock bags, a roll of aluminum foil and a fresh bottle of Stoli.

One by one he took the bullets out of the cup, wiping them thoroughly with the fresh towel, then placing them in the bag. He wet the towel with vodka and wiped down the gun parts, wrapping them in aluminum foil and sealed them all in separate baggies.

I watched, still pondering his words.

Once completed, he put everything into a plastic supermarket bag and called my parents. He told them I'd come to visit a few hours back and had fallen asleep on the couch.

"Your life is now intertwined with this Conny." He said.

"You need to be very careful with this man. His freedom now depends on your ability to stay loyal to him. If he feels that you may betray him, *he will kill you with no hesitation.* You need to prove you can be trusted. Do it quickly, or he will kill you," he spoke gravely. "Take these pieces and dispose of them in different locations so it can never be traced back." Pappy went into the living room and sat on the sofa. "Do it now!" he commanded.

I paged Lou Batz with the code 911.

He called back within minutes.

I took the plastic bag and went outside to wait for him in the cold winter night. Eventually, he pulled up in a black Grand National, a modified Buick racing car with a 5.6-liter twin-turbo. It was a limited-edition vehicle. Only fifty thousand were manufactured per year. "What's up, Speks?" Lou groaned. I could tell that—*here*—was the last place he wanted to be.

"Need this solid, Lou. See this bag? It needs to go away," I replied. "Whatcha got in there?" Terry asked. "Better we just lose it, bro. Thing is, it's in pieces and we need to ditch every part in a different spot," I stated. Lou just nodded. "Alright, Speks, I gotcha," he replied as we pulled away.

It was two a.m. by the time we got rid of it all.

A few parts got tossed in the bay. A few went off the Brooklyn Bridge | We took the barrel straight to the Staten Island dump.

I couldn't stay at my parents' anymore.
++||— *I was all the way in* —

Even a small mistake and I could easily put their lives in jeopardy. I asked Terry if he still had room for me at the house he'd rented.

LOU TOOK ME BACK TO PAPPY'S HOUSE.

He walked me upstairs. "I don't know what you're into, Speks. I know you had a burner in that sack. I got your back on whatever, you know that. But I'm getting married. Whatever little shit I was into, I'm getting out of it. I want you to take over everything. Come see me in two weeks at my social club on the avenue. We'll grind out the details then. Don't tell anyone. Especially Terry. He's good people and I got mad love for him but it's you. You gonna be my man on this," Lou mumbled.

We parted with a hug and kissed on the cheek. "Good lookin' out, Lou," I replied as he walked outside into the snowy street.

When I returned upstairs.

I pulled out the roll Conny granted me and counted it for the first time. It was little more than 2600$. I counted out 1500$ and placed it on the table for Pappy.

I thought, again, about Johra.

His life wasn't even worth 3Large. I sat in a half drunk, half-asleep state | Johra's mangled skull piercing my dome like a purple strobe.

· · ·

128

IN DAYS FOLLOWING.

I rode with Conny on his daily routine, picking up money and delivering dope. He let me hold the 9mm S&W while I was with him and took it back at the end of the day.

Tuesdays were collection days for Pushka.
We made stops to gamblers homes to pick up his cream.
We didn't talk much | *I felt like he didn't trust me.*

I was always on my guard.

I APPROACHED SANDY N. TO OPERATE THE WEED SPOT FOR ME.

He was hesitant at first, but after explaining the profit-potential and imparting him with a thousand-dollar advance, his disinclination turned to enthusiasm.

Conny and I visited the pizzeria daily to collect our skim.

I MOVED OUT MY PARENT'S HOME LATER THAT MONTH.

* * *

CHRISTMAS ISN'T A VERY BIG HOLIDAY AMONGST RUSSIAN IMMIGRANTS.

In communist days, religion was outlawed and besides, most of them are Jewish. In its stead, New Year's is celebrated in the same fashion the birth of Christ would be.

The family gathers for a home-cooked meal and gifts are exchanged. I returned to my parents' home that New Year and offered them my gifts. It was a brilliant feeling, giving expensive things to my family, who had suffered so much hardship. We laughed and drank, but Pappy was unable to attend due to his poor health.

I picked up my first ride on January third.

It didn't get much use while I was driving for Conny.

I drove it to the social-club on a cold Thursday eve where Lou awaited me. A dimly lit storefront, the social club was a hangout for Italian *cusheen's* (*"koo-sheen" is Italian slang for low-level\wannabe gangsters*). Its entrance windows and doors were blacked out. There were a few small tables at the front, a bar at the east corner and a couple of benches for playing cards in the rear.

Lou was pretty well-connected.

His uncle was a Genovese captain who controlled most of the criminal operations in that sector of Brooklyn. It was his social club.

There were a few youngbloods busy discussing the effects of dandruff on the diminishing ocean population of sea-lions or something of similar relevance. They gave me hard looks as I walked to the back to meet Lou.

"Let's go to the office," Lou murmured.

I followed him through a thin plywood door and sat on a small leather chair. Monitors inside were connected to the cameras positioned both inside and outside the storefront.

Lou sat in a large leather business chair, reclined back, and lit a Marlboro. "Drinking vodka, right?" He smiled and reached to open the miniature fridge to his rear. "I got my own, Batzy," I said cheerfully then pulled a quart of Georgi from inside my black mid-length leather.

He produced a bottle of bourbon and poured himself a shot.

"It's like this, Gary, I told you I'm getting married. We're trying for kids. I need to get away from all this. My uncle owns this club, my job here is Cadillac. I pick up dope from one of his people and bring it here once a week. He sends one of his crew in to get the cheddar every day. I spend most of my time in here, like the manager, making sure nothing fucked-up happens." He paused, reaching into the backside of his grey pleated slacks and put a .44 magnum on the glass tabletop. "You understand what I'm sayin' If someone runs up and tries to jack, I'd have to be the one to blast 'em." Lou spoke in a monotonous tone.

He looked me over with his cloudy eyes, inspecting my reaction. I sat composed, arms crossed, ignoring the clapper on the table.

"Once a week I make a run to pick up vig on some of the paper he puts out to the street and bring it back here. His people come by and take it to him," he continued.

I knew the routine | I'd been through it multiple times with Conny. "What you need from me, Lou?" I finally asked.

"My uncle knows I'm gettin' out. He's not OK with it but he's family, he understands. When you called me that night, you had a broken-down pistol in a plastic bag. I'm no dummy, Speks. But I'm also not a killer. The truth is, I'm just not made for this type of work. I need someone I can count on to keep things running correct. I know you're down with some serious hoods—*people talk*. Those clowns out there, they couldn't get laid in a whorehouse with a fistful of fifties. I need someone to step in here and regulate. I don't even want a cut, I just want out," he stated.

Lou looked worried.
He was already on his third shot.

Sitting quietly, I considered his proposal.
"What about Terry? That's your main homeboy number1," I said.

Lou crossed his legs and leaned back.

He held up the empty shot glass with his right hand. For a few tense moments he stared into the glass scrutinizing his reflection. "Close is one thing. Dependable is another," he replied as he moved the glass onto the table. He poured himself another and without hesitation ingested the substance. His lips puckered slightly from the bitter taste. More relaxed, he continued. "I just don't think Terry got the minerals. I know him a long time, Gary. He's more worried about smoking dope then selling it," Lou answered.

He spun his shot glass on the tabletop.

"He's too much of a clown. The regulars wouldn't have a grain of respect for him, prancing around like half-a-homo with nail polish on," he finished.

We chuckled.

"If these mooks don't respect you, they gonna think they can get over. If these fucks step outta line, they need put back in line fast, or it becomes pandemonium. Then the fuckin junkies start not paying. You know what happens next," Lou finished, drooping back in the leather manager's chair.

He had a point.

If the influx of business was in any way disturbed: the Bent-Nose|Grease-Ball in a white pinstripe, with the gold St. Anthony medallion stuck out his hairy chest | *Would be forced to make examples.*

"I'd love to help you out here, Batz, but I'm not Italian," I stated solemnly. Traditionally, Italians more so than any of the other criminal factions had this thing about letting non-Italians in on their hustles. They were beginning to figure out that this was an outdated, largely ineffective, business model.

"I cleared everything with my uncle. I'm vouching for you, anyways, it don't have to be you in here. One of your people can work the place. You know your pinch on this is gonna be nice. I'm talking a few dimes (*one dime = one thousand dollars*) a week minimum," he said.

It sure sounded like a lovely little fiddle.

"Alright, Lou. Give me a week or so to make arrangements. Thanks for this, Batzy. You know I'll let you keep eating," I said.

THE GEARS INSIDE MY THINKER KICKED INTO TURBO MODE.

I couldn't hold down the club myself.

My days were spent driving for Conny and letting him into my arrangement with Lou would be the equivalent of stealing from myself. Conny would surely take over my position, most probably push me out the equation altogether or reduce my slice to crumbs.

Sandy N. was proving himself a consistent, trustworthy associate. He kept revenue RockSteady, I could shuffle him around and put him to work at the social-club. A move like that would be cause for questions, that would almost certainly signal Conny | *He hailed from Odessa.*

I drove to RJ's.

It was in the late hours of the evening, his parents were asleep, and he was out in his backyard with Sal F., barbequing some franks and a half-chicken.

It was around thirty-five degrees Fahrenheit. "A little cold for a BBQ," I noted. Our breath turned into thick fog as we spoke. "Nothing a few beverages won't cure," RJ slurred.

I sat on a cold beach chair next to Sal.

He'd been hanging with RJ for some time, and aside from one quick meet, I didn't know him at all. I courteously produced a pint of drink then offered some to him. "I don't drink," Sal replied.

"How about smoke? You smoke grass?" I asked, removing a bag of my finest from my tight black denims. "Sometimes, but not tonight," he stated.

· · ·

Sal F. was five-feet nine; a thin Italian.

He didn't have the typical Italian features you'd see on most of the Guineas around town. His strawberry blonde hair was cut in a Caesar and although it was short on the sides and in the back, he had a long tail tied into a braid. Sal had shrewd green eyes and a prickly nose that pointed straight at me. Small orange-colored freckles highlighted his pale features.

He was Italian, came off respectable and spoke like a street guy, like he didn't stand for any shit.

I grabbed RJ by the arm and pulled him aside.

"Who's this fuckin guy? How do you know him?" I demanded. "I met him at school. He transferred from the city. His father's some kind of important dude, works security for a foreign dignitary." RJ was slurring but still very coherent. "Yeah, but can he be trusted?" I whispered. "Sal's good people, Gary. I trust him," RJ replied then swigged on his brandy.

"You ready to do some work, Sal?" I asked.

"RJ says you can be trusted, and I have an opening in one my facilities for a motivated and capable person. You fit the bill. You know how I get down," I finished.

I explained the situation and offered to start him off with a modest weekly stipend, with the promise that after having proved himself, earnings would increase | It didn't take much convincing.

Sal was hungry and claimed to be willing to perform. The very next day I picked Sal up and took him to the social club. Introductions were made, and I put him to work.

Sal had stepped into a nice bit of fortune.

He lived half a mile away and was already aquatinted with some of the *cusheen* employees (*drug-dealers, thieves, burglars*) from the neighborhood. Evidently, he'd put in small work with a few of them and they respected his grind. It looked like an easy transition and a sweet deal for me. I would come in every few days to check and make sure that *Everything||was||Everything*, collect the skim left in the safe, and give him his cut.

BUSINESS WAS OPERATING SMOOTHLY, AND EVERYTHING WAS JUST RIGHT.

Fiends were steady buying junk. Collections were coming in mostly on time. Ricky "Kuku" was still losing thousands on the Mets.

GreenPaper was coming in from all flanks.

C hadn't gotten violent since the incident, *It was something we never spoke about.*

Conny was starting to gain confidence in me.

He still didn't let me hold the blaster after business hours, but I felt assured that he wouldn't end my life in the near future.

The pizzeria was cranking, and Sal was doing exactly what he was supposed to be at the social-club. During one of my visits, he informed me of a few acquisitions (*burglaries*) he'd felt the need to supervise. From what I understood, he was carving out a proper slice of cheddar | Conny even gave me a few days off every week to finish up my studies.

* * *

A SUNNY THURSDAY IN MAY, FOUR P.M.

Safely nestled away near the door of my double padlocked room, inside a small fire-safe I had bolted to the floor and fastened together in neat stacks, resided 63,000$ cash money | I'd nary encountered many sixteen-year-old's with money that long.

135

Certainly there were a few somewhere.

Rich prep-school types in Blue-Crested sport coats.

Disgusting Reptiles, engineered to be our future senators. While we break our necks, these scaly lizards train in the latest techniques of how to better enslave the working class.

Around my way you only get that type of paper by hook or by crook. Waiting for Conny outside a carpet store while he picked up Pushka's vig, I sat in the Cherokee Jeep.

Banger at My Side — *With my Money on Mind.*

I felt like Bugsy Segal 2.0.
a Fresh young Gangster.
Loved by the Ladies.
Feared and Revered by the masses.
an Entrepreneur || Bold and Successful.

My pager vibrated, breaking me from my trance.

Louie Batz hit me with a 911 code.

I darted to the payphone, punching in the familiar digits. Lou answered on the first ring. He was livid. Sal hadn't shown for work since my visit Tuesday. He grabbed two ounces of white for a deal he'd arranged, said he'd be back in a few hours, and pulled a *NowYouSeeMe* | NowYouDon't.

One of Lou's uncle's greaseballs was on his way to pick up the skim and if either the money or the powder wasn't accounted for by that night — *Well y'all can guess the rest.* Understanding, I assured Louie there would be a swift resolution with no glitches.

No more than a minute later, my pager went off again.

RJ code 911 | I stood at the payphone for a few minutes before calling back. The situation with Lou was bad but only a prelude of things to come. RJ was bawling. He'd just returned home from his girlfriend's house. She was recovering from a three-day coke binge.

She'd spent the last few days fucking Sal and zapped on the missing cocaine—*best part*—Sal beat her into a near coma, claiming she was pinching from his stash.

I told him I'd be over to pick him up in a few hours.

When Conny returned, I said there was a family emergency and I needed to go. I drove myself to the house, got in the Blazer, picked up RJ then headed to Sal's.

Six p.m.

What had begun as a spirited breeze turned to chaotic winds strong enough to make our eyes water.

Sal's father was away on business.

We swigged on Georgi before entering Sal's two-story dwelling. A small stone staircase lead to a pricey oak door at the front of the house. I knocked on the door, then tried the knob — It was open and we allowed ourselves inside, announcing our entrance. A narrow hallway led to the dining room; its white walls looked freshly painted.

"In here," Sal screamed.

"I gotta take a piss. Be easy with him, RJ. I'll be right there," I whispered, then took a detour into a small commode that connected to the staircase. I washed my hands and my face. The pit of my belly, the one right at the base of the groin was wound as tight as a fisherman's knot and there again was that still small voice demanding I run fast and far.

I opened the door to shouting.

"Fuck you, cocksucker. I'll kill right where you stand," Sal screeched. "Who the fuck do you think you are, coming into my fuckin house, talking that shit. I should plug you right here."

I didn't hear RJ make a sound.

Then I heard it | I knew that noise well enough to understand that whatever strange game was being played was ready to turn into a macabre spectacle ++||— Sal had pulled back the hammer —

Reality took on a hue of greyish yellow and time began to slow down to onehalf of onehalf speed. It was like we had jumped down the rabbit hole then sat right down at the table for tea-time. Just like that scene from *Alice in Wonderland*.

And I was the MadHatter.

I reached into the pocket of my leather, grabbed my switchblade then crept into the next room. At first glance I noticed the crack stem on one of the end tables. Next to it the two-ounce bag of powder, now empty.

Sal stood near a green leather sofa.

He looked a mess. It was obvious he hadn't slept in days. In his right hand, a black .38 snub-nose revolver. The kind NYPD used to carry before getting their pick of Glock19 or P226. Sal held it point-blank to RJ's face — His finger uneasily twitching on the trigger.

I pulled my head back inside.

"Better speak your last words. After you, Imma do your boy Speks. Then I'm gonna go fuck your little cunt of a whore again," Sal belted out a twisted, drug-induced howl.

For a second, he lowered the weapon and sobbed. *He knew he was in a world of shit.* The Guineas from the social club would want their money or he was finished.

I rushed into the room and tackled him.

Sal yelled and raised his burner.

I surprised him, but my charge wasn't enough to knock him to the floor. I wrestled with his right hand as he tried to point the banger at me. He squeezed off a round, nearly missing RJ who stood at the back wall | *Petrified.*

I held his gun arm at bay with my left hand then reached into my coat, feeling for the handle of the switchblade. He fought ferociously, a potent mixture of crack and adrenaline fueled his ire. He almost had the revolver pointed at my forehead when I pushed the button on the knife. The spring instantly released the blade and I thrust it upwards deep into his chest. The shock of the piercing metal forced him to loosen his grip on the revolver. His last gasps of air sounded hurried and desperate.

I'd stuck him right in the heart.

SAL MUMBLED SOMETHING I COULDN'T QUITE MAKE OUT.

Right before I watched the life escape from his eyes. I pulled my knife from his chest and shamefully gawked as purple blood escaped from the slight laceration, spilled down his white tank-top then onto his black jeans. His knees hit the floor and he fell to the left.

++||— HE WAS DEAD —

I sat on Sal's couch, still holding the knife.
RJ hadn't moved from the wall | He was staggered and immobile.

I reached for the phone on the opposite end of the table.
And called the only person I could.

Ψ — Ψ — Ψ

1.
2.
3.
4.
5. *Dahvaye* (dah-vah-aye) is a common Russian phrase sometimes used as a slang statement. Its literal meaning is "Let's go" or "Move it," but it's used by many Russian criminals as a way of saying "goodbye," or "I'll see you soon."

STREETS IS WATCHING

Up in Queens | Shit is for real
   We abouts to get hectic
   Shoulin — Shit is for real
   We abouts to get hectic
   In BK — Shit's for real
   We abouts to get hectic
   Manhattan — Shit is for real
   We abouts to get hectic
   Up in the Bronx | We abouts to get hectic
-Mobb Deep

CONNY TOOK ABOUT AN HOUR TO ARRIVE.

He came into the living room and leaned in to examine Sal's corpse. "Yep, he's dead as a tack." Conny looked up at me, then sat down on the sofa while I explained.

I told him everything | My operations at the social club and my arrangement with Louie Batz. I knew if I didn't come clean, and he later discovered that I'd left out even a minute detail, my fate would be similar to the cadaver formerly known as Sal.

C put his hand on my shoulder.

"Some shit, huh." He let out a detached, emotionless laugh. He stood, fixed the crease on his grey slacks then glanced at RJ, paralyzed in in grief, lost in a trance desolation. He hadn't moved from his position on the sofa.

"You paged me from this phone here?" Conny blandly asked, pointing to the white cordless on the end table | I nodded. He pulled the black Motorola SkyPager from its case and shattered it against the wall then turned on RJ with a look I'd only seen once before.

Conny drew a black Ruger 9mm from inside his leather coat.
He released the safety and affixed it on my comrade.
"What the fuck C! What are you doing?" I hollered.

Conny's finger was already on the trigger, about to squeeze. "Look here, Speks. This is a problem. He ties both of us to *that*." Blaster still at RJ., Conny jerked his head toward the recently expired Sal F. "We're gonna have to push his mute button," he stated.

I jumped in front of RJ. "Please, C, nobody else needs to die today," I pleaded. "No more killing. This man is my friend. You're gonna have to blast the both of us, cause I'm not gonna let him die alone," I finished. Conny lowered the blaster and shook his head. "Get him the fuck outta here," he snarled.

RJ was still rambling.

I shook him until he was free of his delirium then grabbed him by the shoulders and we marched to the back door. *He was finally coherent enough to realize that I'd saved his life.* I handed him the keys to my Blazer and told him to drive right home.

Conny holstered his weapon and sat on the sofa.

He looked down at Sal's corpse and then back up at me. I slumped to the floor, leaning my back to the wall.

Sal's inert face stared right at me. The look of hopelessness hadn't left him, even in death. It activated emotions that blasted jackhammers into the stem of my spine then up into head.

I started to hyperventilate.

I wanted to cry but knew that any show of weakness might anger Conny. Still, my eyes welled up and as much as I tried to force them inside, a few tears ran down my cheeks and onto my chin.

"Don't cry for this piece of shit, Speks. It was him or you, kid. And you did what you had to do." Conny spoke monotonously. "Wait here a tick." He smirked before he stood and exited the room.

He returned a few minutes later with the 9mm S&W that he'd been letting me operate. It was wrapped in a black shoulder holster.

"You know, Speks. By all rights I should've popped you and your little homeboy. You're of more use to me breathing. Your brains work good, and you've shown yourself capable[1]. I always knew you had the minerals. When you're in a tight situation, capable people are the only ones you can count on. There's no such thing as halfway-crooks, *they never around when the beef cooks*," he declared.

His words were deep and heartfelt.

"You not off the hook yet, Gary. The way I see it, you owe me some paper." Conny smirked "What? You thought you were free and clear from payin' on my action? Fuck no, buddy. You owe your homeboy some back pay." He was referring to the weekly money I collected from the social club | *Conny wanted reimbursement.*

"What are we talking about here, C?" I asked. "Ten dimes gonna flush you right." He replied. "Now stand the fuck up and grab this banger" Conny demanded.

I pushed myself up and reached to grab the automatic.

"This is you now, Speks. Treat her proper and she'll shoot straight for you. Demonstrate the fool and she'll treat you like one." Conny gave me a hug and released the pistol. Before I had a chance to put it on, *Conny demanded I pay him a dollar for the gun*[2].

THE SUDDEN RUSH OF DELICIOUS ARROGANCE PUSHED INTO MY WITS.

A euphoric bliss in which my glorious victory over the universe was a not only a reality — *It was my birthright.* I forgot instantly the corpse that lay at my heels. A mere annoyance in a world that was now my ashtray.

MY METAMORPHOSIS *was almost complete.*

Still, there remained the small matter of reimbursing the social club for the drugs Sal had appropriated | That burden would *of course* fall solely on your humble friend and narrator.

CONNY REACHED INSIDE POCKET OF HIS BLACK LEATHER.

He produced a grey Motorola flip-phone.

It was one of the new smaller models I'd been seeing more frequently. Conny picked up his chipped[3] phone earlier that day from one of Pushka's multiple dealerships. This was a virgin industry and C's was one of the very first of its kind.

He dialed the number to one of the TF safehouses.

The piercing computerized sound of keys being pushed resonated through the room, breaking the profound silence and bringing me back to reality. "Yo, it's me. Trash pickup, it's still pretty ripe. Send the rebels," Conny barked at the receiver. He relayed Sal's address to the ally on the other end, pushing up the flip with his chin to end the conversation. "They gonna spotless up this mess, Speks. Probably make it look like a robbery." Conny looked down at Sal as he spoke.

"What about his heater? Is it clean?" he asked. "As far as I know, it belonged to his father," I replied. Conny grabbed the .38 and put it in his pocket. "Alright, let's make like bellbottoms and be out." He giggled as he threw me the keys and we left the house.

I drove myself to RJ's and found my Blazer parked in his driveway.

"Tomorrow, first thing, we gonna call your boy at the social club and fix this right. Then we're gonna put *our* people in there. You're gonna keep making the same skim. Business as usual." C said.

He drew closer and put a heavy arm on my right shoulder then glanced at the blaster as I started the adjust the straps on the shoulder holster. "Cut me out again, Gary, and it's the three R's[4] for you baby-boy. Conny paused, "Oh yeah, have my 10dimes in three days." C demanded. He winked at me before I left the vehicle.

AROUND TEN P.M., I KNOCKED ON RJ'S DOOR.

He answered holding a quart of GeorgiVodka and an already fired-up joint. We jumped into my Blazer and rode around the neighborhood. I reiterated to RJ the facts of the situation.

FACT1 | He was lucky to be alive.
FACT2 | What happened that night — *Never happened*

I assured him, that if he uttered a solitary word about what never happend to anyone | PIPEHOLDING **OG** RUSSIAN NATIONALS:

The kind who call guns Clickers.
The type who call blacks Niggers.
Would be imported straight from the gulag to our front doors.

++||— the End Result —
Closed Caskets, *Mama's Crying* — SlowSinging||*FlowerBringing.*

I looked intensely into RJ's eyes and held my stare securely until I knew he understood. We shook and hugged, and I finally made my way out.

.   .   .

I PICKED UP A GALLON OF GEORGI AND STOPPED AT THE HOUSE.

Inside | The usual suspects were smoking my trees and clowning around. I peeled off my clothes, put them in a plastic bag, cried a little for poor old Saly then took a quick shower and set out for Pappy's.

Pappy was half-comatose from his day's drunk.

Liver disease was in its final stages and it was clear he didn't have much time left. He greeted me with a kiss, and I placed the plastic gallon of Georgi and a thousand dollars in cash on his small table. When I took off my black leather, he noticed straight away the 9mm inside the shoulder-strap I was wearing.

"Looks like you finally grew up. About time." Pappy laughed. He'd already opened the bottle and poured himself a suitable dosage of the potion. "Let's have a look at him," he said. I pulled on my pistol, still uncomfortable with the holster, and after some difficulty, was able to remove it. Pappy laughed, downing his glass, and slamming it on the table.

I put my burner on the table so he could examine it.

He removed the magazine and with a single motion took away the slide and spring, exposing the barrel. "He's a nice one," he said. "Have you named it yet?" he asked, glimpsing me out the corner of his eye.

Masterfully, he reassembled the weapon.

"You must give it a name. There is power in a name. When you name something, you give it life. The name you give it will decide its destiny." he said, clutching the now compiled blaster.

"How about Amanda?" I jokingly suggested. "No," he barked. "You must give your gun a strong name. Name it after a woman and it will behave like one. You need it to be something you can count on when the chips are down and the whole fucking world comes busting down your door. The only thing you can count on a woman to do is break your heart," Pappy stated glumly, as he lowered his head and refilled his glass. "The name must be a secret. Men keep secrets, Gary. Men who hold guns keep many secrets. Anyone who knows the name will be able to find its weakness. That is the ancient law of the warrior."

As he spoke | *I felt as though his words were tunneling into my core and channeling a direct connection to my mettle.*

"With this tool at your side, the knowledge to know when it's absolutely necessary to use it and the courage to do so. Your soul will never be with those cold and timid ones who never knew victory or defeat. Conceal it well and it becomes your equalizer. The ace up your sleeve," he finished.

I poured myself a tall glass of drink.

His words gave me a new focus and cemented my resolve.

They provoked a sensation where I felt myself in the providence of fortune | *It was as though the very framework of the cosmos had opened up to me all of it's secrets.*

"Ace," I said.

Immediately downing the contents of the soiled glass, and in a tumult of clarity, smashing it on the floor. I stood, sheathed Ace, threw on my leather, kissed my satisfied grandfather on the lips, and in a gust of magnificence, ran down the stairs to my chariot.

* * *

IT WAS A CHILLY JUNE.

The winter had been tediously harsh that year.

I'd straightened things out with Lou and squared away the deficit the late Sal had incurred, then positioned a reliable Russian confederate Conny personally handpicked to succeed him.

Both my pizza spot and the club were generating paper.

I felt it was the precise right time to grow my influence. The perfect time to introduce two new devices.

The first was powder.

Conny had been on me for months to pump cocaine from my pizzeria—*I had the obvious reservations*—my appraisal had changed once Ace drew himself into the portrait. I approached High, and due to our close relationship, he supplied us white for considerably less than market value. We sold the powder and started rocking it up into crack.

Our skim quintupled.

I LEFT SANDY N. IN CHARGE OF THE PIZZA SPOT.

He'd outgrown number6 status and now had his own little dope-boys running deliveries. We took a ride in a clean little Acura Vigor with Mag wheels he had recently procured. He made it pointı to show me his blaster.

The second were the Fugazi cellulars.

We started pumping them at both the social club and the pizza shop | They flew out faster than popcorn at the picture-show.

Between the two items — I was bringing home around 30,000$ a month. By the middle of the summer, I was holding well into six figures. But that was just the initiation of what was about to set off the greatest sensation of the X generation.

· · ·

LITTLE GABE RETURNED AT THE START OF THE SUMMER.

The judge handed him eighteen months. He served a little over a year at Rikers and came home on parole. It seemed that all prison had done was bolster his G and make him harder. He put back on his strap and went right back to the grill again.

Conny put him back to work as his driver.

JULY FOURTH.

Terry and I decided to have a BBQ at our house to celebrate the holiday | *Everyone was invited.*

JoJo was featured as the DJ. He was building a strong reputation by working some of the top nightclubs in Manhattan. He was a pioneer of a new brand of sound — Techno. JoJo's music wasn't just hot, it was on fire. He had bookings in such celebrated places as The Palladium and The Tunnel.

Terry prospered selling computer wipes and dope I supplied.

He dressed well and always had plenty of trees but could never hold onto money. When you have heavy sacks of green dope, parasites always materialize.

Terry's number6 was quite a character.

His name was Vinny W. but we called him "Guido" Vinny.

Guido was a short, rounded-out fellow. Not fat, per-se, just round. He stood five-feet six and was about the dumbest mook in the whole damn village. It could be twelve degrees below outside with snow up to your chin, this clown would be outside holding a 40once wearing flip-flops, cut-off jeans, and a dirty wifebeater.

Guido carried himself like a straight-off-the-boat Italian wannabe *cusheen*, incessantly grabbing on his man-parts and behaving like idiot number1. Hence the name Guido, it's Brooklyn slang for a real greaseball Italian that behaves like a donkey and portrays the role of a real smelly bigshit.

Number6 usually don't have anything to offer by way of criminal skills or financial acuity. The lot of them in general mooch off the crew; happy to feed on leftovers. In exchange for this generosity, they do the dirty work.

I'm not talking about "dirty" as in holding-up bank tellers or murdering babies. That type of work was left to the authentic renegade. "Dirty" as in washing dishes or cleaning dirty drawers. "Dirty" as in doing the work that nobody else wanted to do. You can compare them to mail-room workers in a Fortune 1000 conglomerate.

Guido was exceptionally loyal.
A quality you won't find in most number6.

THE JAM WAS BLAZING.

Conny and the little guy even popped in to give me love.

There must've been 150 weirdos packed into the house and another 200 outside, discoing around.

It appeared that something just wasn't clicking. Sure, I was lifted. But these club-freaks were zapped higher than Richard*fuckin*Pryor.

Drugs got you high.
The shit they were on was next level.

Some freak, I didn't know if it was male or female ran right up on me, kissed me square on the lips, and told me it loved me. A handsome bulky male standing behind me stepped between us.

I noticed him instantly — He was one the doing the hand2hands.

Before I had a chance to approach him, he was already near me and introduced himself as Vance M. "What the fuck was that joker zapped on? I've never seen people get like that before, they look like they are-all-the-way fucked up," I exclaimed.

"He was rolling," Vance spoke loudly. I must've looked at him like he was batshit because he went on to explain: "Rolling, you know Xing, on ecstasy," he finished. I still didn't know what he meant—*at the time I don't think many people did*—It was about to catapult on the scene and change the face of our culture forever.

"I brought some up here with me from Frisco. It's caught on big up there," he continued. "Let me get a few of those." I pulled out a handful of bills. "How much?" I asked. "This your party, right?" He produced a large Ziploc bag filled with pink gel-caps. He smiled. "Take as many as you need."

I grabbed ten pills, eager to sample the upshot of this new pharmaceutical, then found my comrades and notified them that I was holding the best thing since AirForceI's.

I SWALLOWED THREE OF THE TABLES.

My logic was faultless.
If one was good — *Three would be more better.*
A half-hour and I felt its effect.

THE BEST WAY I CAN DESCRIBE IT IS AS FOLLOWS:

I first felt a *tingle* in my *toes* and in *my fingertips.*
MY SENSE OF PERCEPTION HEIGHTENED.
*ColorsandSounds*BecameMoreProminent
LoveandPassion Invigorated*my*Thoughts
Time-*accelerated* MakingHours *seem* LikeMoments

I feltMoreInsightful
aComfortableUnderstanding
ofthe Complexities of AllMatters
seemedCloselyWithinGrasp
aDeepEmpathy—Overtook*my*Inhibitions

ItfeltLike, *your*WorstEnemy—wasn't*QuiteSobad*

God became aCosmicBellboy
whomIheld underExclusiveContract
and*WasObliged* toGrantMe *Limitlessfavor*

the TouchofSkin *wasBlissfulQuickening*
and *aKissFromAnother*
became *theMostBeautiful wispofSummerRain*
Everything
tookthe*BlushingHue of*UnrestrictedSuccess
and*forAsLongasitLasted*
Life was*PicturesqueMagnificent*

By the time the sun came up, I was naked in bed with the "freak" who kissed me earlier. As luck would have it, it was female, and I'd expressed my love to her many times.

I was convinced.

Given a small taste of this delicious bonbon, the dopers would feel duty-bound to bring me every last bit of their money with uniform regularity. There wasn't a hawker in Gotham who stocked this originality | I felt like a young Nino Brown in the Russian adaptation of *New Jack City*.

VANCE M. WAS SLEEPING ON ONE OF THE COUCHES IN THE LIVING AREA. I tapped him on the shoulder, waking him from his dope-sleep.

Vance, now here was a handsome guy.

Under a set of different circumstances, I'm positive he could have carved out a successful career as either an underwear model or a gigolo. He wasn't a pretty boy, just one of those rugged, striking types.

Vance stood six-feet-one and was naturally muscular.

He never exercised a day in his life, but when he took off his top, his defined muscles naturally flexed when he made even basic motions. He had a dark healthy tone to his skin and his blonde hair and high cheekbones accented his glowing green eyes flawlessly. His nose was just the right size and pointed upwards giving him the dignified appearance of a nobleman. His voice took a soft, impassive tone and when he spoke you got the impression that you had somehow met him before — He carried himself magnetically.

You couldn't help but like the guy.

"Let's get some chow, bud," I insisted.

Still drowsy, he lifted his head and rubbed the coal out his eyes.

We walked a quarter of a mile to a small coffee shop and sat down to discuss significant matters of urgency.

"So, tell me how I get my hands on some more of those pills?" I asked him. "Well. I could sell you what I got left, about fifty or so." He smirked stupidly. "I don't think you understanding me right, champ. I need a few thousand of these lovelies," I stated. "What I'm gonna need you to do is take a trip back to wherever you scored and bring me back two-thousand pieces," I demanded.

I instructed him to leave me whatever he had left and make for San Francisco before nightfall.

Vance looked at me | Speechless.

When we returned to the house, Vance looked like was ready to jump out the window. Beads of sweat rolled down his forehead, and he nervously ran his fingers through his hair.

I shifted Ace from my backside to the font of my denims.

This gesture was to hint at the fact that Vance was now a guest of the Hotel California. You know, the one where you can check out any time you like | But you can't ever leave.

Guido was just waking up.

He moved into the house a few weeks prior and shared a room with Terry. I motioned for him to sit beside me. "Let me hit that." I waved my hand to Guido, demanding a quick inhale of his (my) grass.

I hit it twice then passed it to a tense Vance.

"Guido here is your man. You and him like Bo and Luke Duke. Y'all are going to take a quick trip." I said merrily. "Vance is gonna be the navigator. The two of you'z hook-up some of them tabs we dropped. I'll supply the paper, a clean ride, and enough trees to suffocate the both of you," I finished.

Vinny nodded.

This was the chance he'd been waiting on.

"No cowboy shit, Guido. Make sure the deal goes down clean. Bring back the pills or the cream, *or your life's on the shelf*" I stated.

I TOOK THE REMAINDER OF VANCE'S TABLETS AND HOLLERED AT CONNY.

We met at Sahara restaurant on Coney Island Ave. While we ate, I educated Conny on the phenomenal objects in my pocket. As expected, Conny didn't disappoint. He was fascinated with the earning potential of this new product, but in order to make an accurate assessment he needed to give it the "acid-test." We headed to one of the safehouses and found ourselves a guinea pig.

It was still early in the day.

We neared our safehouse near the pizza spot.

No matter the hour, you can count on dopefiends of every flavor, shape, and size to saturate the landscape.

Given proper motivation any junkie would swallow a handful of squirrel droppings. For this particular scrounger, 20$ and our promise that his fingers would remain functional were the correct ingredients | Both C and I savored the extent to which our junkie rejoiced in synthetic delight.

WE AGREED TO PUT OUR CHEDDAR TOGETHER | 6000$ APIECE.

Conny didn't like taking chances and installed one of his capable people to come along on the trip and organized transport for Guido and Vance. His man would provide transportation, hold the cream, and most importantly, bring the heater. "Get them ready in a few hours" Conny instructed.

When I got back to the lab, I furnished Guido adequate spending money, two ounces of sticky, and my personal chipped phone. I walked them downstairs as we heard the grey Toyota 4runner blow its horn.

A Puerto Rican named Kalil was driving.

I passed him the 12,000$ in a manila envelope and another few hundred for gas and tolls.

Vance wanted to take that trip about as much as I wanted to eat a basket of chocolate fried cockroaches. "Don't look so worried, Vance. You'll be home soon," I snorted.

* * *

THE LAST WEEK OF JULY.

Radio silence, and they'd already been in Frisco a couple days. The hot phones had probably been cut. Last I heard they'd made contact with a few of Vance's people.

· · ·

AT EIGHT P.M., I WAS CLOSING OUT THE PIZZERIA.

Sandy dropped a line to me earlier. Shifty looking hoodlums had been floating around our pizza spot all day. He said they looked like desperados | *He sounded shook.*

I counted the day's take — 9100$

I put it all in a brown paper bag.

Leftover was a grip of product, probably more than a couple thousand. I never left product behind after closing. If the locals got wind of such a blunder, they would have already begun jackhammering an underground tunnel. Sandy put the junk into another brown bag, and we put both brown bags into a plastic tote. This was the routine — It was something we didn't deviate from.

Sandy wore a black Beretta 9mm. It had a standard eight in the magazine. I told him to chamber a missile before we walked outside.

I pulled out my magazine and smacked it against the counter, aligning the rounds perfect, a practice I had picked up from C. Reinserting the magazine, I racked the slide. The definite sound of the capsule inserting into the chamber broke the uneasy calm.

I walked outside.

My Spidey-Sense was going crazy.

Sparsely placed lamps released their soft yellow light.

Shadows were everywhere as we crossed the street and walked through the first row of brick buildings. A few hundred feet from the safehouse, three indistinct forms outlined a faintly lit area about a hundred yards away | Sandy was shaking and kept looking towards his rear.

A penetrating chill began at the small of my back. It very quickly convened at the base of my groin and almost instantly it made its home inside the capillaries of my heart, its mission now finished. I marshalled every last bit of resolve I had and moved forward.

Fear's grip had fully taken hold.

"Hey! Yo, playboy!" a strict, brazen voice called out to us. "Run your shit!" A slender Puerto Rican with a chrome 4|5 in hand shouted, as he approached. Two loud gunshots were enough to snap me into full mobilization.

I heard Sandy pleading to God.

God wasn't home that night. He tried to avoid spending too much time in the projects. They were just outside the scope of his district.

That in fact might have been the exact setting that Pat was referring to when she meant:

It's-a-Do-or-Die-Situation

I glanced to my side. Sandy had already made a break for it.

One of the bandits fired at him three times from behind a tree. Sandy dropped the bag and his burner and did theGhostFace.

This was no movie.
There was no script.
These weren't actors.
There weren't blanks in those clips.
No directors yelling *"Cut that's a wrap"*.
Only Action ++||— Clocking how us thugs react —

I REACHED FOR MY AUTOMATIC.
Ace in hand, I broke to my flank.

I don't know where I got the Jacobs.

Salty sweat beaded across my forehead. It tendering my eyes with a blurry haze. "He packin' heat," one of the bandits shouted while a single shot whizzed by my torso, *I saw the air break as it rushed by.*

I fired wildly, then lowered my weapon and ducked for cover under a bench I spotted not three feet from me. Before I could make it there safely | I was pierced in my right forearm.

Blood spurted from the mutilation created by the low-caliber slug. Adrenaline tried to fill the wound and drive me further, but it wasn't a clean through and through. The bullet shattered my forearm, my wrist, and created a break in my right ring finger.

Two of them were closing in fast.

The third picked up the bag Sandy released, and vanished into the fog of combat.

I was finished.

I tried to pick up Ace | The shot felt like a hot pencil had entered my tissue. Like a million needles poking into the membranes of my squashy cells. The pain ran up my fingers and into my neck. It was agonizing torture that made the skin on the top of my head throb.

I rolled to the left.

They were about ten feet from me, and the Puerto Rican pointed the muzzle of his chrome to my temple.

I grabbed Ace with my left hand and delivered his parcel to the other thug — It skimmed his shoulder and he stumbled to the right. It left him stunned, and the head-shot originally intended to finish me cracked the bark of a nearby tree.

I remained on the floor and kept firing as they retreated.

Recognizable voices and gunfire soaked into my awareness before neither synthetic nor authentic chemicals could keep me alert and I passed out on the concrete.

* * *

BEEPS FROM THE APPARATUS NEXT TO MY BED SLOWLY WOKE ME.

The smell of old people and Lysol signaled me to that fact I was in a hospital.

I've always hated the hospital.

They make you take your shoes off and put on that ridiculous gown with the slit in the back (the one that exposes your case). It's always arctic cold there. The moans of the ailing fill the quarters like provisions for the 4horsemen to gorge on.

My right forearm was elevated and wrapped in a ceramic cast and my ring finger stuck out from a splint.

Two police entered my little space.
It was detective CoffeeCakes and his partner CrumbFace.

Whenever there's gun violence, the laws have a script they read from. Detective CoffeeCakes handed me his card, sat on a small plastic chair next to my bed then began his index of questions.

I told them that the last thing I remembered was the sweet smell of burnt pork.

CoffeeCakes wanted to notify my parents.

I gave him my uncle Misha's phone number.
Misha would be more than happy to shout broken-English obscenities into CoffeeCakes earhole.

They left.

A young Pakistani intern was right behind them.

He told me I'd need to wear a cast for four to six weeks, and afterwards I'd need to retrain my arm with physical therapy.

SHORTLY AFTER, CONNY AND LITTLE GABE ENTERED THE CHAMBER.
Conny laughed. "Gary Gunz."

and so Began my Legacy.

From that day | *Until the day that I died.*
I was heralded by the street-name of "Gary Gunz".

Well that and the battery of other monikers I was constantly referred to by. There were so many flavors of my name I could hardly keep count.

They called me Gary Left-Gunz.
Gary Crazy-Gunz.
Gary Hard-Gunz.
Gary Mity-Gunz.
Gary Nice-Gunz.
Gary Straight-Gunz.
The forever-popular Gary 2Gunz.
And my personal favorite Gary Gunz-Gunz.

People closest to me just called me "Gunny."

"You're one sick fuck." Conny leaned back and nodded at me. "Those fools were ready to punch your card," Conny said jokingly.

Little Gabe offered me a quart of GeorgiVodka he produced from a brown paper bag — I was glad to receive it.

"One of the fiends told us you were gettin' dropped-on. We busted as soon as we heard," Conny said. "We backed you up, Gary. But you did that shit. You're straight-soldier, bro."

C and Little Gabe sat down near my bedside.

"We know the fools that stepped. They hit one of our spots earlier today," C continued. "The dude you plugged is called Eli. He's a sucker. Use to be down with us til' we cut him loose. He's got no heart. Now the other clown, they call him Junior. He's been doin' the stick+move on our spots for months. He's capable. He runs a little crew in the bricks across town. We thought he might eventually hit your little spot," Conny finished.

"Yeah? Thanks for keeping me informed," I hollered.

Both Conny and Gabe laughed.

"What happened to your homeboy?" Conny lifted his eyebrow. "I don't know. He just burned off," I replied. "We'll handle-up on that afterwards," he stated. "Right now we need to get you back to tip-top. I'll come by in the morning and grab you up." Conny and Little Gabe both shifted to leave — Morning couldn't come soon enough.

Conny waited for me outside as promised.

The doctor instructed me to return in four weeks, to have the cast removed and start therapy — *I've never been a very good listener.*

Conny drove to Brighton, where we found a more sympathetic Russian doctor to remove the cast and splint. He swathed my arm in a brown elastic wrap and told me to move it as a little as possible for the next few weeks. Dr. Kevorkian told me to start exercising. He said it would stimulate quicker healing.

WE DROVE TO CONNY'S APARTMENT.

C's apartment was on the fourth floor of a seven-story building a few blocks from the projects. It was a fairly roomy one-bedroom with a terrace overlooking the highway. Modern furniture and a big-screen television filled the living room. There were trendy black and white photos hanging on most of the walls — They looked expensive.

Little Gabe and two others were there waiting for us.

They were dressed in black denims and long-sleeve pullovers.
It was the middle of the summer; outside temperatures were in the mid-90s. I started getting a familiar nervous tingle.

2PAC WAS PLAYING ON THE STEREO.

The shit constantly hot || On my block
There never fails to be gunshots.
Can't explain a mother's pain when her son drops.

The misty reek of trees filled the house.
There was a small clear baggie filled to the brim with cocaine on the glass coffee table in the center of the room.

Little Gabe gave me a hug. "Gary Gunz."

The other two, both young Russians in their early twenties, introduced themselves as Letno and Tarzan.
Tarzan passed me the already lit trees and as I inhaled the pleasant balmy smolder, my insides thawed and the pain in my arm receded momentarily. We all sat down and pushed our glasses together. Conny withdrew to his bedroom and came back carrying a black vinyl duffle bag in his left hand and my blaster in his right

He put Ace on the table.

Inside the duffle was an arsenal of small arms. Conny left the open bag near the corner of the sofa and returned from his room with black sweat-pants and a black Nike pullover.
He threw the clothes on my lap. The others started doing rails of coke off the table.

Conny sat next to me.

"Singer came by earlier and told us where Junior rests at," he stated — Singer was a local dope fiend who frequented the pizza spot. He'd come by the safehouse in the morning, and in exchange for Junior's whereabouts, demanded five jumbos (10$ bags of crack). A broken knee cap would be his only compensation.

"Retaliation for this one won't be minimal," Little Gabe whispered as he focused on loading the breach of a black twelve-gauge he'd pulled from the duffle.

Tarzan and Letno had both snorted enough powder to gag a giraffe. They wiped their noses, put on surgical gloves, pulled pistols from the bag then filled their mags with slugs from a box of hollows. I got the impression that neither of these gentlemen were gun-shy.

Around my way | The streets gave no forgivenesses.
They were always watching.
Forever scrutinizing.
Looking for chinks in your gangster.
Testing your mettle for weak spots.

There was *no way* I could give a pass here.

Retaliation with extreme prejudice was what the situation called for. Any demonstration of compassion would prove me frail and insubstantial | We parleyed at Conny's until we were all thoroughly Irish.

SUNSET.

Tarzan drove | We piled into an old grey Caprice Classic—The kind plain-clothes used to drive. Letno stole the plates from another vehicle earlier in the day. I sat on the back hump and as soon as we pulled out of parallel-park, reality converted into a grim copious shade of apocalypse.

We traveled about twenty miles and stopped at the L-train trestle on the south side of a large project complex. Those particular projects had a reputation for wretchedness.

If ours was terrible — That one *was Hellish.*

C grabbed the bag out the trunk, sat it on the floor then opened a zipper on the side to produce two black ski-masks and three black half-masks, the kind that cover the bottom half of your face. He handed me and Little Gabe each a ski-mask and distributed the half masks to the other Russians.

Letno sparked a joint.
We passed it around in silence.

Conny took a swig from a pewter flask he'd pulled out his pocket. "*Na Shastyah* (for luck)," he uttered.

We exchanged hugs.

Tarzan picked up the bag and we stepped inside the concrete nightmare. The building wasn't far from the entrance. Singer said Junior was holed up on the second floor. Apartment 218 — We ran up the stairs.

Little Gabe was wasted no time.
He kicked in the door and we burst into the feature.

I stayed in the rear | Behind me were *sinister hobgoblins* craving for *a little bit of the ultra-violent.*

L-G He fired a slug into the first thing he saw.

There were two young men in the room. The first of the men flew back at least six feet by the buckshot Little Gabe's cannon spit out.
He was on the floor convulsing in a dejected death-spasm.

Junior jumped up in shock.

He'd been seated on a rotten beige sofa, puffing on crack he'd jacked me for—*Junior looked real throw'dOff*—His chrome 4|5 was on a wooden table near my brown bags.

"Sit back down," C commanded.

"You know why we here. Say what you gotta say. Make it good and we may just fuck you up bad," he shouted. The twisted smirk on Conny's gave away the fact that he was relishing the moment.

He expected Junior to beg for his life.

Tarzan had already grabbed the two stolen brown bags. He held them in his left hand. Little Gabe was at my left, looking down at the black male he'd murdered—*no older than eighteen*—he lay there on his back. Blood seeped out his mouth, down his face, and from a large hole in his rear then pooled around Gabe's shoes.

L-G pulled out his pistol and started blasting more holes into his corpse. "What the fuck are you doing? He's already dead!" Letno called out | "So what. I'll kill him again!" Gabe shrieked.

Junior sat on the sofa.
There was no way he was walking out of there | He knew it.

"Say playa, let me hit that pipe." He pointed at the stem on the table. Junior didn't cry or plead. This was all part of the game.

And it was past time for the house to collect.

I could tell Conny was impressed with his grit. C handed him the stem then lit it with his own butane lighter.

I held Ace to his dome with my left hand.

The room was in a still anticipation. I tried to squeeze off and fire a shot to his head—*I couldn't do it*—I lowered my weapon. Junior glanced at my bandaged arm and grinned. "So what you gonna do, playboy? You gonna pop me now. Nah, you a heartless bitch," he mocked. Conny brought the shotty up to Junior's chest ready to deliver the finishing blow | *Somebody had to die that night.*

I pushed Conny's shotgun down with my busted arm and pulled up my mask. It didn't matter anyways.

I think there are invisible, pre-set lines that you just don't cross.
Otherwise you keep crossing them one after another.
And after a while | *You're lost.*

Lord condemn me
Or better yet believe me
Or better yet receive me
God, I hope you understand
Forgive me for my mistakes — But I gotta play my hand
And my hand's on an eight-shot semi-automatic.

Junior looked straight up at me and smiled. "You jacked me. It's a package deal, take these missiles along with that" I stated.

I gave him what he wanted.
++|— I put two in his chest —

Ψ — Ψ — Ψ

1.
2.
3.
4. The three R's = the revolver, the river, or the roof

7

NO EASY WAY OUT

We're not indestructible
*   Baby better get that straight*
*   I think it's unbelievable*
*   How we give into the hands of fate*
*   But some things are worth fighting for*
*   Some feelings never die*
*   I'm not asking for another chance*
*   I just wanna know why*
*   There's no easy way out*
*   There's no shortcut home*
*   There's no easy way out*
*   Givin it in*
*   Giving in can't be wrong*
-Survivor

PEOPLE ALWAYS DIE IN THREES.
I don't know why that is.
Just some mysterious cosmic function of the universe.

A few days after Junior departed.

PAPPY WAS READY TO TAKE HIS LAST BREATHS.

He summoned me to come to his bedside. Both my parents were at the hospice. I hadn't seen them in months.

Pumped full of vodka — I stunk like a cabaret.

When I hugged my father, the butt of my weapon came exposed through my leather coat and he jerked back slightly. His look of disappointment apparent.

I had disposed of the burner formerly known as Ace.

I was now packing a trey-5|7 (.357) I'd procured from Shooter, a quirky little Russian who'd been supplying TF with bangers for as long as I could remember. I didn't like revolvers. They only fired six rockets and made me feel like a broke-down Billy-the-Kid.

Besides, they just weren't classy.

A proper gangster kills you with elegance.

In reality, revolvers are easier to conceal than autos. They never jam and don't spit shells, so you won't need to get number8 to futz around collecting evidence. The new Ace wasn't as pretty, but I wasn't about to go outside naked.

THE DOCTORS HAD PAPPY WIRED INTO ALL SORTS OF MACHINERY.

His liver exploded two days prior. It was a miracle he was still breathing. I stood over his bed and felt sickening hurt and compunction. Pappy awoke out the half-sleep he was in and grabbed my bad arm. It sent a sharp piercing pain up into my spine.

"Listen, Gary, I kept alive until you came to see me in order to give you this last lesson," he gasped. "Remember these three things I am about to tell as long as you live," Pappy's voice cracked as he strenuously whispered to me.

"First, the more you love women, the less they love you." He paused, his parched lips chapped from atrophy, struggling to take in breath. "The second lesson is most important. If you're starving, don't eat the first thing somebody hands you. It may temporarily save you, but sometimes it's better to die hungry than to eat shit the rest of your life. This is the most important thing. Gary. Remember this always. It's better to be alone than with people that don't really care about you. If you die with even one true friend, you'll be very fortunate," he finished and turned away.

"Fuck the world if you can" he muttered.

Twenty-four hours later, we buried my Pappy in a Jewish cemetery next to his beloved Betsy.

Wait there for me, Pappy.
Motherfuckers down here | *Got a Russian not knowin' how to act.*

RIGHT AFTER PAPPY PASSED, I JOINED GOLD'S GYM ON FLATBUSH AVE.

I walked into that gym at five-nine and 205 pounds of solid blubber, nursing a busted forearm. I didn't know a lick about lifting weights. It was a strain just to bench the bar. Dr. Steroid types were taking bets on how long I'd last.

After a few weeks of training, I was approached by a tall muscular fellow who introduced himself as Robert P. He offered to give me training tips and schooled me on routine and form. That, and he wanted to sell me anabolic steroids.

ROBERT STOOD SIX-TWO.

Dependent on his steroid cocktail, his weight fluctuated between 260-310 pounds. His brown skin tone matched his dark eyes nicely. He wasn't overly handsome. His nose and mouth were a little unbalanced, and due to abuse of animal hormones, he usually had a bad case of acne on his back and sometimes on his cheeks.

Robert was a brick house. A solid mass of rippling power. He had muscles I didn't know existed.

I gave him a negative on the steroids, but I did agree to enlist his services as a personal couch and trainer. All it cost me was a few sacks of trees and a little Hennessy.

Labor Day weekend.

Guido finally came home and offered some of the best news I'd heard in a long while. They delivered a knapsack; inside was seven grand and four thousand ecstasy tablets | Lance and Guido relayed the events of their excursion.

Upon arrival, they holed up in a broken motel on the outskirts of town. Vance started hollering to his people. That first night, they found a local rave[1]. Vance arranged to link with one of the local suppliers and purchase five-hundred tabs.

Kalil, the driver Conny had installed, had other plans.

His payment would consist solely of a Springfield 4|5 auto pointed square at the dome of the dopeman. They followed this pattern for three weeks, hitting five dealers total.

Right before they were ready to break home, Lance's chief connect finally hollered back. He'd taken the time to perfect the product and produced a superior tablet, much more suitable for mass consumption.

Him, they didn't jack.

They purchased one thousand tabs at four dollars apiece each under the assertion that the price would lessen once we were able to promote the creation and a more appropriate market value was determined. The new tablets were white with brown blotches. They were stamped with a Superman logo and were appropriately named "SupermanS." The white was speed and the brown blotches were diluted heroin.

Fine job, Guido.
++||— Одесса Мама —

I knew the perfect venue for our little friend.

JoJo was spinning parties Saturday nights at NASA, a nightclub on Bleaker Street. I told him to get ten spots on his personal guest list.

There we unveiled our new product.

It was a GrandSlam.
I just sat around and collected money.

I filled every pocket of a beige Columbia fishing vest. After that, I filled my pants pockets. Once they were full, I stuffed paper in my shoes. The very first night, I reached the point where I didn't have any room left anywhere for the remaining dope.

I had to start giving it away.

Retail was twenty bucks a tab. To dealers we wholesaled at a price ranging from eight to ten dollars per unit — We sold out all of our ecstasy that weekend.

Four-thousand pills | Sold.

The dopers just couldn't get enough — We cleared over 60,000$ on the ecstasy alone, and you know every second junkie was sure to pick up sticky-greens or some white as a condiment.

That weekend we took in over 100,000$.

After spreading around some love, I took home 25Large.

Conny and I decided to send Kalil back to Frisco with twenty thousand to institute a means for a more permanent supply. Kalil and Vance took a flight out of JFK that following weekend.

Sandy N. was ghost.

Gary Speks could have given him a pass.

Gary Gunz | He just didn't have that same kindhearted disposition. He was playing life with a man who lived by the sword and followed the code of street law. I wasn't actively looking for Sandy, but he'd be a fool not to know that his coming around would result in a humorless knocking.

Conny wanted me to blast him.

* * *

MONDAY, THE SECOND WEEK OF OCTOBER.

Late in the afternoon.

I was parleying at the pizza-spot.

Kalil and Vance returned safely from their second trip to Frisco. They brought back six thousand tablets that bore the face of Elmer Fudd. Kalil worked out a program of import with the manufacturer. We'd Western Union funds, and he would FedEx us tablets in vitamin jars | The cost to us would be 3.5$ a pill.

We could expect no less than 10,000 units (tabs) of per week.

After securing a P.O. box at the local mail-drop, we started putting Ecstasy at all the hot spots. Palladium, Limelight, Expo, NASA and just about every other popular New York nightclub was under our control. We were first with the dope and came ruthless, ready to stomp out anyone who thought they could vend so much as an olive leaf without our express consent.

I was running the pizza spot personally.

I didn't want to but there just wasn't anyone I could trust with the responsibility. Either they lacked the onions to check1|check2 on the fiends, or they were dopers themselves — A junkie trying to sell dope *is like a monkey trying to sell bananas.*

Conny, Little Gabe, and a few of the TF camp stayed with me most of that Monday. They asked me to join them at the bathhouse on Gravesend Neck Road, a filthy little hole, probably contaminated with all varieties of hepatitis. The OG's required the 200° sauna, and the shish-kebabs were some of the best around. Conny wasted sufficient time there, playing *Durak*[2], with certain gritty Russian hoodlum types. I chose to retire for the evening.

I needed to rest my dome.

EIGHT P.M. I CLOSED UP SHOP AND HEADED FOR MY BLAZER.

Brooklyn's nighttime pokerfaced blackness was ready to pervade.

As I turned my back to pull open the door of my ride, the thundering bang of gunfire exploded the large window of the vehicle, spitting razor-sharp fragments of glass out on the pavement and all over my face | The shot missed my still slightly injured arm by small fractions.

I dipped behind the grill of the Blazer.

Two more missiles aimed center mass barely missed.

The second shattered the concrete under my feet and shot a chunk of pavement at my left cheekbone. It hit hard, taking with it a nice portion of flesh and temporarily blinding my left eye.

My right hand pulsated.
Blood poured down the side of my face.
++||— *I grabbed for my heater* —

173

Two-hundred feet away stood a tall figure.

The way the moonlight shimmered, combined with my wounded eye, obscured who it was.

> Didn't matter:
> There weren't gonna be any discussions.
> *I was about to bring the repercussions.*

I peeked out from behind the front of the Blazer.

Another shot breached the fender. I heard the ting of perforating metal then darted from behind the auto, sending three missiles at the approaching shape. A flash of flame thudded from the muzzle and the brimstone smell of gunsmoke fused with my snout.

As my second slug contacted the top of his cranium, blood sprayed from the right side of his forehead. He instantly dropped his weapon and fell, back-first, onto the cement. I dropped my hands to my knee—w*inded*—as if I'd just finished first at a 10,000-meter triathlon. I don't know how long I stood there | *Breathless.*

Eventually, I collected myself, and started my ride. I was able to catch my last glimpse of a person I had once called friend as I drove away.

> It was Sandy | I'd shot him on the side of head.
> He was dead.

The autopsy gave Sandy's blood alcohol level at time of death .30 over the legal limit. The toxicology report found large amounts of crack cocaine in his system.

I DROVE TO RJ'S.

I parked the Blazer inside the small garage at the rear of his driveway and called Conny. He sent a car to take me back to his apartment.

That night, I got the first of the nightmares.

JUNIOR AND SANDY WERE BOTH ON THE BOARDWALK.

It was a hot-windy day. The sun beat down on my face. We walked peacefully and neared the Cyclone roller-coaster. I was in the middle. The banging clatter of wooden boards echoed harshly as we moved.

I had an ice cream sandwich in my hand.

Sandy turned to me. A section of his forehead was missing and a large crack in his skull displayed part of his wounded brain. He shrugged and asked, "Why'd you kill me, Gary?" I turned to Junior, who laughed loudly. As he bellowed, blood seeped out the two voids I'd put into his chest. The ice cream in my hand melted and in its place was a smoking revolver | I woke, screaming and coated in sweat.

POLICE WERE SNIFFING AROUND SANDY'S FUNERAL.

Lou Batz didn't even want to look at me.

I confided to Terry D. what happened that night. He sounded supportive but I didn't trust it. The whole street knew I had a grudge with Sandy and the consensus was that I'd murdered him where he stood, shot up my own ride with a disposable then planted it on his body after I blasted him.

Terry and the rest had no choice but to act right. If I'd really done Sandy like that, we were now playing a Mans'Game.

And a Mans'Game
++||— *Charges a Man'sPrice* —

Regardless, I needed to move out of that house.

. . .

175

A FEW WEEKS AFTER WE BURIED SANDY, LENNY APPROACHED ME.

Lenny wanted to work the pizza spot. He dropped out of high-school and his father's generosity was wearing thin.

Lenny was demanding his shot.

I didn't want that life for him.

The cost of it was way too high.

I reluctantly agreed but imposed stipulations. I asked Conny to put one of his people with Lenny. I didn't want to lose another friend.

He assigned Tarzan to partner up with Lenny. They worked the spot Monday-Friday and on the weekends, I had them supervise the wholesale of ecstasy at all our nightclubs.

* * *

FEBRUARY 13TH, THE DAY BEFORE VALENTINE'S.

I disposed of the Blazer. I doubted any car dealer would've wanted a shot-up SUV for trade, so I junked it.

In its stead, a crisp Q45 Infiniti.

Black on black with triple limo-tints.

I had a set of chrome BBS honeycombs mounted.

It was the flavors.

I began obsessively hitting the gym. I trained five days a week. It was a wonderful release for me, and the results were starting to show. Robert P. trained with me every day.

Robert recognized my game.

Long money, I was pushing a fresh Q, and always held the heater. He wanted down, and I was just that Russian to put him on. A good manager can recognize his employee's strengths and put them in a position of maximum potential.

I made Robert my first driver.

Most assume that a driver just pilots the auto. A driver, first and foremost, is an enforcer.

There are two rules the driver follows:

Rule number1, the boss is always right.

Rule number2, if anyone tries to prove the boss wrong, it's the driver's primary function to *"show"* them rule number1.

In essence, a driver is a gangster in training.

He spends his waking hours trailing his mentor and learning not only the conventions and regularities of the game, but more so the policy and the infrastructure of the particular brotherhood the boss is affiliated with. The driver's propensity for violence must at least rival that of his bossman. When the driver is around, there's no reason for bossman to ever have to draw his heater.

Bobby had been driving me for more than a month when Conny buzzed me on the chip with an assignment.

C's instructions were straightforward.

Go to the video store located on the east side of Avenue U and determine why the proprietors of said establishment not only refused to allow our dope to be sold from their locale but declined to pay us our weekly tribute — If necessary, use adequate persuasion to inspire a reconsideration of their position in this matter.

It was wet outside.

A chilly breeze blew harshly, further dropping the temperature.

Robert parked the Infiniti at a hydrant next door to the video store. I stepped out the auto and into a mound of rotten sludge that covered the sole of my black Timberland boot with grey mildew.

Rob immediately went to the rear of the vehicle, opened the trunk, and removed an aluminum baseball bat.

We strolled towards the entrance of the shop.

Robert opened the door, ringing an electronic jingle used to announce the entry of regular customers.

We weren't there to buy.
And regular | *Was something we just weren't.*

There was a customer in the X-rated section, which had its own little room with a red plywood door as the entrance. I entered the room and exposed Ace Model3 to the bug-eyed idiot inside, notifying him it was time to make like Michael Jackson and beat it.

Robert stepped towards the counter first.

In seconds a young lady emerged from the back.

My heart stopped at that moment.

Right there | That moment.
I became the withering blossom.
A denizen of a desolate inhospitable land,
Untaught yet obliged to inhabit.
A blossom now reinvigorated by the dazzling sun
Penetrating through a frozen night.
A night that seemed to have lasted just moments shy of forever.

"The owner's not here," she stated gingerly, noticing Robert holding the bat in his right hand. She looked alarmed but not frightened — *Her voice a soothing melody of passive comfort.*

I told Rob to wait for me in the car.

She was a slender five feet three.

Jet black curly hair flowed past her shoulders and down to her breasts. Her complexion was a snowy white.

I was in awe of her natural beauty.

SHE INTRODUCED HERSELF AS JUDI K.

"What are you doin' tonight?" I barely mustered the courage to inquire. "What do you mean?" she answered. "I want to take you out, Judi," I replied. She blushed at my invitation. "You don't even know me." Most women that traversed my circle only cared about your gangster, the caliber of your weapon, and the amount of chips you were holding | Judi didn't look at me like *they* did.

I pleaded until she agreed to go with me to the picture show.

My existence would never be the same.

From that night on Judi and I were inseparable.

Any free time I had we spend together and every moment we shared together was extraordinary.

Time passed very quickly — Four months into our relationship, towards the end of that school-year, Judi and I moved into a small one-bedroom co-op apartment that I purchased on the seventh floor of an aging complex on the corner of Brighton Beach Ave.

I bought the apartment for 80,000$ cash.

JUDI WAS A RUSSIAN JEW FROM ODESSA.

She knew what I did and didn't approve but understood. That way of life was deeply ingrained into our culture.

It was all she could do to bite her tongue.

I was already in too deep.
There was no easy way out for me.

She never tried to change me—Judi loved me for me—She was one of those sweet optimistic people you just can't help but love.

THE MIDDLE OF AUGUST, EVENTS TOOK A TURN FOR THE PECULIAR.
I was paying my usual weekly visit to the social club.
Although Louie and I hadn't spoken in months, business was still business and we had that spot on lock. Lou left it to me fair and square and there was no fuckin' way anyone was taking mine.

Conny put Letno at the controls.
He regulated like the Red Baron flew WWI airspace.

Around the time we'd finished our third *L'chaim*[3], I got the call.

Conny had just gotten popped.

It was just plain, out-and-out wrong. That morning Conny picked up his new driver, a youngblood by the name of Eddie.
Little Gabe landed himself in the cooler again. This time with a "possession of a firearm with intent to kill" charge[4]. With his criminal record and in lieu of his habitual convictions | He was looking at twenty calendars.

Eddie had been driving C for the last month.

They were enroute to pick up the week's ecstasy consignment we'd upgraded to twenty-thousand tablets and shipped in two separate bundles to two separate drops. They hit up the first P.O. box and Conny sent in Ed to grab the goodies. They opened the boxes and undid the packaging then counted the pills inside the vehicle.
Everything appeared to be in order.

On the way to the second pickup Ed gets a call from his mama. She was bedridden with pneumonia and needed her prescription filled. Conny, always sympathetic, detoured collections and stopped at Eddie's to grab the script. Eddie, in a rush, double-parked the truck, leaving C in the passenger seat without doubt sipping on drink and blasting hip-hop.

Just as Conny was about to a swig on the potion, A sanitation truck smashed into the rear of his SUV at around thirty-five miles an hour. The force of the impact sent the Expedition slamming sideways into oncoming traffic and colliding with another SUV (an Isuzu Rodeo) on the other side of road.

The Rodeo slammed Conny square on the passenger side with such force, the door of his Expo completely collapsed on his legs, breaking them instantly.

The driver of the garbage truck, the cause of this event, was zapped on gin and dope.

He was fine.
I mean | *He was in a fucking garbage truck.*

The driver of the Rodeo didn't fare as well.

He wasn't wearing his seatbelt and suffered a concussion with multiple lacerations to the face.

Conny got it the worst.
He caught a major case.

He was rear-ended by a vehicle belonging to the city of New York. That fact alone was worth millions in any court of law. The driver being DUI just compounded the case and made it worth tens of millions — If it wasn't for 12,000+$ cash money, the chipped cellular, and the 10,000 pills found inside his truck, Conny probably would've gotten every single penny of that money.

The crash knocked Conny unconscious.

When the sirens arrived, C was stuck so bad they had to use the jaws of life to pry him out of the wreckage.

Once out they cut open his pants, out plopped two knots of paper. The lawmen, now intrigued, looked inside his auto easily locating the chipped phone and the ecstasy. Conny didn't even have time to throw out the vitamin jars or the boxes they were shipped out in.

Now the supplier, you know, the "scientist" mixing the MDMA with whatever awful substance he considered palatable, that guy was one of the dumbest a mooks in history.

He didn't go to FedEx and drop off the packages.

Nope, this dipshit went and scheduled pickups for every one of his bundles. That meant that FedEx came to his home and picked up the boxes. All the feds had to do was basic detective work, and for our connect and our little ecstasy operation...

++||— It was ShowsOver||*That'saWrap* —

INDICTMENTS CAME SHORTLY AFTER.

They let Conny out on 50,000$ bond.

I'm not talking about 50,000$ bail and 5000$ out of pocket. His bail was 50rocks, a cash outlay of 50dimes to secure his temporary walking papers | C didn't have that type of cash handy.

He put most of his money out to the street, either loaning it to degenerate gamblers or the bookies themselves to cover winnings they weren't prepared to pay out. It was up to me to cover thirty-thousand dollars while Conny unruffled the rest of his capital.

Once out, Conny was put on house arrest.

They outfitted him with an ankle monitor and under court order he could only leave his apartment to visit his doctor or his legal counsel — Not that he was going anywhere with both his legs wrapped in plaster.

* * *

THE SUMMER OF '92 WAS A SCORCHER.

Pohlices jumped-out on the pizza spot and shut it down.

Lenny was fortunate. The spot was doing so well, that in the middle of the day, he'd run out of crack. While he was out to the re-up, the bulls swarmed and collared everyone inside.

Letno wasn't as lucky.
He caught charges.

Narcotics agents, acting on an anonymous tip, raided the social club three days after they broke up the pizza spot. After some negotiating (bribing) with the Italian owners, all evidence seemed to just evaporate, and the social club was back open.

Our people were no longer welcome there.

None of us, myself included, needed to spend any time in the clink. We turned the dope completely off.

I felt somewhat relieved.

THEN THE WONDERFUL — JUDI GOT PREGNANT.

We argued over keeping the child.

How could I bring a baby into this world knowing that my life could end at any minute? I imagined my bastard child roving the earth like a *Ronin*, looking to avenge the death of his estranged father.

Worse yet, a child of my loins, having to endure my struggles. Having to bury his friends and feel horrible lonely destitution that only those solemn few of us could ever know.

Judi put down an ultimatum, if the child went, so would she. Losing Judi would the equivalent of the pope losing his faith.

We got engaged.

I picked up the ring from Jake the Jeweler.

He kept a small booth on the corner of 47th and 5th and came highly recommended from some of the Russian OG's he'd crafted custom pieces for.

I was still sitting on a nice bit of coin.

Judi and I talked about me getting back to school and finishing my final year. I planned for the three of us, me, Judi, and our baby to leave town, move to Long Island. Buy a small home with a backyard a pretty white fence and live out the American dream.

I thought about studying technology in college.

THE FIRST WEEK OF THAT SCHOOL YEAR.

A petite slightly attractive middle-aged assistant principal named Ms. Ladenburg decided to help me.

After reviewing my scholastic record from as far back as elementary school, she enrolled me in a pilot program called co-op (cooperative) education. I attended regular classes two weeks a month. The other two weeks I spent with all of you fine folks, working out there in your world — I sat in class and every now and again retreated to the staircase to sip on potion.

Most of the class knew what I was.
They usually let me alone, teachers included.

Every morning, before class, I met Bobby at the gym, and we trained for an hour. I granted him the *kliytchka* "Baboon," ("Boone" for short) since he was fast to destroy anything that stood between him and whatever he had his eye on.

Like a Baboon, Robert liked to smash.

184

I TRIED TO SLIP OVER TO SEE CONNY EVERY CHANCE I COULD.

Alone in that apartment the walls must've felt like they were closing in on him.

People really didn't want to fuck with C.
He was a damn bakery he was so hot.

Nonetheless, he was able to get work here and there.

Extortion, shylocking, and our other criminal elements were still very much functional. Granted, they weren't operating with the consistency of days previous. Still, people had to eat. The few times a week we had some shit to do, I paged Baboon and it was on.

A few weeks into the co-op program.

Ms. Ladenburg found a job for me. She handed me a folded sheet of paper containing the name and address of Larry Hades then told me to report to him the following day for work at his stock brokerage firm.

EARLY NOVEMBER.

Winter had just gotten its start on the year.
It was usually quite chilly | That year *the chill was bone deep.*

Judi convinced me to leave both Ace and my vehicle home and ride with the rest of polite society on the subway. I took the D train, switched coaches for the N at Dekalb Ave, and finally arrived at my destination — The Rector St. station.

Riding the subways is an adventure all its own.

You find individuals from all walks of life on the New York public transportation system. From the trendy village-dwelling homosexual, to the moneyed businessman. To the reeking vagrant who stinks so horribly he gets to ride under the painfully rigid plastic benches of his own car.

If ever you are ever tasked with locating a group of uncaring, self-involved, mindless DroneVultures, you can easily discover them all packing inside the coaches of your local subway like livestock.

Some of them jabber to each other of futile specifics, yet others talk about the weather outside.

I would often traverse the cars, looking for an empty seat among the mechanical sardines who labored fruitlessly for errands they'd never see complete. Watching the people come on and off at the various stops until it was finally my turn to exit, I would dream of things to come — I would revel in imagining future triumphs and envision my greatness among the profoundly remarkable men of history.

Mr. Larry Hades was waiting for me.

Located next to that famous bull, in one of the lower-numbered buildings on the legendary street of Broadway. It was only two small lower Manhattan blocks uphill from the Rector St. N train station to the building I was scheduled to interview at.

I swigged some vodka from a pewter flask while toiling up the cobblestone walk to greet my future employer.

JLM Securities, at the time, was a fairly small, newly opened firm with its employees numbering in the 60s. The initials were those of the outfit's three principals. A Jewish securities attorney and two German Series 24 license-holders.

I arrived at the firm's greeting area at seven forty-five | Fifteen minutes early and announced my entrance to an attractive young woman and she gingerly directed me to take a seat on one of the couches at either side of her.

I pulled up my pants and sat down.

The smell of old money and construction infused the air with a cologne of stale cigar, freshly cut, wood and plaster.

I waited for my appointment for more than ninety minutes.

9:30AM, Larry Hades greeted me with a handshake.

He was an impressive man, as he walked through the room, you could feel the authority he commanded.

He grabbed my hand with a solid shake.

A young Irishman, he was no taller than five-eight.

Larry had understanding green eyes with the typical fiery red Irish hair and pale freckled complexion.

The most profound thing about him was his voice. It had a raspy, harsh, confidant tone filled with firmness and supremacy. When Larry spoke, I was compelled to believe that he had a monopoly over all the answers — Larry Hades did in fact have all the solutions and he was more than happy to give them to you.

Right after you gave him all your money.

He flashed his gold Movado wristwatch and snickered. "Sorry about the wait, kid. Market opened and I had to do a few quick trades." We passed a small boardroom area[5] where I peeked younger associates, not quite as neatly dressed as Larry, scattered about with receivers to their ears, looking nervous and busy.

We neared a trader area.

OK, TIME FOR STOCK-MARKET LESSON NUMBER1.

Take any stock, bond, or commodity — Let's call it XYZ.

If you're buying XYZ or checking your iPhone to find the value of

XYZ, you would find two prices. One is the *ask* (or offer) price. The other is the *bid*.

These two prices exist for a reason.

The price you pay for XYZ is *not* the price you're able to sell it back at — That's right; if you were to buy XYZ right now for fifty dollars a share and for some eccentric reason, wished to sell it back to the open market immediately after your purchase, you would not get back fifty dollars a share. How much you would get back depends on the security itself, the present market demand for it, and the size of the float (the number of shares available for sale to the public).

If it's a *decent* security sold on a reputable exchange, you'd probably only lose fractions of a dollar. Perhaps an 1/8th or even a 1/16th of a point.

You buy securities at the *ask* price. That's the price at which securities are offered for sale. When you sell, you sell them back to the market at the *bid* price. This is the price at which the market makers are willing to buy it back it. The *ask* is the retail price and the *bid* is the wholesale price.

The difference in the middle is called "The Spread."

Wait a second.. Hey Gunny, I thought spread was something you put on bread *(or something you make in jail after chow-time).*

++||— Not in this case my dearest reader —

The spread is the gasoline that fuels the machine. It's like Gordon Gecko[6] once said, "Money is not made or lost, it's merely transferred from one place to another." So who gets the spread — Where does it go? Did you think the NYSE (New York Stock Exchange) was a not-for-profit organization?

Brokerage houses, and all securities firms, have overhead to pay.

Rent, phone bills, electric, water, offShoreBankAccounts, Stripper assTwerkingLapdances, HugeChristmasBonuses, GoldenParachutes.

++||— *Everything* —

Larry occupied a widow office. It faced a brick wall and was next door to the J in JLM securities. I sat in a small cozy black cloth office chair as Larry Hades slipped into the large manager's chair.

"You know, I graduated from your school," he commented.

I nodded feeling somewhat uncomfortable. All of this seemed foreign to me. "Tell me 'bout yourself." Larry spoke with a Brooklyn accent. I kept it short and sweet. "Nothing much to tell, Mr. Hades. I cut some classes last year and they put me in this program so I could graduate," I said nervously. Larry gave me the once over, then stared hard into my eyes | I didn't flinch.

I stared right back for what felt like five minutes. We didn't speak for a long while.

Finally, Larry broke the silence. He smiled and said, "You passed, kid." Larry told me to come in the next day. "We'll set you up with some numbers to get. It don't pay much. But it's a start." He abruptly stood. "Alright. Break out, kid. See you at seven a.m.," he hollered.

Judi was ecstatic when she heard I'd clinched the job.

The next morning I reported for work at a quarter to seven and ushered directly into Larry's office.

He was already at his desk, sipping coffee from a blue and white disposable cup. Larry directed me to take a seat at one of the boardroom desks near his office. Some of the rookies had already begun their telephone assault on the wealthy.

It was a loud area of the floor.

The character sitting directly to my right introduced himself as Walker. He was fancily clothed and no older that thirty-five. The mook across from me was Mark Rimson. He looked old and used-up.

Both were Series 7 brokers.

I sat for about twenty minutes conversing with them.

They were extremely energized over the company's new IPO (Initial Public Offering),[7] by a small media company that specialized in publishing children's books and producing PBS shows.

Larry came out his office holding a stack of index cards with people's names and addresses hand-written on them. "Call up information and get me the phone numbers for these," he grunted, tossing the stack on my small table before returning to his office.

Walker glanced through the partition separating our areas and eyeballed the cards. He smiled. "Good leads there, Gary." "That fuckin Larry must've scored on his last fische-ing[8] trip" he stated, staring longingly at the cards. I worked the next six hours straight, ignoring lunch, getting numbers for the cards.

Something about holding that phone.

Something about the lulling frenzy of the trading floor | People ran around like orchestrated bumblebees.

All around me | *Fortunes were made and lost.*
The beautiful shouts of brokers resonated throughout the room.
They were like the proclamations of Viking pillagers.
++||— THEY WERE DEMANDING BLOOD AND BONES —
And anything less than total victory | Was considered forfeit.

It was two p.m. and I'd completed my stack of lead cards. I didn't need to sip any drink or smoke any trees that entire time.

I was too enthralled; I was located directly inside the core of the world.

. . .

I ENTERED LARRY'S OFFICE AND HANDED HIM THE CARDS.

Larry perused them and looked up at me angrily "Don't waste time getting women's numbers. We don't pitch to women," he stated. "Why not, Larry?" I inquired.

He threw the entire stack at me.

"Cause I fuckin said so. Pick up those fuckin' cards and tear up the women, and next time you come in the office, fuckin' knock," he shouted, his face turning redder than normal.

My right hand pulsated.

I left the cards on the floor and returned to my desk to collect my leather and made for the exit.

Larry approached me and put his arm around my shoulder.

"Sorry 'bout that, Gary. I had a real bad morning. A piker (small fish) decided to reneg[9] on 3000 shares of dogshit that tanked and now I'm stuck with the hickey[10]. I didn't mean to fuck with you like that. We don't call women because they like to nag and ask a lot of questions about bullshit. Women don't know how to make decisions, and if you catch them PMS-ing, they just rip on you hard. I don't know, Gary. I didn't make this shit up. I'm just telling you like someone told me. We don't pitch the bitch" he stated apologetically.

I walked back to my desk with Larry and sat back down.

The market closed at four p.m.I was expected home in a few hours. When Larry offered to buy me lunch, I declined.

That was a mistake.

The market may close at four, but the retail end of the business just starts cranking around five p.m. Most retail brokers, especially the hungry ones, the churners-and-burners[11].

The realSavages | *Their work* is never done.
The cream got them fiend for massive ill-schemes.

Ten to four.

Larry dropped another stack of index cards on my table. "Get these and you can break out," he said. "I thought we leave when the market closes," I replied. He laughed. "Look around, Gary. You see anyone leaving?" The boardroom bustled with activity, more even than earlier in the day.

"Let me school you some." Larry sat in my small black swivel chair and put his left hand on the arm of the seat. He fumbled in his pants pocket and pulled out a pack of Marlboro Lights then reached into the same pocket and produced a black ivory lighter. He deeply inhaled then tilted his head back to exhale.

The assurance of his unchecked wisdom was dominating.

"Most people don't get home til' six. That's why we're still here. Brokers make the most money in the whole fucking world and we don't do shit. Sales is speed. In this business, if you don't sell, you starve. It's that simple. You know when its prime time to call and ask for an order. Anytime you can pick up a telephone is prime time. I don't care if its two-thirty in the fuckin morning. If you think you can get a trade out of your client, you call that fucker. If you want to make it in this business, stake your claim. I'm the first in and last out, that's why I'm a producer. Now get on that phone and start cranking, cause tomorrow you're gonna pitch some of those numbers. I got a feeling about you, kid. I think you're gonna be a superstar," Larry exclaimed.

"Here's something you can hold onto, Gary," he stated, walking towards his office. "Stocks go up and down | But the commission always stays the same."

He closed his door and left me to it.

His inspiring words caressed my covetous nature and slaked my thirsty dreams.

I called Judi and told her I'd be home late. It was close to eight o' clock when I finished getting numbers for that stack of cards.

THE NIGHTMARES CAME AGAIN THAT NIGHT.

Sandy, dressed in all white, sat behind a dark mahogany desk. There was a giant bloody hole on the top left of his head, and when he swiveled the chair, the light shone on the slick parts inside.

His brain throbbed. When he spoke, thick purple blood leaked down his face and onto his white outfit. He handed me a small box, gift-wrapped in silver and green film. "For you, Gunz," he snickered, urging me to accept it | I took the box.

Trembling — I ripped off the paper while Sandy grinned. I awoke in a murky sweat before I could make out what evil lay within.

SEVEN A.M.

Larry was waiting at my desk with a yellow legal pad and a ballpoint pen. "Start writing," he rigidly stated. "Those cards you got numbers for are names of known degenerates that invest serious money in the market. You're gonna call them and qualify them. Don't tell the wife you're a broker. Their wives don't want them spending more money on stocks. That means less for shoes and handbags. Tell them you're with UPS or FedEx or something," Larry insisted.

"What do you mean 'qualify' them?" I asked.

I wasn't a phone rookie.
Selling wipes taught me about slamming orders.

This right here was straight *TakeOvertheWorld||NWO shit* — I wanted to squeeze as much out of Larry's beneficial comprehension as possible. "You want to figure out if the guy on the phone is a piker or a whale. Here, write this down," he said.[12] His science sensitized the hairs on my neck. By the time we concluded, it was about lunchtime.

Larry left me to start dialing.

I applied the style I developed selling wipes to this new task and it worked marvelously. That first day I was able to get eight leads for Larry. Around nine p.m., I managed to peel myself from my chair.

Some of the brokers gathered around during my qualifying pitches and called me a natural.

They were certain I was going to be the next multi-millionaire.

For the next month I called information in the mornings. The afternoons — I spent qualifying. I scored more than one-hundred leads that month for Larry, many of which he called back and opened accounts with.

I rarely attended my classes.

Larry had a special relationship with Ms. Ladenburg and as long as I kept my leads numbers past expectations, he smoothed over any fracas my poor attendance might have caused.

* * *

CONNY WAS SLOWLY RECOVERING FROM THE CRASH.

He was still on house arrest.

Five times that month, Baboon and I went on assignment to flex our muscle and collect C's paper. Plenty of people turned their backs on him. He had to let the street know that he was down, but never out. The street loves you when you're up on high.

When you're down | You can't find a homey to troop your beer with you.

Hit with a two-four it's difficult.

194

Officer SpongeCakes never had probable cause to search Conny's vehicle. His Lairs were talking about a sentence of time-served as a possibility. And the rumor was that Little Gabe might be coming home early after volunteering for a "shock" rehab program in prison.

By the new year:
Things couldn't have looked better for Judi and I.

Larry handed me a U-4 application (the compulsory background check and fingerprinting required by the SEC to file for a Series 7 license) and promised to send me to classes so I could take the exam that year. My Judi was going into her fourth month of pregnancy, and she just glowed with the bliss of anticipation. *It made me feel incredible.*

Yeah, things were great.
++||— *Except for the nightmares* —
They came two or three times a week | Always the same.

SANDY, DRESSED IN WHITE, STILL BEHIND HIS MAHOGANY DESK.
His fractured brain bled down his face.
Sometimes Junior would be there too.
He whistled *Rock-a-bye-baby*.
Sandy laughed and handed me the gift-wrapped box.
Every time I opened it, the contents of box would become more discernible — Finally it became clear what lay inside.

Please, dear God.
Oh please don't let it be.

Ψ — Ψ — Ψ

I.

195

2.
3.
4.
5.
6.
7.
8.
9.
10.
11.
12.

8

THE HARD GOODBYE

In the lonely light of morning
  In the wound that would not heal
  It's the bitter taste of losing everything I held so dear
  -Sarah McLachlan

I HADN'T WORN ACE IN MONTHS.

He dangled in his holster on a wooden pole, in the portion of my closet which stored clothing I just wouldn't wear. Collecting without a banger was like putting WD-40 on a rowboat.

> *The more I thought about it.*
> The more I wanted out forever.

MID-JANUARY '93, LARRY ASKED ME TO PITCH STOCK ILLEGALLY.

His reasoning was obvious. During the short time I'd been obtaining leads, I had far surpassed any of the seasoned veterans in the office.

I was an animal on the phone[1].

"How can I open accounts without a license?" I inquired.

"You're gonna use my name. After seeing how you work, I trust you enough to let you do that. I already ran it by the owners. As long as you sit in my office and the rest of the boardroom doesn't know our business, they're fine with it," Larry stated. I looked at Larry sort of sideways. "Wouldn't that be against the law?" I asked.

It's common for callers to use their broker's name to pitch stock illegally. Big brokers don't have time to waste, cold-calling new accounts when they can be demanding large trades from established clientele. They pass the cold-calling off to their unregistered callers.

Prohibited practices such as these are commonplace at some of the largest retail brokerages in the nation.

I was apprehensive and playing coy, but Larry caught on fast. "Look here, Gary Gunz. Ms. Ladenburg told me about you. It wasn't luck that got you this job. I asked for you personally," he barked.

I sat up in my chair.

"Let me tell you a little something about *me*. I got bullet holes in my U4. I'm a convicted felon. I should never have gotten a 7. In fact, I'm only blue sky[2] in 7 states."

His words were filled with vain assuredness.

"I told you I went to your school, right? You probably didn't know I use used to sling dope out the projects across the street. I asked for the hardest-case Ladenburg had. I was you, Gary. Six years ago, I plead out to felony probation for selling cocaine to minors. The fuckers said I'd never amount to nothing. Take a look now. I run shit here. Let me key you into something. The best hustlers make the greatest brokers. All we do here is sell legal dope to rich junkies. You work hard, you got boatloads of talent, and now I need to give you a shot. The same shot someone like me, gave me. Take the shot, and be what you were destined to be. Take your shot now. Because people like us, straight from the bottom, don't get too many shots to pull up to the top." The vein on his forehead turned purple.

He leaned back in his chair, nodding slightly.

"Alright, I'll bite. Right after you tell me how I get paid," I stated.

"Ten points (10%) on every account you open, that's how. If the joker sends in 10,000$ you make yourself a dime. Every two weeks I cut you a personal check for the commissions. Raise me half-a-mil, and you're staring at fifty large. Open quality accounts, and I'll toss you some points on the trades." He seemed excited.

I was almost closed.

"I'll show you how to 1call-close these dummies. Just that knowledge alone; you should be paying *me* for that," he finished then stood to offer me his hand as a binding contract.

We shook, sealing the deal.

The next three days were spent watching Larry's every movement, taking notes, and learning once and forever the persuasive arts of the 1call-close. We weren't talking people into buying pruned dogshit with company money for a free promo.

These people were real.
They were using their own money.
And the stakes were for keeps.

When the stakes are high — You damn sure gotta do.
Anything || To get your piece of the pie.
++||— ELECTRIFY —
Even die for the cash.

199

++||— THE ICALL-CLOSE —

It's the most prevalent tactic in the history of telephone sales.

Icall-closing, takes aptitude, discipline, and a stone-cold heart. Discipline comes naturally to most first-generation immigrants. But it's the things I've seen and the shit I did that made my heart cold.

The Icall-close Rule#1

For every possible objection the prospect has to buying, you—the salesman—are armed with at least three credible rebuttals. There's no reason in the world you should ever take "No" for an answer because the sale is assumed. Whether he knows it or not, the mark you've got on the phone bought your shit before you even called to sell it to him.

Fact is, your chances of closing are reduced by 80% on the second call. If you allow the client the opportunity to "think about it," you've doomed yourself. The element of surprise is on your side. Your call isn't expected, so you need to catch the mark with his pants down and get him to commit to something — *Anything.*

Opening the account is the hardest part of the business. The mo-mo you're calling doesn't know you from a hole in the wall, and if you don't close him quickly — He never will. Once a buying relationship is established, his confidence increases exponentially, and future business comes much more willingly.

Every sales pitch for every piece of bulletin-board bullshit, 504d deal, and all other scam-concoctions that I've ever sold reads the same | In truth, every Icall-close looks exactly alike. All you need to do is fill in the blanks and read it with passion.[3]

Sure | I could probably author a best-selling novella on the nuances of the slam-sell — *Yah, I think I'll do that* | Right after I learn to repair the ignition manifold in a rocket-propelled hydrofoil.

You wanna learn sales, go see Zig Ziglar.

I'm confident that, for three grand and the right index-finger of your first-born male child, he'll send you some DVD's on his patented techniques | For now, *it's back to your regularly scheduled tragedy.*

I picked up that phone to pitch stock,
++|| *— Like Arthur pulled* Excalibur *from the stone —*

IN FOUR WEEKS I OPENED 60 ACCOUNTS FOR LARRY HADES.

Results like that were unheard of on the street.

I'll tell you something about Wall Street, there may be 1.5 million people working in thousands of offices. But what you really have is the smallest street in the world. Everyone knows everyone, and if you're not inside, you're outside, gazing in through a thin, dark-tinted glass. People talked about me, *about my talent* | It filled me with imminent promise.

Judi objected.

She didn't like me putting my neck on the line and jeopardizing our future. "Why don't you just wait until you get your own license? What good are you really doing other than making Larry rich?" she insisted. She could always see the big picture a lot clearer than I could | GeorgiVodka+Dope helped stamp out that voice of reason.

The paperweights in school, didn't care whether I came to class or I worked right through school — I was just another number to them. Ms. Ladenburg had some kind of fishy arrangement with Larry. She was probably getting a kickback, or maybe the salami, possibly both.

Near the end of my second month., I'd opened a total of 103 accounts. Even the owners of the company stopped to pay homage to my talents.

I felt important.

MARCH 14TH.

Conny called and indicated that a crucial matter needed my attention — I asked Larry to leave earlier than usual.

It was around three p.m. when I left my desk.

I reached the Rector St. station realizing I'd left my leather attaché behind. It contained some of my best prospects.

The green-eyed mo-mo's in the boardroom would love nothing more than to sticky-finger it.

I rushed back upstairs.

The door to Larry's office was cracked open.

He was inside with one of the other senior brokers, talking about me. I stood in the far corner of the boardroom, out of sight. I could just hear Larry's voice. "This kid is making me a small fortune. You know what kind of trades I'm scoring off his accounts. It's fuckin sick. Who would've thought this little shit had this kind of talent. You know he actually thinks I'm gonna let him get a 7. I'm holding onto this kid as long as I can. I'm gonna jam his paperwork so far down the bottom he won't be registered til' he's fifty years old." Both bellowed in laughter.

They were clowning:
But I was the one wearing rubber shoes.

Larry's words ricocheted in my ears. I left the bag and darted out of the office.

I recalled Pappy.
"Be careful, Gary. Don't trust anyone, Gary"

I SAT ON THE TRAIN WITH MY HEAD DOWN.

Perhaps Larry had mistaken my kindness for weakness. Judi would know what to do, she was better with matters like those.

I drifted off to sleep.

It was the same dream.

The same one every time I rested my glimpsers. Sandy handed me the box—O*n impulse*—I took it. Junior was screeching "Rock-a-bye-baby." Blood leaked from his puncture wounds as he whistled.

I undid the wrapping in a panic and opened its top.

The underdeveloped lifeless fetus of my unborn child was inside.

It bled through the bottom of the container.

I dropped the box to the floor, looked at my bloody hands, and fell to my knees | By now I would have woken up.

This time was different.

When I looked up, Sal was there. It was the first time I'd looked into his face since I pierced him. Unlike the others, he wasn't bleeding from the stab in his heart. Sal put his hand on my cheek, and said, "I'm sorry." I snapped back to life three stops from my station.

I was scared | *Shivering.*

There was plenty of time to walk it off after the subway stop, which was a few blocks from where I'd parked that morning

A QUARTER TO FOUR P.M.

I exited the subway at the Kings Highway station. I'd parked the Infiniti a few blocks from the exit that morning. I called Boone (Baboon) and told him to gear up. I'd roll by to pick him after my meeting with Conny.

The meet with C was scheduled for four-thirty at El-Greco Diner, located on the corner of Sheepshead Bay and Emmons Ave.

I pulled into the parking lot at four p.m.

It was early and I decided to walk across the street to Ginger-Rose, a fashionable barbershop frequented by many hard Brighton youngbloods | I needed to get my fade right.

I was greeted with the smell of expensive chronic.

Its smoke took on a green tint from the multi-colored hub lamps inside the ceiling — Trendy house music played on the stereo.

There were stations for seven stylists, each of them into some sort of swindle. Hip knickknacks were scattered throughout the floor. A red disabled motor-scooter was parked next to a wall of twenty-one-inch television sets formed into a battery, all displaying the same images. Collages of custom fades covered the walls | Many of the people pictured were felons of a diabolical nature.

Brother Will was there to salute me.

He was a gruff Russian TF member.

A petty thief and a known heroin fiend. He sat in one of the metal folding chairs waiting his turn at Jimmy the barber.

Jimmy too was a TF soldier | The barber gig was a good cover for peddling any contraband he came across. He had a good little racket there. As long as he kicked up skim to his captain, he was allowed to operate in a prime location. The fact that he gave a damn good Caesar was just a bonus.

BROTHER WILL WAS TWENTY-TWO YEARS OLD.

He stood five-four, was of a stocky build, and had sharp high cheekbones. His skin appeared thin and bristly from comprehensive drug abuse. He'd just finished an eight-month stint at Rikers for burglary. He wore a huge ornate TF tattoo on his back.

The last few months, he was spreading paper around real thick. *Word was* | He and his little set had a line on a very lucrative hustle.

"What's good, player?" he said merrily. "Chillin' here for a second. About to sit-down with Conny at the grease house. Figured I'd tighten up my dome. What's crackin' with you?" I replied.

I examined Brother Will.

All his threads were CrispNew||HighDollar. The oversized aftermarket diamond bezel affixed to the white gold Rolex on his left wrist was shining correct | He was Representing *Heavy.*

Jimmy the barber called on me, passing over two other waiting customers. They didn't acknowledge that I had cut them.

They knew me by reputation.

Brother Will spoke as Jimmy put a black polyester cover around my neck. He grinned. "Same shit, Left-Gunz. You know how we do." "Actually, Will, I don't know. But I hear you're into that new shit," I stated coldly. "Nah, Gunny, we just doin' what we gots to. How 'bout you, bro? They tell me you're gonna be a daddy. Props to you," Will replied.

He was avoiding the subject.

"Ya, I got a shorty coming. My lady's in the city right now getting an ultrasound. Imma find out if it's a boy or a girl," I cheerfully stated.

Brother Will's cell rang, and he excused himself into a far corner to take the call. "I gotta peel-off, Gunny," Will hollered, already at the door. He crossed the street to the El-Greco parking lot and entered the driver's side of a late-model yellow BMW M3.

I was looking at a known neighborhood loser wearing a 15,000$+ wristclock, push off in a 40,000$ vehicle | This was a mook, who not even a year back was begging me for my leftover crumbs.

The whole thing struck me sideways.

Jimmy finished up my haircut right around the time Conny pulled up to the diner.

C WAITED FOR ME INSIDE.

We sat in the fourth booth on the right side of the smoking section. The two cups of coffee he'd ordered were on the table.

I sat with my back facing the door and glanced out the window.

El-Greco is located towards the end of the slips where most of the party and fishing boats dock. I had a clear view of the bay and the small wooden footbridge that separates Sheepshead Bay Road and the affluent Manhattan Beach area.

The sun was still out, but barely.
Twilight was on its way.
The ordinary citizens of the city casually wandered the sidewalk.
Some warm ++||— Some bitter freezing —

C's finances were thinning out fast — Something that usually happens breakneck, once the parasites grip their razors into you. Between the plundering lawyers and the weekly fees for his house arrest, he was barely breathing.

"What's Good, Conny," I said, motioning the sloppy Georgian waiter away. "Something came up, Gary. This fool Gene is into Pushka for a hundred rocks. Been on a bad losing streak all week. I got the word this morning. It's getting out of hand. Pushka wants the money by ten tonight. The job got passed to me. He knows I'm hurtin' and gave this to me as a solid. I need you to go over there and bring this paper home. I need this, Gary. Bad. I know I can count on you. You been there for me, brother. Pushka's giving me ten points off the top. That's ten dimes to me. I'll lay a quarter on you for the pickup. How does 2,500$ sound?" Conny's tone was anxious, he looked worried. I pulled the flask from inside the pocket of my insulated coat and handed him a taste — He grabbed it and swigged deeply.

"I'll do this one for a dime, bro. I feel your pain. I got you on this. No worries," I replied then took back the flask to get a fast sip on the Georgi inside. "Good lookin' out, Gary. Gene's gonna be at his apartment waiting for you at six tonight. Meet back here at seven sharp. Pushka's gonna send one of his people to grab the paper. Take our cut, hand him the rest," Conny stated, he sounded easier, more relaxed. "Count on it, bro." I finished and sat back while he gave me the rest of the details.

I knew Gene T.
He was a short, overweight, small-time Jewish fraudster.

Gene was a gambler of the most degenerate nature and a drug addict who fancied exclusive greens and fish-scale white. Any money he may've accrued through insignificant illicit activities was all spent chasing that stallion.

He was into the usual cons.

Credit card fraud, cell phone scams, calling card fraud, and the occasional insurance scam, *all petty,* nothing complicated.

He rolled with two of his cousins. They were involved in most of his scams and shared his affection for illegal imports. I'd met with him and|or his people on frequent occasions to either deliver dope or pick up vig. It was "criminals" like them that kept thugs like me in business.

"You know, C, I'm a little skeptical on how-the-fuck this zero is gonna come up with that type of coin," I said. "Supposedly he's got it. I hear he's into something huge. If he don't, you know what to do."

Conny pointed to his arm, indicating that physical persuasion might be required.

"Strap up, Gary. Play it safe." Conny stood and gave me a hug.

Shattering one of Gene's body parts wasn't exactly what I wanted to be doing on a Monday night | I *hoped it wouldn't come to that.*

I JUMPED IN MY RIDE AND SPARKED A JOINT I'D ROLLED EARLIER.

Inhaling deeply, I coughed from the hot bitter-sweet smoke that filled my lungs and carried my mind to a more secure condition.

I got to Baboon's at five-thirty.

He lived close to the diner in a basement apartment he rented from his mother. He jumped into the driver's seat, pulled his Glock, pumped one into the hole, and concealed it into a holster he'd fastened inside his gym pants.

On the way to the meet, I called Judi.

She asked if I could meet her by the 42nd street D train station in a few hours to take her home.

Some fast business came up — She would have to take the subway home. I promised to meet her at the Brighton Beach D train station. We spoke for a few minutes more.

—||— It was a girl —||— I was so happy I almost cried.

I told her I loved her.

NIGHT HAD ALMOST COMPLETELY FALLEN.

I directed Boone to block the hydrant on the corner of Sheepshead Bay Road and East 14th where Gene lived. Robert fixed his burner as we neared the door to the apartment building.

I scanned Gene and his cousin, Elliot F., a tall, obese Jewish lout, fast-walking out the apartment and moving towards a crisp black

Mercedes hard-top convertible. It was one of the new spiders Benz had released. The sticker was almost a hundred thousand, and there was a waiting list.

"Yo, Gene," I yelled. "What's up. Where you jettin' off to? You and me, we got some business," I stated calmly, nearing striking distance. "Was waiting for you. I got shit to do, Gunz. I can't wait forever, you know." *Gene was just as obnoxious as I remembered him.*

"Look here, Gene. You're down big this week and Pushka needs his cream. You know what I'm sayin', right?" I stated coldly. "What do you think, bro? I was trying to dodge you?" Gene and Elliot both laughed.

Shame I didn't find it funny.

"Run the paper," I demanded.

"Walk with me to the whip," Gene said and started again toward the Benz. I followed him while Boone stayed behind with Elliot. "You know, I been hearing things about you. I hear you're tearing it up there on Broadway," Gene said. "Little something," I responded, noticing the diamond-covered, tri-color Rolex Day-Date on his wrist as he opened the trunk and pulled out a small black lambskin handbag. "All of it's in here," he said loudly as he handed over the bag. I clicked open the stainless-steel lock and glanced inside at the ten small stacks of freshly minted bills. "No need to count it, Nice-Gunz. Take my word, it's all in there," Gene stated.

I reached inside the tote and examined the bills.

As soon as I closed the deal and Gene and I parted ways, the liability of delivering one hundred rocks was on my shoulders.

Last thing I needed was a bag of counterfeit.

The department of treasury uses restricted paper.
And a special brand of ink that has a unique fragrance all its own.
Bound in its original bank-wrap | *It smells a lot like a sack of garbage.*

IT'S A PENETRATING ODOR.

It cannot be mistaken for anything other than what it is. That smell of "clean" money, to many, intoxicates more than a hot-rail of fish-scale raw.

Something about its smell.
It cuts through conscience, morals and integrity.
It infiltrates directly to the crux of man's animal nature.

"Boone," I called for Robert, "grab this bag and count it out." He retreated inside the Infiniti to follow the order. "What the fuck you into, Gene?" I asked impulsively, curiosity getting the better of me.

Gene looked at Elliot and there was a brief pause. "All here, Gunny," Baboon yelled from the driver's side of the vehicle.

"That's what I'm sayin' Gary. We got something here, a real gem. This is the fuckin *new* shit, and I got work for someone like you. This shit here, it's gonna make you a millionaire fast. You do like money, right?" He waited for a reply. I gave him a stiff look. "Alright, what you got for me?" I replied. "We hit a real lick here. I can't talk now, but I promise you, we're fixin' to put you on," Gene affirmed as he and Elliot climbed into the Merc. "We're gonna holler at you," Gene said, sliding the coupe into drive.

Boone looked at me bewildered.

"I don't know what they're into, Gary, but it looks like they hit the fuckin lottery," Robert said, his voice tainted with resentment.

"They're keeping it all QT[4] for now. Tell you what. I really don't give a piss. I'm gonna be a father, bro. Real talk, Rob. I got responsibilities now, to my family. I know you want down. Same here, we talking some big markers, man I'm not blind. I see that shit. But the writing's on the wall. Whatever-the-fuck they're doin', stakes is high," I said anxiously. "Get us to El-Greco. We need to drop this here," I said, indicating the leather bag. "I got your back Rob. We're still shining. You know I won't let you starve." I put my hand on his shoulder for a moment while he drove.

SEVEN SHARP.

We pulled back into El-Greco parking lot and walked through the two sets of double-doors then past the John Gotti look-alike who acted as both host and bouncer.

Pushka's man stuck out like racing stripes on a school bus | He was the greasy-bald Russian with the thick gold herringbone and wrinkled leather jacket who enjoyed sipping considerable quantities of vodka-straight, breaking chins, and smoking odd black cigarettes.

I sat parallel to the middle-aged man and twitched my head upwards, acknowledging my capabilities. "You have something for me?" he blurted with a heavy Russian accent. Having already lightened the skim, I slipped the leather tote under the table. "I took out our share," I notified the man with the porkchop fingers.

"You Gary Gunz, right?" he asked. "Yeah. I'm him." I shook my head, flattered that my name had somehow reached the top. "I thought you'd be taller," he said as he got up to leave.

Baboon drove himself home.

I GOT TO THE STATION.

All I could think about was Judi getting home, seeing her bright smile, and the insanity of the day being done. The Infiniti's white dash clock read eight o'clock sharp. I tilted the seat back and enjoyed a few sips from a fresh quart of GeorgiVodka I'd purchased on my way to the train station.

The eight p.m. train ran ten minutes late and had let out its passengers | Judi wasn't among them.

I turned up the stereo.

++||— *2Pac* —

> *Dear Lord if ya hear me*
> *Tell me why || Little girl like LaTasha had to die*
> *She never got to see the bullet. Just heard the shot*
> *Her little body couldn't take it || Just shook and dropped*

8:25p.m | I saw the first of the Ambulettes pull up.

Somehow | *I knew all along.*

By the time I made it upstairs and pressed past the crowd of spectators, four police and two paramedics had cordoned off the perimeter. A small crowd had formed to witness the misfortune.

Snippets of their conversations clued me in. "He just stabbed her, stole her bag, and ran off. Police are looking."

My heart was inside my throat.
I couldn't breathe.

NOT JUDI.
Please not Judi.

I made it close enough to see the puddle of blood ooze from under her dress and stream down into two shopping bags whose contents were scattered about the concrete pavement.

Sprawled on the freezing pavement.
Judi lay on her back.
Paramedics were at work trying to save her life.

I pushed my way past one of the uniformed police, and the others chased after me. Two more police grabbed me before I could reach my Judi. I screamed and fell to my knees. "Please, help her!" I yelled.

I tried to force my way through. "She's my wife. Help her!" I cried. "You can't see her now. They're trying to save her. Let them do their job, sir," The fat uniform emotionlessly stated.

They strapped Judi to a stretcher and two paramedics carefully carried her down the stone staircase to the street level.

I threw off my jacket and broke free of the officers holding me by the sleeves then ran to Judi and grabbed her hand | It was covered in blood. "Baby, baby please don't die," I begged.

Tears leaked down my face.

"Be brave, Gary, for me, for our baby — *Be brave.*" Those were the very last words Judi ever said to me. They were quite possibly the last words she ever spoke on this earth.

She was pronounced DOA at the hospital.

Four lawmen tackled me down — One of them delivering a right jab to the back of my head. After a few minutes a detective offered me a hand. I slapped it away and got up on my own.

The dick told me what witnesses said had happened.

Two young males, possibly in their early twenties, (1black|1white) followed Judi off the train. One pulled a large hunting knife and demanded her purse. Judi dropped her purse to the ground and impulsively screamed for help. The black male panicked and thrust the oversized blade directly into her stomach. The other grabbed her bag, and they both ran out the same north-side street level exit — *Not before the black male pulled the knife from her gut.*

No one in the crowd was able to give an accurate description of the two.

At the hospital a teenage looking Pakistani intern informed me that both my Judi and the baby had almost immediately perished.

The knife struck my baby's neck — *She died instantly.*

Blood loss, realization of the baby's death, and the trauma of the wound caused a massive cardiac arrest that paralyzed the flow of blood and her central nervous system — *That's what killed my Judi.*

I CANNOT BEGIN TO EXPLAIN TO YOU IN WORDS | MY SADDENED READER.

The physical, mental, and spiritual anguish, of losing the irreplaceable one who you love the most. It is a pain reserved for the accursed sinners of an implausible fiery hell. It's the overriding dark-blackness of inexplicable cataclysm — *Its absolute devastation.*

It escapes the grasp of all rationale definitive.

WELCOME TO BRIGHTON:
Where the youth get blinded by stardom.
Where Russians get murdered at random.
Nobody seen | Nobody heard it.
++||— *Just another funeral service* —

The hours that followed are hard to recount.

Somehow, I ended up at Conny's apartment, a shattered wreck. I didn't have the heart to call Judi's mother. I made Conny do it. Both he and I sat there for a long while before he made the call.

Conny put the word out on the street.

Somehow, Judi's bag would turn up.

The two who killed her were probably dopers looking for a fix.

Sure enough, around two a.m., Tarzan paged Conny code 911 from one of the safehouse numbers. "We need to go outside and make this call," Conny calmly stated. "You can't go anywhere C. You're on lock," I replied, still numbed | I couldn't believe any of it was true.

My head spun in a kaleidoscopic reality.

"Fuck that," Conny shouted. "You and me brother, we're gonna handle this shit. Let this be the reason I go away. You're in no condition to go anywhere alone. Blood4Blood|Eye4Eye we're in this together—Your beef is mine. I'm holdin' you tight, Gary. We're gonna get these fucks. Right is right, Gary. It always will be," he said.

I didn't care about a damn thing. Not even revenge | *I just wanted to see my Judi again.*

But Conny was unstoppable.
Right is right every day of the week — *Including Sunday.*

The ride to the safehouse was hazy | I cried a lot.
She didn't deserve this.
Maybe I did.
Not her.

C and I traveled unarmed. They were watching Conny too close to keep a heater at his house. Neither one of us were packing.

I drank from a liter of Absolut. It wasn't helping the pain. Neither were the dozen or so Vicodin Conny gave me to swallow.

I heard the dogs bark as we neared.

Tarzan opened the door to the safehouse.
The usual villains I'd grown accustomed to seeing were inside: Letno, Zorik, Sloan (Pig), Arthur "Animal", Serge, Chuck "Who likes to fuck", Kazuole (Asshole), and a few others.

Bobby "Tiger" was there too.

He was that dangerous ++||—*SoontobeFamous*— type Russian Bobby was one of the youngest Russian captains in history.
I'd never met him.

His reputation preceded him.

BOBBY GREETED ME BEFORE I COULD WALK INSIDE.

He was a short, pudgy but solid, sweet looking fella. The type you would expect to get beat up for his lunch money in elementary school — Perfect example of never judge judging a book by its cover.

"I'm sorry for you, Gary," he said, handing me a 9mm chrome Taurus. "I can only imagine your pain," he stated. "This cocksucker was trying to pawn off some shit for crack at one of our spots on Kings Highway. One of my guys looked inside the bag and found your girl's wallet," he said.

I took the blaster, slumped on his shoulder and attempted to cry. But there weren't any more tears | *Only murder lent structure to my thoughts.*

I checked the chamber of the weapon.

There was a slug inside and the safety was already off.

Sadistic brilliance jammed into my soul, taking control of my movements. I walked inside that apartment with resolve and purpose.

++||— MURDER —

++||— *Death* — ++||— KILL —

It was a small room.

A torn brown sofa stood upright to block out the windows. Two pit bulls, Prince and Rock, were chained to a rust-covered radiator.

In the middle of the room, head slumped, and tied to a chair, sat the killer of my family — I ran up and pistol-whipped him hard across the face, instantly drawing blood.

He was barely conscious, he'd already taken a nasty beating.

I smashed him again and pulled up his head. I wanted a look before sending him straight into the waiting arms of hellish Satan.

. . .

Y<small>OU KNOW</small> | T<small>HERE ARE DEFINING MOMENTS IN A PERSON'S LIFE.</small>

These are the very moments in space|time *that circumscribe your destiny.* Not just in this world. But in the celestial fabric. In the dimensions beyond any notion of organic existence.

All roads lead to those moments | T<small>HERE'S NO ESCAPE.</small>
And the choices you make will delineate your passage.

"I know this fuckin' guy" I shouted

"*Holy Fuck.* I know this piece of shit!" I yelled, amazed by the twist of fate that led me here. I was looking at someone I had grown up with. It was my childhood friend | Vlad.

Vlad looked up at me with a helpless|hopeless stare. He picked a terrible day to die. I pointed the automatic at his doomed soul. He didn't beg for his life — He didn't need to *from me.*

I lowered the pistol, allowing it to drop from my hands to the floor then reached into my pocket and threw the knot of paper inside, watching as some hit Vlad in the face, as the rest scattered all over the floor. Turning my back, I walked out of the room just in time to hear them release the dogs. They tore the life from him bit-by-bit.

I should have known they were gonna kill him.

++||— P<small>EOPLE ALWAYS DIE IN</small> T<small>HREES</small> —

C<small>ONNY WALKED WITH ME DOWNSTAIRS.</small>

He handed me a small green velvet box.

"I wanted to be the one to give this to you, Gary. They found it in her bag," he stated grimly. Inside was a yellow and white-gold, custom made necklace with a small star-of-David pendant in its center. In the middle of the yellow star was the letter G in white gold.

It was my birthday gift.
Judi stayed late in the city *getting it for me.*

THE NEXT FEW WEEKS REMAIN AN OBSCURE MIASMA.

Weeks clouded in distress and uncertainty.

The only thing that I can recall unquestionably is the presence of intoxicants of every earthly design conceivable. Anything I could locate to numb the pain and provide courage for the chore of undertaking the inescapable.

Eventually | I staggered home.

To Judi's and my home.

I cannot accurately determine how long it had been since the day of her passing. My guess is close to two weeks. The sauce, the drugs and the people providing it did a perfect job at ensuring I didn't sleep a wink.

Conny was gone.

The federals picked him up for bond violation.

His lawyers couldn't do a damn thing about it.

I wasn't going to see Conny for a long while. He subsequently plead guilty to all counts, throwing himself at the mercy of the court.

Mercy, now that's an interesting concept, more like a luxury, reserved for small children, the wealthy elites, and God himself.

Too bad mercy wasn't on the roster for the judge presiding over Conny's fate. He got hit with 11sticks (calendar years). I wouldn't see him again for nine. His home would be the maximum security Federal Correctional Facility located in Allenwood, Pennsylvania referred to as "Allenwood." Conny took those nine sticks for me.

++||— *He'd never let me forget it* —

* * *

218

I sifted through Judi's things and some others we'd prepared for the baby | The pain *was so much more than I could bear.*

I showered, attempting to wash away the grime of that life.
A life I had never asked for | A life *I no longer wanted.*

Everything that held any brief flicker of meaning had passed.
I wanted | I *needed* to see my Judi again.

It was time to *Snuff It.*

I shaved, dabbed on some cologne, then went and put on my best suit. Once I was dressed and ready, I walked to the rear of the closet and grabbed my oldest friend. I wiped away the dust with a t-shirt and wrapped the hard leather holster around my shoulders.

Ace model3 was a Browning High-Power 9mm semi-auto with a high capacity mag. The slide had a glossy chrome finish. The rest was a hard plastic polymer | He was a fine banger, real pretty. I pressed the release and the still full magazine popped into my left hand. In one fluid motion, I reloaded the mag, slid one into the hole, clicked off the safety and returned him back to his bay.

Some things you can never unlearn.

Reaching into the pocket of my dirty jeans, I retrieved a half-full pouch of fish-scale powder, dumped its contents on the glass coffee table, then promptly drew in the sticky-sweet powder.

Its bitter iodine taste overflowed my senses and penetrated the recesses of my cranium, creating in me the will to ignore my deepest inhibitions and carry out acts most dastardly and implausible.

IT ALL SEEMED SO TRIVIAL | *My pathetic plight.*
I sat with my hand on Ace and enjoyed the moment.

Then the crash.
Like a being pecked to death by a gang of ducks.
Truth is whatever hurts most when you run out of dope.
The baselessness of your actions become the only solid reality.

I drew Ace from his holster, put the barrel in my mouth and bit down hard enough to feel the gums on top of my two front teeth bleed — *I swear I'm so sick of this world.* As I squeezed the trigger and every calculated millimeter drew nearer to the end, *all feeling of hope left my soul.* Hope: *the pathological belief in the occurrence of the impossible.*

Then the phone rang.

It was a bizarre clatter of a buzz that I at first chalked up to illusion. After all I'd been under the influence of mind-altering chemicals for weeks. Hallucinations *at that point* were commonplace.

Still, it kept ringing.

I tried to squeeze and just end it all , but the deafening ring undermined my focus. It was almost like the very spirit of Earth was conspiring against my demise. I dropped Ace on the cushion of the leather sofa. Fuck it — I'll answer the fuckin thing and then call it a wrap.

My main homeboy#1 was on the horn.

Mephistopheles himself needed to holler at me. He impromptu clued me in that my time was far from up. I still had a job left to do. I had his soldiers to prepare.

++||— *I still had people left to kill* —

Once I'd made arrangements with Satan, I put Ace back in his sheath, then called Rob and told him to come over and help me get cleaned up. He brought GeorgiVodka and Vicodin, after drinking a pint and swallowing a dozen or so tablets, I was finally able to sleep. I slept for two days recovering from that bender.

Boone remained at the apartment to look after me.

When I finally awoke, I put on a clean pair of denims, a black sweater, and my Timmy's. I opened the safe and handed Boone twenty dimes. "Hold onto this, bro. We may need it, we may not. It's better to have it than to go knockin' on doors later," I stated, as he tucked it into his inside jacket pocket.

I scribbled some paragraphs in a yellow notepad on my desk, tore the paper and put it, along with my house keys, into a padded envelope then into the back pocket of my denims. Ace encircled my shoulder and I looked at the Baboon, "Let's go, son. we ain't comin' back here," I remarked | I let the door lock from the inside and followed my driver down the stairs.

I will Never Forget:
The extraordinary moments I spent in that seventh-floor flat.
—||— *I would gladly return there if I could* —||—

and Everything I left behind was Important.
✳ *Even if it was yesterday* ✳

Before we reached the Infiniti, I dropped the envelope into the mailbox on the corner. It was a note I'd written to Judi's mother.

It contained my deepest apologies, the keys to the apartment, and the combination to the safe, which, coincidentally, was her daughter's birthday. There was over a hundred thousand in cash inside, and the deed to the apartment, which was worth another hundred or so.

I took nothing.

Just Ace and the clothes on my back.

I never visited Judi's grave, nor did I speak to her mother again.

I can only hope that money was enough to ease the pain, if even for a fleeting second — *although I doubt it.*

BOONE DROVE ME TO CHUCK'S APARTMENT.

Chuck "*Who likes to fuck*" was number6 who hung around the old pizza spot. It was a cute *kliytchka*, considering he had one of the ugliest mugs you could ever be so unfortunate to gaze at.

That's how he got his name | *Sure, he liked to fuck.*

The girls though, they'd rather eat white dogshit.

Chuck lived in a small two-bedroom apartment on the second floor of a high-rise. He might have fallen off the ugly tree and hit every branch on the way down, but he was reliable and lived alone.

I informed him I'd be occupying his spare bedroom while I looked for a place of my own.

He knew me too well to give me any lip.

Chuck's street smarts paralleled those of Prada-purse-wearing Park Avenue socialites. But he didn't ask questions, he wasn't against holding the iron, and he was skillful at operating items such as laptops, credit card scanners and various other technological gadgetry. "You're with me now, Chuck," I stated, sitting in the corner of his worn leather sectional. "Boone, go see Shooter and get him a Jammy," I commanded. "Be back tomorrow by six a.m. The three of us are goin' to Broadway. I just got a line on what that Gene fool is doin'," I finished. With that, Baboon left to carry out my instructions.

. . .

THE NEXT MORNING.

Boone returned with a black 9mm Ruger semi-auto for Chuck.

We all hopped into the Infiniti and made our way to downtown Manhattan via the Battery Tunnel.

Sitting in traffic that morning, I felt like myself again.

We parked in one of the public lots, paid for the day, and made towards our appointment on the eleventh floor of one of the many aging buildings in the two-hundred numbers of downtown Broadway. The construction itself was located directly across from one of the entrances to the Brooklyn-Bridge. It was a busy area approximately a quarter of a mile from the bull.

We entered the lobby.

Security was light.

An off-duty NYPD stared at a monitor behind a crumbling desk. So long as his thirty dollars an hour kept coming in, he nary cared.

Had he asserted even the slightest trace of awareness, he would have noticed that all three of us were strapped. We walked right past officer ShutEye and right into the elevator waiting on our arrival.

The degenerated hallway of the eleventh floor was nearly in ruins; rusty pipes were exposed, and the trashed, white paint flaked from the walls. It was an unmarked door, but I knew where to go.

I just followed the noise.

A girl, no older than seventeen, sat behind a dilapidated wooden desk. Although it was early in the morning, she looked hauled-out exhausted. Behind her, a partition separated the small reception area from the rest of the office.

"Tell Felix that Gary Gunz is here," I said. She promptly picked up the black handset of her Merlin Supervisor phone and relayed the message.

. . .

A FEW MINUTES LATER, FELIX G. SLITHERED INTO MY EPISODE.

We followed Felix into his tiny office in the far corner of the space. As we walked, we passed through a boardroom full of about twenty or so of the saddest bunch of zeroes I'd laid eyes on.

Every one of them was of Russian descent, most were known criminals, and more than half were TF members. Brother Will sat in the far-right corner of the huddle of ruined tables. He smirked as I walked past and continued to mumble into the handset in his left hand | I entered Felix's sloppy office and took a seat facing his desk.

++||— My men stood by the door —

Felix was a plump Russian in his late twenties.

He had red chubby cheeks, shifty brown eyes and slim rigid lips. His mug was a greasy mess and he wore a '50s bouffant for a hairdo. Felix stood around five-eight but slumped his back. It made him appear shorter. He wore a cheap brown suit and dirty black shoes.

Felix was a nobody.
Someone I'd never waste my time palling around.

"The Mensch[5], glad you could make it," he stated. His was a whiny shriek of a voice reserved for sad unfortunates who could never find their place in the world and were always searching for some sort of condolence.

Some had started calling me "the Mensch" when I declined to pull the trigger on my fiancée's murderer. Although the federals would later list it as one of my aliases, it was a *kliytchka* that never quite stuck.

"My cousin, Gene, asked me to call you down here. We heard you're a natural for selling stocks. You know that's exactly what we doing here. Selling stocks," Felix said.

I just nodded and waited for him to continue.

"We want you here, Gunny. We need your talents to help promote some of the companies we're selling. We think you can make a lot of money with us," he said as he removed a soiled white handkerchief from his left pant pocket and wiped the sweat from his brow.

He proceeded to tell me just how wonderful some of these small companies were — *How great it would be for any investors involved.* He offered me twenty points cash for every share of his stock I sold.

I continued to nod until he finished up his pitch.

"Felix," I said, centering my gaze directly on his eyes.

I stood up and slightly adjusted my denims and set my hands on that small area above the knees then moved my head inches from his face affixing my gaze directly into his cloudy yellow orbs. I needed pathetic Felix to understand that if this was a game.

++||— I wasn't playin' —

"Say Felix, When my father fucks my mother, It's not with his fingers. You understand me kid? This whole shit here, it's a fuckin' scam. I knew that coming up here. What I need to know is exactly how it works," I remarked, the upper portion of my lip twitching.

I fixed my jacket in a way that allowed him to see the butt of the blaster dangling from my shoulder. "Either you walk me over to Gene and let me hash this fucker out with him or we're done, you and me," I stated.

Felix sat still for a moment.

He replied by disparaging me with a few choice Russian obscenities | Perhaps whatever unique cocktail of narcotics he'd earlier ingested had worn off and he overlooked who he was barking at. Before he could finish, Baboon reached for his heater. "No need, Boone, we're leaving." I stood up and made for the door.

"Wait, wait Crazy-Gunz. I'm sorry, bro," Felix whined. "Let me talk to Gene. I know he wants you here." he finished. He returned shortly and we walked five offices over to see Gene.

Gene stood at the door and asked to speak to me alone.

I entered the spacious office.

There was a large glass table facing the door in the center of the room. In the corner, a black leather couch and two comfortable looking manager's chairs with a glass coffee table in the middle.

It was a corner office with a panoramic view of lower Broadway. Gene sat in one of the manager's chairs and I took a seat on the couch. "Sorry about your girl, Gary," he said.

I was sick of the empty condolences.

"Happens," I replied, prompting him to skip formalities and get to the particulars of exactly how-in-the-fuck I was gonna get this paper.

"What you got for me, Gene?" I asked.

This prompted Gene to burst into his programmed sales pitch.

"Gene let's be real here, you and me," I said. "Game recognizes game." I stood and began to make my exit. "Hold on a second Gary." Gene followed me toward the door. "You're swinging wild, bro. Shoot at me straight, and we're gonna blow this shit up like nitro. You know what I bring to the table. Keep the save-the-world bullshit for the clowns in the boardroom. Either you talk to me 'RealTalk' or Imma bounce," I stated.

Gene knew I wasn't buying the pitch.

He had no choice but to break it down. True to form he left out the meat and only gave me the potatoes. Give a man a fish and he eats for a day. Teach him to fish | He opens up his own fishery *and tells you to Gitfuk'd — Only after years* was I able to combine all the pieces.

So that I may be able to recite it to you now: How we were able to bilk corporations, trust-funds, both rich and poor individual investors, for hundreds of millions$ It's a textbook example of white-collar crime | Bear in mind, this was only the prototype.

There were many more that followed.

Let me spin it for you really quick.

It all starts with a shell company.

A shell company is what remains of a stock when it hits donut.

The price of any stock increases based on speculation and anticipation — I submit to you this scenario: XYZ, a small biotech organization with less than twenty employees, has uncovered, through some miracle of modern science, the cure for the common cold.

The whole world gets excited.
They start talking about it on 20|20
All the bigshits are tickled purple — *The common cold is cured.*

XYZ Company now requires a large infusion of capital.

The next step seeks out an underwriter. After all, they do have the miraculous common cold cure | Riches await.

The underwriters create an Initial Public Offering (an IPO) and XYZ is now a publicly traded company. Everyone wants to get rid of the cold, and XYZ is the only house on the block with the patented technology to provide the antidote.

It's all about supply and demand.

XYZ's principals are sitting on billions in stock options. Investors who got in early also enjoy the benefits of a successful run.

It's like a fairytale.
That's just it | *Fairytales* aren't real.

When XYZ's new wonder-drug was found to produce harmful side effects such as heart disease, cancer, and, in some cases, death.

Investors start dropping XYZ like a handful of hot charcoal.

The stock is devalued by the market it traded on and delisted to a poorer market. Subsequently, XYZ Company closes its doors and the principals take nice long vacations, getting laid, paid, and sipping lemonade in the shade | Thanks to good old Joey taxpayer:

++||— Одесса Мама —

That's what a shell company is.

XYZ Company may be out of business, but the stock certificates still exist. By law, it must remain registered with the SEC and the NASD.

Here's where the scam creeps in.

You—Being that dashing Russian G, find yourself running low on wine and prostitutes. You need to hurry on up and get this paper.

The following formula is a blueprint to millions:

Step1 | Find yourself a fairly reliable number8 with a clean criminal history. Preferably a dope-fiend, who can clean up well enough to deal with bigshit banker types.

Step2 | Go see your boss and pitch the proposal to him. You need to keep him in the loop or it's the 3R's.

Step3 | Open a corporation. The type of corporation doesn't matter. But a plain old Class-C Corp is easiest.

Step4 | Pay a visit to the world-renowned law firm of Dewey, Cheetam and Howe. They'll go to just about any length to procure your business. I always found it amusing to watch them bite into each other's asses. Pay Mr. Cheetam his retainer and you'll be able to accomplish some of your main goals.

The rest *is easy like Sunday morning.*

Goal-A | Locate and purchase a shell company.

This one shouldn't be hard at all. There are plenty of shell companies out there, I mean tens of thousands of them. It shouldn't cost you more than 20-40,000$ to buy up the millions of shares you need to have a controlling interest in the defunct shell.

Goal-B | Mr. Cheetam files an S-8 form with the SEC and merges your new corporation with the shell company you purchased.

This process is called a "reverse merger". Now you have yourself a publicly traded company, which you control, for the bargain price of roughly fifty-thousand dollars.

You might be asking yourself.

Why not forgo all this TomFoolery.
Just take your corporation public.

That reason is simple.

Your goal was never to trade stocks and bonds.

You've got dope to sell, people to extort, and weapons to smuggle. Legitimately trading in securities would interfere with the program.

A public company needs a business plan, earnings, a product or a service, and a desire to stay in business longer than a few months. Besides, underwriter fees would be well into the six figures and would require a loan all in itself.

All of that is superficial | The real reason you don't want to take the legitimate route is just that.

++||— *It's legitimate* —

When any new security is offered, The SEC mandates that a red-herring (prospectus) must sent out to all potential investors.

The first few pages, standard business jargon with names and profiles of all of the company officers. I'm talking full background here. From their past employment history, to where they went to college, to the color of their wife's panties, everything must be disclosed. The next pages are about the company's financials where it says, most of the time in bold writing — More than likely, *you're going to lose all your money.*

That's the beauty of merging as shell.

You don't have to send a prospectus to any of your marks. It's not an IPO issue — Your company is already public.

The law does not mandate any disclosure whatsoever.

That was the case until April 2004, when laws were amended to accommodate for the "abuse" of form S-8 (which was used to circumvent the registration and prospectus delivery requirements of the securities act of 1934). But by that time the damage had been done. We abandoned the pump-and-dump sometime in 2000, in lieu of far more lucrative ventures.

Now it's time to get this party started.

Summon the posse of battle-ready young dreamers ready to Fight2Eat and get to pumping shares of your chop-stock[6].

And pumping stock is easy as:
Bye-Bye Miss American Pie.

GENE AND I AGREED ON A THIRTY-FIVE PERCENT CASH PAYOUT.

The stock of the day was a sporting goods company claiming to have an exclusive contract with the NHL to supply protective gear and uniforms for next year's season. It could have been an outfit selling shit-on-a-rope.

Like I gave a fuck | Thirty-five points was a sweet deal.
++|— *And I was fixin' to spit out fire —*

Before calling it a deal I decided to slide a wild-card.

"Listen here, I need to put together a squad. I got some medieval cats I wanna bring in to push this shit. Gremlins, I'm talking about. Put some paper on it. So I can spread love," I stated, then nudged my head up slightly and puckered my lips in that prominent, know-it-all way. "What do you need from me?" Gene replied. "Twenty thousand, cash. In advance. You can take it out of my chop when the money comes in," I stated.

He refused.

Parting a degenerate junkie like Gene from his precious skim:
It's equivalent of taking the TVremote from an overweight gambler | On *Superbowl Sunday.*

I appealed to his greed | He reluctantly gave in.

Gene went to his desk.

He reached into a small leather handbag and fetched two bundles of freshly minted Benny's still conjoined in the bank-issued bands labeled 10,000$ and handed them to me. I took the cream and smiled then tucked the money into the left inside pocket of my leather and we left the office.

I revealed a few details of the scam as we walked to the garage.

Telling your soldiers too much information could be poisonous. They just wouldn't know how to handle all the data. Either they become gluttonous or get frightened. All they needed to know for now was they had each earned a thousand-dollar bonus | That would be enough to keep them loyal.

It was still early in the day.

I directed Boone to drive to Primorski (pree-more-ski), one of the oldest Russian establishments and home to some of the slimiest gangsters in the gangster business ++||— *It was a place I frequented —*

I instructed Chuck to wait for us in the auto while we grabbed some chow and potion.

Tarzan sat at one of the tables towards the front.

He stared at a plate of herring and potatoes and had an almost empty bottle of Absolut to his left. Another usual by the name of Dima (Dee-Mah) sat with him. We called him Fat-Dima for self-explanatory reasons.

TARZAN WAS A SLIGHTLY OVERWEIGHT, FAIR-SKINNED RUSSIAN.

He stood at five-feet-seven and hid his portliness well.

Calm grey eyes, freckled cheeks, thick lips, and a pointy chin were some of his distinct features. He had a mane of dirty blond hair, often wearing it in a mess. Now this Tarzan is not to be confused with the original Ludwig "Tarzan" Fainberg. Although I never had chance to encounter Fainberg | I can't say that I would've wanted to.

This Tarzan was a different fella.

++||— Equally as brutal —

It was rumored Tarzan had strong ties to a gentleman I will refer to as "Roman." This guy Roman, one of the original Gasoliners, was like the Russian Nicky Tarantino in the Odessa adaptation of the movie *Casino*.

The story goes like this.

Roman had a daughter — *A real looker she was.*

At age sixteen she was already turning heads. Not only did she look like a supermodel, she was one of the brightest and most talented musicians in her prep school. She played the harp, piano, clarinet, saxophone, and a variety of other instruments. Roman loved watching her perform at Russian restaurants such as National, Primorski, and many others.

She was a real bright spot on an otherwise bleak landscape. Her voice was heavenly and could make teary-eyed even the most dispassionate felon.

After one of her performances, she was raped by three intoxicated classmates from her prep school who cornered her on the way to her vehicle. Fearing she would expose them they murdered her and disposed of her body in the contaminated waters of the river Hudson.

The youths stole her vehicle and were quickly apprehended and taken to the local jailhouse.

Roman was crushed | His only child was a victim of the violent lifestyle he'd tried desperately to separate her from.

Two of the youths had "accidents" while detained for arraignment. Accidents meaning their jailers palms were greased while that same Russian, the one with the gold herringbone and the meathook fingers, was sent in to MakeItRight.

The third attacker was a special case.

His father, one of the more prominent district attorneys in the borough, used his leverage to rescue his only son from his fate. The boy was released to his father's custody. It only bought the kid a few more hours and a far more horrible death.

That night, Roman's people broke into his home, grabbed the son and father then took them to the basement of one of Roman's illicit establishments.

Roman had the father tied to a wooden chair.

One of Roman's conscripts held the father's head, forcing him watch as Roman gouged out and ate the eyeballs of his murderous son. Next Roman slowly cut out the boy's tongue, he went ahead and ate that too. Finally, Roman hacked off all of the boy's fingers and toes. He let his father continue to watch his son bleed out for twenty or so minutes. At last content with his retribution, he stabbed them both (son first then father) in the neck with that same dull knife.

All-in-all, not a very pleasant fellow

Tarzan was an alcoholic of the worst quality.

Sober, (which he often was not), Tarzan was a funny guy. Shit-faced, he morphed into a vile|sadistic, heartless demon.

In his mid-twenties, he was already a respected member of the Russian underworld. He was a smart criminal, a pretty rare find among the zoo of mooks that lurked the avenue.

What Igar, Tarzan B., couldn't accomplish with his mind, he'd be more than happy to try with his knuckles. He was there when I plugged Junior. He knew I was capable and demonstrated the proper respect given only to one's equals.

Fat-Dima was his number6.
A talented number6, but number6 nonetheless.

I sat down for *L'chaim* with them.

It was too early in the day for the live music, but the expensive stereo system transmitted the sounds of Misha Gulko.

Прибыла в Одессу банда из Амура,
В банде были урки, шулера.
Банда занималась темными делами,
И за ней следила Губчека.

Эх, Мурка, ты мой Муреночек!
Мурка, ты мой котеночек!
Мурка - Маруся Климова,
Прости любимого!

Речь держала баба, звали ее Мурка,
Хитрая и смелая была.
Даже злые урки и те боялись Мурки,
Воровскую жизнь она вела.[7]

I TOOK OFF MY LEATHER.

Carefully, I hung it on the seat, and spilled a line of crushed fish-scale onto the beige tablecloth.

"You wanna hit this shit?" I asked as Fat-Dima filled an empty glass with the remainder of the Absolut, then pushed it toward me. "No doubt." Tarzan motioned for the Benny I'd converted into a sniffing-straw. He smirked, then snorted the powder. "Whatcha up to, Gunny?" "Just got put on with Gene T," I stated, recounting a few details to Tarzan. He shifted his head towards Fat-Dima and snickered.

"These fucks here. If they don't bring the vodka fast, I'm gonna break faces," he barked, making sure it was in earshot of the curious waiter who hid in the far corner of the hardwood dance floor.

As the frightened young waiter disappeared into the kitchen to obey the order, Tarzan laughed louder. "Dumb fuck, I should break his head on principle, standing there, nosing around when people[8] talk business. You know something, Gary. Me and the fat guy here, we just hooked into something like what you got with Gene. Looks to me like this shit here is the way," he said.

I dumped the rest of my drug sack as Tarzan continued.

"Bobby Tiger shot me a line on something him and Trigger been working on. We just got back a few hours ago from checking it. I'll be fucked in the mouth if it isn't the same fuckin' thing you're telling me about," Tarzan said as he formed a fresh rail.

I bellowed hard after he finished speaking. "It seems like the Russian community is really coming together on this one here," I said. "Yeah, Trigger was on blast. Made sure every last one of us looked at his tri-color Rolex Prezzy. All those fools looked cashed-up to the gills. Bout time we got some of that paper." Tarzan slurred his words and bobbed his head drunkenly. Tarzan liked to speak with his fingers, often waving them around excitedly.

The waiter returned with a liter of vodka in a clear crystal container and placed it in the center of the table.

He couldn't take his eyes off the burner dangling from my shoulder. Didn't matter to me | He was just background scenery in a much bigger picture.

Tarzan ++||— *He wasn't having it* —

In a drunken stagger he jerked from his chair, flinging it behind him and onto the floor. "You like looking at guns?" he shouted in Russian, pulling a dull black 9mm Glock from the rear of his wool grey pants | I watched as the young waiter stood frozen in panic mode.

Tarzan pulled back the slide allowing a missile to insert into the chamber, then grabbed the waiter by the collar of his white button-down shirt and put his blaster millimeters from his eyeball. "Here, have a look, you stupid fuck. Look close. You like what you see? *Tell me motherfucker.* Tell me you like it," he screamed until the waiter nodded.

Tarzan finally released the waiter, slapping him flippantly on the cheek with his left hand. The kid scrambled to Tarzan's backside to pick up the chair he'd knocked down, putting it back in place.

He tucked the Glock and fixed his pants.

Before Tarzan sat back down, he swung at the container of vodka the waiter had placed on the table clear across the room, shattering it against the wall. "Don't bring me this cheap house shit. You think I drink this lowlife shit? You bring me the name brand. Show respect to people when you see them," he sneered as he calmly sat down.

"You believe these cocksuckers Hard-Gunz?" he asked. "Ruin my whole fuckin' lunch teaching these animals some manners. Someone has to teach them how to behave. I feel like the director of a cemetery. I have all these people under me, but nobody fuckin' listens" he waved his hands in annoyance | He snorted the remainder of the powder on the table. "This is the motts (good) shit Gunny. You get this from your connect?" he asked me as he raised his head.

"Nah, I don't fuck with him no more. I got it from a friend of mine," I replied.

I'd lost touch with High.

He changed his number, and I was no longer interested in dealing pharmaceuticals. Baboon picked up this sack of white from Terry D.

He was eager to make cream and expressed interest in linking up when the opportunity arose. They would both be happy to know that it was almost ThugTime. "Imma bounce," I said. "Make sure you stay in touch. Hear anything 'bout anything, hold me down."

We shook hands and I returned to the Infiniti Q.

The next morning was my first day at work.
I was ready for action.

Larry left numerous messages for me.
I put my dick on him.

This was my time to climb | *It was my time to shine.*

I sat next to Brother Will and made myself at home.

"Who do I see for some leads?" I asked. "Go holler at Gene, he's in his office," he stated, still holding a receiver to his ear.

Baboon sat next to me and took three bacon, egg, and cheese bagels from a brown paper sack we'd bought at the coffee shop adjacent the building. "What's he do? Hold you dick?" Brother Will remarked as he continued to dial. "Nah, fool. He holds your mother's," I replied.

Most of the office burst into laughter.

It was those very few moments of comradery that I will always cherish. Those brief moments of elation you can never find in normal business settings.

Most everyone in the place had a heater.
++||— *Everyone was ready to pull* —
You could cut the tension with a dull jail-house razor.

Chuck "not the one who likes to fuck" Dickens said it best:
It was the best of times. It was the worst of times. It was the age of wisdom. It was the age of foolishness. It was the epoch of belief.

Blah-motherfuckin-Blah.

I handed Brother Will my pewter flask and offered him some potion | He gladly accepted. I sent Chuck to see Gene for lead cards.

He returned a few minutes later with a cardboard box filled with client account statements from various firms such as Paine-Webber, Shearson, Gruntal, along with many smaller companies. There were over a thousand names, some of which belonged to the wealthiest people in America.

THAT FIRST DAY, I OPENED EIGHT ACCOUNTS | *OVER 60,000$ IN ORDERS.*

I caught the tail end of that deal and it wasn't long before the stock went to the zero it was designed for. I did manage to place more than 70,000 shares at prices ranging anywhere from seven 7$–13$ a share. I raised close to a million *and was paid out 300,000$.*

A Hasidic Jew named Avi came to the office every two weeks with a suitcase full of freshly minted Benjamins | It was promptly dispersed to us in brown paper bags.

The firm was "owned" by a mo-mo who stumbled in once a month to gather a check for the agency (the standard commission charged on the buy and sell of securities) and his ten percent for letting us to operate under his series 9|10 license (you need to have both for SEC to let you be principal|owner of any brokerage house).

He was a clown of the most comical order.
He picked up almost all his money in pharmaceuticals.

I MET A FEW PROMOTERS DURING THIS TIME.

The most notable was a plump, cigar smoking fatty named Bert. He as well, brought cash.

The job of a promoter is to advance the sale of a particular issue. *Wall Street is a small street* — When the genuine bigshits caught wind of our pump-and-dump, they sent their double chinned blockheads over to unload some of their own penny stocks.

That's how it works, ladies and gentlemen.

The larger brokerage houses wanna eat too.

They send in their proxies to see if they can dump their own shady securities. Seeing as how they can't crank them out of their own boardrooms, they pass them off to the more unsavory elements.

Namely ourselves.

You would think they were above slimebag boiler-room operation chop houses | *Think again.*

It's like one big happy family, black sheep and all.

++||— Одесса Мама —

JULY '93.

After setting myself up with a loft in the very trendy TriBeCa area of Greenwich Village, sliding into a pre-owned all Black Merc 300e, and putting on the RolexPrezy|DiamondBezel, I was still sitting on over 100Large cash money.

It was time to call the cavalry.

I shot a line to Terry.

He was still tight with Rick Kuku, and they were still small-timing pharmaceuticals and pushing wipes.

I invited them to join the team making cream.

Ricky declined, he claimed to have something going with the Genovese and needed to stay grounded.

I handed Terry ten thousand in cash, *a sign-on bonus*, and instructed him to round up some of the demented fools he associated with. He was more than happy to accept my offer.

Terry would be working directly for me, pumping out our next deal, a network marketing company that sold whole food nutrition, environmental solutions, and health and dietary supplements throughout North America and Japan — *What the company really did.*

Pay me a 35%cash rip on every share I sold.

TUESDAY MORNING, THE SIXTH OF JULY 1993,

Terry came up to the office with Guido-Vinny, three young cretins who he declared to be his callers, a shifty young female named Lucy, sister to one of the three, and a pleasant surprise. My old chum Lenny R.

I put Terry and his crew up in a partitioned area of the workplace Chuck had sheet-rocked in anticipation of their arrival — Right next to the private office I'd strong-armed from Felix.

Terry's deal was straightforward.

He kept every account he opened and was only allowed to trade them into our chop[9]. I would front the bill on his callers, paying each of them a modest draw against any business they did. He'd manage the callers by sitting on their necks all day, making sure they sweated out every penny of their draw. Whatever accounts they opened we split right down the middle. His skim would be 20% on everything. Payable whenever the brown paper bag hit my desk.

Under normal circumstances anyone coming into the organization had to open forty accounts for their sponsor (the person who brought them in) before they were allowed to start opening up accounts for themselves. *Terry was like family* | In the interest of seeing him get cashed proper, I omitted formalities.

Lenny was a special case.
I needed someone to handle my book of clients.
It was quite large and too much for one broker to handle.

Whenever an employee leaves the firm, whether it be stock, real estate, car sales, travel agencies, hand-release massage parlors, or trapp spots, any and all accounts owned by the former representative by default go to the largest producer.

Most organizations have NDAs for potential staff members to sign, dictating the fact that all clients are property of the company and cannot be taken in the event of termination.

Chop-house boiler rooms work similarly.

The primary difference resting in the fact that anyone attempting to "steal" accounts would receive multiple thrashings to the cranium.

Although there's no written agreement, it's understood that, after leaving the firm, if you attempt to call on any of your former clientele, you run the risk of starting a war between your former employer and your current one.

I was top cock at this particular henhouse.

I'd seen more of than my fair share of hoodlums come and go. Either they fell flat on their face trying their hand at the graft, or they just didn't have the minerals to fight.

Mercy didn't exist in my dojo — For every idiot that left, there were more accounts for me to smash on.

Lenny was a good kid, but he wasn't a soldier.

Had I sat him the boardroom with the vipers, he would get bit by their poison fangs. Instead, I spared him the misery of battling not only for business, but for his respect among the bitter|callous ones I called my brethren.

Just because I said so, Lenny never had to open one account. I taught him how to trade my book and ask for the big money. Undoubtedly, I saved the choice degenerate buyers for myself.

We controlled the phone *Like Napoleon.*
Like a half-Mongolian warrior.
|| *Drafted* ||
Into the brutal armies of Genghis Kahn.
++||— *Like a motherfuckin' stock phenomenon* —

January of the following year.
The new junk we were pushing tanked to zero. Among my unit we were holding close to a million dollars. Four hundred thousand *CashMoney* | Belonged to your courageous friend and satisfied narrator.

Early in the month Gene called me into the office.

The conversation we had went as follows:
"You made yourself some change this year, Gary. You been doin' a good job," he stated shrewdly, reclining in his manager's chair. "So did you," I replied. "You know me, baby. Gary Gunz shine like marble, *Slang remarkable,*" I continued as I took a seat on the sofa.
"What's on your mind, Gene?" I asked.

"I got a new assignment for you, Gary. Something big I think you're gonna love. You know we're done with this stock. The shit's at zero and the next deal is gonna take a month or so to finish. Boss decided we can't have a capable guy like you sittin' idle. You're goin' to Cali," He informed me.

Gene always had the finest greens. He hastily rolled together a sizable amount of his best product. As he twisted the joint, chunks of green sticky flew from the ends and onto the carpeting.

I looked around.
The office was filled with excess.
Expensive knick-knacks carelessly strewn about.
Mixed together with the musky odor of exclusive trees:
It was the intoxicating fragrance of greed.

Gene had his feet up on the glass top of the Mahogany desk.

"Cali, as in California?" I shouted, then grabbed the half-smoked fatty. "What-in-the-fuck's an ugly Russian like me gonna do up in Hollywood?" I hollered. "We got something for you down there. Lots of work. Lots of paper," Gene said.

I sat back and listened closer.

"You're gonna need to bring some support. Take two of your best. Tomorrow head to JFK. six a.m., flight 112, three passes waiting for you at the Tower-Air terminal. You'll find out everything when you get down there." He stood as he finished speaking and reached into his black attaché.

Gene handed me a small zippered black pouch.
100,000$ greenCashMoney was inside.

"Consider it an advance. Comes straight from the top, Gunny," he finished.

I opened the bag and counted the money.

That morning, Lenny and Baboon, each 10,000$ richer, arrived, bags packed, at the Tower-Air terminal of JFK.

I was already shit-faced drunk and waiting for them.

We took the seven-hour, non-stop flight to San Diego, California where a black Lincoln limousine, the operator of which was the personal driver to the instigator of our mission, was waiting with instructions to take us to our final destination. To meet with said instigator.

++||— A gentleman known as "THE DENTIST." —

$$\Psi - \Psi - \Psi$$

1.
2.
3.
4.
5.
6.
7. Arrived in Odessa gang from Cupid,
    In the gang were Uhrki, cut-throats.
    The gang was engaged in dark affairs, and Gubchek was watching her.
    Oh, Murka, you are my Murenochek!
    Murka, you are my kitty!
    Murka - Marusya Klimova,
    Forgive your beloved!
    The woman kept her speech, her name was Murka, she was dodgy and brave.
    Evil were the Urhki and they were afraid of Murka | She led the Thieves' life.
    Loosely translated from the Gulko classic
8.
9.

THE HAMMER

Doin' bids around here is like a baton
    Get home, pass the stick, and another man's gone
    Another man's dead from another man's lead
    Another man starves while another man's fed
    Another man grinds another mans' doin' time
    Get the picture
    If not | Then another man's blind
- Anonymous

SLAVIK|SLAVA,
    AKA—The Dentist—Is infamous among the Russian émigré that populate the island of Brighton.

Brighton:
Many men are hard to find
++||— Many witnesses go blind —

Brighton:
OG's get props from bandits.
On the block — Stay Glocks cocked.

Brighton:
Where everybody wants to be Pac.
The dramas never really stop.

Brighton:
Where they say it's pohlices I should fear.
++||— *But it's my own kind doing all the killing here* —

It is rumored that Slava was a former KGB from communist days of old. During his tenure as a professional hitman, his favorite recreation was torturing his marks by pulling out their teeth ıbyı and smashing them into powder with a mallet before finally killing them. Hence his *kliytchka* | All I needed to know was that he was a soulless criminal genius.

TWO P.M.
We arrived at Slava's villa on the outskirts of a small town called Bonita, which was located exactly fifteen minutes from the Tijuana border. His home was a mansion spanning twelve acres of land, complete with indoor and outdoor swimming pools, Jacuzzis, tennis courts, and Mexican nationals armed with Kalashnikov 4|7's patrolling the roof-tops.

Before boarding the airplane.

I managed to hide an ounce of trees and a quarter of white in my underpants — I twisted a joint on our way to the meet.
By the time we pulled into the long driveway *my high had settled.*

. . .

THE DRIVER, A SLIM BALDING RUSSIAN.

Carried our bags to the entrance, and as we approached the ornate front door—*I got that feeling again*—like this whole thing was wrong | Like this was the very last place I was supposed to be.

SLAVA GREETED US WITH A SMILE.

Immediately, I questioned the validity of his gangster.

The Dentist, former chief enforcer of Marat Balagula[1] and criminal engineer of diabolical schemes designed to defraud honest Americans, looked like the town drunk straight out a cheap Irish novel.

Slava stood five feet, three inches tall, with gaunt pencil legs and a protruding belly. His rosy features resembled those of a man who'd spent much of his adult life sipping from large flasks and indulging in various forms of mind-altering psychedelic substances.

Not quite the boss-looking, pinstripe-suit wearer you see in the movies. Barking orders and pointing fingers at those he requires terminated.

Slava invited us inside.

He began addressing Baboon in our native tongue.

"He's not Russian. He can't talk to you," I stated in Russian.

I jerked my head up slightly, acknowledging the fact that it was me he needed to communicate with.

"Who are you?" Slava asked. "I'm Gary, the man you invited down here," I once again stated in Russian. "You're Gary," he affirmed. "I thought you'd be taller." He spoke in English but with a harsh accent.

I laughed. "I get that all time."

He escorted us downstairs to his game room.

A full-sized Brunswick pool table stood in the center of the space. There were two large burgundy leather sofas and four matching recliners on the left side of the room. A few dated arcade games stood next to three pinball machines across the room. In the center sat a high-dollar television and stereo surround-sound setup.

As we took our seats, his mother—an elderly, infirm, crumbling and overweight Russian woman—brought down a bottle of ice-cold Absolut then placed and poured goblets for each of us on a glass coffee table.

SLAVA POINTED TO THE WALL, SHOWING OFF HIS GUN COLLECTION.

It featured two original Nazi issue Lugers as well as an original Nazi issue Beretta M.1935 | I wasn't as excited as he was.

"Can we smoke?" I asked.

Slava approved and I produced my bag of greens as well as a packet of EZ Wider papers, crumbled the weed, and twisted a fatty.

I toked on the trees.

"You brought me all the way down here for something. Holler at me then," I insisted.

Slava sat on one of the recliners and quaffed up the vodka in his tall drinking glass."I'm putting together a new deal for everyone in New York. Should be available by the end of the month. Lots of money in it," he spoke strictly in Russian. "But I got something different for you. I want you to manage a sales office here in San Diego. It's going to be a special place, where you'll be selling a very special company," he continued to speak, and I continued to nod.

"I'm starting a coffee company. I want it to be something real. Something I can leave to my children when I die. Not this bullshit I'm selling now. I want this company to be as big as Starbucks. That's where you come in, Gary. I need you to take the lead on this thing and help me," he finished. "I don't mind helping you, Slava. You have lots of respect in the community and I want to be a part of what you do. But what's in it for me?" I replied in Russian.

"Take a walk with me, Gary. We'll talk more," he stated, then stood from the chair and filled both our empty cups with more potion.

Slava put his arm around my shoulders.

We walked through a screen door, past the Olympic-sized pool in his backyard and into a small wooded area towards the back of his property. His driver followed closely but not within earshot of our conversation.

"I need you to work with one of my guys down here. My most trusted captain, Ruslan (Roos-lahn). He's been working on my deals from a small office at one of my business. We need to build a sales force for my new company. It's a new type of stock deal you've probably never pushed before—it's a hard sell, but you can do it right. I need you to recruit brokers and supervise the office until it gets on its feet. Then you can go home. Your compensation will be slightly less than what you're accustomed to. This is for real. I need all the capital for business expenses. How does twenty points sound to you?" Slava asked.

I STOPPED WALKING FOR A MOMENT AND OBSERVED THE LUSH SCENERY.

He had was a beautiful home — *this* Dentist *character.*

Not the type of place you get from scratching out a 9-5 in corporate America. Not the kind you acquire from exercising compassion for your fellow man. In my line of work, it certainly wasn't the kind you got from maintaining rigorous honesty in your business affairs. "Twenty points sounds like I'm on the next flight home," I replied.

I turned around and strolled back to the game room.

"Wait a minute," he said. "Tell you what, Gunny. I need you for this job. I'll go as high as thirty. Still five points less than your norm, but on the next go, after you get back home, I'll front for your own office and pay you what I'm paying Gene—I'm talking fifty points—Just stay here and work this thing like I know you can." Slava puckered his lips and nodded slightly, probably sensing my response.

I nodded and held my hand out for a shake. "I'm up for that. You heard about me. You know I do whatever it takes."

Slava grabbed my hand sternly and would not let go.

He applied heavy pressure to my fingers as he leaned his head to whisper into my ear. "Good, Gary. I knew I could count on you." His spittle assaulted my cheek as he spoke. "I'm glad you mentioned that, because there is one more thing." I could smell the biting aroma of rotten potato mixed with the unmistakable stench of concentrated alcohol on his breath.

"There is a Georgian over in West Hollywood.[2] He runs a bookmaking operation from inside a small camera store in the Sherman Oaks area. Ruslan will show you exactly where. The Georgian owes a lot of money. He's been causing me much troubles." Slava smiled. "So you need me to collect," I answered. "No, Gary Gunz. The time for that has passed—*It's final notice time.* The Georgian..." Slava raised his scrawny left arm and with his middle finger slowly touched the underside of his chin.[3]

He finally let go of my hand.

I drew back a few paces, not quite sure this surreal moment was actually taking place. "I didn't come down here for that, Slava. You know I respect you, but this is not what I do. I sell stock. I don't murder people," I whispered to him.

Slava laughed. It was more like a bellow.

"You do whatever I tell you. You forget your place in the organization. Besides, you already took the money," he remarked as we walked back to the house. "What do you mean I took the money? I ... I didn't take any money," I stuttered. "Gene gave you the money, didn't he? He told me you accepted," Slava stated. "I accepted that money as an advance for selling product. He didn't tell me anything about a hit," I muttered — *Sweat ran from my forehead.*

I tried not to panic.

"Whatever Gary Gunz. You took the money, the rest is unimportant. I expect you to carry this out like a professional," Slava stated coldly.

THE RULES TO A CONTRACT HIT ARE AS FOLLOWS:
Prior to accepting payment, the assassin has an opportunity to decline. After the paper transfers hands, the mark is living on borrowed time. Once the money is acknowledged, a timeframe is determined in which "the work" must be completed.

Extensions are rarely granted.
The entire sum is paid in advance.
There is no getting out of the deal *for either the assassin or the mark.*

If the contract is not fulfilled on time, not only is the reputation of the hired gun marred, but his life and the lives of those closest to him become jeopardized | The gun becomes the mark

I knew the rules — At that point there was no turning back.
Like it or not, I had a job to do.

Pappy told me this would happen.

Run around try to be down and I'll be trapped in.

Never paid no mind.

Grabbed the heater.

Started blasting.

++||— And now I'm no longer laughing —

"Why don't you have one of your people take care of the situation? Why fly me down from Brooklyn for a problem in your own backyard?" I asked coolly. Slava giggled. "You ask too many questions, Gary."

I opened my mouth to speak, but he beat me to it.

"You know I knew your grandfather. He was a great man with much esteem in the community. I learned many things from him. He would be proud of you here with me," he remarked, as he put his hand on my shoulder. "You should have asked these things before taking the job. That's OK. You're new here, you probably didn't know. For now you need to do this work like your life depends on it," he finished.

Slava wasn't smiling.

Neither was I.

We walked back to the house in silence.

I sat on one of the leather recliners, grabbed a bottle, filled one glass to the brim, and poured one for Slava. "*Zah Bratvooh* (for the brotherhood)," he barked drunkenly as we clanked glasses. "*Na Shastyah*, (for luck)," I replied as we downed our drinks.

Lenny, Boone, and, I were promptly escorted out by the driver and taken to the Hilton Residence Inn in the La Jolla area of town.

WE CHECKED IN AROUND EIGHT P.M.

Were told that Ruslan would be by in the morning to meet us

252

with further details. I enlightened my comrades about the true nature of our trip to Cali | Boone took it better than Lenny.

I took a bag of white from the pocket of my denims and spread it on the brown hardwood table in the corner of our double-bed suite.

"Hit on this, Lenny. It's gonna settle your head," I commented as I cracked open a Philly, dumped its contents in the trash, and filled it with buds from a Ziplock bag.

Boone agreed to drive.

After many attempts to curtail Lenny's involvement, he finally convinced me he was ready to hold the hammer. None of us slept that night. We stayed zapped on white and vodka attempting to annihilate any sense of morality we may have had.

* * *

QUARTER AFTER NINE NEXT MORNING.

Ruslan knocked on the door.

Young and thin, He stood five feet four inches tall and was of Russian-Jewish descent. His nappy brown locks receded to form a small circular island of hair resembling that of Bruce Willis as John McLane | He had a hard-boiled look to him.

He was a killer.
++||— I could tell —
It takes one to know one.

I opened the door and allowed him inside.

"Looks like you'z been havin' a party without me," he remarked, inhaling the lingering scent of sweet sickly smell of burnt cocaine and green stickys. "You must be Gary Gunz." His bullying green eyes scanned me for weakness.

Ruslan stuck out his right hand, dropping the jet-black nylon duffel in his left — Still in a condition of inebriated transparency, I grabbed Ruslan's hand and nodded. "They call me Komar," (Mosquito) he stated, taking a seat on one of the beds. "Slava probably told you about our little problem down here. We need to fix it fast. We got seventy-two hours to close the file," Komar stated. "We got much to do. Get dressed and we can get started," he finished, igniting a Dunhill cigarette.

Lenny got in the shower first.

Robert Baboon sat near me on the bed.

"Why call us from Brooklyn? You look capable to me bro. I mean don't get me wrong, the paper works and I'm not complaining. But this shit just don't add up," I said. "It's like this, Gunny, the Georgian's causing us a lot of trouble—" Yeah, I know," I said impatiently. "Slava already told me that," I continued.

I was out of drugs and anxious.

"Let me finish," Komar said.

I grabbed the half-empty bottle of Georgi off the table and took a heavy swig hoping it would take some of the edge off.

"He borrowed a lot of paper from Slava. Must have been around a lemon (a million) for a dope deal he set up with the monkeys (black gang-bangers) in Long Beach. The fucker kept the paper and the dope then fucked-off Slava. He's brother by marriage with a well-connected Armenian we've been doing business with for years. He knows we don't want our supply cut. And nobody needs a war. He's just laughing it up at all us idiots," Komar stated contemptuously.

He dropped his cigarette near the black duffel and stomped it out on the red industrial carpet. "This fucker's gotta get smoked without the Armenian finding out we did it. We go in there and make like we're robbin' the place, then wet everyone." Komar couldn't resist letting out a repulsive half-smile | He loved his job.

"What do you mean everyone?" I queried.

"He's never alone, Gunny, he always has at least one bodyguard with him. Most of the time two or three. We're gonna need to finish them too." He continued. "We gotta make these killings clean. I mean this Gary. It's *our* lives on the line." he stated.

"So let me figure this now. Why would the Georgian go to Slava for cheddar to buy his dope from the Shvatzah's when his brother got all the paper and dope he needs?" I asked after polishing off the rest of my vodka. "His brother-in law is a true player down here. The Georgian's a joker. He runs his book and no one takes his clown for serious. He already did some deals with his brother and beat him too. So now he's cut. He can't do nothing to him though. It's his brother-in law, family by marriage. You know how those nasty Muslim Stalin's do Gunny. He's married to his only sister, they got kids and the whole shit. Slava already went for a *raazbohr* (sit-down) with the Armenian," he continued. "Nothing." Komar nodded. "The Armenian's a businessman. He won't assume someone else's debt. He told Slava to write it off as a loss. Told him 'Charge it to the game.' From what I heard, they didn't leave off on great terms, but still dealing with each other as long as Slava leaves the Georgian alone. That's why he brought you in. If we put local guys on this, they talk and it's straight war. We needed out-of-towners," he finished coldly.

Lenny walked out of the bathroom and got dressed.

Robert Baboon took his turn.

Komar unzipped the black duffel bag.

Protruding from the top was the barrel of a slick black Heckler&Koch USP9SD 9mm semi-auto. He pulled the weapon out with his right hand and dug for a few moments with his left eventually finding a Brügger&Thomet Impuls IIA suppressor. Komar screwed the silencer onto the weapon in a fluid motion.

My internals blistered.

He set the pistol on the bed and motioned for me look inside the handbag. I pulled out a Berretta 92SB Compact. An attractive 9mm semi with polymer grips and the standard satin black finish |The silencer was already affixed to its barrel. I clutched it with my right hand, pointing it at the floor, at once feeling its disparaging preeminence.

There were two more firearms inside the black nylon duffel. An evocative all-black Glock 19 9mm with a 10+1 magazine and a chrome-plated Randall Service Model 4|5 with black mahogany grips and a high capacity mag. Three boxes of 9mm Remington hollow-point slugs, a box of 4|5 Golden Saber's, a small container of latex gloves the—kind with the powdered chalk on the inside—three black hooded pullovers, and four black ski-masks lay at the bottom of the bag.

I pondered the lives of those about to perish:

Casualties to the barbaric animosity of fate.
It was a chilling moment | After all, it would be my hard hand that would carry out judgment for the few important ones that decide such matters. *Who and why* were unimportant to me;

++||— The bringer of peril —

I was merely a cog in the tangled carousel of bias and inequity.
AND LET IT BE KNOWN | *This is how* YOU *made me.*

"Let's get to getting," Komar announced. "You got any more of them greens?" Komar asked as he reached into his pocket and pulled out a large Ziplock packed with fish-scale cocaine and began to dash it on the table. "Nah, we done burned out bro. Maybe some crumbs." I answered, producing the few remaining buds from the baggie in my pocket and laying it on the table. "No worries, I know where we can get plenty. Let's chief this here and get some ID's, then we'll go and pick us up some," he insisted.

We left our number and headed for Komar's transport, a

champagne Lexus LS400 with matching interior and Lexus factory chromes, then drove to a small apartment complex near Balboa Park.

AROUND ONE P.M.

We arrived at our destination, a shady complex of apartment housing near Balboa Park. Komar knocked on the door of a second-floor apartment and we were greeted by one of his number6. A pimple-faced greasy youngster by the name of Vitya (Veet-yah) quickly ushered us into a dark, dreary mess of a living room.

The intense smell of crystal-methamphetamine smoke permeated the air. The nasty furniture reeked of cat urine.

I wanted to hit fast-forward *and call the whole thing a wrap.*

"These are my friends from out of town. They need IDs," Komar barked. He produced four pieces of paper from the jacket pocket of his blue and white velour track suit. It was too hot out to be wearing the full set — *Komar was just too gangster to give a fuck.*

I recognized the papers.

They were the same ones I called on to push my dogshit to. Lead cards complete with all the information we would need to fake our new identities. That was probably one of the very first forms of modern-day identity theft.

Let me break it off to you real quick.

++||— *1Time2SetItOff* —
++||— 1Time2Represent —

In order to buy my phony stocks, you had to give me all your private information—*all the goodies*—Your DOB and SS# and whenever we could persuade you credit card numbers.

So there you have it: We pilfer all your money *and* steal your identity too.

You don't even have to buy our garbage for us to have your info. Most of the shanty lead-cards I've worked with come "pre-approved" with all the vitals already filled out. In the chop-stock industry we trade them like baseball cards.

I mean *why-the-fuck not?* After all, you're dealing with Career Criminals — We suck out whatever we can then keep on moving around.

++||— Одесса Мама —

Komar carefully selected four client leads from the same geographic location. We took turns taking our digital likenesses against a sky-blue cardboard background number6 assiduously created for this precise purpose.

Using templates of the actual state-issued licenses stored on one of his homebrew personal computers, he created exact replicas of out of state drivers' licenses minus the numbers, then laminated them with a machine he kept on a separate countertop.

This particular identity crime predated the holograms which are now standard practice on most state's identification cards. But those too, can be duplicated with fabulous ease.

That still wasn't enough.

Vitya's next move was to forge us credit cards.

He used a Motorola credit card replication machine. An antiquated device that allowed for the reprogramming of the magnetic strip on the back of credit cards.

For obvious reasons, these devices no longer exist.

Komar's number6 used stolen MasterCards, then reprogrammed the strip with fresh numbers and expiration dates from a typed three-page list he pulled from a drawer in one of his desks.

The work wrapped up close to seven p.m.

Komar stopped at one of his dealer's places to pick up supplies for the express purpose of getting our lungs right. We retired to the room at approximately eleven p.m. It was the second night in which we didn't sleep a wink.

Komar returned around nine a.m.

He looked as throw'd off as the three of us.

"We need to get us a hoopty," he announced. We each took a turn at the shower and dressed in formal apparel. Dressing the part is vital in accurately carrying out the crime. In order to properly exact any type identity crime, it's important to believe that you are the person you're impersonating. Any sign of hesitation will lead to the discovery of your potential fraud | And most certainly handcuffs.

Komar emptied the contents of the black duffel.

We put on latex gloves before we wiped the blasters with a wet towel. When those were thoroughly clean, we wiped down the shells.

I loaded a slug into the chamber, locked the safety on the Randall semi then adjusting loose the belt of my tan khakis, tucked it into the small of my back. Before setting out on the four-and-a-half-hour trip to West Hollywood, we twisted a few Andre's for the road and prepared two full pints of room-temperature Georgi.

THREE P.M.

We pulled into the Enterprise rental terminal at LAX and introduced ourselves as salesmen who'd just arrived for a seminar. Within twenty minutes, we'd procured a dark blue Ford Taurus SEL sedan. I drove the Ford, following Komar to the top of a four-story parking garage where he left his Lex. He hopped in the backseat of the rental and we drove to a Motel6 near Canoga Park — The part of town where they filmed all the porno.

I charged Lenny to rent a room with his concocted documents.

. . .

Approximately seven p.m., we checked into to room 112.

A degraded double-bed suite that smelled like stale sex and cigarettes. We spent the following hours smoking cocaine mixed with trees from a pipe Komar supplied.

It wasn't easy to sleep that night.
All I could think about was Judi and Pappy | I hurt inside.

* * *

We went for some breakfast in the morning.

One p.m. | *We returned to the room and got ready to turn it on.*

Komar animatedly explained the situation. "We do this in daylight. We send Lenny inside to scope the spot, see what's-what. Me and Gunny are gonna run-up and blaze. Boone covers the back door in case anyone tries to run. We do everyone then open the till. I don't give a fuck about the dough, but if there's any paper just take the shit and burn-off."

Komar's voice took on an excited, high pitch.

He snatched the pipe from Lenny, lit it with his butane lighter and took a deep inhale. "After me and Gunny get back we honk one time. Baboon runs back and we peel. No mistakes. We need to be in-and-out in less than three minutes."

We dressed in black denims and dark colored tops.

Komar poured the final *L'chaim* before we rode to deal out death. "A silent moment for the departed," I said, holding up my quart of GeorgiVodka and spilling a few drops on the carpet.

. . .

I HANDED LENNY THE RANDALL 4|5 AND THE KEYS TO THE FORD.

Komar grabbed the duffel and jumped in the shotgun seat while Boone and I sat in the back and I sparked up a Philly laced with white. The motel was only a few minutes away from our target.

Komar pushed the music on.
It was Rozenbaum, playing one his classics, "*Utki*" (hoo-t-key).

Я помню, давно учили меня отец мой и мать
Лечить так лечить | любить так любить
Гулять так гулять
стрелять так стрелять
Но утки уже летят высоко

Не жалею | что живу я часто, как придётся
Только знаю
что когда-нибудь в один из дней
Всё вернётся
обязательно
опять вернётся
И погода, и надежда,и тепло друзей[4]

I inhaled the last few tokes of the Andre as we pulled into a side street near the camera store — *My mind was in another world.*

Thinking how could we exist through the facts.

The Georgian's shop was on top of a small hill with nothing around it. "Leave the iron and go see what we're facing," I instructed a pale-faced Lenny.

"Look for a fat bald guy with a thick beard. That's our Georgian. Keep your cool bro. Buy some film or some shit," Komar barked as he unzipped the duffel, handing both me and Boone a pair of latex.

We put the gloves on and got ready.

Within a few minutes Lenny returned to the vehicle with a brown paper bag. "I bought some film," he said, taking his seat at the wheel.

"There's three of them inside. I saw the Georgian. Behind the counter. There was a tall, built dude with blond spiked hair also behind the counter and a skinny, slimy looking Russian with dark hair playing a joker-poker machine in the left-hand corner of the store," he finished.

An edgy trepidation welled up inside my hub.
For a few seconds there was a sort-of aura around my being.
It released me from the balance of impartiality.
It imbued me with limitless audacity.

"What's the store look like?" Komar asked.

"There's a couch on the left-hand side, soon as you walk in. Glass counter in the center of the store with a small wood door right behind it. Shelves on the right with expensive looking frames and film and some gambling machines on the left side of the store," Lenny answered. "Alright, fellas. It's now," Komar exhaled and at the same time flicked his cigarette out the open window.

He handed both me and Robert the masks then passed us the blasters. We checked our holes again, making sure the killing slugs were in place.

"Showtime," Komar blurted, pulling down his mask.

Boone, loaded burner facing the ground, ran to the back door. Komar and I exited the vehicle and marched toward the front. The element of surprise is pivotal in such situations, we *had it on our side.*

KOMAR KICKED OPEN THE STEADY, GLASS ENTRANCE.

I RAN INSIDE, QUICKLY SCANNED THE AREA.

The first of the silenced missiles made a severe *pop*. The others were much quieter — None any less forgiving.

I shot the Georgian 3Times in the pecks.
Spun around | Shot IvanDrago 1Time in his neck.

Blood spurted on some of the picture frames. It splashed on the glass counter. Within milliseconds another *pop* poisoned my left eardrum.

Komar stood over Baryshnikov.
He begged, in Russian, for his life.
++|| — Two headshots put him to rest —

Komar was panting. "Get the register," he commanded.

I sprinted to check the till for money and stepped in a pool of purple plasma leaking out the Georgian's core. *He was muttering profanities.* Not even thinking — I put 1 in his dome.

His head bounced off the hard tile floor.
And with two small convulsions | He was *Patrick Swayze.*

I smashed the register. "No joy, bro. I can't open it," I muttered. "Fuck it," Komar screamed, running over to the register and knocking it to the floor. He manically grabbed one of the shelves and sent its contents crashing to the floor.

"We need to move," I mumbled.

"I know bro. Hold up," Komar said. He produced a large sack of cocaine from his pants pocket, opened it and sprinkled its contents on the counter. "Let the cops think it's drug-related" He snickered.

I left behind a trail of blood-prints as we darted out the shop and jumped into the hoopty, gasping for air.

LENNY HONKED | A few seconds later Boone hopped inside.

We peeled off like it was New Year's morning.

Komar directed us to stop at the nearest convenience store.

"Hop out and get some Windex, tissues, gasoline, and aluminum foil," he instructed. Lenny returned with a plastic bag containing kerosene and Reynolds Wrap. "*I said gasoline. Fuck it its flammable.*" Komar hollered | THE LOOK IN HIS EYES *was Unexplainable.*

A QUARTER TO TWO P.M.

We returned to the lot and neared the Lex.

Thoroughly, we sprayed the entire vehicle with cleaner and wiped down as much as we could with paper towels then quickly changed into our formal attire disposing of our hoods and denims into the trunk. I took apart the two blasters we'd used and handed the barrels and silencers to Lenny who put them into a plastic bag then into the backseat of the Lex. *Without the barrels* | The burners would be useless to Officer FrostedKreme in the ballistics lab.

Bonne wiped the disassembled tools and threw them back into the duffel. Komar fashioned two long pieces of aluminum foil into square-shaped receptacles for the flammable liquid he poured inside them. He placed one in the front seat of the Ford and the other in the open trunk. We threw our falsified papers into the passenger side of the vehicle before I flicked my Newport into one of the improvised disposal devices.

--||— *It ignited immediately* —||—

The fire rose to the matted ceiling, at once causing a vinegary aroma and spreading quickly throughout the car. By the time Komar flicked his Dunhill in the trunk, the interior of the auto was engulfed in flame.

. . .

"WELL, BROTHERS, HOW DO WE COORDINATE A *L'CHAIM?*" KOMAR SAID.

We took our positions in his Lexus sedan and peeled off just in time to hear the unused ammunition combust and to witness the rental's windshield burst | We drove back to San-De, in near-complete stillness.

AROUND SEVEN P.M.

We returned to the motel and sat down to eat some Burger King. It was the first time in days I'd eaten a "normal" meal and was quick to devour my portion — *Boone di*dn't touch his at all.

"I'm gonna see the boss and tell him it's done. I'll be back in a few," Komar stated as he walked out.

TEN P.M.

Komar returned to our number, fashionably dressed in a black Armani and sporting a fresh Rolex Day-Date. The jubilee band was stern from newness, the caustic aftermarket blue diamond dial presented a shrewdness that undermined wisdom.

"The Dentist's happy with our work. Got us some prizes." He sneered, flashing the bling on his wrist. "He got matching ones for all of us. I got yours in the Lex. Fellas, Get dressed right, we're gonna' get saturated. I'll wait for you downstairs," he said, then walked out the room.

KOMAR DROVE TO MISSION VALLEY AS WE PUT ON OUR ROLLY'S.

We drove about forty-five-minute to a still-under-construction Russian eatery in which a brother had a controlling interest. The liver was first-rate.

It felt like old times | It did.

THREE A.M.

We returned to our room and continued our bender.

Adding some prostitutes to the mix, given the present circumstances, seemed the right thing to do at the time.

Finding said company is effortless.

Just have a fistful of Any J's and look on the Interweb under the heading: "Sleazy Streetwalker." Almost immediately classless broads will materialize to claim the aforementioned Jacksons and offer their list of pay-for companionships. It's real easy with their kind. *The more you have*, the more you get.

Boone was starting to worry me:
He was reclusive and almost unapproachable.

Komar left around six the following evening.

I wanted nothing more than to end all this with some sleep. Besides, we were almost out of dope. I wanted to save at least a little to wake up to. Going to bed after four days of smoking cocaine is tough | *Try doing it after a triple-murder.*

Crashing off cocaine is different for everyone.

The thoughts that race through your mind cannot be explained in clear-cut terms. All the amphetamine-induced answers you thought were ingenuous become fruitless and bare — *It's a terrible place to be* — The romance of the narcotic world peels away like layers of burnt flesh. It's only then that the ricochet of actions perceived as faithful become skewed with the sureness of truth pending.

IT'S THOSE FIRST FEW MOMENTS THAT ARE THE MOST DREADFUL.
Right when you stop ingesting the substance.
That's when the fear prowls into your forethought.
The internal violence is staggering.
You don't want to stop | YOU'LL DO ANYTHING TO GET MORE.
++||— *Anything impossible* —

WHEN I WAS FINALLY ABLE TO SLIP INTO SLUMBER, I DREAMED OF HOME.

I returned to my childhood home, where innocence dwelled, and convictions had not yet been abandoned.

Adam sat at my grandfather's table. He looked at me as if I were once again that awkward child who longed for the acceptance of friends — I smiled and stood to hug him. Adam bowed from my embrace and walked back into Pappy's living room, where a smoky white glow waited to whisk him back to the heavens.

"What have you done Gary. What have you become?" he said.
I couldn't respond | I just stood there in a state of dread.
"It's not too late," he whispered.

I woke to a frightening bang

A sound I knew all too well — I jerked out of my safe position on the couch and grabbed my heater. Lenny was on his knees near the bathroom door, his own vomit on the floor next to his feet. "What the fuck, Gary?" he cried as I ran over to investigate.

Robert "The Baboon" sat on the commode, slumped over. The right side of his brain was stuck on the small white ceramic tiles of the wall parallel. Bits of his cracked skull along with brain particles gathered mostly on the shower curtain.

His cracked face was frozen in a look of eternal dismay.
Blood splattered all over the room.

Booby's right hand held the still smoking Glock9mm. In his left, a sheet of aluminum foil shaped into a homemade crack-pipe. The miserable smell of blood and brimstone permeated the room. I went to my dear friend Robert and held his head in my arms. For a moment, *reality escaped,* and his body was still animated.

I wished it was me that bit that bullet | *It should have been.*

Rest in peace, Bobby Boone.
I'll see you when I get there.

"We need to go. Right now," I barked.

"What about Bobby?" Lenny demanded. I gulped. "He made his choice. We need to leave him and save our own asses." I tried to speak evenly, but the words staggered from my mouth. I pictured them as brain matter, haphazardly strewn across clean white tiles. "Grab whatever you can and do it fast," I said, already packing a small bag.

Within minutes we were dressed and at the payphone down the road. I dialed The Dentist and told him that our room was compromised.

Shortly after, His driver arrived.

He quickly took us back to the villa.

I relayed the details of Robert's suicide to my employer over a fifth of Georgi. "It's the nature of the business, Gary, *people die,* It happens. Does he have any family" Slava asked. "Only a mother back in Brooklyn," I replied. "Make sure she understands that it was an accident. You see to it that she gets taken care of," he said sternly. "We take care of our own. I'll send some friends to clean up. We don't need any extra attention"

"I understand," I said.

"You and Lenny stay here tonight. Tomorrow Komar will take you to an apartment about twenty miles away. He'll take you to rent a car from one of our brothers. We need to start moving this new product in the next few days. I'm counting on you Gary. Don't let something like this discourage you from doing what you have to do," Slava stated.

++||— My time for choices had passed —

THE NEXT MORNING.

We snacked on a traditional Russian breakfast prepared by Slava's mother. Komar picked up some greens and we drove to the apartment. A spacious two bedroom on the third floor of a newly built complex close San Diego's business district. Komar handed me the key and as soon I pushed open the door I inhaled the newness of the freshly painted walls and noticed the modern furnishings.

It radiated a pleasing softness.

We quickly put up our bags and all three of us took seats at a small metallic oval-shaped breakfast table. While Komar poured out some trees from a gallon-sized Ziplock onto the table's red hardtop, I glanced out a closed window that looked directly down on the outdoor parking garage — A young couple pushing a trendy blue three-wheeled stroller opened the door to their auto. It prompted me to recall a life that was once so bright — *So simple.*

A forgotten life.
No longer accessible.

We each took a turn on Komar's pipe.

Lenny recounted the details of what happened to Robert Baboon.

He and Robert finished the rest of the coke while I slept. Robert just couldn't wrap his mind around the fact that he'd murdered. He started saying that we were all going to hell. He blamed me. He wanted to smoke me while I slept — *Then kill himself.*

Lenny tried to stop him.

Robert, the bigger of the two, flung him into a wall. It knocked him unconscious. Bobby had the Glock to my temple — *Poor Bobby*, he just didn't have the minerals to click it. He went into the toilet and freebased the rest of the white. When it was done.

He decided it was time to snuff it.

* * *

MID-AFTERNOON.

Komar drove us to a car rental dealership where a silver Mustang 5.0 GT convertible waited for us. It seemed like the last few days had hardened Lenny some.

Lenny was my driver by default.
Until he died | Or someone better came along.

We tailed Komar to the Emerald Shapery Towers, in the center of the San Diego business district. Once inside we took a glass elevator up to one of the higher floors where Komar opened the door to our new office — Only a small black leather office couch rested in the vestibule. The three of us sat on the sofa and Komar broke down Slava's "legit" deal. A coffee company he was touting as the next Starbucks. A brief explanation was all it took to encapsulate its true nature.

++||— Fraud pure and simple — [5]

Slava already had everything in position.
The only thing I had left was to put away 1MM$ worth of his dogshit and catch that big bird home.

•   •   •

PLACING 1MM$ WORTH OF PRODUCT IS A LOT EASIER THAN IT SOUNDS.

In most cases, two or three big clients will gobble up everything.

Logic dictates that the mo-mo's you burned on your last product(s) would be reluctant to play again.

> That would probably be the case;
> *if we lived in a world where things made sense.*

Most of the same losers bought my garbage repeatedly. I'd use an altered name and say I was calling from a different company and *1MoreAgain* | They lost all their money.

The coffee company was broken into 40,000 units at 25,000$ per unit. The yoke of selling 1MM$ worth of his coffee company bullshit was on Komar, Lenny, and myself. *It took almost eight months of hard pounding the phone* | We put away all of it.

In the meantime, we were paid thirty points of a 1MM$ on a three-way split. That would leave 100,000$ for your hoodwinked friend and narrator.

> Right | And MikeJackson never diddled little boys.

Slava paid us only half in cash—*The other half*—stock options for the exact same garbage we'd just got done pumping. I wasn't pleased but arguing with a man like The Dentist was dangerously unproductive. Between the dope, prostitutes and partying in Tijuana.

> I was lucky to break even.

At the end of it all I was just glad to be going home. My gladness wouldn't last long.

When I was young.
I thought I'd seen it all.
Experience kills a weak Russian who isn't strong.
She sure is a hard teacher | Experience.
++|— She gives the test first and the lesson afterwards —

* * *

I CALLED AND NOTIFIED CHUCK OF MY PENDING RETURN.

He'd been holding it down at the Manhattan office making sure that my presence, even if physically scarce, was still understood.

Christmas holiday '94 sometime Friday afternoon, I landed in Newark LaGuardia airport | Chuck was there to meet me.

He drove us directly to café Arbat.

There was a homecoming party in my honor.
Tarzan and Terry D. along with their full complement of number6 and number8. Brother Will, Arthur Animal, Kazuole, even Bobby Tiger greeted me home.

It was a fine night to be home.
We packed Arbat *tighter than a frog's asshole.*

Letno and Kalil were first to run up and hug my neck. Little Gabe was once again back home from the clink. He looked his usual BoutIt|BoutIt.

Gene T. was the nowhere man.
++||— *He fryer'd me good and I wanted to see 'em* —

I spent the weekend partying with the brothers and tending to my most important affairs.

. . .

LENNY WAS FINALLY BLESSED WITH A *KLITCHKA*.

Ruslan nicknamed him Spider (he looked like Spider from Goodfellas). It fit him well.

Spider stayed with me at my TriBeCa duplex.

THAT MONDAY MORNING, WE WENT UP TO THE OFFICE.

Terry was the new PowerPlayer.

He had been building himself quite a reputation.

During my trip, he managed to be the lead broker on two heavy deals, netting close to half a lemon.

Terry looked the part too, dressed up in Hugo Boss pinstripes, the Gucci manbag, and demonstrating a 2tone Rolex submariner. He wasn't shy about showing me how far he'd risen while I was away. "You seen the new Cadukes (Cadillac), Gunny?" Guido Vinny stated. Terry and me got matching black Eldos in the garage," Guido continued. "You know I been away on business. But I'm happy for y'all " I answered.

They were sure to know the nature of my business in San-De.

News in our community travelled fast.

I only said it to stress the fact.

++||— *I was ready to kill for mine* —

"Where's Gene at?" I asked Terry.

"He went on vacation a few days ago. Gene's in Europe somewhere in the sun. Better than me. I'm fuckin' here with these do-nothing idiots," Terry said, sneering at his cold callers.

His sales force had grown substantially. Before the trip he had three callers and his assistant, Lucy | He now had ten.

He was definitely on the come-up.

"So what are we working on now?" I asked Terry.

"Some private placement bullshit Gene's trying to make us pump. It's not my style really. I like regular stock. Much easier to sell. We just closed out a deal a few weeks ago and we're doing this while we wait. Fuckin' Gene owes me almost a hundred rocks on the last bullshit and now he wants me to sell this loser. Fuck that cocksucker in the mouth. I'm just popping accounts on blue-chip until he pays me. After that, I'll flip 'em into the next cash-out," Terry said angrily.

"You know when he's getting back?" I inquired. "Last I heard, not for a couple weeks. He better come back soon with my money, that Russian cocksucker," Terry snapped.

His last comment turned almost every head in the boardroom.

"What-the-fuck you'ze looking at?" Terry shouted as he stormed out of the office. "He's just hot. Gene owes him money up to his dick," I announced to the onlookers.

Perhaps now the picture is becoming a bit clearer.

Waiting on those royalties, it was like as like waiting on a baby. This isn't your ordinary 9-5 | The same people that control the stock also control the cash. If you don't get paid on time, you can't hold the corporation liable.

Fuck | There is no corporation.
There's only the furry hat Jew with a pouch of cash.
++||— And the Russian with the heater —

I HOLLERED AT SLAVA.

He instructed me to find adequate office space, put a deposit on the facility and recruit a sales team. The Hasidic Jew, Avi, would reimburse me for expenses. The new product would be ready within the month | My payout would be fifty points, as agreed.

. . .

THERE ARE MANY MISTAKES A CRIMINAL SHOULD NEVER MAKE.

Very important *RuleofThumb*. When dealing with con-artist better than yourself — Never invest *your own precious skim* into empty promises.

I SPENT TWO WEEKS SCOURING THE AREA FOR OFFICE FACILITIES.

I finally settled for a space on Broadway close to my former boss Larry Hades | If you ever find yourself in a position where office space in Manhattan is required, you'd better be ready to part with a sizable chunk of paper.

By the mid-'90s, building managers were tired of small companies renting space for a few months then moving out without honoring their lease. Either you show a track record with multiple years of profitable business and accredited references or be prepared to pay the entire lease in advance.

It took almost a month, a bit of manipulation, and close to 100,000$ to rent a 3500sqft space. Furnishing the office with pre-owned furniture and electronic management equipment was another twenty large | My staff was growing weary as well.

I'd taken over almost all of Conny's old crew.

Little Gabe, Letno, Chuck "Who Likes to Fuck", Lenny "Spider" and all their number6 and number8 respectively, almost thirty lawbreakers were under my command.

I instructed them to stay away from selling dope and the usually petty crimes and strongarm tactics. They don't net enough profit for the risks involved and the attention they bring.

Thirty heads equaled thirty mouths to feed.
Even when there wasn't any product they still needed to eat.

THREE MONTHS LATER:

Gene was still ghost.
Avi the Jew didn't come with reimbursement.
Slava the Dentist still didn't have a new product.
And I was under 130,000$ in the CashBox.

For Joey Americana it sounds like a lot of paper, but when you've got my kind of expenses with no new revenue coming in -- 100Large won't even buy two months.

SLAVA MENTIONED THAT A DEAL WAS DAYS AWAY.

Once we started the new pump-and-dump, he'd repay my cash outlay by kicking up some extra cheese. I figured it a good time to holler at Terry.

That's right when everything went to shit.

LITTLE GABE, LETNO AND I HEADED TO GENE'S OFFICE.

I greeted him with a hug. "What's good, Terry?"

"Good you came, I been needing to shout at ya," Terry replied.

We followed Terry and his number6 into a small conference room and took seats to discuss the issue at hand.

"It's like this, Gary. I been talking to a few friends of mine," Terry said smugly, as he stood to brush cigarette ash from his navy blue suit trousers. Letno produced a small flask filled with Southern Comfort and passed it around the table. "Ya, so what's up?" I asked anxiously. "Well Gary, we haven't had a good product in a long time and your boy Gene hasn't been back for months. No one knows when he's getting back. He owes me over a hundred dimes," Terry said.

He walked around the table.

"What I'm saying, Gary, is that you need to pay me the bread Gene owes and collect from him. I'm through waiting for my money. You're the one who brought me in with him so that means if he can't pay," Terry let out a short anxious pause. He was breathing heavily. "You owe me his debt," Terry said as he drank from Letno's flask.

His statement took me by surprise.

Terry D. was invoking street-law.

In reality, he was speaking truth | If someone I'd vouched for failed to compensate on debt he legitimately owed, then I would become responsible for said payment.

That's if he had the Jacobs to collect.

"I came by to holler at you about coming to work with us. Of course for a better payout then where you're at now. I been talking with the Dentist. If you didn't know, I did some work for him in Cali. He's got product for us in a few days. But what-in-the-fuck is this here you're sayin' to me now? You're sayin' I fuckin' owe you something?"

Pausing for a moment, I looked down at the dilapidated brownish carpet. It was marred with cigarette butts. Empty bottles and trash were pushed into small piles in the corners.

I looked directly into Terry's eyes and took in a quiet but deep breath. I clenched my hands . "I don't owe you a plug fuckin nickel, you motherfucker." I stood and shouted. "I known you since we were kids. And now you come to me, talking how I fucking *owe* you something. *How about* FuckYou," I stated, keeping an even tone in an effort to maintain my composure.

Terry walked closer to me.

Everyone sitting at the table stood at once.

"Take a look around, Gary. I own this fuckin' place. Everyone works for me now. Gene isn't in the picture 'cause I don't want him here. He done moved on. And the Dentist, I'll skullfuck that cocksucker. I need his deals like I need a second nose. We been steady pumping our own chop here for months. How about you come work for me buddy?" Terry giggled in an anxious tone.

"I think what you need to do is take a moment and think about where you are. 'Cause this ain't yesterday, slick," Guido Vinny said. Two tall, well-dressed Italians stood near the office entrance.

I was pretty sure they weren't there to bake us Calzones.

++||— Tensions were sky high —

By the time I turned my back on my childhood friend, Terry D. had a modified chrome S&W snubnose hammerless 5shot pointed a few feet from my forehead. "Now what, Gary? Are you gonna kill me too? Like you murdered Sandy?" Terry barked. "It's like that huh?" I said in disbelief. "Yeah, bitch, it's like that," Guido Vinny replied, his right hand already near the center back area of his worn denim jeans.

TWO THING YOU CAN'T EVER DO WHENEVER YOUR G IS BEING TESTED.
Never give in to bullying, even if the chips are stacked against you. And under no circumstance can you ever allow one of your subordinates to pull a jack-move. If ever a gangster is faced with such a challenge | Death is preferable to dishonor.

I instinctively pulled Ace from his sheath.
In milliseconds I had him pointed at Terry's forehead.
Terry was no killer

When somebody wants you dead.
You'll never see it coming.

"Now let me tell you how the Fuck it is," I said.
L-G and Letno reached for their heaters. "Nah fellas, no need for any more iron," I urged. "Hear me now Terry, if you wanna do this

little dance for old times' sake | *Bring it*." Once the best of friends, we were now both staring down the barrel of each other's blasters. "We can die right here together." My voice was steady. Calm. We all realized that it was one wrong move.

They'd be using chalk in there.

"Now we're all gonna put away our burners and me and my people are fixin' to walk out of here. You and me, we done on all aspects, our business ends today. RightHere||RightNow. Or every last one of us here can get right to it," I stated. I'd called his bluff; the show was over.

++||— *For now* —

We simultaneously lowered our weapons and left the room. "And Guido, you fat-fuck, better work out your chest. You got a weak heart," L-G added. "See me in the street, you better wear a vest G.," Letno hollered.

We carefully exited the office.

WE NEVER DID GET A NEW PRODUCT.

It's actually rather amusing, what happened to the Dentist.

Gene was pinched by customs agents while crossing the border with an insignificant amount of black-tar heroin and more than a 100Rocks duct-taped to his belly. He was withdrawing the cream from an overseas account in the Cayman Islands in relation to the fact that he was a degenerate junkie-gambler who forfeited another quarter of a 1MM$ to Alex Pushka's book-making operations.

The federals were called.

Y'all already know. In a New York minute Gene started chirping. It wasn't long before he told them everything. And I mean *Everything*.

Lettermen aren't the ordinary brand of lawmen.

They don't play hero and do jump-outs for insignificant bullshit. The federals have infinite time and the resources to give you enough rope to hang yourself dead. When they finally decide to indict, they have enough evidence to guarantee a 97% chance of conviction.

97% let that absorb for a moment.

Punishments are severe.
Years are doled out in football numbers.

The dirty cheese-eating rat (Gene) swore them depositions on most everybody he knew. But his word alone wasn't enough for indictments. The allegations of a junkie-felon wouldn't hold water in a court of law. But it was enough to sanction wire-taps and further surveillance. The federals released him under the premise that once indictments were handed down, he would agree to testify in open court.

SLAVA HAD BEEN UNDER FEDERAL SCRUTINY FOR SOME TIME.

Lettermen were looking for any reason to sting him hard.

After Gene fingered Slava as the mastermind behind a new wave of financial crimes, they prepared a strike-team to take him down. Gene provided details on all the Dentist's previous stock swindles.

The one they focused on was the coffee deal — They assumed it as crooked as the rest of his shanty ventures and indicted him for wire, mail, and securities fraud. The feds figured that once this case was cracked, they'd be able to secure easy convictions for the rest of his crimes.

Early April 1995, A mixed team of Federal agents from the FBI, ATF, and INS staged an assault on Slava's Bonita Villa.

Quietly neutralizing his security, they burst in through the back door hooting and hollering about "Freeze," and "Nobody fuckin move," and "Where around here do you keep the donuts?"

It was like a regular episode of Cops | It was.

Slava's obese wife and Bigfoot half-retard son were tackled to the ground and handcuffed. Slava drunker than CooterBrown shouted Russian obscenities when they burst into his bedroom.

When the feds pushed him down the stairs, his elderly mother stumbled out of her bedroom which was adjacent to his. A nervous young federal pointed his Mossberg Pump straight on her | Slava's mama had a heart attack and died on the spot.

To their dismay, the federals soon discovered the coffee company they'd indicated as primer for their takedown was fuckin MC-Hammer, *Too legit to quit.* Upon careful examination of all business records the feds realized that the spotlight of their entire indictment was really a legitimate deal that could never secure a conviction and were forced to drop all charges against Slava the Dentist who subsequently decided to cut his losses and disappear into obscurity.

Here's the kicker | Before Slava did the Keyser Söze, he sued the federal government for the wrongful death of his aging mother and was awarded over 1MM$ in damages.

Hows about that for Одесса Мама.

So | Where does that leave your misled friend and saddened narrator? Up a creek of shit with tiny yellow paddles.

After suffering a heavy deficit, I was forced to close up shop.

The glory days were gone and everybody was doin' bad. *Everyone's lives were up for grabs.*

SHORTLY AFTER, TERRYS OFFICE WAS RAIDED BY THE SEC.

They rushed in SWAT-style with enough local police dressed in riot gear to subdue an entire housing project. They collared everyone they could get their hands on.

More than fifty-two felons.

Before being placed inside the paddy-wagon, agents recorded everyone's faces. There was little or no evidence to obtain jail time for the salesmen. They were unregistered representatives working illegally under a licensed broker's name. They just wanted that boiler room shut. Video recording all the offenders was a sure-fire way to get their message across. The government had never encountered securities fraud on such an organized level and really had no precedent to work on.

They probably could have booked them on trumped-up charges, but it was the organizers they wanted. They blundered on Slava. The only other leader was Gene, who'd conveniently signed a deal granting him immunity.

All they really had was a plain old structure-fuck.

TERRY AND GUIDO WERE "OUT-OF-TOWN" WHEN THE RAID CAME.

They'd been tipped off by Ricky Kuku who, as a result of his connections with the Genovese clan, was alerted of the pending action. They left everyone in the office, including their loyal sales assistant Lucy, to burn.

GENE PUT TOGETHER QUITE A LIST OF PLAYERS FOR INDICTMENT.

My name was among them.

One junkie's word wasn't enough — Two on the other hand, plus an eye-witness account of fraud and murder, was plenty.

* * *

JUNE '95,

I opened a small office above an electronics store on the corner of Flatbush and Avenue U and put my people back to work.

I sent a kite to Alex Pushka requesting a *raazbohr* to talk about a joint venture — He knew me to be stand-up and capable.

In the meantime | It was business as usual.

I went against my better judgment and invested whatever scant resources I had left into street pharmaceuticals. It was only temporary, or so I figured. I put Letno and Spider in charge of procuring dope and pumping to the fiends. I should have known that history always repeats itself.

SOMETIME AROUND MID-JULY.

I gave up my duplex in TriBeCa, went back to living with Chuck, then traded my Benz 300 for a fresh Black Yukon 1500 from the dealership.

The knock came at about 4:30 a.m.

As a general rule of thumb, when any law enforcement agency comes to pick you up, it will always occur in in the very early morning hours. Chuck woke me. The laws wanted to see me.

I came to the door in my underpants.

Three FBI agents awaited me at the entranceway.

Two wore the signature black suits. The third, a rookie looking youngster, was in grey suit trousers and a casual white top. I was barely awake and hung-over stiff.

I thought the whole thing was all a dream.

"You're Gary Govich," the senior agent stated. "We have a warrant for your arrest," he said before I had a chance to confirm. "You need to get dressed and come with us," another demanded.

"Can I brush my teeth?" I asked. The senior agent nodded, and they escorted me inside to brush my teeth and get dressed.

The federals aren't the local JumpOut beat-cops.

They're much more educated. They practice etiquette. They treat you like a human being when you cooperate with their orders. I followed them downstairs, un-cuffed and we stopped at the local store for coffee and cigarettes.

I was driven to downtown Manhattan.

When we arrived at their bullpen, they cuffed my hands behind my back and took me through a side entrance into a brightly lit, recently renovated interrogation room. My left wrist was cuffed to the beaten steel table. There was a large video camera both at my rear and in front of me.

I stared into the two-way bulletproof window and shortly after, another agent entered the chamber. An aged white gentleman with a droopy chin and tired eyes. He wore an electric blue necktie around his fat neck and his suspenders looked worn.

He introduced himself as Senior Agent BaconFace.

"You know we got you by the dick, right Gary?" He chuckled then sat down in the wire metal chair beside me.

Agent BaconFace moved in close.
His breath smelled like he'd been using shit-flavored toothpaste.

"We've watched you for a long while but never had anything solid. Aside from your friend Gene's sworn deposition, that is," he remarked, dropping a manila yellow folder on the desk. "Yeah, well, Gene's a junkie and a habitual liar, whatever he told you." I laughed. "Can I smoke?" I asked. "Sure, Gary Gunz," BaconFace replied.

There was a long silence before I spoke.

"What else you got?" I asked gingerly. "We know about your stock operation in San Diego. The local cops picked up your friends Lenny Spider and Letno yesterday on drug charges. We got them selling an entire bird[6] to undercover police," he remarked.

I was starting to get concerned.

"Letno held his water pretty good. Spider, on the other hand, he sandbagged you, Gary Gunz. He sold you out in exchange for immunity. We're getting ready to book you for eight different RICO predicates, including criminal enterprise, drug trafficking, securities fraud, and murder. You're looking at a minimum of fifty years, possibly life," he sneered.

"You got the wrong guy," I shouted. "Sure, I worked in the chophouse. But I never even sold a thing. I was the handyman. They called me the Hammer. I used to repair the walls when they got angry and threw telephones at each other. Sometimes I loaned the brokers money for points. But that's it. That's as far as it goes," I insisted. "Murder?" I yelled, surprised. "Criminal enterprise?" I continued. "Man, you got the wrong Russian. If all you got is Lenny, you got nothing," I concluded.

"We got him, and we got Gene. That's enough to keep you here for stock fraud, wire fraud, mail fraud, and we'll just go ahead and book you on the rest. Let the judge figure it out. Spider's an eyewitness to murder, his testimony is all we need," Senior-Agent BaconFace affirmed.

"Give us the Dentist. Sign a deposition today. I mean right now, and we let you walk. We know you did the hit for *him*. We've been after him for years. We don't want *you*. Sign the paper and go home."

The agent opened the folder to show me both Gene and Lenny's deposition as well as a pre-typed deposition for me to sign. It implicated Slava in a slew of crimes that would surely seal his fate.

"I told you, Agent BaconFace, I'm a nobody here. I got nothing for you. They call me the Hammer because I fix shit. If you need a drywall patch, holler at me. If not, go on and book me and let me call my lawyer," I said then lowered my head and accepted my lot.

BaconFace looked like someone had just sucked all the jelly from out his donut | It was a tough decision to make.

I could have sold out Slava for my freedom
Not Me | I just wasn't built that way

I would have walked on out.
Had me a cheeseburger then went home.

Then what | I was in one of those catch-22's.
Life was over no matter what I did.

Least I could do was go out with honor

Honor | *Now there's an interesting concept.*

—||— Honor is expensive —||— In the *mafiya* it's reserved only for those who can afford it. Holding less than 20,000$ cash, I couldn't afford much if any at all | Certainly not a normal lawyer.

Dignity on the other hand *is every man's right.*

Welcome to Brighton:
Where living in the city *is like living in the times of* Frank Nitti.

· · ·

THE FEDERALS DID EXACTLY WHAT THEY SAID THEY WOULD.

They went ahead and booked me for everything.

After seeing a judge, I was remanded to MCC's (Metropolitan Correctional Center located in lower Manhattan, adjacent Foley Square and across the street from the Federal courthouse) general population and held, pending trail ++||— *No bail* —

IT TOOK ALMOST THIRTY-SIX HOURS FOR A HOT MEAL AND A PHONE CALL.

I called my mother.

She was the only loyal person I had left.

I listened to her cry before she slammed the phone on me.

and so the story goes:

A young man with plans to make CREAM.[7] *Which fell.*

I went to jail at the age of twenty.

IT WASN'T OVER, THOUGH.

++||— *Not by a LongShot* —

♔ ♔ ♔

♔ ♔ ♔ ♔ ♔

YOU CAN BET JEWELS ON IT.

♔ ♔ ♔ ♔ ♔ ♔ ♔ ♔

1.

2.

3.

4. Translated: "I remember a long time ago, I was taught by my mother and father, If I heal, I should heal, If I love I should love, If I shoot, I should kill. To them, I wave my hand (if they could only see me now).

I don't regret that most of the time, I live how I must. I believe that one of these days, everything will come back. Absolutely, everything will return, even fortune, even weather, even the warmth of friends."

5.
6.
7.

PART 3

The Cost Is High

✳ ✳ ✳

10

BRATAN

И ничего что я не стал академиком
  Не прошла мимо меня жизни красота
    Пусть кому-то и трудны понедельники
    А мне полегче если рядом братан
    Пусть кому-то и трудны понедельники
    А мне полегче если рядом братан [1]
  -Alexander Rozenbaum

ALL ROADS LED TO INCARCERATION.

It was only a matter of time.
Frankly I'm surprised it didn't happen sooner.

I was placed into a tank of thirty violent prisoners on the seventh floor of the facility's male housing unit.

Once I was inside, years of dope|alcohol began to wane leaving only detoxification to take hold of my psyche.

· · ·

AFTER GAFFING ITS CASE AGAINST SLAVA,
The government needed something concrete to save face and put him away for good | They required my testimony.

A FEW DAYS AND IT WAS ON LIKE DONKEY KONG.
The word was put out — I'd turned government informer and was pending transfer into witness protection. Inmates sought to purge me of any ability to communicate with the laws by way of attempting to break my jaw.

++|— *I fought so much my knuckles hurt —*

Sometime during the fifth day.
Two bosses (prison guards) entered the tank and placed me in handcuffs. Due to consistent squabbles and "for my own good," I was transferred to protective custody. They escorted me—*with my legs shackled to my arms*—to an elevator which stopped on the tenth floor, an area of the facility reserved exclusively for violent and troublesome offenders.

THAT'S A FUNNY TERM "protective custody."
It's solitary confinement—with commissary privileges
Jail or prison time of any sort is rough.
Solitary is the next level.

They put me in a 6x9 cell.
Ripened white paint flaked from the walls

It reeked of torment.

The bed was situated in the center of the room with about a foot and a half on either side of it to the wall. It was a metal slab with four legs bolted to the floor and fitted on all corners with special equipment to hold straps—if necessary.

An aluminum toilet|sink combination sat in the front left corner.
The toilet and the sink shared a water line.

There was no bedding.
I wasn't allowed to bring the grey burlap bed-rag nor any of the toiletries I was issued into the cell.

THE FIRST FEW DAYS, I SCREAMED A LOT.
It fell on deaf ears — When my shouts became too bothersome, an overweight bossman and two of his colleagues entered the cell, stripped me naked, strapped me to the bed, and beat me until I pissed and shitted myself.

Inside the cell, the lights were on 24|7.

That didn't stop giant cockroaches from crawling all over me while I slept. A camera, designed to deprive one of any privacy, was affixed outside the door. Its positioning allowed them to peer into a small slit of a window.
They checked on me around the clock | *"For my own safety."*
There was a small speaker imbedded into the wall next to the door. It squawked; a loud noise that resembled music. There were two silver buttons under the speaker. The first was a "call" button used to alert them if I had a medical problem. The other was there to control the volume of the radio | Neither button functioned.
Climate control wasn't a factor when designing the facility's tenth-floor solitary region. There was neither air conditioning nor heat in the cell. During the day, temperatures rose over a hundred degrees, and at night, went as low as the teens.

Alone with just my thoughts:
++||— *Time drew out like a blade* —
I replayed everything over|over *and over* again.

The same conclusion every time.

How and why I got there was unimportant *and getting out wasn't an option.* Any prisoner will tell you — *Prosecution and Persecution are the same.* When inside, truth and justice are hollow words.

Ideals available only to those who can afford them.

I was broke, busted, and disgusted

My fourth day of segregation, they shackled then escorted me to another room on the second floor to meet with my attorney, a young Anglo appointed by the courts | He reiterated what I already knew.

I was deep inside a massive cluster-fuck.

"Just sign this affidavit, and it'll all be over. I can have you home in twelve hours." He smiled, presenting me an already typed statement which he just happened to have handy. What waited for me on the street was far worse than the hole.

You don't have to be in jail to be doin' time.

I sign that paper *and my life's over* | Literally.

I wasn't worried about me.
People like Slava had no reservations when it came to, say,
Strapping a bomb to my mama's car.

𝄇 I REFUSED TO SIGN 𝄇

The government lair told me that the feds planned to drag this out as long as it took. They intended to file reset after reset to keep me locked in that hole as long as they could. Federals have limitless time and resources and a war of attrition is how they meant to do me.

. . .

SHACKLED, I WAS ONCE AGAIN ESCORTED BACK TO MY HELL.

I was allowed one fifteen-minute call to my family every week.

Food was (usually) delivered three times a day. It consisted of 2tone-turkey or another form of mystery meat, a sloppy vegetable, and a tiny carton of milk. It was handed to me in a Styrofoam tray through a 2x12 slit in the door.

I didn't get to eat every day.

There were days all I received in the form of sustenance was a cold cup of coffee at night—*Any complaints*—would result in the boss with the Rollie Fingers mustache strapping me to the bed and smashing me unconscious.

My hands went through the same hole the food did any time they opened the door for any reason.

I was allowed three showers per week.

The shower room was roughly ten paces, I was walked there wrists bound to ankles | In shackles.

The shower room door was made of reinforced steel, similar to my cell. Inside was a rusty overhead nozzle that trickled brown-tinted water. The shower lasted no more than four minutes and I was un-cuffed only after I was back inside my room and the door was locked.

They watched the entire shower through a slit in the door. Often there would be women watching me shower and laughing at me.

I had an hour of "recreation time" every five days.

For which they led me—*shackled*—down the hall to a small, outdoor cage, which was only slightly larger than my indoor cage.

There was a homemade stationary bicycle that had no resistance. They never put me inside that outdoor cage when other prisoners were around. Sometimes they made me wait, shackled, for extended periods of time until the cage was cleared.

It's the uncertainty that steals your sanity.
Not knowing what time of day it is — What day of the week it is.
Unsure whether you can battle through another episode of
You—||++Against++||—You

It made me sick all day long.

I would have gladly snuffed it if I could.

The feds held me by my dick so hard:
I couldn't even kill myself without their permission.

Twice during my imprisonment, I was escorted to the federal court building. Both times the government reset the case to a later date. The law gave them a year to reset the trial proceedings, after which they could change around a few of the charges and re-arraign me | They were playing with a loaded deck and had a limitless supply of wild-cards up their sleeve.

Early April '96, I was locked up for nearly nine months.

Hope for me was a deluded belief — *distant even in thought.*

Commissary never made it to my hole.
I lived off whatever food I was given.
I lost almost sixty pounds.

My skin was filthy with scabs where bugs had bitten off chunks of flesh in my sleep and my genitals were infested with a weeping rash from compulsive scratching. I hadn't shaved in almost eight months. My beard and hair were covered in lice the size of my thumbnail.

I abandoned all thought of fleeing that white hell.

There have been studies, by some pretty important bigshits about the effects of extended periods of solitary confinement. All of them have affirmed similar deductions—*Solitary confinement isn't anything-nice.* It's designed to drive a person to the extreme limits of their mental, emotional, and psychological capabilities.

In a statement issued by Stuart Grassian MD, a highly respected psychiatric bigshit, on his evaluation into the short-term and permanent concerns of solitary; *"Effects determined difficulty with thinking, concentration, and memory. They also included panic attacks, overt paranoia, self-mutilation, and auditory and visual hallucinations."*

In similar clinical analysis conducted by other bigshits of similar renown, it was determined that solitary confinement produced auditory hallucinations in as little as a few days, with visuals following a week or so later. The length of time it took to produce such effects was dependent on the psyche of the test subject.

I started hearing voices during my sixth day of solitary.

They started as knocks and whispers, but eventually turned into screams. Visual hallucinations quickly followed.

They were never pleasant—*I knew it wasn't real*—I guess it was just my mind's way of coping with confinement. It didn't stop them from driving me smash-the-walls crazy. The boredom breached me like a dull knife, leisurely prodding at my innards.

I began playing with my own feces.

I spread it on the walls and on the slab I slept on.
Sometimes I smeared it on my body and face.

Wikipedia describes Coprophagia as the consumption of feces, from the Greek *copros* (feces) and *phagein* (eat).

Many animal species have evolved to practice coprophagia. Other species don't normally consume feces but may do so under unusual conditions. Only in rare cases is it practiced by humans — Cooped up in a 6x9 all day every day is a pretty rare case.

I don't know why I did it.

Probably because it was one of the only things I could do. *The monotony was so severe* | I no longer cared. Anything to break from the noxious nothingness of solitary.

PERHAPS DICKENS PUT IT BEST;
I was dead to everything but tortured anxieties and horrible despair.
A more dejected, brokenhearted, wretched creature:
It would be difficult to imagine.

I repeatedly prayed to God.

He wasn't home | Instead were the souls of those I'd murdered. *They often cackled at my misery.*

I WAS INSANE IN THE MEMBRANE
※ *Crazy insane*||Got no brain ※

* * *

"GOVICH, YOU GOT A VISITOR," AN OVERWEIGHT BOSS-MAN SHOUTED.

I could have two monthly visits from anyone on my approved visitor list. Nobody I associated with dared put their name on that list. Approval meant a full background check.

My parents came the first two months.
I refused their visits.

I lived in a world of facts, of a reality I thought I understood. I believed myself to be center of the design and I was certain I knew all the answers. But I had to face the truth about what I'd done to hurt those around me and in hurting them, what I had done to myself.

I didn't want my parents to see their only son in the condition I was in ++||— *I didn't need another boulder on my heart* —

THEY ESCORTED ME, IN SHACKLES, TO THE SECOND FLOOR.

I was placed into a room with a middle-aged chubby gentleman who introduced himself as Marty M. He dressed in a luxurious dark navy suit, wore a teal blue shirt with a white collar, and monogrammed white cuffs. His gold collar-stay accented his blue white and gold Hermes tie.

I recognized instantly | *He represented the law firm Dewey, Cheetam and Howe.* I'd seen enough of his type to know. "My client, a chap you may know by the name Alex P. has retained my firm to provide legal counseling for your case," he stated joyfully.

He spoke with an English accent.

I quickly grabbed the Snickers bar he slid across the small green table and fuddled with the wrapper to open it as he continued to speak. "I scheduled a motion for this afternoon to plea for bail on your behalf. The presiding judge is a close friend to one of our firm's partners. I think we can arrange something in the area of half-a-million. I'm hoping we can have you released in the next twenty-four hours." He smiled as he spoke.

His words were murmurs.
I was more concerned with opening the chocolate bar.

When one's arms are shackled to their legs, even the easiest things become quite impossible. Marty unwrapped the bar and placed it on the table. I grabbed it with my mouth and devoured it quickly. Chocolate smeared on my face and beard. Marty M.

produced a white satin handkerchief and wiped the smudges of chocolate from my skin.

"How have they been treating you?" Marty asked.

"How the Fuck do you think? Like an animal in a cage," I yelled. "My client has taken a personal interest in you. He's going to make sure you get out of here as quickly as possible. Just sit tight for a few more hours and we'll have you home." Marty smirked. I giggled. "Sit tight? Where the fuck am I going?"

It was the first time I'd laughed in almost nine months.

"Problem is, Mr. Marty, I can't afford half-a-lemon in bail money. I can't even afford a half-a-hundred. So I don't know how the fuck we gonna do this here," I stated. Marty chuckled, then placed his card on the table. "Mr. P. has pre-arranged everything for you. He's handling our legal fees and posting any bail money required. You must mean a lot to him. We'll be in touch, Mr. Govich. See you soon," he finished then left the chamber.

I could still taste the chocolate and peanuts as I was escorted back to my hole on the tenth floor.

Straight away, placed neatly near the toilet.

I glimpsed the large brown bag containing the commissary foods I'd ordered months ago | It's startling the kind of miracles a pay-for-attorney is able to work. In the following six hours I was escorted, un-cuffed, to the shower room, then handed a Bic razor (the plastic kind with only one blade) and allowed ample time to shave and shower.

No corrections officer watched me through the slit in the door.

I felt almost human.

Some time later I got the announcement. "Mr. Govich, your bail has been posted," a friendly female voice declared.

. . .

It was the sound of sweet music — I didn't believe it.

Often I had hallucinated those words, only to wake up to the guffaws of my slain victims and the winter flummox of my very personal, never-ending nightmare.

I'd forced myself numb to the pain long before.

Even if I was getting out, I was leaving the frying pan and jumping straight into the fire. My newfound benefactor was none other than Alex Pushka. One of the most notorious Russian gangsters, to ever walk the city of Brighton.

Brighton: Where all the felons are licensed.
Brighton: Around it hangs the iron curtain of silence.
Brighton: Where ordinary Russians walk frightened.

++||— *And you can go insane from the sirens* —

A few long hours later.

I was taken into another holding tank in another area of the facility. It was my final stop before processing out. There were a few other prisoners there waiting for their walking papers | I quickly cut past and was released to a locker room area where an older guard handed over my musty clothing. They stunk a rotten odor, but I was glad to smell it. Two guards escorted me to another door, and I was outside.

Free like OJ — *All day.*

Close to eleven a.m., the first week of April '96,

300

I was released from the south side exit of MCC and walked without delay to the corner of street. It was an area where vehicle traffic was permitted. Autos anxiously waited for their loved ones.

Sounds and sights of the city blanketed me in fright. The natural ebb and flow of New York traffic scrambled my head into a byzantine perplexity | *It didn't seem genuine and at the same time all too real.*

My head and stomach throbbed:
My body unprepared for re-entry.

I squinted to look around.

I recognized Little Gabe immediately. He stood with Letno and Tarzan near a black Lincoln Continental. I walked up and nodded.

None of them recognized me.

"What's the matter, you'z too good now to holler at yer boy?" I stuttered. "What the fuck? Is that you Hard-Gunz?" Tarzan responded. "Who you thought it was, bro?" I tried to snicker. "Shit, look at this. It's the return of the motherfuckin soldier." Tarzan hugged me. "Let's jump in the limo, Gunny. We got a surprise for you," Little Gabe declared.

Letno opened the backseat door.

A familiar mesmerizing fragrance cuddled my lungs with it's warm sugariness. Once inside, the plush cushioned seats of the late-model cruiser instantly absorbed some of the ordeal. In moments we crossed the Brooklyn Bridge, passed the Gowanus expressway, and were onto the Belt | I decided to enjoy the moment and rest my glimpsers.

> When I opened my lids
> *Sandy's bloody stare strobed directly into my core*
> I screamed.

"Bro, bro," Little Gabe said.

"It's me Gary, it's just us. They told us you spent your whole stretch in seg. When they had me locked on Rikers, I did six months in solitaire. I know what you goin' through. Just give it some time. Few weeks, you'll be normal again," L-G reassured me.

"You got some trees? Spark them shits," I said.

Letno was already twisting up a Philly in the shotgun seat.

"Don't get too John Blaze. We got a big surprise for you tonight. Besides, Pushka said not to let you get too fucked up 'til he can holler," Tarzan said.

"What the fuck happened, brothers? Why would you let me rot in there?" I asked. "For starters, your boy Gene had a sworn deposition naming you as the head Russian. They were trying to give you leadership role in a criminal enterprise[2]. He was easy to fix though. He went to work with Bobby-Tiger and Trigger. When they found out about his deal with the feds, they broke his head open with a handset. After that, he developed a speaking problem. Motherfucker had his jaw wired for four months. When it healed, they broke it again and knocked out four of his teeth. He won't be talking to the feds anymore. After they fucked up their case against Slava, they had nothing on him either," Tarzan replied.

"Your homeboy Spider, he was your problem number1. Nobody forgot about you out here. This fucker, though, he was like the invisible man. Turns out, the feds had him safehoused in downtown Brooklyn. They were gonna put him in the rat-house (witness protection) after he testified. Man, he knocked on everyone, not just you. You were their point man, Gunny. He fingered you as the triggerman in some hit in San Diego. They figured if they could stick that on you, maybe you'd roll. Few weeks ago, we got tipped about where they were keeping him. Old friend of yours actually. Just rolled into one of ours spots and hollered. At first, we thought it was a setup. So we reached out to Pushka, we been working his deals for a minute, you know while you were out." Little Gabe giggled, then passed the blunt to me. "Who tipped you off?" I asked.

Everyone laughed in response.

"You gotta see for yourself, bro," Letno stated merrily.

"Spider's up there with Elvis now. Turns out he likes to swim in cold water. Polar bear club or some shit." Little Gabe cackled. "Pushka told us to hit his mute button. He slipped and hit his head on a rock somewhere deep out in the ocean," Little Gabe finished and grabbed a gallon of Georgi they brought and took a heavy swig.

"After Spider ghosted, the feds had nothing. Pushka sent his lawyers. He posted 750Rocks to get you sprung. Hearing's scheduled for next week to drop the whole fuckin' case. We just wanted you home. Feel me?" Letno said excitedly. "Motherfuckin' warrior you are," Letno said. *He handed me my Rolex and Ace, wrapped up in his holster.* "Kept it real clean for you, Gunny. Knew you'd be home soon to grab at it," he finished.

I reached for my trusted ally.
My third eye flashed the marred faces of my victims.

With my left thumb and forefinger I simultaneously touched my temples | I shook it off then took Ace and put him on. As I wrapped the familiar holster around my shoulders my head instantly cleared.

++||— It felt like I had never left —

"What happened to Chuck?" I asked.

Everyone laughed.

I laughed as well. "I must have missed a whole lot of shit."

"Your boy Chuck, he's a sick fuck. This is the funniest shit. This fool won the lottery. I'm sayin', he played some small jackpot and won nine fuckin lemons. Took a quick payout almost 3MM. Fool moved to Florida and opened up an SUV accessory place or some shit. Lucky bitch. Still can't get laid though, ugly motherfucker," Little Gabe barked | Everyone including myself relished the euphoric moment.

WE STOPPED AT A SEVEN-STORY APARTMENT COMPLEX ON OCEAN AVE near the Kings Highway intersection.

"Let's get you cleaned up. Cool-out at my spot with me for a few hours before we show you your surprise," Letno said as he and I exited the vehicle.

We took the elevator to the sixth floor.

Adjacent to the staircase was Letno's three-bedroom apartment. He opened the beige door and I entered his home. Just a few hours earlier I was in a solitary nightmare — *Haunted by devils.*

I left solitary.
So did my demons.
✻ *They followed me* ✻
Reopening my wounds.
Gashing at my injured heart.
Tormenting my battered soul.

It looked like Letno had been makin' it just right. Various ornate knick-knacks were scattered about, and the apartment was filled with costly furniture.

A tall slender black-haired Russian youngblood in his early twenties walked out one of the bedrooms and into the living area. "This is my boy, La-Onda Mark, from Borough Park — Pushes a black Pathfinder truck," Letno stated. "Met him through Pushka's cousin

Sammy Movemaker. He workin' with us up at the lab. Sounds pretty good on the phone," he finished.

Mark's features resembled those of a Mexican illegal. Letno called him "La-Onda" because he reminded him of the gangsters in the movie *Blood In||Blood Out*. "Heard a lot about you, Gunny. Pleasure to finally meet you," Mark said.

I stood to shake his hand. "Past time for a *L'chaim*." I snorted.

"No doubt," Mark replied, already walking towards the spacious kitchen. "I'm gonna go get your whip, bro. We've been storing it in your Uncle Misha's garage on 86th. I'll get it washed up and ride it over here. Put on some of my gear. Pick something nice. We'll sort everything out for you later," Letno stated.

He pulled his mobile to dial a cab then put on a light black leather coat and made for the door. "Don't get him too zapped. Pushka wants him literate for tonight," he commanded Mark. "Motherfucker, you keep on pouring *L'chaim* till I say word," I yelled.

I finally showered around three in the afternoon.

I sat on the sofa and removed the high-capacity magazine from Ace. Gold hollow points with steel cores were stacked in his magazine. There was already one in the hole — I cradled him in my arms then placed him back into his sheath.

Letno returned in time to blaze another fatty.

"She's downstairs, just like you left her," he said.

"Looks like you fellas been doin' alright," I remarked. "Yeah, you know, Pushka been good to us. He's got plenty of product. You're gonna put us back in the box, Gunny. When the street hears you're back in the game, it's gonna get wicked," Letno said excitingly.

I laughed.

I WAS CRYING INSIDE ⊧*Dying inside*⊣

WE DROVE TO THE NATIONAL RESTAURANT.

Clouded always in dreams of greater things, it's one of the oldest and most lavish restaurants in Little Odessa.

The National Restaurant is an extension of the International Food Deli, the oldest international deli on Brighton Beach. The two establishments are across the street from each other. The restaurant takes up two floors, and like many Russian restaurants in the area, doubles as a night club.

International Food was the very first store of its kind in Brighton. It started a trend that revolutionized Brighton's entire Russian community and set the standard for the entire country to follow.

I can recall a time when the two-floor, twelve-hundred-square-foot store was a filthy shack shoebox.

But this here is America.
All you need here is a dollar and a dream.

The owners of the International Food Corporation came to Brighton on the same flight as my parents | Today they are the sole proprietors of a food dynasty that controls more than thirty separate corporations, employs thousands of migrant Russians, and whose value has been appraised at more than a hundred million USD.

Their success has been noted in many contemporary publications such as *The New Yorker* and *Forbes*, and their names popped up on Fortune 1000 more than twice.

HERE'S A LIL' SOMETHIN FOR YOU.
Probably won't read about this one here in Fortune magazine.

My grandfather was a close friend of Elena's (one of two sisters who came to America on the same *Aeroflot* as my family). It was Elena and her sister who supplied the initial seed money to rent the abandoned space.

Here's the 100Million$ question.

Where in the world did Elena get the initial 50,000$ for renting and renovating the space? Simple Answer. She had it with her when she took the flight to JFK.

Whoa now.. Hold up Gunny | *Whats this BullShit you're saying to me now*? Didn't you say that during the communist regime you had to fork over all your valuable possessions to the state and were allowed to leave with only a hundred dollars per person?

Well, my wonderful reader | I did.

But in Elena's circumstance, as in the case of many Russian immigrants, there was the option of trying to hide some of your treasures and attempting to bring them with you when you left.

Risky business, that was.

Government officials looked through luggage and even checked body cavities. Failure to comply would result in the revocation of one's exit visa and immediate transport to "the Zone."

Elena had about a hundred dimes in diamonds that she just wasn't ready to give up—*And they were just too large to swallow.* She put them inside her vagina and went about her most important affairs. *Small problem*: Government was familiar with this ploy and, on exit day, a high-ranking KGB came to the airport and retreated with all the women to strip them naked and look inside their sweet-spots.

Elena started to panic. Last to be searched Elena and her sister disrobed. The director of the investigation Comrade Communist a known pervert approached the pair. She knew that, if discovered:

++||— It was closing time —

Elena played her final card — She started pleasuring herself. This aroused "Comrade Communist" so much, he almost released in his pants. Left fully pleased, he decided to send them all on their way, to America — Land of the free *and home of the scam.*

* * *

A FEW MONTHS LATER.

Elena's son in-law, Pasha, had himself a eureka moment.

I'm talking about a blockbuster. It took some greasing—Bureaucrats back in the motherland granted Pasha exclusive import rights. Pasha fixed it so that popular imported European cold cuts, smoked herrings, European pastries, and many other foods became available exclusively through a small shop he opened on Brighton 3rd.

He called it International Food.

Within only a few years time business was a-boomin. Pasha bought the property and expanded the store. Based solely on his success, other stores sprung up all over Brooklyn | Pasha became their wholesaler and soon after started making the meats himself.

The International Food family is the story of American dreams come true.

All you need here in America is a dollar and a dream.
Well | *Maybe a few diamonds more than a dollar.*
++||— Одесса Мама —

WE ILLEGALLY PARKED THE CAR OUTSIDE THE ENTRANCE.

I threw the keys to the valet standing outside. "Do your fuckin job," I shouted in Russian at the young valet.

It was good to be home.

We walked through the first set of doors and came into the front vestibule. Luxurious cigar smoke imbued the air with a sweet fragrance of wealth and victory.

We neared the doorway to the main hall and glanced at a few of the many photos of famous bigshits—both Russian and native—that adorned the two spiral staircases. There were wonderful little modern vases, expensive original paintings, hundred-year-old lamps imported (stolen) from Odessa.

A Russian national with a thick unkept mustache smoking a funny looking cigarette nodded upwards to signal our entrance into the main hall.

I pushed the clean white, cherry-wood-accented revolving doors, walked past bronze, 18th century figurines, and entered the scene — Inside the gold and brown hall, at least 150 friends and associates greeted me with cheers. Everyone who mattered came out to welcome me back. This entire production — All of these people | *All for me.*

Господа и Дамы.
Мы представляем вам Сейчас.
Еще один раз.
Одессит и Бандит.[3]

Brooklyn's own native son.

Grisha"*Gunny*"Govich.

And just like that ++||— I was home again —

An older Armenian waiter quickly ushered me to my table.

I sat with my mother, father, and uncle Misha. Tarzan approached and sat down beside my father. "We're so happy to have Gary home," he said in Russian. Tarzan was already bent shitfaced.

I was working on fast joining him.

I TURNED TO SEE RJ STANDING AT MY BACKSIDE.

"And there he is. Gary Speks," RJ slurred.

I stood to embrace him. "You Irish fucker, man if it isn't good to see you RJ," I said. "That's Detective RJ to you." A sideways smirk formed around his lips. He instantly flashed a gold NYPD detective's badge that he pulled from his rear pants pocket. "But you can just call me brother." He kissed me on the cheek.

"Walk with me, Gary. I need to talk to you," RJ requested. We proceeded to the front balcony, and stepped directly inside the VIP section of the restaurant which had been especially partitioned off for me. I instructed the overweight Russian thug|bouncer to refuse entry to anyone until we finished our business.

We sat at one of the four empty tables.

I grabbed a sealed bottle of Absolut then poured us both a tall drinking glass full. RJ pulled a small flask containing his favorite blackberry brandy. "You know I keep my own, Speks." He laughed as we touched our bottles together, both of us taking deep swigs on our potion. "I haven't seen you in years and now you pop on up. I mean, I'm glad to see you. But where you been?" I asked. "You know Gary, I heard about your girl and what happened. I'm sorry," RJ said, *Unlike the never-ending stream of simulated condolences.* I knew RJ's wasn't artificial.

We lamented for a moment.

Then RJ caught me up on what he'd been up to.

"After high school, I went to college. One semester in and I just didn't have the money to pay anymore. My family made too much money to qualify for any grants. You know dad's got connections. We're fourth generation Law Enforcement. They started really putting the blocks to me to join the force. Fuck it, so I did. I breezed through the academy. Shit, I didn't even have to take a polygraph. I didn't do one fuckin' day in the blue and whites. Not a single day in a patrol car. I didn't even have a precinct to report to. Dad got me posted right inside 1PP (1 police-plaza: police headquarters in downtown Manhattan). After a year I took the detectives test. I work intelligence down there. Mostly paperwork bullshit. For now." RJ paused and swigged hard from his flask.

"When I heard the feds had you in seg on some trumped-up bullshit, I acted. I had to. I work closely with the feds on some of their cases. I got close to the agents working your case and I got inside their files. It didn't take long to figure out who their snitch was. I went to go see Little Gabe. It's not like he was hard to find. He keeps a pretty high-profile." He laughed.

"When I found out it was Lenny, I just almost pissed myself. I knew when I exposed him, he was a goner. Gary, I just couldn't have you rotting in there. I owe you, brother. You saved my life. And I'm not saying we're even close to even, but this one here, it's a start," RJ affirmed. I tried to mumble something, but it was incoherent because I could not find the words to express my gratitude.

I stood, embraced him, and cried.

Alex Pushka, along with two others, walked through the front doors of National Restaurant at eight p.m. I was still upstairs in the VIP when he requested my presence in the main hall.

Pushka was everything I expected him to be.

A Russian Jew, closer to fifty, he stood at a stout five-feet six.

I scanned his thick black scalp and graying beard. Both were immaculately groomed | His very presence demanded the highest level of admiration.

Pushka beckoned me to sit beside him.

At once his incisive black wrinkled eyes were able to lacerate whatever mettle I imagined myself as having. His was the detached, manipulative gaze of a master villain. It was one of those moments when the butterflies in my belly wanted to flutter out and escape from their nest. "Why don't you sit down, Grisha. I've been waiting to meet with you," Pushka said. Although he was fluent in English, he spoke only in Russian | *All the time.*

I affixed my attention to his 36mm tri-color gold Rolex presidential wristwatch. The aftermarket bezel, blessed with more than 3karats of diamond and the entire face encrusted in pink diamonds, matching the gold tone of the bracelet.

In Russian culture (*mafiya* culture specifically)

Your wristclock is considered an entity of its own.

It identifies your position in the pecking order. It's an outward demonstration of your accomplishments | It articulates the strength of your G.

Alex Pushka's was remarkable.

"Would you like some Cognac?" he casually asked. "I prefer vodka," I answered. "You young people nowadays. You only like the cheap dogshit that the government has taught you to like. Me, I prefer the finer things." He paused for a moment. "I see you like my watch." He laughed slightly.

I confirmed.

"A trinket, it's nothing but pink gold and yellow diamonds. I played the hand that I was dealt and I never bluffed my way out of trouble. No matter how hard they tried I never let them knock me to my knees. I stood up like a man. Like your grandfather. He died standing," he said coldly. "I want to welcome you home Grisha." He only called me by my Russian name | It was a sign of sincere affection that I relished.

"I understand what you went through inside that jail. I did six years in 'the Zone' because I wouldn't talk. My first years were in solitary." Pushka leaned back and pulled up his black silk turtleneck sweater, exposing a tattoo, six stars circled by a snake, on his belly (the stars symbolized his years spent in prison and the snake is the symbol of a high-ranking member of the "thieves in law").

He then pulled up his right shirt sleeve and presented a large tattoo of an upside-down spade (the mark of a thief) then put his hand on my shoulder. "Sure, I was scared—*But I was never afraid*—[4]It was one of the greatest experiences of my life. I would not trade my time there for a million dollars. It taught me how to be the man I am today. I greatly respect what you did. These children today, they don't understand honor, family. These things mean nothing to them. All they want is money and drugs. Grisha, you are special to me. The government authority, they tried to make you kneel and you would not. I love you for this, Grisha. To me, you are family. To me, you are like a son," he said, then stood and kissed me on the lips.

"Come with me to the stage, Grisha. I want to make a toast," he said as we approached the elevated hardwood platform.

A popular group called The Rose Sisters performed their Russian pop-hit "Atlantic-City." They ceased immediately and turned the microphone over to Alex Pushka | He didn't even have to ask.

"I WANT EVERYONE'S ATTENTION," PUSHKA DEMANDED IN RUSSIAN.

The room paused to listen.

"There is an old French legend. An angry girl told her lover to go rip out his mother's heart, to prove his love for this girl. So he murdered his mother, then tore out her heart. But while he ran to the girl with his gift of love, he tripped and fell. And the mother's heart said, 'Are you in pain my son? Are you hurt? Will you be alright?' That is when the boy understood that unconditional love was with the one he had killed. It was with his mother. He returned to his hardened beauty then killed and buried her. Let us drink this drink, for unconditional love. Let us drink tonight for our brotherhood. For that which we are strong. For the everlasting help and support of each other. Let us raise our glasses for you, Grisha, and for each other." He finished by raising then sipping from his porcelain teacup.

The hall erupted with screams.

I WAS AT HOME AMONG THE BROTHERHOOD | Home at long last.

I FOLLOWED PUSHKA INTO THE VIP.

We sat alone and conversed about the future.

"I'm sorry about your lady. None of us find enough kindness in this life, as we should," Pushka said. "You know, Grisha, I'm a businessman. I made an investment in you. I have many honest business ventures. Let me tell you this, my son, the problem with making an honest buck is that it's too hard. Too many people are doing it. The margins are too low. I'm interested in profits. I don't care what we have to do. Except drugs—we don't get involved in drugs— You see what happens when you get involved with that garbage. You go to prison, people die. Some of your friends are already working on my deals. I want you to take this over. Like a manager, you understand most of these are children. Without supervision there is no guarantee that profits will be high. For this, I make you my son. You are under me and no matter what you cannot be touched. I want you to put together your crew and become the *Bratan* that I already know you to be," he whispered.

I poured a tall glass of Absolut and continued to listen.

"I want you to understand, we didn't become people to peruse our own destinies. We became people because we had no other choice. You do whatever you want but you never forget that. I will teach you my law—*man's law*—Never forget you owe me enough to honor what I say as the truth. You never forget from this point that you are my *Synok*, and so you represent me and my *bratva*. Drink whatever you want, whenever you want. But never use drugs. Never sell drugs. This is my law. You will be great, Grisha."

He formally anointed me into his family and made me his *Synok*[5]. Alex Pushka stood, kissed me once more on the lips, and returned to the party.

++||— And there sat I —
Synok of the *Pushkatzkaya* brotherhood.
Captain of the Red-Army | *My very own brigada.*

Every *brigada* has a name. I'm not referring to the name of the crime family (which is always the surname of the *Atetz* who initially established it). I'm talking about a nickname, a *kliytchka* recognizable by the entire street | Ours was called The Red-Army, or RA for short.

* * *

The party started to disband around four in the morning.

I was thoroughly content with the outcome | Alex Pushka gifted me keys to a two-bedroom duplex across from the world-famous Radio City Music hall. It was a furnished dwelling he'd allow me to reside at until I could get on my feet.

He also left me with the address to his mansion in Dix-Hills Long Island and instructed me to meet there with him within forty-eight hours for further orders.

Six a.m.

They turned the music off and turned the lights on. A few of my loyalists stayed to finish the night. Members of my *brigada* and *Bratan* of the Black Tulips (Churnayee-Toolpahnee) with some of his *patzanee,* were still clicking *L'chaim* | Bobby "Tiger" was *Bratan* for the Tulips. He was by far one of the more serious gangsters in Brighton.

His father, an original Gasoliner, was hit with fourteen calendars for money laundering and conspiracy to commit murder. Most of his assets were seized during the indictment, but he managed to keep a small restaurant on Avenue W and Bedford. During his incarceration, Bobby T. assumed ownership and ran his operations from the back.

BOBBY TIGER WAS "THE PRINCE OF BRIGHTON"
✳ His G was a birthmark ✳

As prince he had divine right to take whatever he wanted whenever he wanted to take it. He described it as "Stealing bread from the mouths of the Decadent." Kinda like a modern day RobbinHood — *except pudgy* ++|| — And Russian —

You could drop Bobby in Montego Bay Jamaica buck naked.

BY THE END OF HIS FIRST WEEK.
You'd find him belly full in a warm bed.
A crew of brute monsters at his disposal.
Jamaican women scrubbing his dirty drawers.

WITHIN A MONTH.
++|| — Bobby T. would be SupremeRuler —
The original Jamaican Doon|Dadda *the type to murder blood clot for fun.*

THE DAY MY JUDI PASSED.

Tiger was the pudgy fellow who tendered me the banger.

Bobby alone was a mitigating force. He was far from alone. He managed to befriend a Gambino button-man. A goodfella whose name is unimportant | Let's call him George. Together, they controlled much of the drug and gambling traffic in the entire Russian area of Brooklyn. Bobby also aligned himself with another Russian national who bore the *kliytchka* of "Trigger." As you can probably guess—he didn't get the name "*Trigger*" because of his love for piña coladas and getting caught in the rain.

Trigger was responsible for the financial element of the Tulips operations. This meant the stock-scams, white collar crime, and all similar essentials fell under his jurisdiction. He was currently doing time for unlawful possession of a firearm.

THE LAST OF US SAT AT A TABLE CLOSER TO THE STAGE.

I sipped on warm vodka straight.

Tarzan shouted obscenities at the wait staff for turning the lights on and demanded scrambled eggs — We laughed as he threw handfuls of leftovers at the nervous attendant.

I listened to Bobby T. recall his knifing of a young Russian we called Sasha *Dleeny* (dleen-ee; it means "long." It's a *kliytchka* usually used to describe a person who is tall, thin, and gawky).

"We were over by Sahara, Jerry Albania was driving, I was sittin' in the back with my lady. This ugly son-of-a-cunt comes up to the window and starts asking me for work right there in front of my girl. I told him, nice at first, not to bother me when I'm with my family. But this fuck, he just wouldn't let go of it. He keeps talking. So I told him to come closer to my window and I poked him. Right in the gut. It was the funniest thing Gunny, when I pulled out the jigger, it had this nasty yellow slime on it. I was like what-the-fuck. I'm thinking it was the fat from his belly. But this skinny fuck got less fat than a salad." Bobby snickered.

Everybody laughed

Bobby "Tiger" linked up with Pushka early in the onset of his criminal career. Truth be told, he never needed Pushka to make a name for himself. He was one of the founding members of TF, and like Conny, sat on the council. Bobby had a strong following long before being anointed *Bratan* in the *Pushkatzkaya* brotherhood.

Bobby was no dummy | He lacked the resources of a criminal brotherhood and knew that on his own, although a serious player, he wasn't capable of achieving the monetary wealth and respectability that a brotherhood like Pushka's could grant him. He was Pushka's *Synok* long before I was and was first in line to be his next *Bratanok*.

Bobby had a weakness that would eventually prove to be his downfall. He loved to dirty his hands, involving himself in petty crimes like burglaries, small drug deals and other random acts of aggression with his *patzanee*.

He also loved to enact violence on civilians[6]. The laws really don't give a motherfuck about gangsters jacking and killing each other off. It makes their job a lot easier. When you go after civilians, *that's a whole other deal.* You're intruding on their turf. When that happens, they look to put a stop to you quick.

"So what the fuck we working on now?" I asked.

"Pushka's been laying some sweet deals on us. He's able to hold the price for a while so we can put away plenty of shares. Actually, we just closed out of a deal," Tarzan replied. "But that's not the problem we got right now, Gunny," L-G said.

I tilted my head upwards, waiting for him to continue.

"Shooter, the fuck we all been getting our burners from. He went and got himself killed," Gabe said. "He was selling a half dozen gats to a *grazny* (dirty) Uzbek. Fool came with a fully loaded clip, slammed that shit in, then blasted poor Shooter dead." Little Gabe finished by slurping down the remainder of his glass. He stood and grabbed a still full bottle from the other end of the table, titled his head back and took a hard swig of Stoli. He staggered a small step back then wiped his puckered lips with his shirt sleeve. "Really, who let this cock-sucker die. Number6 is not allowed to die without permission," he blurted.

Everyone laughed.

"This does pose a problem," Bobby stated. "We're out of disposables, so don't use what you got unless you're willing to walk around naked for a while," he said. "I can guarantee you this, Gunny. The fucker who comes up with some firepower is in for a real sweet payday. The street is screaming right now," Bobby finished.

My wheels were spinning.
I surely wasn't allergic to money.

"Let me think on that, Bobby. I need to get back in the game. What type of numbers we talking here. Say two dozen jammys?" I asked. "I know what I can do. I'm thinking three dimes a grip. Dozen smokers net you fifty. Two dozen score you one hundred. Would be a nice little lick for you," Bobby stated. "Let me work it for a few. I can probably come up with something," I replied.

A few more hours passed.
A few more *patzanee* left the party.
All that remained were Tarzan, Letno and Little Gabe.

AROUND SEVEN A.M.
Tarzan broke out the cards for a few hands of *Durak*[7]. "I wanted the rest of these fucks to burn-off before I came to you, Gunz-Gunz. You know I work with Bobby mostly. But me and you got history. I need your help here, brother," Tarzan said.

I could tell he was off about something.

"What's wrong T ?" I asked.

"It's like this, Gunny, I got into this telephone card hustle with a Hasidic Jew called Manny. This cock-sucker's been holding out on me. I did all the paperwork for him, but he's not paying me any of the points he promised. I know he's banking big paper on the deal. He owes me over a hundred large. I can't tell Bobby about it. I wanted to keep him out and didn't tell him in the first place. If he finds out now, after the fact, you know what I'm talking about," Tarzan said.

"Well I know he wouldn't be looking to buy you an ice cream cone," I said. "Let me handle-up on it." I stated gingerly. "Have him come down to Café Arbat tomorrow night at seven for a *Raazbohrnayk.*

Tell him *Pushkatzkaya* wants to see him," Little Gabe insisted.
++||— He was already assuming the role of my *Pareyn* —

"We're gonna deal with it, T. You sit this one on the bench. You're already emotionally involved. We can't have you jumping out on this fool. Just come by my new place in the afternoon with all the paperwork you have on it," I said.

And with that we parted for the day.

GoodNight | GoodNight
— Ψ — *Parting is such SweetSorrow* — Ψ —

---

1. Translated:
    And it's OK that I didn't become an academic. For the beauty of life did not pass me by.
    Let someone else have the difficult Mondays.
    For me its easier if near me is a gangster.
    Let somebody else have the difficult Mondays.
    For me it's easy because near me is a gangster.
2.
3. Translated:
    Gentlemen and Ladies.

We Present to You Now.
OneMoreAgain.
From Odessa. He's a bandit

4.

5.

6.

7.

11

CAN'T KNOCK THE HUSTLE

I don't wanna live no more
   Sometimes I feel death knockin' at my front door
   I'm living everyday like a hustle
   Another drug to juggle
   Another day Another Struggle
-Christopher Wallace

INTEGRITY.

Every year since 2005, Google has listed *integrity* as one of the most searched words on the web. Here is the Merriam-Webster Online Dictionary definition of "integrity"

Pronunciation: in-'te-gr&-tE.

Function: noun.

Etymology: Middle English integrite, *from Middle French & Latin; Middle French* integrité, *from Latin* integrat-, integritas, *from integr-,* integer *entire*

1: firm adherence to a code of especially moral or artistic values: INCORRUPTIBILITY

2: an unimpaired condition: SOUNDNESS

3: the quality or state of being complete or undivided:
COMPLETENESS

DEFINITION 1 IMPLIES A FIRM ADHERENCE TO A CODE.

I like that.

It doesn't define the code, it merely mentions that there *is* one, and strict obedience to it defines your personal level of integrity. It gives no right or wrong, *no black and white definition* | It really doesn't provide a concise explanation.

It *does* mention moral soundness. But one man's morality is another's imprudence. What I deem to be corrupt conduct, another may perceive as incorruptibility.

So the definition of moral integrity would indicate that someone like Adolf Hitler for example, had a recognized concept of integrity. It would even suggest that—based upon his devout belief, adherence to his own personal code of moral values, and his sincere willingness to die for his principles—his level of integrity was high.

My personal integrity *denoted a very specific code of values and standards that I dutifully obeyed.*

We believed ourselves special people:

Chosen to enrich this dirty world through our example of rigorous standards of living which were based on a code of beliefs that far surpassed the standards prescribed to us by the fraudulently distorted laws of a bias land based on inequality.

It was a fancy way to dress up the truth.

Fact is: We were cheats, thieves and murderers | Plain and simple.
Still, I fancied myself a provoked warrior in honorable combat.
And in the warrior's code | There's no surrender.

I DROVE MY YUKON.

Traffic was light, in less than hour we arrived at the midtown Manhattan address Pushka provided.

L-G sat shotgun, Tarzan and Letno followed in a silver Mercedes cruiser. They picked up Movefaker and La-Onda Mark on the way.

We pulled into a pay-for-parking lot adjacent Radio City Music Hall. Little Gabe stuck his head out the window and motioned to the Hispanic attendant, who steered us into a reserved area on the floor level of the facility. L-G snickered. "See, Gunny? We got this motherfucker on lock." We parked and exited our vehicles, then Letno approached the young Latino, dressed in a black and white security uniform, seated behind a ramshackle plexiglass front desk. He slipped a thick white baggie into the slot where moneys are normally tendered | The Latino returned us two vouchers good for monthly parking.

We walked up the ramp to the face the outside daylight.

I swigged heavily from a small pint of vodka I kept inside my pocket. "When are you gonna stop drinking that dogshit? It tastes like fucking turpentine," Tarzan barked. "Around the same time your mother stops selling her asshole," I replied.

The address Alex Pushka provided was a short walk over.

It was in a building with aging architecture and dirty glass doors.

An older, balding Russian dressed in burgundy and grey doorman's apparel stopped us at the entrance. "Where do you go?" he said in a thick accent. I reached into my pocket to produce the paper Pushka supplied with the address and apartment number on it, "accidentally" exposing Ace's grip to the now frightened doorman. "I n... no want trouble here," he stammered. "Nobody wants trouble. I live here now," I said in Russian.

I presented the paper to the doorman.

"Alex told me to stay here for a while," I proudly stated.

"You know Alex, right?" Little Gabe winked at the small man. "Yes, I know Alex. He own this building. He cousin to me," the doorman said, then walked behind his desk and reached for the phone. "He no tell me you coming to stay here. I call him to make sure is OK," he said forcefully. "Alex is my cousin, too. Check-it, old-timer, he's all of our cousin's.

Look here, homeboy," I pulled open my jacket and glanced towards the magazine end of my sidearm. *"He's his cousin, too."* I smirked. "So you go on ahead and call Cousin-Alex. Let him know his *Synok* just came home," I said mockingly. The doorman put down the phone. "I am sorry, cousin. I did not know you were also cousin to Alex. I call later. Welcome home," he replied, already escorting us to the elevator. "Reward our cousin," I directed Letno, who was already peeling a Benny from his roll.

We took the elevator to the thirteenth-floor.

It was a penthouse-style apartment that boasted all the trappings of a luxurious Fifth Avenue tenement. Nicely equipped with three bedrooms, four bathrooms, and a terrace overlooking the cityscape.

Marble and gold inlays garlanded the walls of the living room and extended into the bedroom. There were three giant black leather recliners and a large black leather sofa bed in the center of room, a decorative oriental style rug beneath them. There were two small retro lamps on the glass end-tables, providing dim lighting for the oversized area. In the very middle of the room a glass-top table, its legs decorated with green wrought iron leaves.

I threw my leather on the sofa.

We sat around the center of the room as L-G tuned the small telly to NY-1 news channel. Letno poured four grams of white from a foggy Ziplock on the glass table. Tarzan crushed it with a playing card he produced from a deck he kept in his pocket. "My cousin really knows how to do it big," Movefaker said gleefully. "He's my cousin too, remember?" I chuckled.

From then on: Alex Pushka would be forever known as "Cousin Alex."The *kliytchka* would carry into his everyday life. All of the street, Feds included, would refer to Pushka as *"the Cousin."*

La-Onda Mark started making chokers. Tarzan took some of the white and twisted it into a Philly blunt. When my turn came, I went against my better judgment and slammed one. It wasn't gonna do me like it did Adam or Sandy, or any other junkie fuckers.

My G was too bold.

++||— My heart was too cold —

"Tarzan, you know how to reach this fucker Manny?" I asked, tasting the wet iodine flavor of the chalky powder as I coughed. "Yeah," he replied as he picked his head up from the table. I could see the white residue attached to the hairs inside his nostrils. "He stays at an office in Borough Park. It's inside an apartment building, right behind a body shop he owns. His office is right up the stairs. He keeps equipment for the telephone cards in a back-room. Cameras everywhere, Gunny, he's real paranoid," Tarzan finished, then did another line.

"Is he packing?" I asked. "Not him. You know his fake religious Jew bullshit won't let him carry iron. That doesn't stop his *goyim* cronies from holdin," Tarzan coldly stated.

I nodded."Pathetic."

I KNEW HIS TYPE.

Manny was a Jailhouse-Jew.

He found religion in the New York penal system. Before being incarcerated for the kidnapping and rape of a minor, Manny was a mook like any other. After recognizing he could get better chow and extra holiday privileges if he grew a beard and wore a beanie, he decided to *"follow his calling."* In general, Jailhouse-Jews were regarded as ordinary con-artists and pretty lousy crooks.

Do-anything weaklings that fabricate lies in order to please their lawmen handlers were vermin to men like me. Useless jellyfish, they wear wires, sign statements, and tell on everyone they can | Men sit it out.

++||— I sat it out —

"Get him on the horn. Time we sort this thing out," I demanded.

Tarzan dialed a number on his cell.

The symphony of digital beeps and dashes carried an echo through the stillness of the room. Soon, a lampoonish Russian voice mumbled greetings. "Manny it's me," Tarzan said.

I grabbed the receiver from his hand before he could continue. "Hiya Manny, it's Gary. You probably don't know me. You may know of my family, *Pushkatzkaya*," I stated. "What, what, who's this?" a slow, coarsely broken voice replied. "Who I am is irrelevant to you, Manny. What *is* of importance is the fact that you and my associate Tarzan have a good amount of business left open," I said contemptuously. "I don't know who you are, my friend, but whatever business Igar and I have is between the two of us." Manny replied in a soft, controlled voice.

"Let me tell you who the fuck I am, homeboy," I barked at the receiver | Specialized Personnel in Executing Killer Shitbags

|| AKA *Speks* ||
AKA *quick to burn down a house of cards.*
AKA *quick to squeeze off on bodyguards.*

"Now, Imma tell you one more again. Tarzan is my associate, which means any business you have with him, you have with me.

And now that we know each other, I think it's time we meet in person. Be at Café' Arbat tonight at seven. Please bring what you owe. Next time I won't ask nice. Go check my record," I insisted before flipping the phone closed."

I NEED TO GET SOME Z'S BEFORE WE MEET THIS FOOL,"I SAID.

I retired into the bedroom.

"Yo, anyone heard from Kalil?" I shouted into the other room, already undressed. "He been doing some work for Bobby Tiger," Tarzan said. "Since you were in the clink, Bobby scooped up lots of your crew and been givin' them work," Letno affirmed. "He's a real generous guy, that Bobby. Real smart, too. Reminds me of a monkey trying to fuck a football," I answered.

Everyone responded with laughter

"Gabby, go holler at Tiger. Tell him we need to 'borrow' Kalil for a *raazbohrnayk* (a sit-down where there will most likely be violence involved)," I ordered. "I'll see y'all in a few hours," I concluded.

It would be the first time in almost a year that I slept on a mattress with sheets. They felt soft and inviting. It was a profound and peaceful sleep | *There were no nightmares that night.*

I awoke, then took a long swig of my pint.

In the next room, my *brigada was* playing a few hands of *Durak.* "Clean up and let's roll," I said.

6 P.M., WE ARRIVED AT CAFÉ ARBAT.

I was already well lit before Kalil showed. He gave me a kiss on the cheek. *"Privet Bratan,"* he said in broken Russian. I laughed.

"Since when did a Spanish fuckhead like you learn Russian?" "Hanging around, backstabbing Jews, you learn what you need to stay alive," he whispered in my ear.

I reached for a crystal glass, filled with vodka, and raised it high.

"For unconditional love," I stated.

"To the Brotherhood," everyone replied.

"What you've been doing for Bobby while the federals were jerking my cock?" I asked Kalil. "Collections mainly," he replied. "He been keeping you green?" I inquired. "Green enough to live. It's been a grind. I'm low man in the pecking order. But I've been getting by," Kalil grimly stated. "No more of that shit. I'm home now. We back up in the green-land," I said.

"You got something in mind, 2Gunz?" Kalil asked. "Few things. For now Tiger's got you on loan with me. Way I see it we were together from the bang. Just 'cause I had to sit on the bench, it don't mean loyalties change. Imma holler at the Cousin." I confirmed.

8 P.M., THERE WAS NO SIGN OF MANNY.

"L-G, hold it down here while I go see my cousin," I said. 'Tomorrow early—*Ring the Alarm (assemble the men)*—I stated coldly. "Kalil, you drive." I passed my keys and grabbed the rest of the Absolut.

It was a misty night.

We rode in silence on the Belt to the Long Island Expressway, taking exit 51 to Babylon then route 231-N—from which it was a short mile and a half to Alex Pushka's Dix Hills mansion.

Pushka's property spanned three acres of land.

His white and grey three-story house was not dissimilar from the other affluent homes in the area. Unlike Slava, there weren't any armed men with Kalashnikovs on the rooftop—Just a fancy steel gate with the letters A-P embossed in the hub of an oval-shaped crest in center of the gate.

Kalil picked up the intercom phone.

A large camera was mounted atop the right side of the bulkhead. The device swiftly rotated, turning its watchful eye towards the center of my windshield. "Gary here for Alex," Kalil stated.
The gate slowly opened, allowing us entrance into the cold world inside.
We drove up to a covered carport and parked in the leftmost spot. The mansion's roof was held up by stone and concrete pillars, etched with pictorials of medieval combat. Kalil and I walked up a stone path to the front entrance.

I KNOCKED ON THE SPANISH MAHOGANY 3LIGHT|3PANEL DOOR.
An attractive, dark-haired slender woman with deep laugh lines and a pale complexion answered and escorted us inside. She appeared more sophisticated than the women in my circles but wore an excessive amount of perfume.

It was a sweet sickly smell.
The one *where you know* it's overpriced.

I never cared for its kind.
It was almost offensive.
It gave too little and cost way too much.

She was there for the money.
How could I blame her.
++||— So was I —

"Alex has been expecting you. Your friend can wait here," she said, motioning to a cramped foyer next to the entrance with a small sturdy wooden chair and a round glass-top coffee table covered in magazines. Kalil sat while she escorted me to an elevator toward the rear of the spacious living area.

The smoke-tinted glass elevator took me to the third floor.

I exited into a beautifully decorated den.

The walls and the ceiling were dressed with block paneling and stained with a dark natural wood color, bringing out the deep grain of the expensive lumber. The rear of the room was a wall-to-wall bookcase, filled with pricey looking tomes consisting of all the classics.

I quickly surveyed the walls of books.

Psychology, Philosophy, Ancient and Modern Sciences. Most of the issues looked like they had been read multiple times. With no formal education whatever, Alex Pushka taught himself to expert.

++||— *Taught himself to be master* —

As though it was at the core of the whole known universe, a deluxe handcrafted European-style imported desk lay in the center of the room. Alex Pushka sat behind the desk, looking cozy in a large, well-appointed black leather manager's chair. The smoke from his Cuban created a swirl of vapor that reflected off the brokers table lamp in the corner of the desk. As I walked towards him, his gaze never left the computer screen in front of him.

"Sit down, Grisha," he insisted, waving toward two small manager's chairs in front of the desk.

I took a seat and produced a pack of Newports.

Pushka pulled a DuPont lighter from his pocket and lit my smoke then pushed a large marble ashtray toward me. "Would you like a drink?" he asked, pushing a button on the bottom of the desk. The wall panels on the room's left side opened to reveal a small deacon's bar. "Sure," I said. "Pour one for both of us," he stated.

I stood and returned with drinks for Alex and myself.

Alex clicked his mouse and shut down the screen of the terminal, grabbed his drink and leaned back in his chair. "Are you enjoying your stay at the apartments?" he asked. "It's a nice place. Beats the shit out of prison." I grinned then leaned back. "You know when I was released from the gulag in Russia, I returned to Odessa and my brothers embraced me just like you. The same faceless government robots tried to steal everything from me. They will never see anything or anybody again. Take anything from me, Grisha | *And from you I will take everything*. That is our law. That is what makes us men." he said, still reclined in his chair, pulling from his Cuban.

"I allow you three months to get on your feet and move out of my apartment. When people rest in my house, they don't make any trouble where they sleep. My doorman yesterday. That wasn't very nice. This man was trying to work for me, and you try to frighten him. Why do you do this Grisha? Why do you disrespect my house like this?" Alex demanded.

"Alex, he was a *frayer*[1], a nobody. I needed to teach him that when talking to people he needs to show the respect they deserve. How could I have known he was your man?" I ingested the potion an returned my glass to the table.

Pushka silently stroked his beard, initiating a careful tension. *Minutes felt like hours in our hard silence.*

Finally, he let out a diminutive smile and slightly nodded his head. His voice now calm and exacting. "In the future, understand that anyone who works for me is under my *krisha*[2] and cannot be touched by anyone. This is law."

Alex Pushka placed both elbows on the extravagant hardwood top of his desk. He unfastened a gold bar-shaped cufflink from his left side than carefully rolled up his monogrammed shirt sleeve and glanced at his timepiece.

AN **IWC** Schaffhausen PorscheDesign.
Its dramatic detail was hypnotic.
++||— *A clock of rare power* —

It could *only* be worn by a ChiefCommander.

Pushka pushed the release, then slowly placed the gunmetal grey titanium wristclock close to my left hand. "It fits you perfectly, Grisha," he whispered — I held the artifact in my palm, closely admiring the tint of greenish hue of my features in its flawless sapphire crystal.

"The lawyer, Marty," Pushka paused momentarily.

"He will come by the office in a few days to hand you some papers. You must sign these papers. He has prepared a deal for you. You will receive a minor felony conviction for unregistered stock trading. Your punishment will be time served an ACD (All Conditions Discharge) and probation for two years," Alex continued.

"I wouldn't sign a postcard for those *moossaré*.[3]" I scoffed.

I quickly returned the clock to the counter, folded my arms then jerked back my head. Just the thought of concession made me feel dirty | Disrespected.

"I understand this, Grisha. Unfortunately, I need back the bail I posted for you. I cannot afford to tie up such a considerable amount. My business requires that I have liquid assets ready at all times. As long as they have an open case, the cocksuckers, they *will* be watching you. If they're watching you, they're watching me, you understand. We don't need this. I know this is a tough position for you. I would consider this a great favor if you close this for me." Alex leaned forward. He was inside my comfort zone, invading space that I considered personal.

He crossed his hands intertwining his fingers.
They were covered in prison tattoos.

Alex Pushka stared directly into my eyes, demanding my immediate answer — I felt like a voter in one of those third-world elections where there's only one candidate running and failure to participate warrants an immediate public termination.
"I do this for *you,* Alex," I said.

As though I had a choice.

Pushka pushed back his chair, then leaned across the table and put his right hand on my shoulder and pressed down firmly "Most of the brothers are actresses, trying to play the man's role. You are a true man. Very good, Grisha, I will not forget this. *Please,* Grisha, do not be unkind to an old man." He stared off into the distance for a long moment, then gracefully moved the IWC from its position on the desk and into my lap.
I removed the gruesome Rolex I had received from Slava as a cruel reward and feigned the mandated gratitude for its sacrificial replacement | *A profound scarlet-letter.*

"*Spaziba,*" I solemnly replied.

Pushka smiled as he walked over to the bar.
"Now what is this business you have with the Hasid? This Manny owes us something, eh?" He smirked as he poured drinks for the both of us. "Did you not think I know of your affairs? It's my rightful duty

to know everything." He laughed while putting a fresh glass of cognac atop a small placemat on the desk.

"Now let me tell you what you *don't* know. Your friend Tarzan has been playing both sides of the fence. *My fence.* He tried to cut a deal with Gene to partner with him and retrieve Manny's debt. Gene is slippery. I understand you and him have open business. Gene went to Manny and settled for a much smaller amount, took that money and paid up to his *Bratan* Bobby Tiger. Tarzan was completely cut out. Now he's trying to force his way back in." Pushka sat in the chair next to me and held up his glass.

I clicked glasses with him and devoured the fluid inside.

"So what now, Alex?" I asked.

"Now..." he paused. "Now I teach you how people handle these things," he stated. "Tarzan tried to take away from his *Bratan*, his rightfully deserved cut of money. He is wrong. He gets nothing. And if not for current circumstances..." Alex paused again, this time raising his right middle finger to his jugular vein.

I gulped.

"Relax, Grisha. I cannot afford that now, I'm about to lose another *Bratan* for at least three years. Luck has smiled on him today. Regardless, I'm putting Tarzan back with you. He is your people. Control your people. Make sure this never happens again. I will not be happy with you if it does. As for the Hasid, Gene had no authority to act on behalf of the brotherhood. He didn't counsel with his *Bratan* in advance. This makes any dealing invalid. Manny owes the full debt, plus interest for late payment. 150,000$. Explain this to him persuasively, Alex instructed. "And if he disagrees?" I asked with a smile.

"I said *persuasively*, Grisha."

WE ENJOYED ANOTHER *L'CHAIM* AND SAT BACK FOR A MOMENT.

"The money will be divided as follows. You receive forty points. twenty points will go to me, and the final forty will be passed on to Bobby Tiger. Tarzan gets to live another day. He should be grateful for that," Alex said. "Tiger, what's he got to do with this?" I queried. "I'll tell you what," Alex answered a bit angered, "When the debt occurred, Tarzan was under the *krisha* of Bobby. He owes Bobby his fair share." | "But forty points? Isn't that a little much?" I demanded.

"Give this to him, Grisha, he is in the right. If he wants, he can take all of it. I spoke to him and asked that he be fair with you. Besides, he's going to bunk with his father for the next three years. He needs a bone right now," Alex insisted.

"Prison?" I inquired. "He's a soldier. He can take it. Good timing. His partner, Trigger, is almost home. He'll be in charge of The Tulips for now." Alex sprawled back into the recesses of the small leather chair. "Pour us another drink, Grisha," he commanded.

"I need Kalil with me. He's also my people, and with Bobby gone, he'll just be on idle," I stated.

Alex was silent again.

"I will do this for you, Grisha. Kalil is a talented man, perhaps he is better with you. But you do something for me." He smiled. "Bobby has been educating an Albanian. I like this child very much. He is like a second son to me. It would be a shame to waste his schooling. Take him with you for a short time and finish his studies. I will make all the arrangements," Alex confirmed "Thank you, Alex," I said as I stood to exit. "Finish your drink," he insisted | I thought of Pappy as I picked up my drink for our final toast of the night.

"For unconditional love," Alex avowed.

"To the Brotherhood," I answered.

"One more thing, Grisha." He sat back down behind his desk and clicked on the screen. It was a colorful hazy blur of sharpness to my inebriated glimpsers. "This thing you have with your friend, Terry, it's embarrassing to me. He's at Hanover-Sterling (a boiler-room brokerage run by the Genovese cartel) now making a loud noise over how he disrespected the Russians. He is starting rumors like one of those old grandmothers waiting to die. Help him with this," Alex stated coldly, his eyes already attached to the screen.

"With pleasure," I answered.

"I'll see you tomorrow at the office. *Goodbye Cousin.*" Alex Pushka snickered.

* * *

FOR THE TIME.

Kalil would adopt the role of my driver and closest confidant.

"I need you to find Lucy, my old sales-assistant. Start by looking at her mother's house. Be mellow when you talk to her family. We don't wanna scare her off. Just find out where she's at, then we'll make our play," I charged.

"About this Manny fucker, we're gonna see him first thing tomorrow morning. First we need to pick up some supplies," I continued, directing Kalil to take the Brooklyn Bridge into Greenwich Village then to a magic shop next to the NYU annex building.

I had roughly twenty dimes in cash left.

Hardly enough to run the shop for a week, but more than sufficient to hash out a plan so I could triple my cheddar then double that with some OG's.

My mother held my twenty while I sat.

We stopped there first.

I left Ace in the vehicle.

Though I wasn't strapped, she knew what time it was—*a mother always knows*—nonetheless, she was happy to see me. I sat with her for a moment and we drank some of her wonderful Earl Gray tea.

We reached the magic shop close to midnight.

In the city that never sleeps | The night was still young.

I entered the store, purchased the required supplies and, within minutes, placed the five large bags in the trunk of my Yukon.

I instructed Kalil to park in a pay-for lot around the West 4th area and meet me in one of the bars across from the shop. We kicked it there till daybreak, swigging on vodka, sniffing YaY, and simulating a feeling of satisfaction.

I awoke early the next day (around eleven) with both a stunning hangover and a strange woman in my bed. Kalil was in the other bedroom in a similar condition.

We sent the ladies home via taxi and hollered at Little Gabe.

"Meet at the kebab-house on Coney Island Ave and Ave K. in two hours. We going to that dance today. Everyone's invited. Real fancy place, so dress appropriate. Dress your best,[4]" Kalil announced cheerily. I asked for the phone. "Hey, Gabby, you know this guy, Jerry Albania. I got a special invite for him. His cousin really wants him to be there. Make that happen," I said. "On it, Gunny," he replied.

KALIL AND I PULLED UP AT THE KEBAB HOUSE AT AROUND ONE P.M.

Most of the crew were waiting on us.

We sat at the corner of the storefront in a collage of small metal tables that had been pushed together to form a large one. It was an old run-down establishment. The mauve colored paint had long begun to chip from the edges of the wall. There was a small stage towards the rear of the eatery, adjacent to it a tiny bar. At the very rear left corner, the entrance to the kitchen.

What the place really was — A Washeteria for a majority of the more prominent Georgian brotherhoods.

The whole place stunk of decay and hostility.

It was rare that a member of an Odessan organization was given entry into a Georgian establishment | I was the exception.

While the ambiance may have been unpleasant, the kebabs were excellent, and it provided a quiet means of assembling my *brigada* and hashing out my plans discreetly.

I inhaled the aroma of charcoal and burnt meat.

The owner of the place, a friend of Pappy's was heavily connected to Georgian brotherhoods.

He stumbled out to greet me with a hug and kiss on the lips.

He was a short, olive-skinned man dressed in 1970s Russian-style formal wear. An expensive gold nugget clock decorated his aging wrist | *While he may have been short in stature,* he was great in power.

He looked a lot like Stalin, and reminded me of a happy Roman dictator, cheering as unlucky peasants were ripped apart by lions | All for his pleasure.

++||— *All for his amusement* —

"Tarzan, I'll deal with you later" I stated. "You know what you did. Don't worry. You're gonna walk out of this OK." I barked.

I screened the table.

Little-Gabe, Kalil, La-Onda Mark, Letno, Arthur Animal, Kazuole, Sloan, Fat-Dima, Tarzan, Bugsy and Jerry Albania were all present and accounted for. "Where's Movemaker?" I questioned. "Nobody could reach him," L-G replied. "He a faker, Hard-Gunz. Last time we did work, he ran out the room and pissed himself," Letno said.

"I'll tell our cousin he couldn't make it," I said.

Letno laughed. "Cousin knows he's a clown, we keep him around like a mascot." Kazuole, a thin young-looking, dark-haired Russian, poured our cups full of potion. "Just as well then, brothers." I stated cooly "For everyone who don't know, Jerry the Albanian is gonna be riding with us until further notice. Raise your glasses for him," I demanded.

"To long life, happiness, and unconditional love," I said.

"*The Brotherhood,*" everyone replied in unison.

"From now until forever, I decree Jerry our brother—*I will never regret or take back these words I say*—This is the law." I walked over to Jerry grabbed his arm and pulled him in close for a hug then kissed him once on both his cheeks. "Welcome, brother."

The group cheered.

I pointed at the bottle of Absolut next to my plate of kebabs. "Pour another for Conny in the clink, come home soon brother."

The instant our glasses touched the table, Little Gabe poured a third glass full of elixir. "A moment of silence for our fallen brothers," he said dourly.

"Today, brothers, we take our respect from the Hasid Manny. This man has accrued a very large debt. It's time we give him a past-due notice," I said. "Tarzan's gonna take us up to his office, then we're gonna explain to this man that taking from the Red Army is like taking from yourself. It's a lose-lose situation," I finished.

"Gunny, I already told you, the place is full of cameras, security, and all that shit. Even if we get close enough to him to take out his bodyguards, he'll see us coming and slip out a back door. He's just gonna run, especially if we come with this kind of force," Tarzan said.

"Yeah. You're probably right. Let's forget about the whole fuckin' thing and let him keep our 150Rocks. *Fuck*, we might as well bend over and stick out our assholes for every other worthless loser to fuck our ass," I said, holding my head down towards the table.

I put my hand on my chin.

"Now that I think about it, we should all go to the six-o[5] walk up to the desk Sarge and turn in our gats—*forget about all this shit here.* Let's get jobs as shoemakers and cab drivers, start paying our taxes, and voting for congress." I said.

Agitated, I stood up.

"Why don't you just shut your fucking ugly face before I break your lips. Just do what you're told," I commanded. I poured Tarzan a glass of potion and waved him to the rear of the table.

"KALIL, GET THE BAGS."

Before I could finish, he jumped to his feet and moved hastily to the Yukon then quickly returned with the bags I purchased from the magic shop — I dumped their contents onto the table, exposing three costumes complete with dark coats, black Miller dress hats, fake side curls, and three kits for fake beard and mustache appliqués.

"When in Rome brothers..." I laughed "We fuck the Romans in the face." I went on to describe the plan. "You understand now what I'm talking about. Tarzan takes us to the spot, and we infiltrate inside, dressed like Hasidic Jews, we should be able to get far enough past his security to cut off his oxygen.

"Me, Letno, and Jerry Albania dress up and get inside. Jerry and Letno, y'all neutralize the help. I'm going straight for bossman. Once we're clear, we'll buzz up the rest of you. Nobody dies if nobody has to die," I started distributing the gear.

· · ·

"ALBANIA, YOU HOLDIN' IRON?" I INQUIRED.

Jerry lifted his dark sweater, revealing a black rubber grip.

"That'll do just fine, better not be afraid to pull. Do-or-die time, homeboy," I stated.

I handed Tarzan one of the cheap white paper sheets that were used as placemats and he quickly drew the layout of the office area, the regular position of the guards and the approximate location of the safe —The three of us carefully put on our disguises | We started toward the office of the Hasidic Jew known as Manny R.

* * *

THERE WERE FOUR AUTOS IN OUR CARAVAN.

My Yukon took the lead position. Kalil drove and Letno rode shotgun while I sat in the back with a skittish young Jerry Albania.

"First time, Jerry?" I asked. "Nah, Gunny. I been with Bobby on a few jobs, but he always kept me driving. I never went inside," he stated. I moved closer to Jerry and whispered, "You know how they say it gets easier every time you do it?" "Yeah," Jerry replied.

"*It don't* | It's the same fucking shit. Every time you do, it's another stone on your soul | It damages you more, every time," I lamented.

"You sure you wanna do this, fam?" It was a rhetorical question and an outright lie. All of us were already dressed out *for our dance with the fiendish demons of red* — There was no backing out.

Still, it sounded nice to say.

Real humanitarian.

"NAH, GUNNY, I'M IN," JERRY SAID.

"Good, good," I said. I placed my hand on Albania's shoulder and squeezed. He was sweating so bad his fake beard nearly slid off. "Don't worry so much. We all do what we must," I stated affectionately.

We reached Borough Park.

We parallel-parked, in the mostly Hasidic neighborhood. It was a run-down, fairly deserted part next to the L-tracks.

There was a schoolyard nearby.

We stopped near a three-story tenement flanking our target structure. I instructed my *brigada* to follow closely behind, but not within detection — A*nd, in the event of gunfire,* to introduce extreme prejudice. We entered through a hole in the chain-link fence which ended in a gated opening.

The entry was open and unguarded.

I led us through a small graveyard of wrecked autos and various car and truck parts at the center of the lot; weeds and other plants grew within the carcasses.

To the right, a busy auto repair shop with four open bay doors. Noises of pneumatic mechanic's tools shattered the silence.

Directly past the shop, a large steel-reinforced metal door lead into a three-story brick structure, which housed our mark. As we approached the door, a bulky video camera encased in a fortified enclosure swiveled towards us.

I rang the bell.

Almost instantly, a squawky voice came over the intercom. "Who is it," it demanded. "*Svayee* ("friends of yours")," I replied.

The door buzzed open.

"It worked. OK let's move quick," I whispered.
We darted up the stairs, Letno and Albania led the way, blasters

on the ready—I quick walked behind them. My heart pounded fiercely, with every step up, it thumped harder and harder.

At the top of the feeble stairs was a cramped office space.

Five small desks, papers scattered atop, filled the area. There was a larger manager's desk towards the right, behind it was a door, and another door towards the left side. Two sullied windows faced brick walls. An appealing young woman wearing traditional Jewish garb sat at the desk facing the staircase | Two middle-aged Russians dressed in dark clothing and leather coats were seated behind desks.

Letno straight pointed his Ruger at the first of the men.

"Stand the fuck up both of you. Real slow," he commanded. "I said get the Fuck up, I'll Fucking kill you," Letno screamed.

Albania trained his revolver on the terrified woman.

I didn't know who was more terrified | Her or Albania.

I entered last, ripping off my fake beard and mustache. Nearest the door, a pale-skinned balding, bearded national with incisive blue eyes slowly reached for something inside his desk. He reminded me of *"Uncle Fester"*. "He's going for a gat," I shouted.

The woman started crying.

Letno's finger on the trigger.
++||— Squeezed it —

Bullets started flying.

The first scraped Festers' shoulder. The next landed right in Uncle Festers chest. The recoil launched him from his chair and sent him flying into the desk directly behind him | Blood spurt from his side in a laceration style pattern.

Without hesitation Letno pointed his blaster at the Russian2theRight | *He immediately stood,* both hands raised. "Get on the floor, face down, both of you" Letno commanded. In moments, Russian2theRight and the Jewess were in the center of the room, lying face down on the floor.

I looked down at the two.

"Where's Manny?" I asked. "I'm gonna ask nice this one time. Then it won't so nice." I said.

Festers' blood was starting to pool around the them.

The monitor on the reception desk flashed images of both the front and back doors. The *brigada* gathered at the front awaiting entry. I motioned to Albania — He quickly depressed a button below the desk. "Hey, look at this." He pulled up a sawed-off, nine-inch single-barrel Mossberg with a modified stock that was suspended from the bottom of the desk with Velcro. "Give it here," I sneered as Albania tossed it over. Jerry searched the desks, opening drawers and scattering papers about the quarter. He recovered two more burners, a snub-nose .38 and semi-auto S&W 9mm.

Little Gabe was first up the stairs.

Tarzan, Fat-Dima, and Kazuole right behind him.

"The rest are covering the shop downstairs," Little Gabe stated, slightly winded from the run upstairs. "You see this shit, Gabby?" I said, holding up the shotty. "Old girl had this under her desk, she was gonna shoot us up."

"Who's this pathetic yuk?" L-G indicated the wounded Russian laying face-up. "Looks like he got himself into a massive wreck," he continued. "We die the way we live," he said to the unconscious man before pulling out his Glock9milly and holding it up to the man's dome. "No Gabby, he's gonna bleed to death anyway. Just leave him alone," I said sharply. Little Gabe mumbled something, sheathed his gat and approached the woman.

He crouched on his knees and got closer to her face.

"Were you gonna shoot my friend, you filthy bitch?" he whispered in her ear. *Silence* | He kicked at her ribs. "I asked you something. When people speak to you, you need to answer," he said quietly.

He didn't care about her reply.

++||— *He only rejoiced in her agony* —

"That's his daughter," Tarzan shouted.

"What?" Gabby screamed, pulling the woman up by her long, dark hair. "And when were you gonna tell us about daddy?" he screamed as he dragged her by the hair towards the back room. L-G butted the woman's head against the door then kicked it open.

Tarzan and Fat-Dima followed behind.

"*Manny, oh Manny, where are you. Oh Manny, where can you be,*" L-G sang. A loud crash boomed as, I assumed, the woman was flung against the wall, then came metal crashing against metal, and finally indistinguishable gunfire.

Believing the girl shot dead, I sprinted towards the room.

Dense grey smoke made the air brittle with particles of foul speckle. She was unconscious on the floor of Manny's computer room | A pistol-whip to her temple assured it.

The server room was packed with computer terminals and seven racks of complex infrastructure equipment entangled in an octopus of wires. They led into a satellite relay system in the rear right corner of the tiny room then to the outside through a two-foot hole in the brick. Tarzan toppled one of the racks, causing it to crash into the tables housing the terminals and demolishing most of the pricey equipment and L-G fired two rounds into the other racks for dramatic effect.

It worked.

Manny, A frail, bearded skeleton of a man, emerged from the other door at the far end of the office.

He'd been hiding in the bathroom.

"Please, please, enough. My daughter, my beautiful daughter." He was teary eyed and almost in shock. "Don't worry, Manny, your daughter's alive. Look," I grabbed him by his collared white dress shirt and turned his head into the now destroyed server room. "More than I can say for you. You're a dead man walking if you don't bring us our money," Tarzan demanded. "Jerry, check him out," I instructed. Jerry frisked Manny head to toe. "He's clean," Jerry replied. Manny let out a sigh and straightened his blue pinstripe trousers. "I'm Gary. The guy you spoke to yesterday," I said.

Manny stared.

"I apologize for the dramatic entrance. You wouldn't meet me at the café. I had no choice but to come to you. Let's have a seat and talk. I think we can work everything out," I encouraged. We sat facing each other, in two of his uncomfortable office chairs.

"Please, look at Victor. He's dying on the floor. Please call him an ambulance," Manny said. He spoke now with a hint of a Jewish accent I hadn't heard before.

He sounded almost sincere.

"His life is now in your hands. The faster we work this out, the quicker he gets the help he needs. Be fair, Manny, you owe me a considerable amount of paper. Bring me my 150,000$ and we can forget about all this and leave like gentlemen," I said. "Gentlemen?" Manny questioned. "You're terrorists, running into my business, harassing me and destroying my property. I'm a legitimate businessman. I have connections" Manny yelled. I looked at Tarzan and Fat-Dima, prompting F-D to deliver Manny a stern backhand.

Manny massaged his face.

"Perhaps you finally understand the dire nature of your situation," I said. "We didn't come here to hurt you. But…" I paused. "Allow me to state to you the facts." I leaned back in the chair. "Fact one, your businesses are as legitimate as mine. Aside from the phone card fraud Tarzan helped you with, we know about the immigration fraud, the sweatshops on Delancey Street, and the whorehouses on 5th and Broad | We didn't come here for a rub-and-tug.

We know you, and you probably know us," I said.

"*Pushkatzkaya.*" Little Gabe nodded.

"That's right Mr. Manny, I represent the *Pushkatzkaya* Brotherhood. Perhaps you're already familiar with our *krisha* due to your dealings with Gene T.," I continued.

"Be advised that whatever dealings you may have had with Gene are not pertinent to your original arrangement with Tarzan. These dealings were not authorized by the brotherhood. Whatever money was paid to Gene is between you and him. It has nothing to do with our business today," I affirmed."Gene told me that I covered the debt. I paid him thirty grand. You're telling me I still owe you one-hundred thousand?" he questioned. "No Manny, I'm telling you that you owe me 150,000$. You've accumulated interest for non-payment. Please don't make me repeat myself again," I stated harshly. "That thirty dimes you paid Gene is your beef with him. I just want my money," I finished, then stood to fix my trousers.

"*Now*, Where's my Fucking money?" I demanded.

"I don't keep that kind of money here, I will get it for you. Just give me a few days, and you'll have it all," Manny pleaded.

I looked to Fat-Dima — He responded with another harsh backhand to Manny's right cheekbone. "He's lying," Tarzan observed. "I should kill this motherfucker right here," he said, pointing the muzzle of his burner to the back of Manny's cranium.

Manny's daughter was beginning to regain consciousness.

Little-Gabe grabbed her hair then applied a chokehold with his left arm and placed the barrel of his blaster to her temple. "We don't need this any more than you do. We just want the money. Take us to the safe, get us the money and we leave. Look at your friend on the floor, he's dying for fuck's sake. Look at your daughter. It's not worth it," I said.

"*Please, Daddy, just give it to them,*" the girl whimpered.

"I don't have a safe. Just give me some time. Please," Manny repeated. "Is money really that important to you?" I said mockingly. "Dima, *convince* the gentleman," my left eye twitched slightly as I spoke. Instantly, Fat-Dima produced a SOG easy-open skinning knife with a perforated edge. He inserted the blade into Manny's thigh.

Manny screamed.

Unfortunately, his office happened to be in an area of town where screams go unnoticed. F-D pulled the knife out and blood gushed from Manny's leg.

I looked over at his daughter—She was still crying.

"OK, OK. Take whatever you want. Please, just go." Manny hobbled over to the safe, reached for a hidden latch in the carpeting and exposed its face to the open air. A few tense moments passed as he dialed the combination then opened the door to a midsize MS1D drop safe.

"This fucker's loaded," Tarzan announced.

I pushed Manny aside and moved over to the unit. Inside, freshly minted Benjamin's, still in their 10,000$ bank-issued separators totaling 325Rocks.

I quickly counted 150,000$ and returned the rest to the safe.

"What the fuck you doing, Straight-Gunz? Take it all!" Tarzan exclaimed. "That would put us in the wrong. We didn't come here to rob Manny. We came here to collect. That's it. Let's ride," I announced, watching as my *brigada* piled out and I closed the rear.

I threw a ten-thousand-dollar stack on Manny's lap before exiting his office. "For Victor," I stated.

It would either pay for a hospital or his funeral.
He gets what he got — *The game is the game.*
++||— Only the players change —

WE MARCHED OUT OF THE COMPOUND—*A CHORUS OF laughter.*
It was a great day.

None of us had to die.

Somewhere past the chain-link fence, Albania puked up his lunch. It was the last time I would see him show any form of weakness.

*   *   *

WHAT CAN I SAY: THE NEXT FEW YEARS WENT BY RAPIDLY.

GeorgiVodka mixed with Trees+YaY created a hazy fog of nightclubs, gunplay, and sleazy women of every variety. A slimy blur that I either wish to not remember or as much as I try | I just can't.

We put our heads down and went to work.

Work of all sorts | Gambling, extortion, weapons, drugs, but mainly stock schemes and other forms of white collar crime | That was our real bread and butter.

We were ✧ to Stocks
✧ *Like keys were to locks* ✧

Although time passed quickly — It did not go smoothly.

December '98, I sent Kalil and Bugsy to Florida to control and maintain a large hydroponics marijuana growing operation that had originally been started by former TF members a few years prior.

Kalil headed there—on my request—to make sure we were getting our fair share. He remained there for four years (until the DEA finally pinched him) — It became a fundamental element of the Red Army netting us on the average twenty-five-thousand monthly.

I convinced Lucy, my former sales assistant;

To rejoin the team making cream.

We now consisted of eighteen cold-callers and a giant cache of losers buying phony stocks from us daily.

The federals got Bobby Tiger the good one.

He was already well into his first year of incarceration. Law Enforcement had been gathering evidence against Bobby for years, putting together sealed indictments, really doing their due diligence.

Shame they could never get anything to stick. Folks were just plain old scared of Bobby. And with good reason— *Bobby was for real.*

You know what they say: A scared witness is a blind witness.

They feds needed to get crafty.

They set up a sting for Bobby that they knew he would fall for.

He favored a local Russian nightclub named BLOW as an outlet for his heroin distribution and kept a small office in the back. The feds sent in a confidential informant wearing a wire.

They knew Bobby was too savvy to fall for an easy trap. So they came up with something else. Instead of the informant attempting to broker a deal with Bobby and get him pinched for intent to distribute, they made the mook go inside and hit on his wife.

Bobby ran out the back room with a cattle prod and almost beat the poor louse to death | The feds rushed inside in their usual grandiose style, heaters out, shotguns, dogs, donuts—*Everything.*

They got Tiger on more charges than a DeWalt Battery Pack.

Interfering with an investigation; witness tampering; attempted murder (of said witness), and finally the ever-popular resisting-arrest. Although my personal favorite was assault on a federal agent—he got that one for spitting right in the lead investigator's face.

The feds didn't have a great case | It was entrapment.

Beating the charges meant walking out free and clear. Losing meant a minimum of 20sticks. The feds have a 97% conviction rate. *Why bother?* When they offered him a plea deal of three years — He took it.

Me | I was the invisible man.
Every time the feds got close to me, RJ would tip me off.
We'd burn everything down to the ground.
Then move the fuck around.

In return, I steered him towards enemies he could easily lasso and look like the hero. We set him up with some expensive trim, and squashed any gambling debts he incurred at our numerous parlors.

RJ keyed us into some very interesting loopholes.

He was also instrumental in setting up a gun running operation from the Midwest. With RJ's information, we procured, on average, between fifteen and thirty weapons a month. I paid him a small fee for every burner we imported into NYC — It worked out well for everyone.

I had RJ on the lookout for Terry D.

Terry had been working with the Italians for years and was becoming more of an annoyance every day. He was a real earner for the Genovese, his operation netting on average 100-150Rocks a month. They surrounded him with bodyguards. That all made Terry a pretty hard man to touch. Guido Vinny was still driving for him.

We'd unsuccessfully attempted to snuff him near his favorite brothel on 5th Ave | Amateurs handled the work.

Guido spotted the team and quickly snatched Terry into his Lincoln stretch and somehow | *They got away.*

++||— In Retaliation —

We found Little Gabe's body Inside the dumpster at one of our Manhattan offices. He was *twenty-five years old* when he died.

++||— *Salute* — Gabby
❣ YOU DIED THE WAY THAT YOU LIVED ❣
Hope you find lasting Peace.
Hope *you find* Truth *my brother.*

THREE WEEKS LATER.

We discovered Letno's charred body, burned to death in an "accidental" house fire at his Staten Island residence. We suspected these to be the actions of another Russian brotherhood.

Letno shacked up with the daughter of a prominent gangster whose name—for the purposes of insuring that I continue to remain in the realm of the living—I won't mention.

Daddy didn't approve of the couple and warned Letno on several occasions to leave it alone. When the father heard they were about to elope.

He decided to *handleIt.*

Letno was *twenty-seven* when he passed
✠ HIS HAND CLUTCHED HIS GAT WHEN THEY FOUND HIM ✠

* * *

THE LONGER TERRY AND GUIDO WERE STILL SUCKING UP AIR:
++||— *The deeper my fury ran —*

It didn't stop me from fucking with him.

I had a special bullet made for him—a custom .45caliber replica that was about the size of shotgun slug. I sent it out to a jeweler in the diamond district to be dipped in 24karat gold and custom engrave his name in fancy writing on the casing.

Then another artist (a former member of TF), who owned a small t-shirt shop in Greenwich Village painted a picture of Terry with his brains blown out the back of his head on the same shell.

I had the bullet put in a plush velour box, the expensive kind you get for an engagement ring, then messengered up to his office.

Around the same time we found out about Letno.
I MET MY FUTURE WIFE | Tamara.
My mother introduced us.

An attractive young Russian girl who didn't speak too much English, she'd only recently arrived from Odessa Russia (eight years before we met) and was still very naïve. She was seventeen when we went on our first date. I wasn't looking for a wife or even a girlfriend at the time | That's how it usually happens.

When you're not looking.

She wasn't Mila Kunis.
But she definitely didn't hurt the glimpsers.

I brought her to my condo apartment.
An upscale two-bedroom condo with a terrace that overlooked the ocean in a predominantly Russian area of town, fairly close to Brighton Beach.

Tamara didn't give in to my advances.

But we did see each other again.
Only because I gave her an extra cell phone I kept around the house. Tamara came from a poor family that could never afford such an expensive item.

The trinket fascinated her.

She took it, and so began our courtship. Later on, she told me that she only saw me again to return the phone. By then, I wooed her with my charm and humor.

Translation: I bought her *expensive shoes* and *designer handbags*.

I told her I was a stockbroker, a business owner, and an investor. It wasn't long before she found out that I was, in fact, a criminal, a conniver, and a scoundrel—*She always knew*—I drank a little more than a lot | We started living together in the beginning of 1999.

Tamara was in her last year of high school.

I was in my last year of securities fraud.

Lawmen had become increasingly wise to our pump and dump.

By the latter half of '99, common stock fraud and 504(d) private-placement deals became so rampant among the brotherhoods, the government had no choice but to shut it down.

Soon after opening an office, setting up shop, and manipulating the paper | *The feds were already onto us.*

They were like a dark rain cloud that followed you everywhere. No matter what—*We couldn't shake them.* Nobody was making any cream — Including the Cousin. Life had become a perpetual state of paranoia, constantly watching our backside — We were all at each other's throats. We had to do something with the quickness, before we murdered each other for scraps | It was a dangerous time.

I walked around with a boulder on my shoulder.
Streets were cold.
It was a cold war.
And I was a cold soldier.

It was either go to prison time *or* Time4SomethingNew.

Tarzan had that covered.

He invited me to his Staten Island town home, located close to the dump, to help him bury a box of hand grenades in his backyard.

There, we hatched plans for a new white-collar fraud. Tarzan had the paperwork tucked away, neat and nice in a yellow manila envelope | *All professional like.*

One look, I knew straight off.
Like *Steve motherfuckin Winwood.*
++||— We were back in the high life again —

LISTEN CLOSE OR YOU MIGHT JUST MISS IT | IT'S A HEARTBREAKER.

Prior to our involvement (destruction) of the currency trading market. It was completely unregulated.

I mean this here baby was a virgin.

What is the currency market?

A very valid and interesting question.

The currency trading market also known as the FOREX (FX) exchange is a legitimate marketplace where substantial money can be made, or in my case... Lost|EVERYTHING|Lost

As a matter of fact, it's the largest marketplace in the world, with over 1.8 trillion$ changing hands every day. Making money in currency trading happens the same way it's done in any other market, on speculation.

The devil here is in the details.

If you're new to the market, here's a brief synopsis of how it works:

The FX market allows you to buy and sell currencies against each other and speculate on the differences in exchange rates. These rates may be influenced by world economic and political events, currency rate differentials, as well as many other factors including extreme weather conditions (hurricanes), acts of terror, et cetera.

Making a transaction on the Foreign Exchange Market is simple. The procedures are identical to that of any other market.

Here's the relevant real-deal Holyfield.

Let's say you go on vacation to Mexico for instance.

You know how they always say you can buy things like silver and leather jackets cheaper in Mexico | Well, it's true.

You know why? Cause your American dollar is worth much more in Mexico. It's worth more due to the rate of exchange between the dollar and the peso — The currency exchange rate is in a constant state of flux. Even if the change that occurs is in fractions of a penny, it still means a whole lot if you're entirely based on exchanging currencies for the fractions of pennies that make up the difference.

That's all nice and well and everything — That is, it might|could be, If we were ever interested in making money for anybody other than ourselves, Jake the Jeweler, the Merc dealership—*most importantly*—the Dopeman.

What we really had was a vehicle that permitted us to go back to the same skells that bought our worthless dogshit stock and pitch them this new currency garbage—*It was something they'd never heard of before*—Something that was so sexy a sell that they practically begged for it.

The beauty for us was two-fold.

The obvious fact that the market is unregulated means that the SEC, NASD, Attorney General, and every other nameless federal agency are rendered impotent to our involvement.

Unregulated means just that:
No regulations of any kind.

We didn't have to buy up floats.
There was no outside market-maker to bribe.
No waiting for the fathead lawyers to file papers.
Absent was the Hasidic bagman with his pouch of *shekels.*
There wasn't a 50-50, 60-40, or even 70-30 cut with shady promoters.
There was only ++||— All4UsandNone4You —

Once we positioned an investor into units of currency, they had no way to check on their investment. It's not like you were able to look in the newspaper and check the exchange rates of the Yen in comparison to the Ruble — Nope, all they had was our monthly statement. I'm sure it would not surprise you to know, *that every single month*, without fail, they were in the green. Yeah, them, me, my *brigada*, and especially | Cousin Alex Pushka.

We owned this thing 100%, soup to nuts.

It didn't have to go to zero until we said it did.

So who do you turn to, when you finally figure out you lost everything? The answer is *nobody*. That's exactly what the first mo-mo's deduced. Right after they gave us all their money and they lost everything | 1MoreAgain.

They called the FBI and were told that it's outside their jurisdiction then instructed to call the SEC who told them that this was not a stock so they in fact need to call on the FBI. And right around the time that lawmakers got to figuring out the what's and how's of it all:

++||— *Every last one of us* did the Keyser Söze —[6]

When I first showed Pushka the paperwork that contained the prototype currency scam, he was skeptical. As a matter of fact, he was downright apprehensive. He didn't think it was going to work. Pushka felt that individual investors, after taking a massive beating on common stock, would never buy into something like this.

It just sounded too good to be true.

JANUARY 2000 — ALL BUSINESS HAD COME TO A HALT.

Pushka had no choice but to let me run with it.

After Mayor Rudy cleaned up New York's Italian criminal element. He put his sights on just about every other form of crime. White, black, green collar | He nary cared. Mayor Rudy needed warm bodies locked in jail-cells.

That included us.

Pushka put up front money for a small office in Staten Island.

It allowed six for employees. He gave six months to turn over a minimum of half-a-million$. I was held personally accountable. I tapped Tarzan, Fat-Dima, Fred-Lover, and three rookie callers.

We named the front "RidgeCrest Capital."

It made us sound like we were the best thing since pickled herring | Truth is — *We were.*

MARCH '00.

We were roughly two months into our currencies operation and we had already thumped out over 700,000$.

For a long while, things weren't too great financially and people kept dying | *Fortunes change so quickly when you're living on street-time.*

A quarter of 8p.m., I arrived at Gambrino's restaurant to commemorate my twenty-fifth birthday | Tamara was at my side.

It was her first introduction to the brotherhood.

I was leery showing her this side of me. But we were starting to get serious, and I thought it was time for her to inhale some reality.

About twenty of my *brigada*, ten or so members of the Black Tulips, and RJ had gathered to greet me and gift me blessings.

Cousin Alex was expected to arrive later in the evening, seeing as how I had a sack of money for him to count.

Bobby Tiger grabbed me at the door.

He'd been out of club-fed for only a few months and already heavily back in the game. I told him to bring his wife to keep with Tamara while we talked business. "Gary 2Gunz, looks like you did it brother." Bobby cheerily kissed me on the lips to salute me.

I laughed. "Just doin' what I do, baby. Truth is Tarzan's the one who cooked it up. We're just making our play. Like Bo and Luke. The only way we know how."

Bobby and Tarzan had long since reconciled.

"Tell me Gunny, how the fuck do you get the cheese on this thing. I mean, I understand the selling part, but how is it that you pull the cash out?" Bobby whispered, directing me towards the bar where two tall porcelain cups of vodka were awaiting us.

"It's easy, Bobby. Real old-school," I replied already gulping down most of my potion. "The trick here is associations. Cousin Al wanted us to do the whole thing for self. He said he needed to see that it worked before he took a major role in it. We needed to outsource a little," I sneered as I downed the remainder of the liquid and slammed the empty container on the table, demanding more.

"Fat-Dima has a connect with a check cashing (run by the Genovese). We get the checks sent to a dummy office in the city. We send in number8 to pick up packages every week and cash 'em. Now that Cousin sees the payoff I can turn everybody on—Одесса Мама" I proclaimed.

"You did good Large-Gunz. This is a real winner," Bobby said, his arm around my shoulder. He led me into a small area in the back, where there was a table piled with gifts.

Just before entering, he whispered a final warning to me.

"Look here Gunny. Your cop friend, he's running up a serious marker with me and my man George there," he stated, glancing at the Gambino button man.

"How bad is it?" I asked. "He's into us for over fifty Rocks. That's just this month. I know you've been covering him for a while. But things are slow as fuck. We need him to slow down a little," Bobby stated grimly. "The way I see it, RJ is a fucking investment. Especially now that we're ready to take the fuck over —*we need him now more than ever*—Besides, you know he's bringing in the iron for us," I replied. "I understand Gunny. I do. Please, just tell him to chill for now. George is asking." Bobby nodded.

"I got it. No worries," I said confidently.

We raised our glasses to toast and I looked over at Tamara.

She looked like she fit right in with the pack. Tamara had come a long way from the poor immigrant I discovered. I dressed her up real classy, Gucci, Chanel, Prada | She looked knockout stunning.

TWENTY PAST TEN.

We were all righteously loaded—full of booze and pharmaceuticals. "Speks, look who I found lingering outside," RJ slurred. His arm was around the familiar face of an old friend Vance. "Fucking-A bro, where the fuck you been hiding at buddy?" I shouted, embracing my estranged comrade.

The hardened group around me scanned him uneasily.

"He's alright, brothers," I confirmed.

I grabbed Vance by the shoulder and took him into the small bar area away from the crowd then directed the barman to pour us some potion. "For real Vance, where you been?" I demanded. "Here and there. I been wandering around trying to make it. Went back to school for a while. Didn't go too good so I went back to Cali, but I missed it here so I came on back," he said merrily.

I scanned him closely.

Although he dressed well, he looked dirty.

Not obviously so, more like a hidden dirt, the kind of grime that builds up under your fingernails and you can't get rid of easily.

"So what brings you out here to see me buddy. How the fuck did you find me anyways?" I inquired. "That's the thing Gary. I didn't come for me, I came for Terry. Remember him?" He said evenly.

"What in the fuck are you talking about?" I demanded.

Within seconds, Vance hopped back, reached into the front of his fresh jeans and pointed a rubber grip .357 snub-nose to my forehead.

It was the perfect moment for him to smoke me | The door was no more than twenty feet to his left and everyone else was in the other room. His hand shook — *He hesitated.*

I grabbed the revolver and threw it on the ground.

He just stood there shocked for a moment, as if an old camera reel had suddenly stopped to some macabre black&white picture-show immediately after the horrible ending.

I pulled Ace from the backside of my trousers and struck him once on the temple | *Purple blood* spilt from his skull.

I grabbed my friend Vance by his thick black locks and flung him into the other room, his body hit the chair-rail on the side, and he fell hard to the sullied tile floor. "This motherfucker just tried to kill me," I screeched, kicking Vance in the sternum.

"Kill the music!" I barked.

At once, Fat-Dima and Tarzan ran towards me. Fred Lover was

already switching on the lights. "This cocksucker just tried to shoot me in the other room. I snatched his pistol. This piece of shit was supposed to be my friend!" I announced, stunned.

There were more than a few blasters pointed at Vance.

He squirmed on the floor. "I'm sorry Gary," he cried. "Shut the fuck up," I howled, kicking him again in the ribs. Bobby-Tiger retrieved his .357 from the other room and brought it over to me. "Look at this Gunny. I took the shells out, and you gotta see this," he bellowed | Tiger spilled the slugs into my palm.

They were painted in the same fashion as the one I had delivered to Terry. Every of them had my name etched and painted in red.

"Get her outta here, for fuck's sake," I demanded

He and Fat-Dima gabbed Tamara and took her jacket from the coat-check counter. She had witnessed the entire event. *Tamara didn't cry or scream in fright*—She just kept her head down and walked out calmly. Before leaving, I noticed her cold, glazed-over eyes | Heartless and unmoved.

It frightened me.

"GET HIM IN THE BACK," I DEMANDED.

The rest of the brothers grabbed Vance by his pants and shirt collar and dragged him to the small dark door in the very back corner of the party room. "RJ, you might wanna leave right about now," I said grimly. "Nah Gary. I think I'm gonna stay, brother," he slurred.

I sat on the worn greenish couch and stared down at my once friend. There were seven or more brothers in the room with us. "How'd you find me Vance?" I asked — *His failure to respond resulted in violent blows to the face and kicks to the groin.*

I lit a square and inhaled deeply.

"You know you're gonna die. It could be tonight or four days from now. The longer you live, the more it's gonna hurt. Let's make it fast and easy. Talk to me," Bobby said casually. George and Fred Lover started burning his neck with the tips of their cigarettes.

"Enough!" I shouted.

I sat Vance up on the couch with me. "Get him a drink," I instructed | Instantly number6 returned with some vodka.

I passed it to Vance.

"I'm so sorry, Gary. You know I never wanted to hurt you," he said as tears streamed down his cheeks. "Was that before or after you pulled the gat on him?" Bobby asked. "Chill Bobby, let him talk," I said.

"I ran into Terry a few days ago at Palladium. He looked like he was doing great. He was so happy to see me. We got stoned than he offered me a job with him. He let me stay at his place with him and Guido. I was living on couches, surfing for months. My parents kicked me out. I had nothing. I was so grateful to him. I'm so sorry Gary." Vance choked on almost every word.

"So what happened then?" I asked.

"We were getting high on coke and Special-K. That's when he offered me 10,000$ to do you. Of course I refused. He told me I owed him. Terry told me I had to do it or he'd do me. I didn't know what to do," Vance affirmed. "It's OK Vance," I said while he cried on my shoulder. "How did he find me?" I queried. "I don't know, Gary. He just told me this is where you'd be tonight," he stated. Cool, cool— Now tell me where he lives at," I said.

Vance sobbed for a long moment, then revealed the data.

I ordered the boys to cuff him.

RJ bound Vance's hands behind his back with his duty shackles. I stood from the couch and put my arm around Bobby. "We can't do him here. Too many witnesses. Barman, owner, waiters, they all seen this. Cops gonna pinch all of us," I whispered. "Ya, plus it's gonna leave a big fuckin mess." Bobby chuckled loudly.

Vance started to cry again.

"Hide the cuffs and walk him out of here. Stuff him in Lover's trunk. Me and Lover are gonna drive to Terry office. We'll merk him the same way they did Gabby. I'll pop him twice in the face and throw him in the dumpster. You stay here and wait for our Cousin. Tell him it's all gravy," I whispered.

We paused for a few final *L'chaim's.*

HALF PAST ELEVEN.

We pulled out of the restaurant — High as paratroopers—Me especially, I hadn't slept in days.

Fred lover and I drove in virtual silence to Terry's Wall Street office | By the time we made the turn at Rector Street, my heart was pounding so hard, it almost came up through my throat. I swigged from my pint of Georgi and sniffed a hearty bump of flake off my truck key. Fred did the same. We stopped next to an escalator located in the middle of two corporate tower.

The street was empty.

I quickly exited the vehicle and fast-walked towards the backside as Fred Lover pushed on a button right under the left side of the instrument cluster — The trunk popped open and a nearly comatose Vance begged for his life. Fred wasn't there to hear it. He waited in the car. "You're gonna need to trust me, buddy." I assured Vance. "Just get up and walk out with me," I whispered. As we neared the dumpster he panicked and screamed for help. I couldn't afford to get pinched.

With the butt of my pistol—*I cracked Vance hard*—in the back of his head.

His knees buckled and he dropped to the floor.

I sheathed Ace and grabbed Vance by his hair, pulling him to face level. The undersized dumpster was almost filled to the top and already open, it reeked of foulness — It didn't take much *to tip him over inside of it.* RJ didn't need his NYPD handcuffs turning up on a stiff. *I unshackled Vance then took a last look around.*

"OK Vance, its nap time," I said.

"Make sure I never see you again," I whispered in his ear.

I fired my blaster twice. The shots shattered the night stillness with violent acuteness. Neither bullet hit him — *They weren't meant too.*

"Peel out of here fast," I shouted.

We took a side-street shortcut to the bridge and cleared it in minutes.

It felt strange and cold
++||— *All of it did* —

Ψ — Ψ — Ψ

———————————————

1.
2.
3.
4.
5.
6. Keyser Söze: The villain in the movie *The Usual Suspects*.

12

CRUEL SUMMER

Hot summer streets, and the pavements are burning
   I sit around
   Trying to smile, but the air is so heavy and dry
   Strange voices are saying—things I can't understand
   It's too close for comfort
   This heat has gone right out of hand
-Bannanarama

THE EARLY WEEKS OF NOVEMBER 2000,

I returned from Jamaica a few days prior. Tamara and I had *a wonderful honeymoon.*

                   We were no longer starving for bread.

OUR CURRENCY SCHEME WORKED BETTER THAN ANYONE HAD EXPECTED.

After the prototype reaped more than significant benefits, Cousin

Alex green-lighted a full-scale—*Medieval*—SwordSwingLikeConan operation. Cousin took all the 700k we raised on the RidgeCrest fraud and—using the affluence of his more astute partners—flipped it into a plush two-story office space in mid-town Manhattan.

This here was the perfect front.

We filled it with all sorts of wonderful eye-catchers. Company logos were everywhere. Wall-mounted flat-panel big screens, hand-crafted wood furnishings, block paneled walls and ceilings — The place looked more for real than the Lehman Bros. flagship office.
We figured it like this:

If It's *really* our goal to defraud and steal:
Why-the-fuck-not just steal every single thing we can?

It goes a little something like this right here:
We fabricate a phony track record and financials, then hit the pavement and recruit every single broker we know, from every single legit company on the street.
Once we showcase the office and pitch them the product, we easily con(vince) them to bring their entire book of clients and flip everyone into our "for real" FOREX fund. We made this shit so appealing, any broker, registered or unregistered fell for it — Hook, line, and swindle.

++||— *They bought the entire dream* —

We had them believing that they were no longer garden-variety stock-brokers, They were "*Money Managers,*" and as "Money Mangers" the entire sales staff, worked our deals for a monthly stipend of the total sum of their client's investments as well as a percentage of the profits | It was just so simple to close *these insatiable parasites.*

Every once and again, one of the fish would inquire how it was that we were able pay them their sizable commission and still show consistent profits of 10-30% monthly. "That would be due to the virtually undervalued and untapped market and the strategic knowledge of our highly proficient trading desk," a well-dressed number8 would answer.

That would usually appease them.

Those that pressed for more information would find themselves the victims of misfortune. A broken nose via a phone to the face—*for example.* Most didn't care so long as their monthly check was accurate.

Within three months, we had just about every talented manipulator in our net. By the time I came home from Jamaica we had more than sixty reps promoting our counterfeit treachery.

First week of October.
Our sales force had put away more than *ElevenMillion*Biscuits.

The play here — We kept it real simple.
We reach 20million CashMoney.
++||— Then we *GhostFace* —

40% goes to Cousin Alex Pushka
30% to the Black Tulips.
The rest to the Red Army | Namely, *your humble friend and narrator.*

Five million GreenMoney
❊ **Одесса Мама** ❊

That was before things got complicated.

In the meantime, RA and the Tulips drew 50,000$ cash a month to cover *brigada* expenses and leave a little for the dome-piece.

I had another little something on my mind though.

Tarzan, Kazuole, Jerry Albania, La-Onda Mark, Fred Lover and Sammy Movefaker met with me at the National restaurant a few days after my return.

Fat-Dima, *Unfortunately* — He couldn't make it.

Truth be told, Fat-Dima's days of *"making it"* ended when he betrayed his brothers. A few days after Vance attempted my murder, RJ provided us with a taped recording he appropriated from the police clubhouse.

I listened, outraged, as Fat-D spoke with Special Agent BaconFace and agreed to wear a wire. "He told the Genovese where you were gonna be on your birthday, Gary. He was moving H and ecstasy for them and got pinched by the locals. He sold you out to Terry for fifty large. That's what our other snitches tell us. They offered him a hundred to do it himself. He didn't have the onions. They say he sold out Gabby, too. Told them where he'd be when they killed him," RJ informed us. "How about our new shit. He knock?" I responded anxiously. "Nah Gary. He was gettin paid big on the currency." RJ affirmed.

That was in early April '00.

Near the end of April, that same year.
We were sending flowers to his wife.

It was a beautiful service.
Good music, lots of fare.

He was Tarzan's number6, which made F-D *his* problem.
I wanted no part of it.

Rules are rules —||— *HE KNEW THE GAME* —||—

WELCOME TO BRIGHTON:
Birthplace of Killers.
Where the mothers raise their sons
To grow up *and be Guerillas.*

PROGRESSIVELY, MY USING HAD TAKEN A TURN FOR THE TERRIBLE.

I was terrified of the nightmares. The emotional violence keeps me up for weeks at a time. I got to drinking and sniffing more YaY than ever. Somewhere around this time, I discovered prescription meds. It didn't affect my hustle — Nothing *could knock my hustle.*

The dope made me feel good. It made me work harder. It gave me selective memory and a powerful feeling of control.

* * *

2:15AM NOVEMBER 9.

I was half-awake looking at movies while Tamara slept in our bed. Hard knocks to the front door of our apartment broke my calm.

Full paranoia had taken hold. I reached for my heater and crept up to the door. I assumed it was lawmen or agents coming to finally take me away.

It was far worse.

RJ bobbled inside and gave me the news.

Lou C.
"Louie Batz"
Was dead at *twenty-five years old.*
Breast Cancer | I just couldn't believe it when I heard.

373

My darling reader, *saddened*, I PRESENT IT TO YOU NOW:
The true-life-story of a principled man of virtue and character.
He married his high school sweetheart.
Never cheated, stole, or murdered.
Went to work, provided for his family, and loved his child.
The story *of a man who sought only justice and* Truth.

I know he found it.

I knew what to do — More opiates. Handfuls of Vicodin ES and Norco chased with GeorgiVodka would dull the abrasion.

The funeral was two days later.

Terry D. would be there.

I hadn't heard from Terry since the Vance encounter.
After clearing things with Cousin Alex, we dispatched a faction to the address Vance provided. They staked out the place for three days. Nobody was home. Had we know that Fat-Dima for a dirty cheese eating rat | We nary would have wasted our time.
No matter now: *Fat-Dima* was permanently on silent-mode.

And an old friend was dead.

NOVEMBER 11TH 2000.
A chilly wet start to the morning had yielded a small bit of sunshine by the time we showed at the Bensonhurst Prospero & Son Funeral Home. It was a casual non-foreboding place located near the 86th street L-tracks and across from a small car-wash.

As we drove nearer, my mind's eye filled with memories.

I reflected on the days of long past.

Cruising down the avenue in Louie's coupe.
The four of us | Me, Sandy, Lenny, Lou Batz, and Terry.
Best friends forever.

Lighthearted, completely unaware of the complexities of life and the looming defeat of innocence | It seemed like a lifetime ago.

IT HAD BECOME EXACTLY LIKE THAT OG REVEALED TO ME:
Cash ruled everything around me.
It was a terrible way to live.
But *it was my life.*
For better or worse.
++|— *Till I rested my eyes in back of a hearse* —

We drove up in a three-car caravan, most of my *brigada*, a small element of The Black Tulips, and an ambassador from the Red Fellas, a ruthless band from another *Bratva*, mostly based out of Moscow, we had dealings with.

Terry's Cadillac SUV and another four carloads of both Genovese and Bonnano family associates were already parked outside.

I instructed my people to wait in the cars on standby, grabbed Fred Lover and Tarzan, then walked up the four steps to face the towering ten-foot French doors that marked the entrance to the hall.

Two Italian wet-looking reprobate types eyeballed me. I stared back | *Tarzan mumbled something in Russian.*

++||— It was about to go live —

RJ and Ricky Kuku stepped out to cool off the tension. "Ricky. It's been a while," I noted. "Yeah it has, Gary. I hear you fellas tearing up some new shit," Ricky said. "Just makin' it, same as you. No better, no worse," I replied. Ricky Kuku, our former boss during the computer wipes scheme, was instrumental in bringing Terry D. into the inner circle of the Genovese family. He was a key player and a captain in their cartel — *There were rumors of his personal hand* in Little Gabe's murder.

I wanted to pop him right where he stood.

Today wasn't the day for any of that. I came to pay my last respects to a longtime friend and see him off right. "You know we need to fix this disagreement of ours somehow, Gunny, before it gets worse," Rick said as he stamped out his cigarette. Perhaps he was genuinely interested in squashing our beef.

Another day perhaps.

"I'll see you later Rick." I nudged my head up as RJ escorted the three of us inside.

We approached the guest log at the door of the screening room. Annie, a thin dark haired slender-cheeked woman of twenty-six years greeted me there.

Annie was Louie's wife.
I hadn't seen her for over ten years.
She was more striking now than ever.

"I'm glad you came, Gary. Terry's inside with Guido. Please Gary, I'm begging you, for Louie's sake, no trouble here." As she spoke, thick tears gushed down her rosy cheeks, blotting her eyeliner and distorting her blush. "I loved Lou, he was my heart. Annie, if there is anything I can do..." I paused and reached into the internal pocket of my black wool overcoat to produce a thick manila envelope containing ten thousand dollars and handed it her.

She stared in disgust for a second, as to reprove me for deeming Lou's life worth any form of monetary compensation whatever.

She took the money.

Annie leaned into my shoulder to hug me, she jumped back, eyes wide in disbelief. She identified the holster on the left side of my chest. "How dare you bring that inside here you son-of-bitch!" she screamed.

RJ rushed to her side to calm her.

"Get that thing out of here. Get your people out of here too. They didn't know my husband. They have no business here. How dare you bring them and that thing in here? How dare you..." she trailed off, her words dissolving into sobs. I said nothing, just stared at her for a moment longer, then handed Ace to RJ and instructed my men to wait right outside.

"I'm sorry Annie." I tried to grab hold of her. "Just say your piece and get out of here Gary," She demanded.

I nodded and went into the viewing room alone.

It was a blandly decorated area with comfortable cushioned folding chairs, two small gift tables, complicated trim and wall-to-wall paneling | Giant reefs of flowers were scattered about.

Among the flowers, positioned next to the coffin in the rear center of the hall, was the assortment I had sent.

A malicious feeling of loss loomed over me.

I approached the dark-stained mahogany coffin.

Terry D. and Guido Vinny were seated on a small bench to the right of the coffin staring bleakly in my direction.

Terry was dressed expensively, he looked aged though. Not mature. Just old and odious, as if the game had cost him more than he bargained for. I nodded to him slightly before kneeling over the small altar and looking at my compatriot.

Cancer, my dearest reader, is an equalizer.
It doesn't make friends or enemies.
Rich or poor —||— Young, old.
Cancer don't give a Fuck.
It comes and takes you when it wants | No matter who you are.

I was stunned to see Louie. A once vital and handsome man had turned into a pathetic tired shell. He was bald, from the chemo, and had withered down to under one-hundred and twenty wasted pounds.

He fought to the acidic end.

Treatment after treatment. Pain on top of pain on top of hurt on top of misery. He wanted to live — *And I just wanted to die.*

God Bless you, Louie Batz.
It's true what they say: Only the good die young.
I made myself shed a tear for him.

++||— *I had to force it* —

I sat down next to Terry and stared at Guido.

"Give us a moment," I said softly. "It's alright, Vinny. Go get us something to drink." Terry nodded. Guido, forever number6, got right up and made his way to the door.

I produced a pewter flask full of Georgi from inside my suit jacket, uncapped it, reached into my pocket and grabbed a handful of Vicodin. I tossed them in my mouth and gulped deeply from the flask before passing it to Terry.

He grabbed it and drank down a heavy mouthful.

Terry snickered. "Still drinking the same garbage?" His jovial mood soured fast. "You know, Louie always loved you more than anyone," he said coldly. "No he didn't, T. He loved us all. He loved Lenny and Sandy too," I said. "It's fucked up, all this shit between us. I know you blame me for their deaths, I can't change that. I wish I could. I wish it could be me that died for them. I hate this life Terry. I hate these phony friends, the lies and pain we have to accept, for what, a Mercedes and Rolex watch? I wish I would have known," I finished. "Yeah. I wish I would have known too," Terry said, then slumped over and looked at the ground.

I passed him my flask and he drank from it again.

"Louie knew," Terry finally said.

I chortled. "He did, didn't he? He knew all along. Look where it got him Terry. It got him dead." "Yeah, he's dead. But he's not murdered or missing. He's at peace. With a clean soul. Mine is stained," Terry said | "Mine too, Terry." I nodded.

We sat for a long while, knowing that once we got up, we would go back to being who we were.

Guido returned with a bottle of Johnny Walker Black-Label and poured four plastic Styrofoam cups full. He positioned one on the altar for Louie and poured a little on the carpet for those who'd perished prior.

"Old friends," Terry said holding up his cup.

"Good memories," I replied.

We gulped down our drinks and hugged.

Before leaving, I took off my Rolex, a two-tone submariner black-face and placed it on the altar. I looked back to see Terry do the same.

I drank heavily for the next few days and mourned my friend.

* * *

BUSINESS CONTINUED.

The *Pushkatzkaya* brotherhood moved our clubhouse to a discreet office located above the storefront to a poplar clothing retailer on Kings Highway, near the Coney Island Avenue area.

We assumed ownership of the store from Fat-Dima. He found it prudent to will the store over to Tarzan just hours before his departure.

It was a diversified place to say the least.

It served three purposes.

The first, being a legitimate retailer, allowing for the laundering of a substantial amount of money. Secondly, it was an ideal locale to hole up and hide out from wives and disenchanted mistresses. Finally, it acted as a sweatshop, producing perfect replicas of popular name-brand velour jumpsuits — We supplied them to many of the trendy retail shops on the avenue and other stylish areas.

Nearby, next to a Turkish eatery, was one of our most lucrative gambling spots. RJ and his left-hand cop buddies were regulars who kept large tabs with us.

Our principal play was the currencies trading.

It was a nuclear-explosion.

The days of the common stock scam were at a full close. Whereas before, you may have been able to scratch out a pathetic living swindling in this particular affair, as of June 15, 2000 the feds shut down the entire show[1] (or so they thought).

We were always one step ahead of the feds

The Italians got caught with their pants around their ankles. They play Bocce-Ball.

Russians play chess | We're strategists.
Most upper-echelon *Bratan's* have PhDs.

After the feds sunk their teeth into many of the Italian unfortunates, we were the only viable game in town.

Everybody was coming to us for a piece.

Into the third month of 'o1 we had just about every important brotherhood funneling their white-collar crime through us.

We opened up a second office for the influx of criminals — We needed to keep them apart from our "legitimate" agents at the headquarters.

BY MARCH 4ᵀᴴ, WE WERE WELL PAST OUR GOAL OF 20M$.

After meeting with Cousin and taking an advance of 250,000$, we determined that a new goal of forty million would be a more appropriate figure in order to make a gracious final exit stage-left.

At a glance, you could venture to say that commerce was in perfect health, our concerns were all in order, and we were cashed up to the neck bones.

It's only deep under the surface that you find the truth.
In this life | It's always like that.

You see the very fundamental basis of being the skipper is that you need to keep your crew in line. From the top down to the bottom. By "in line," I mean you can't give them too much...ever.

Cousin Alex almost never paid all cash and he never paid me on time. It just wasn't in his best interests to get me flush. The only person he was looking to make rich was himself. He paid me but mostly in items that I could pawn off for considerably less paper.

His preferred method of payment was diamonds.

Most often, he gave me a pouch of diamonds instead of a bag of cash. Sometimes he'd hand me watches, Rolexes, Pateks, Concords, and other jewelry — I always accepted.

What else was I gonna do?

The times I did complain, he looked at me crooked, as if I were insulting him and being insulted was not something Cousin Alex Pushka took lightly. Besides, by that time he'd unquestionably identified me as a full-blown addict.

As long as he gave me enough to pay my people, prance around town like I was a bigshit, and above all, get my head right, I remained dedicated. Between my skim from our other various interests, and my take from the currencies, I was lucky to net a 100,000$ a month.

Although in frayer terms that type of money is a small fortune, when you're living street-life, no matter how much you get, it never lasts.

You're always thinking of that next big score.

That giant pile that's almost within your grasp, but never touchable.In the meantime, you spend more than you make. And the money you have, well, that slips right through your fingers | *It's as if you never even had it in the first place.*

Tamara spent plenty too.
She'd grown accustomed to my lifestyle.

Tamara went shopping with the other wives and girlfriends. She savored the thousand-dollar floral arrangements I sent to the Manhattan lawyer's office where she worked as a paralegal. She reveled in the 600$ shoes and Cartier jewelry I showered her with.

Every so often, I stumbled home, zapped shitface on cheap vodka and smelling like overpriced perfume. She'd scream and cry — She would tell me I was a criminal and she didn't need my "dirty money."

Tamara would have these wonderful moments of pious morality. When I woke up the next day and reached for my Vicodin, I usually found her cleaning one of my firearms and requesting a ride to work.

After delivering Tamara to her office I would polish off a pint and ten to twenty pills then stop at the McDonalds drive-thru on 5th and 11th, kick back and look at Jerry Springer in the custom dash-mount monitor of my gun-metal grey Lexus GS with BBS titanium Type-G wheels. I traded the Yukon for the Lex and had all the emblems taken off | I was Gary Gunz in the Grey "G" with the *Type-G's*.

TRIPLE **G** | It compounded my image.

The whole fucking thing. That entire world was about image. I could summarize my life in one word.

—||— *Illusion* —||—

It was all a deception, designed to perpetrate. To generate trickery. It was a life-and-death game of make-believe. I had become a master of deception and duplicity. I had no tangible identity or purpose. I masqueraded as whatever I needed to be; whenever I needed to be it because that's the only way we operated. We were cunning and manipulative | But we weren't real.

I dreamed often of the big payoff at the finish.

My hard-won pot of gold at the end of the treacherous rainbow. With it would come the liberty to go and do anything I longed to do.

With it would finally come the freedom to be who I was meant to be. And if I didn't know who that was, well then I would just buy the answer | It was close enough *for me to taste it.*

GeorgiVodka and dope would numb me just right.
I just needed them long enough to grab it and move around.

When I finally got full up on dreams and dope | I made my way to work.

I spread my time out between both the apparently illicit office and the one we made look like the real thing.

We paid the Russians peddling our product green cash. Their payout was anywhere from 20-40% of the gross with a bonus promised at the end. Fred Lover (my new driver) and I would personally mule the cash from one of Alex's legitimate businesses, a bakery in Brighton Beach, to the office every week.

By the last week of August 2001 we were like the clearing house for every major Russian player on the east coast.

My beef with Terry had grown somewhat tame.

We'd rough one his peoples — He'd scuff-up one of ours. Nobody was seriously hurt, just a few black marks and scratches. It was mostly for show. Neither one of us could afford any fresh 187's. We both had too much at stake.

TEAM TERRY SOMEHOW MANAGED TO SLIP THROUGH THE CRACKS.
His crew was one of the last ones standing.

When I saw him at the funeral, his securities fraud was already in full tilt. I heard murmurs of 50-60Million$. In the meantime, with the streets as hot as they were, he wasn't making any gambles.

RJ bought a small house three blocks from my condo.

His down payment was almost entirely made up of graft money we'd kicked up to him for services rendered.

He came over three or four times a week and we would stay up until dawn, drinking our fill and binging on narcotics. We'd chat about current events, history and our political views, but we mostly talked about the paper with pictures of the presidents that's dead.

I promised RJ a million dollars as payment for his integrity, unwavering friendship and loyalty.

He often proclaimed me his forever brother.
Unfortunately | *Friends in this life are measured in monetary figures.*

In the morning, Tamara would sometimes make eggs for both of us and join in our conversation.

* * *

THE MORNING OF SEPTEMBER 11, 2001.

I was driving alone down the LIE, on my way to Pushka's Dix Hills mansion, when I heard news of that first airliner crashing into the towers. We scheduled a meeting to review the particulars of a few numbered Cayman Island accounts Pushka set up for me.

Our snake oil was almost all bought up and we were about ready for the big dust-off.

Tamara called around nine.
She told me about the first hit — 1 World Trade.

We assumed that it was an accident with a small private plane.

The press didn't release too much information in the beginning. *Most New Yorkers thought that the first one was an accident.* We just blew it off and resolved to meet up around dinner time. By the time I arrived at the Cousin's, the second airliner had hit the south tower at 2 World Trade | We knew by then that it was an all-out terror attack.

I picked up the equivalent of 50,000$ in cash and other valuables, then left before the towers collapsed.

We looked at the crashes on our tellies for hours. Every network *Replayed them Over&Over* | Somewhere around eleven a.m., everything just stopped.

IT WAS LIKE THE WHOLE COUNTRY WAS FROZEN IN TIME.

The authorities closed all of the highways going into Manhattan around noon. Landlines and cellular phones were pretty much useless. Calls just weren't going through no matter how hard you tried. I managed to make it back to my apartment before it went into total lockdown.

I needed to get into Manhattan.

A few of the *brigada* were positioned in the towers running a small credit card fraud. I was worried for them and Tamara who was also stuck in the city — Only first-responders were allowed passage.

I went to RJ's grabbed his extra badge and patrolmen's uniform. All I had to do was flash RJ's tin and I was allowed free reign on the roads and entry into the city.

I regret doing that.

When I got close to the debris, I saw unthinkable carnage I wish I could forget. The senseless unfairness of it all was too much for many to bear, myself included | It evicted all sanity from the psyche and deviously plundered the heart.

I lost a good friend in those towers. She was a beautiful caring person, full of love—*she had nothing to do with my gangster life*—she was just there being wonderful.

I miss you, Jamie.

* * *

THE NEXT FEW MONTHS:

A blur of drugs, gambling, parties, restaurants and prostitutes.

I plummeted further into desolation and hit the bottle harder than ever. I ingested any form of narcotic or pharmaceutical I could get hold of. September 11th was at the forefront of our thoughts for years, but the first few months were the hardest. The telly kept displaying the planes crashing into the WTC from every angle.

Over and Over and Over | Again.

They kept showing the people inside the towers and the surrounding areas, torn from the rubble and gripped in fear. It drove me insane every time I looked at it. It was a terrific validation for me to delve heavier into my addiction.

For sheer respect to the fallen.

I will not discuss many of the fraudulent activities that surrounded the tragedy. To this day it's a very touchy subject that even slimebag Geraldo types can't bring themselves to talk about.

But if only for the sake of truth and continuity I must recant this one deplorable swindle.

—||— *Forgive me if you can* —||—

IT TAKES A SPECIAL BRAND OF VULTURE TO ATTEMPT TO PULL OFF SOMETHING LIKE THIS.

I only heard about after it was over.

Immediately following the catastrophe, the country was in a state of frenzy. Authorities and salvage personnel flew in from all over the world to help with the rescue and cleanup effort.

Gene T. and his cousin, Fat Elliot, decided it would be beneficial to their depleted bank accounts to form a fraud NPO (non-profit organization) that dealt in raising money for the clean-up and reconstruction of the WTC.

So they did just that.

They diverted their entire operation into scamming the individual investor via an appeal to his compassion and patriotism. It worked like a charm. They raised two million dollars in just over a month and half. *The problem*: there was never an NPO created, nor were there ever any plans set in motion to form said NPO.

It was pure fraud, clean and simple.

++||— Not for pussies —

Had they filed the appropriate paperwork with the city and federal establishment and given them the required 20% minimum, they never would have gotten into the jam that they did.

Both Gene and his Fat cousin were confidential informants for the Attorney General. BaconFace had been letting them operate for years within the *Pushkatzkaya* in order to build a case against all of us.

Specifically | Cousin Alex Pushka.

They felt as though they were untouchable. After all, the feds were letting them earn for years on multiple frauds they'd been intimately involved with and unprosecuted for. They thought that this one here would just be another con in a long string of cons.

They could not have been more wrong.

There are some things more sacred than even the most important investigation. Shitting on September 11th was a huge mistake for Gene and his fat cousin.

* * *

MID-NOVEMBER.

A frigid morning that year gave way to an even colder day.

It was the day Elliot F. got picked up by his handler, Special Detective Cheesy Poofs.

The entire crew was in disarray.

RJ notified me early in the afternoon that Fat Elliot was a narc.

He didn't know until the pickup. It was one of those things they kept close to the vest — Even from insiders like RJ.

Cousin Alex already knew.

Looking back, I can assume that Pushka had someone on the take much higher up the food chain than RJ. Nobody could reach the Cousin the entire day | What came next *was far worse.*

THE MORNING OF NOVEMBER 20, 2001.

I was stuck in BQE traffic when I got the call from Fred Lover. "Gunny, you... you there, bro?" Fred stuttered. "I'm here" I managed a reply after pulling over on the side of LIU hospital.

That's when he told me.

"You sure about this Freddie?" I asked.

Fred Lover told me again. Our office was locked shut with a handwritten "Office closed" sign taped to the door. For a moment I thought it was all a big joke, I thought that they *were funning me.*

Cousin Alex wouldn't answer his calls. Bobby Tiger wasn't answering either | No one had to tell me what happened: *I knew*

I'd been fleeced by the best in the game.

I'll never forget the feeling—fruitless desperation fueled by dismay and laced with disgusting regret. It was a feeling of uncompromising heartache. I switched my phone off and turned around, towards my favorite, full-naked gentleman's club in Queens. They opened early and I could spend the rest of my day sniffing dope and drinking GeorgiVodka.

I CRASHED HOME AROUND TWO A.M | Pockets on empty.

Soul on empty.

THE MORNING OF NOVEMBER 21ST.

I dampened my hangover with Vicodin tablets in a jar I kept inside my nightstand drawer. Early morning, I received the phone call | Terry D. and his entire crew had been stung hard.

It was one of those bittersweet victories.

If not for the fact that I'd just been duped out of my fair share of 20M$, I would have smiled.

THIS ONE HERE | IT'S A REAL COMEDY.

A sad tale told by an imbecile.

Suggesting tragedy.

The following is an account from an accredited national rag-sheet. To protect the identities of certain parties of interest, namely myself, I won't go into too much detail.

. . .

THE FBI ARRESTED 20 MEN TUESDAY MORNING ON CHARGES OF running a massive pump-and-dump scheme that defrauded thousands of investors out of more than $50 million. Two alleged ringleaders — Terry D. and Ricky Kuku — are said to be associates of the Genovese organized crime family.

The arrests and charges comprise the third major bust of an alleged Mob-infested boiler room operation in the past 9 months.

According to an indictment handed up in Brooklyn, the group ran three brokerage firms from 1998 to 2001 and used them for "pump-and-dump" scams.

Tennis star ----- ---- and NFL player ----- --- were duped in the scheme, a source close to the investigation told The Associated Press.

---, identified in court Thursday only as a professional tennis player, was scammed out of more than $600,000 during a three-month period, said the source, who spoke on condition of anonymity. ---, a former --- ---- ---------- linebacker, was identified in court only as an NFL player. The amount of money he lost was not disclosed.

The indictment says that the group's brokerages ----- ------- And -------- Capital employed a posse of cold-calling telemarketers who hyped the stocks of four companies: ----- Technology Group, -----, --- Industries and ------ ----- -------.

The brokerages amassed blocks of stock in each company before the marketing team sold it to unsuspecting victims, promising fantastic returns. When the stocks rose on the sales, Terry D. and Ricky Kuku dumped the brokerages' holdings, reaping a $50 million windfall. The indictment also alleges that the group laundered its profits in overseas bank accounts and paid a cut to the Genovese family.

According to the indictment, the brokerages refused to execute sell orders from clients who tried to cash out at a profit. In at least one instance, a broker who tried to honor a client's sell order was threatened at knife point.

· · ·

THOSE ARE THE FACTS.

How they got that way, that's the comedy.

IT ALL STARTED WITH RICKY KUKU.

Making a fortune duping wealthy individual investors just wasn't enough for Terry and Kuku | They wanted More and Better.

++||— *It cost them everything* —

And everything counts in large amounts.

Terry went after the biggest fish he could find, Ricky's next-door neighbor. Rick lived in a fairly middle-class area of Staten Island, nothing fancy, just suburbia. He had a pretty, white house with a cedar picket fence. He often parked his crisp silver Mercedes 500S in the driveway for everyone to see. It made him feel like a champion when his neighbors come up and gawked at his car. He would tell them narratives of his wonderful brokerage business and how much money he'd made for himself and his most valuable clientele.

"If only you would have been involved in our last deal, I could have made you a fortune," Kuku told his neighbor, who lived in the house across from him. He didn't just tell him once; he pounded it into him. Kuku kept flashing his gold Rolex presidential until finally, the poor old sap just couldn't take it anymore—*He needed a taste*—Ol' boy was practically begging Ricky for a piece of their next product.

Kuku gave it to him.

He installed him into a fine piece of paper that went from twenty-five cents to seven bucks, then back down to donut. Got the mo-mo out just in the nick of time too. Made his neighbor a nice little sack of money—*Of course he wanted more.*

That was all part of the plan.

Ricky Kuku's neighbor just across the way was *also* a braggart.

He couldn't keep his yap shut about the giant pension fund that he and a few other bigshits controlled. This idiot was retired police and as it turns out, had inaugurated into a managerial position for one of the largest pension funds in the city.

Terry and Kuku decided to tighten the bolts and really put the blocks to him. They kept this pigeon on the hook for almost a full year, installing him into product then selling him out right before the big nothing. It was a simple plan: cash the sucker up to his gills, gain his trust just enough to grab a sizable chunk of the pension fund, and the Grand*finale.*

++||—Keyser Söze—*forever&ever*—

Possibly, it was Notorious BIG who said it best.

"Never sell no crack where you rest at. I don't care if they want an ounce. Tell 'em bounce." That means don't shit where you eat. You're the one who's gonna have to smell it.

I guess they must've thought that was their big break. It was worth compromising the rules for their shot at the title.

I might've done it too.

That wasn't the real issue though.

Chances are, their project would have popped off and set them up for life, if not for that fact that someone in their inner circle was secretly Secret Detective TastyCakes in disguise.

Guido Vinny, Terry D's loyal number6, had been collaborating with the feds since '97 when they bagged him on cocaine distribution charges. Guido was running a side business, trying to put together a little scratch for a new herringbone rope-chain, or a Cadillac, or maybe even a replacement for the front tooth he'd been missing for years—he ended up selling over a kilo to a plainclothes.

They made him an offer: Wear a wire and sing when it comes time for trial or do fifteen calendars — Guido choose the wire.

It seems like most everybody does.

They talk a lot though, about honor and loyalty. Where was the honor when the feds came charging into the homes of your comrades just before dawn? They came on your dime, Guido Vinny.

Live with that shit if you can.

Terry and Kuku got busted just in time for the paperwork Kuku's neighbor signed to not go through. They weren't about to allow a couple of modest shitheads to swindle 500M$ from the police pension. They had just about enough of Terry and KuKu's little operation. The dope, the white-collar fraud, and the murder.

They got them for everything.

Neither Terry D. nor Ricky Kuku were getting out the clink till *all the saints* come marching in.

As for Guido Vinny.

Your textbook example of the perfect mo-mo. After testifying at three trials, he got indicted for the murder of Little Gabe. Terry did what we like to refer to as "the BackFlip" and signed indictments back on his main-homeboy#1. He agreed to testify in exchange for taking the death penalty off the table.

I celebrated the news in the usual way.

Isolating myself in a Manhattan bar and getting open on Vicodin, GeorgiVodka, and a sprinkle of cocaine mixed on the side.

It was way past quitting time, but I was at the point where I couldn't function without it. I needed it to put sensible thoughts together. I would use it as a tool to help me figure a way through all this mess, then draw back with some answers.

I STILL DIDN'T HAVE THE ONIONS TO TELL TAMARA:

That it was *all-over-Jehovah.*

NOVEMBER 22ND BROUGHT MORE BAD NEWS.

I met with Sammy Movefaker and La-Onda Mark toward the middle of the day. They came knocking on my front door (I turned off the phone) and requested a sit.

We met at The Sheepshead Bay diner for some coffee. Movefaker informed me that Cousin Al had been alerted by some of his loyalists to the feds closing in and took an early exit.

All of our accounts were compromised.

++||— We lost everything —

Pushka played out his hand to the end.

You see, if the swindle gets busted up and profits get seized, I can't hold anybody accountable for my skim. I would be forced to charge it to the game and maintain my commitments to the brotherhood.

How convenient.

He slipped me a paper bag containing 50,000$ in cash.

"Cousin wanted you to have this. For your loyalty," Faker said. A micro-smirk appeared on his chapped lips.

Faker knew what this was all about.

It was his moment to laugh it up at my expense and he was delighted. "Cousin will be in touch with you when he gets back. Keep your ears open Gunny," he affirmed.

We retreated to his black SUV, lit up a fatty, and sped off downtown for a massage and oral pleasure at Nu-Look.

The next morning more of the same.

It had all become a dark-water-floodstorm, focusing its cruelty directly on its primary target — Me.

The feeling of impending doom never left me. No amount of dope seemed to wither it away, it just dulled it long enough to miss the brunt of the attack but still catch the backlash of its recoil.

Fred Lover called early in the morning.

He was presented a legit job at a prominent brokerage. Fred was leaving the *brigada* and sought my blessings (a clean and safe way out). One of his current girlfriends put him on. Her daddy was some smelly bigshit with great power over others. At her request, daddy plugged in Fred Lover. *I didn't care anymore* —||— I gave it to him.

I HEARD THE WORST OF IT THAT AFTERNOON.

Tarzan, my confederate from the jump, was in a bad mess.

He ventured into another business deal without my knowledge. The Manny business didn't teach him a lick. Tarzan was a bull-headed risk-taker who valued the thrill more than the reward.

It was the finish for him.
The last risk he would ever take.

This time Tarzan put his trust in the wrong people.
This particular scheme involved identity fraud in a tiny

Pennsylvania town. His number8 got picked up at the mailbox he initiated for the hoax and entered into a deal with Officer CoffeeStains to sting Tarzan. It earned Tarzan a five-to-seven-year stretch in federal lockup. They wanted him to knock all the way to the top.

Tarzan decided to do his time like a soldier.

It was his Jewish temper that got him a knife through the windpipe by an Aryan-Brotherhood gang-banger.

He never even stood a chance.

Wherever you're at, Tarzan.
I hope you're playin' it close for me.
Knowing you | Its right on the wire.

YOU'RE FREE NOW BROTHER.
Free *to not grind* | Free *to soar with eagles.*
You're *free to* go home.

♛ I will NEVER forget you ♛

THE SAME NIGHT, MORE BAD NEWS.
RJ was under formal investigation by IAB (InternalAffairsBureau). I wasn't surprised | It might have been his bolstering, or the eighteen-karat gold Concord timepiece he flaunted that gave him away. Whatever it was, he needed to distance himself from me for a short while so his PBA rep could tidy things up.

It didn't matter anyways ++||— It was over —
The whole entire thing had just whisked right by.

I was left with a meager 125000$ to try and pick up the pieces. Shit, if I was pinched, my legal fees would easily double that.

TIMES HAD GOTTEN *Passion-of-the-Christ* HARD.

I felt wrapped up *tighter than a mummy.*

BY THE END OF THE MONTH I FINALLY TOLD TAMARA.

She didn't take it well. She mockingly told me that she had known all along — I paid her no mind — We were married only in certificate. I slept on the couch and she took to the bedroom.

Ingestion of booze and prescription tablets had slowed to what I believed a manageable level. I relaxed for a bit and decided that I might try to go legit. Go back to school and possibly learn a skill. Leave Tamara, go somewhere nobody knew me and start fresh.

I dreamed of it often — *I felt like it wasn't too late for me.*

CHRISTMAS '01.

I was looking at colleges to enroll at. Tamara and I were on speaking terms and every once and again would even get a little intimate — Perhaps things were turning back around for the better.

In this life, you always reap what you sow.

Not too long ago, I mentioned the distinction between mankind and other animals. I prematurely concluded it lay in the fact that humans have impressive race-cars, shopping malls and HBO.

That's true | But the real difference is that we're the only species on the planet that put other species and even members of our own inside cages.

CONNY K. | WAS GETTING READY TO COME OUT OF HIS.

$$\Psi - \Psi - \Psi$$

I.

13

SOMETIMES YOU GOTTA WALK ALONE

I walk a lonely road
   The only one that I have ever known
   Don't know where it goes
   But it's only me
   And I walk alone
   -Green Day

SYNCHRONICITY.
I've had incident to examine this theory.
I offer to you now, a very strange concept.

I NOW RELAY IT TO YOU AS PRESENTED BY WILKEPDIA.COM.
   "*The experience of two or more events which occur in a meaningful manner, but which are causally inexplicable to the person or persons experiencing them. The events would also have to suggest some underlying pattern in order to satisfy the definition of synchronicity.*
   Carl Jung coined the word to describe what he called "temporally coincident occurrences of acausal events." Jung variously described synchronicity as an "'acausal connecting principle'" (i.e. a pattern of

connection that cannot be explained by direct causality), "meaningful coincidence" and "acausal parallelism". Jung introduced the concept in his 1952 paper "Synchronicity — An Acausal Connecting Principle"

It differs from mere coincidence in that synchronicity implies not just a happenstance, but an underlying pattern or dynamic expressed through meaningful relationships or events.

It was a principle Jung felt encompassed his concepts of archetypes and the collective unconscious, in that it was descriptive of a governing dynamic that underlay the whole of human experience and history — social, emotional, psychological, and spiritual.

Jung believed that many experiences perceived as coincidence were due not merely to chance, but instead, suggested the manifestation of parallel events or circumstances reflecting this governing dynamic.

Events that happen which appear at first to be coincidence but are later found to be causally related are termed incoincident."

Huh?
You know, It's definitions like these...
That require further defining.

THAT'S WHAT ALL THESE INTELLECTUAL-TYPE BIGSHITS DO.

They make these things up to seem important and academic.

I envision a dozen or so really smelly bigshits sitting around a long dark table with dim lighting, holding small, expensive looking crystal glasses. Some smoking cigars, others with tablets and pencils. The rest adjusting their neckties and diligently debating the significance of sophisticated applications of conjectures like these, and their bearing on the human statistic.

Truth is | No one really knows much of anything at all.
That was me | I knew too much and understood too little.

STILL THIS SYNCHRONICITY BUSINESS HAS SOMETHING TO IT.

Probably not the way Mr. Bigshit is describing, but in a more traditional sort of way. Allow me to present it to you in a more digestible format.

In life there are absolutely no accidents.
Everything happens the exact way it's supposed to happen.

The Buddhists, Hindus and most other Eastern cultures believe in the law of Karma.

WILKEPEDIA.COM SAYS THE FOLLOWING:

The explanation of karma can differ per tradition. Usually it is believed to be a sum of all that an individual has done, is currently doing and will do. The results or "fruits" of actions are called karma-phala. Karma is not about retribution, vengeance, punishment or reward; karma simply deals with what is. The effects of all deeds actively create past, present and future experiences, thus making one responsible for one's own life, and the pain and joy it brings to others. In religions that incorporate reincarnation, karma extends through one's present life and all past and future lives as well. It is cumulative.

KARMA IS REAPING WHAT YOU SOW.

You alone, through your actions, are the creator of your experiences. There's no timeframe for when your positive or negative karma kicks in. It just happens, leaving you in the thick of it. Actions you take today can bear fruit at any time and continue to blossom until reaching finality.

In Conny's case, it took a few months more than nine sticks in Allenwood for his actions to reach conclusion.

They finally did though, and they had to cut him loose.

Me | My karma kicked in when I smoked that first fatty with Adam, or maybe it happened when I stole that first comic book. Probably when I eighty-6$^{\text{'d}}$ the Georgian.

In any event, it was close to reaching the end for me.

Mine and Conny's paths were shared — Our karma twisted into a cluster of perforated lumps that ended the same way it began, with only one sure conclusion ++||— Violence, hurt, and probably murder —

Everything comes full circle eventually.

FEBRUARY 2002.

MoveFaker opened an insignificant clothing store in a ramshackle strip mall directly across from my old high-school.

The store carried urban wear. It was a fresh brand of outfit.

First introduced onto the scene by the legendary rapper LeftDaHood, this new style targeted the underprivileged listeners of hip-hop music | Project kids proclaiming "thug life" and abandoning school for the dope game.

Urban brands designed overly loose and saggy bottoms so youngsters could play make-believe—pretend themselves G and stylishly wear their jeans down around their knees and hang their drawers all the way out the back. Some even had hidden pockets for dope and pistols | It was actually a pretty good idea faker had.

His store was only a few meters from the projects.

Plenty of good customers there.
Especially on the first and fifteenth.

When I drove up to grab a few velour warm-ups, Faker attempted to present his hardest G and "represent" for Brighton.

I was desperate to get away from fakers.

His clowning entertained me momentarily but mostly I paid him no mind at all. It worked well, I grabbed whatever I needed and chunked him deuces. Few days later he hollered at me about an overweight friend holding a blank prescription for 120 Vicodin with five re-ups. A rare magnificent providence that I could not allow to escape.

Within minutes I arrived at his store.

I abandoned the Lexus G by way of head-on collision on a busy intersection. The adjuster and the witnesses said it was entirely my doing. I obviously didn't see it that way.

Good for me New York is a no-fault state.

I opted for a more inconspicuous vehicle, a late-model black Dodge Durango, with leather seats. I picked it up for ten thousand cash from one of the shysters on Coney Island Avenue. It read 48k miles, but knowing those scammers, the odometer was probably adjusted. No matter, I got it for a good deal and if things got tight, I'd just burn it and get back more than my investment.

I put it under Tamara's name because, by that time, my twenty-plus accidents left me practically uninsurable.

I entered the store which consisted of two rooms.

The main room was a shallow eight-hundred square feet in length and about seven-hundred feet wide. I noticed the entire left wall was upholstered with a type of plastic material that allowed special hangers to be affixed to it. There were fifteen or so such hangers, each displaying a different brand of velour jump.

There were a few standing clothing racks scattered about that were dangling mostly demins and t-shirts. A 4x6 service counter made of beige granite style Formica stood in the near right corner next to the forward bank of windows. An unused cash register sat atop the counter | Within moments a modestly attractive young brown-haired female greeted me at the back-room door.

SHE INTRODUCED HERSELF AS YALLENA, (YA-LEEH-NAH).

At five-feet seven, she carried a pleasant slender looking figure that didn't hurt the glimpsers.

Immediately her penetrating heavy hazel-grey eyes fixated on my position. They were silently appraising a monetary value to put on my essence | She just couldn't help herself.

Outwardly, she appeared a young female, early—mid-twenties.

Inwardly, *I felt a bizarre quality of affluence.* It covered the whole of the space she occupied. Her eccentric behavior and controlled mannerisms made it obvious that she had been trained for years, by masters, in proper womanly manners, and had long ago been apprised of her rightful place in this world.

She looked very expensive.

From her brow line down to each individual polished toenail *everything* appeared perfect—*too perfect*—It was like she bought her bodysuit at "The Perfect Store." As Yallena neared me the scent of her exclusive fragrance attempted to lacerate all prior apprehensions.

Her smile, Stoic ++||— Frigid —

She drew herself closer. "Your Gary?" she invaded my space to offer counterfeit affections. I received them with my own special brand of FuckYou. I stood quiet for a moment and did not say or do a thing. "I'm sorry I offended you, Gary. It's just that Sasha (Alex aka Faker) has told me so many funny stories about you. I feel like I know you," she said.I continued to purposely ignore her and walked casually towards the back room.

It was as though she did not exist to me.

GARY GOVICH

The creation factory rarely produced her model.
Although highly sought after, I knew what she really was.
Everyone knew.

A faulty design indeed.
The blueprint had been modified.
She only came with one solitary emotion.
And ignoring her kind was the only way to summon it.
I glanced at the only authentic expression she could produce.

Fear.

Yallena was the youngest granddaughter of Elena, one of the sisters whose initial funding opened *the 1&only* National restaurant. This made Yallena the heir of more than 13million$. At least, that's what she looked like on paper.

She was thirteen years old when Sammy poached her one day from intermediate school. Sammy was almost twenty.

If you're thinking that would make him a nasty ChoMo, you've probably got a very valid argument — Russian culture would tell you otherwise. Granted, a filthy pedophile he may well be, but meeting Yallena was the only thing Movefaker ever did right in the whole of his pathetic so-called life. I say this for having millions of greenbacks, It just won't buy you any smarts.

Yallena stood by this loser through thick and thick.

There was never a boring day with Sammy.

If he wasn't strung heavy on dopesacks, he was out gambling away paper he didn't have. On the rare occasion he managed to acquire a crumb or two, he'd spend it on more dope, prostitutes, or some other valueless contraband item.

He was lowlife scumbag number1.

I only came to see him for the script he claimed to have for me. After that I would ghost like his cousin.

Too bad things don't always work out the way you plan.

Particularly when alcohol and dope come into play.

The back room was a partially unfinished 100X40 office area. Exposed and torn sheets of drywall challenged every angle. The rear of a semi-working particle-board, wood-colored desk faced the door. A thick whitish smolder flooded the area.

Sammy turned from behind his cracked manager's chair and faced me. "You need to hit this shit here, Nice-Gunz. It's the killers," Sammy stated, attempting to pass me a half-smoked white-owl cigar cracked open and re-created with hydroponic greens.

"Nah, I don't roll that way no more. I put that shit away. Too messy, smells too bad," I replied. Once graduating to opiates — I no longer found the sticky's appealing. The pills were much more discreet and their effect got me much more Irish.

"So you got that script for me?" I demanded.

"Sure, Gunny. My bro Oleg left it with me. Just go to his pharmacy on the corner of Brighton and Ocean Parkway and get it filled. They're cool over there," he replied handing me the prescription.

"Tight, Sammy, how much?" I asked. "Just leave me two C's. He's my boy, says he gonna have lots more," Sammy continued.

"Good lookin' out." I stated, turning to leave the room.

"How you like the shop?" Sammy interjected before I could make my escape — I took a second to pretend to look around, though all I was thinking about was the bliss script in my hand.

"Its tight. Seems a little empty though," I stated, commenting on the obvious lack of inventory. He smirked. "We just getting started.

Only opened the doors a few weeks ago. Yallena wanted me to stop grindin' so she got her family to lay out the paper for this spot."

I wasn't surprised.

Making an idiot out of himself was the only thing Sammy was capable of without help from others. Getting out of the game was probably the best idea he had since he discovered jerking off.

"I wish you luck with all that Sammy. Hope it works good for you," I stated, anxious to leave and fill my script.

"Actually, I wanted to shout at you about coming partner with me," Sammy declared. "I need someone who's handy with the steel. You see what's goin' on out there — Savages out there. If they wanna bumrush and jack, I got nothing for 'em. You're a lot more capable than me. I know you not doin' anything right now. This would be a good break for you to go legit or even just make a nice lick." He finished speaking and took a seat on a tall bar chair behind the counter.

"You serious about this Sammy?" I paused to consider his offer. "Serious like a fat girl on a moped," he exclaimed. "It don't look like much now, but I'm opening accounts with major vendors. We're gonna fill this store up with nothing but the cleanest gear. Not just for the animals across the street, for Russians and everyone else," he stated. "See, Fast-Gunz, people got lots of respect for your hustle. When they hear you're in this with me, they're gonna come and see us just on love. Feel me?" Sammy leaned back in his chair waiting on my response.

"So what do you need from me?" I asked, waiting for the catch. "Nothing. Just come in here and post up. Maybe help me call some distributors and con(vince) them to let us carry their gear," he replied. "Let me chew on it for a day. I'll pass by tomorrow let you know," I insisted. "No pressure, Gunny," he added as I finally left to procure my medication.

There was no consideration needed.

It sounded just like what I needed to legitimize and possibly even get in good with the National people.

WorstCome2Worse:
I'd shanghai the entire spot and take everything.

I TOLD TAMARA THAT NIGHT ABOUT MY NEW VENTURE.

She wasn't happy with my decision. Unless large amounts of GreenBenjamin's were involved, she wasn't happy with anything.

The next day I started working with Sammy Movefaker.

Couple days after that, I'd persuaded some of the more popular distributors to let us carry their apparel.

You would think those corporate business types jumped on the chance for a retailer to push their fashions. It's much more complicated than that ++||— *Business without a firearm usually is* —

Clothing companies, especially real trendy ones, are exclusive about who they let carry their inventory. Having money to buy it isn't enough. They need to be sure that your store is set up adequately to display their product, is reputable and stable enough to persevere through a few bad seasons. They usually don't open accounts with business that don't already have an established track record.

They always require financials and references.

Another major obstacle was zoning. If your retailer is within a thirty-mile radius of another shop carrying the same brand, chances are, you gonna be shit-outta-luck. Most reps establish exclusivity within a certain zone and won't offer new accounts a chance at all. If not because of the contract they signed with your competitor, then for the sole reason of not flooding the market and diluting the brand.

Talk about a shitty deal.

Here's a new business attempting to get on its feet, but nobody wants to mess with you because you're too new —*Some American dream* — How in the fuck are you supposed to die old when nobody's letting you live? The answer to that was just warm and familiar enough for me to do it: cold call prospects who never heard of me and didn't want much of anything to do with my affairs. All it took was the right cocktail of alcohol|dope, mixed with a driving dose of opiates, and I was on the phone making it happen.

Opening accounts was a tough task — But it's what I did.

Smooth talk alone wouldn't do the job. Every representative I spoke with required further swaying (a cash bribe).

Faker was hardly around the shop and didn't have anything to invest. I myself wasn't averse to the idea of pitching in some of my own paper. After adding fifty dimes of my own money, Sammy added me to the S-Corp as a 50|50 partner. Towards the end of February 2002, 50,000$ lighter | I was a business owner.

Desperation returned.
I was always discontent and irritable.
Thug-time was close — *I could feel it welling up within.*

Every time I swigged the Georgi or ate a handful of reprieve, my high would settle quickly and I'd reflect on past misdeeds.

I felt deserted | No matter where I went or who I saw.
++||— *It was me against the world* —

* * *

MID-MARCH 2002. BEFORE NOON MID-DAY.

Conny walked into our clothing store.

I was in the back room brokering a deal with Ecko Unlimited when I heard the ruckus up at the front. I hung up with the rep who I'd convinced through two-thousand dollars in graft and a quarter-ounce of white to allow us distribution rights, and came out to probe.

There he was, the exact same way I recalled him.

He didn't look a day older.

Prison has that unexpected effect on a person. You don't age in there. I've seen it time and time again on criminals coming home from big stints | They come back looking exactly the same way they came in. It's like they were frozen in time, sucked into a time|space warp where all things cease to transpire — I call it the phantom-zone, you know, the one where ChrisReeves Superman banished General Zod, Ursala, and the other ogre-looking fellow.

Loneliness becomes a physical pain that hurts all over.
It's a place where you can drift and never even know you were gone.

Forever fear | Inescapable fear wherever you turn.
Wherever you look.

That's prison.

"What's up, brother?" I exclaimed, approaching Conny for a hug.

"Gary Speks What the fuck you doin' in here? You're the last person I expected to see," he said, surprised. We hugged for a long moment and I kissed Conny on the cheek.

A dear brother had finally returned home.

We left for lunch at the kebab house on Coney Island and Avenue K. Conny broke it down to me smooth, told me all about the cooler.

Ten years in there will change a man.

411

He was released sometime in early January, then sat home for a couple of weeks lingering in freedom.

> The world changes enough in a week.
> Leaving jail after a decade — Nothin' looks the same.

Coming home from prison is a culture shock.

Inside | You think, plan, and anticipate all day and all night.

All you can think about is finishing your time, getting out, and coming home. But when you get out, you realize just how much things have changed and all the hours you spent arranging your movements somehow get cancelled as soon as you draw in that first breath of sovereignty. You realize, that although time has stood still for you, it's moved rather quickly for the rest of the world and it becomes increasingly hard for you to figure your place in it.

I call it "ThawingOut." The process of being reinserted into the world from a long incarceration.

"So, what you're saying to me, C."

"You telling me you're out the game forever?" I asked while we waited for our order of lamb. "Nah, Gary, I'm telling you that I'm not just jumping on the first thing I hear about anymore. There's people up in Allenwood doing thirty, forty calenders — *Life*. Shifty motherfuckers, sharp like shark teeth, still they got jammed up. You know why Gary? Cause the feds are smarter. They're the real criminals. They got all the dough in the entire bakery. Next time I turn anything on, I'm making sure it's quick and off the grid. I'm not going back in there, not for nothing," he stated sullenly.

We ate the rest of our meal in silence and I drove Conny back to the store. "There is something Gary," he said before we exited the vehicle. "You know I heard about that shit with Pushka, how it went down," Conny affirmed.

I sat still, curiously awaiting his announcement.

"It's like this, Pushka had two 4K[1] motherfuckers in his unit, real close to him. One of 'em been cooperating with the feds for years. They had him stone cold on that currency shit y'all were pumping out," he said grimly. I listened closer and inhaled deeply from my Newport as he continued.

He named Sasha I. and Vova M.

I knew who they were. I first met them at the homecoming party Cousin threw for me at National. They were the two Russians that accompanied him | I didn't associate much with them.

SASHA RAN HIS OWN *BRIGADA*, THE LEATHERMEN.

It was a long-established crew that could be traced back to the days of the Nayfeld brothers. There were about fifteen trusted men in his group—*every last one a murderer*—His was something like a hit squad specializing in sophisticated robberies and contract killings.

A fully anointed *Bratan* gathering intel for the government. Sasha had been working as a CI for more than ten years.

What could he do?

They had him on dead-square for murder.

The feds didn't do much to save him from the double-tap to his backside. They found him dead, with his tongue cut in half at his New Jersey home right before Cousin Alex did his GhostFace.

VOVA, HE WAS MORE OF THE ACADEMIC TYPE.

He kept the books for Pushka. One of Pushka's most trusted associates, Vova was there from the blast. He and Pushka kicked it as far back as the Odessa docks. On the sneak tip — Pushka's loyal assistant was quietly embezzling millions from his holdings.

Cousin found out by chance during our currency run — Vova got sloppy, he attempted to move more than 1.5MM$ into one of his personal overseas account. That's how the FBI was alerted. They traced the wire and started pushing-up on Sasha for info.

Sasha gave them Vova.
Vova, he gave them *everything*.

All the accounts froze at once.
Most of our graft was lost instantly.

Pushka's loyalists leaked the news to him before the feds closed in tight | Cousin Alex Pushka handled it like a professional.

Sasha got two sleeping pills.
Vova got the horns.

Alex Pushka doctored the paperwork clever enough to pin everything on Vova. The whole swindle went down as though Vova were the skipper. He received leadership role along with the twelve other charges | The government knew it wasn't Vova.

They didn't give a good GodDamn.

He was the one they had, and although he was singing like Luciano Pavarotti, all the evidence ended with him as the principal. It was an easy win for them, resulting in eleven calendars in lockdown and over 1MM$+ in restitution.

++||— Poor Vova didn't make it through his first year —

"So you're telling me Pushka really lost everything and had to lam it?" I inquired. "C'mon Gary, you know better. He didn't lose everything. He still came-off. He just didn't get as flush as he would have liked. He should have straightened you out better than he did. Conny shrugged. "He isn't coming back for a long minute. *Pushkatzkaya* is gonna have to go on the back burner," he said.

"What about Bobby Tiger? Nobody's been able to reach him since that shit went down. Pushka got him flush right?" I demanded.

"Bobby been in rehab. Checked himself in about a week before you closed shop. He had a bad GHB²problem. Couldn't stop. The fool almost stroked he was doing so much. He's been back for almost a month, just staying QT." Conny finished speaking then pulled out a small flat pewter flask from the inside pocket of his black leather, drank deeply then passed it to me.

Conny reached for the door handle.
StoneFaced he looked directly in my eyes.

Conny put his hand on my shoulder. "I been hearing shit about you too Gary. That you're heavy putting—*that's that shit*—in your bloodstream. People are gettin' worried about you," he stated sadly.

"What fuckin people? Man, I'm out here maintainin'. I got into this clothing shit with Sammy. I'm makin it JustRight, C," I barked with conviction. C'mon Conny. You really believin' that bullshit these streets puttin out. Those fuckers out here are trying to see your homeboy falloff flat-busted. Not me brother. Not on my watch," I finished, pulling open my grey fur-lined black suede and exposing the shoulder holster I wore on the inside.

Conny paused then took another swig.

"I been thinking about getting out of this shit forever. I got something we need to jump on. I need you to get down on this with me Gary," Conny demanded."What the fuck, C? You just said you wasn't getting' into the same old bullshit?" I replied. "Tell you the truth I been thinking about reaching out to you for a minute. I just came into the store to see if I could get some jump-offs and there was Faker, looking as lost as neck-tie at a tractor-pull. That shit was disturbing Gary. Like it was meant to be," Conny said.

"I don't know Conny. I'm working with Sammy now. I just sank in fifty Stones — *My money.* I know what you did for me. I'll never forget it. I want to take a crack at this for a minute and check how it flips. If you need some cash, a few dimes to get it poppin', I got that," I said.

"I'm straight," he replied quickly, looking insulted at the offer. "I need more than a few grand. I need a few lemons. I got the *new-way,* brother. But if you don't wanna mess with it yet, that's cool. I'll check you tomorrow, we can catch up a little more," Conny stated.

He exited my Durango and made his way back to his apartment. Conny came by in the morning as promised.

We kicked it proper | Everything seemed fine.

Just below the surface, reality awaited.

Sammy Faker had been gambling away the company's prudent capital since the start. I set into business with Sammy under the pretense that I would be the one calling the shots and if things became volatile — *I would just grab the banger and regulate.*

I was too busy looking for dope and playing bigshit to realize the irony of the situation I was in.

The first few days of May 2002 would clarify everything.

One evening, Bobby Tiger and a few members of his Black Tulips pulled into the parking area of my shop. He apprised me of the fact that Movefaker had amassed a debt of over 200,000$ with his bookmaking operation. He hadn't paid his vig in almost three weeks and was on his final notice.

Bobby was aware of my business with Sammy and had come down as a courtesy | He called it "courtesy," but it was more like a warning. Faker committed our business as collateral.

And it was past time to pay.

THE PROBLEM:

We had absolutely no money in reserve. Aside for a few hangers and a couple pieces of inventory, the store was worthless.

We'd ingested and gambled away everything.

As half-owner of the store, I was responsible for half the debt. I could have told Bobby the truth. I wasn't aware of Sammy's movements and fuck him and his debt.

Bobby was a talented hood.
He knew I would never do such a thing.

A real gangster *never shirks on debts.*
If I did | I would put my own reputation on the line.
I had to man-up and pay.

Bobby would never maneuver like this if times hadn't taken a turn for the harsh. He was starving for work | *Everyone was.*

Since the feds had busted up the stock fraud rackets and Pushka ghosted from the currencies you had to take things real carefully. All things crooked were slowly drying up. Gambling, dope, and whores were just about the only things left. When just the scraps are left, the sharks turn on each other and cannibalize.

++||— It's that type of party —

I cut a deal with Bobby, promising to repay him in two 50,000$ portions for my half of the debt. The first half would come in three weeks. The next shortly after.

I wouldn't pay him in cash.

Instead, I'd bring him the next best thing. Ten pistols, Two AK's, One rifle, and about 2500 rounds of ammo. It wasn't quite the hundred rocks, but since the street had been dry for a while, he accepted graciously.

Conny was present when I made my arrangement with Tiger.

Knowing this would be the catalyst to get me back in the game, Conny couldn't stop smiling. And I couldn't help but think that he arranged this whole dramatic piece of misfortune.

We took trips looting whatever merchandise was left into the trunk of my Durango.

I closed the store for good.

That night I dropped a line to set up a meet with my contact in SLC Utah. A short, lanky, balding Russian by the name of Boris A.

RJ had dealt with him for years. He was my guy though. After Boris lost his Series 7 and got banned from the industry for illegal trading, he decided to go legit into real estate brokering — He moved to Utah. Boris figured if he moved far enough his past wouldn't follow him.

In his case it didn't. Within a year he was a registered realtor with the state of Utah. It's not that Boris couldn't resist some extra income, Thuggin' was just in his blood. When I reached out to him, he was more than receptive towards my offer of ten points on all profits.

The plan: It's simple but risky.

There's an ancient saying among the Uhrki of Odessa.
He, who doesn't risk *never* drinks champagne.

There are only two or three states in the entire Union where the straw sale of a firearm is legal, and fewer where firearms don't have to be registered to the owner | Utah fits both criteria.

A straw sale is the person-to-person sale of a firearm.

Let's say for instance that you're a gun collector, or you have a surplus handgun and you need some extra coin. All you need to do is pop up at a gun show or place an ad on a website like GunsAmerica.com, wait for someone to react, and sell your gun. You need to ask the buyer if they're a felon or planning to use the firearm for illegal purposes. When they answer no to both questions, you have every right in the US of A to sell them your weapon.

I've never heard of a criminal admitting they were planning to hijack a money truck with the blaster they were about to buy.

The advantage here is two-fold. First, is the lack of a National Crime Information Center (NCIC) background check as required by the federal government when buying a firearm. Thanks to our bill of rights and gun clubs, it's required, but only in the states requiring it.

In firearm friendly states, the NCIC check is optional. You can thank lobbyists and the gun makers themselves for that.

Aside from straw sales, you can go to any gun show and pick up a firearm and just walk on out. In lieu of incidents like the one at Waco, if you're planning on purchasing more than a few, I wouldn't advise the latter. Pohlices of every flavor crowd gun shows, scoping for anyone looking to amass an arsenal.

The straw sale is probably your best option.

A state like Utah also doesn't require registration of weapons. A fact that's critical for a criminal like me — looking to use it for illicit activity. If a registered weapon is recovered in, for instance, a homicide or robbery, even if it's wiped clean for prints, it can eventually be traced back to its original owner by way of the serial number. An unregistered weapon may have had a previous owner; in fact it may have had many owners, but it was never registered. The only way it could ever be traced back is through ballistics. If it's something like a murder, most lawbreakers will dopr their smoker at the scene.

If it's been wiped clean.
It's just another untraceable burner.

Having done our homework.

We hollered at Boris to procure us a rent-house or apartment from his real estate listings with an identity that we'd "borrow" from some of our clients' personal information. A residence was crucial, we couldn't just book a hotel room and stockpile heaters under the bed. Some foreign-speaking housekeeper would surely find our stash and either notify law enforcement or alleviate us from the burden of keeping it — Around the time we notified Boris of our future journey, he would place advertisements in various local buy-sheet newspapers.

The ads would read something like this:

Need Extra Cash? Sell Us Your Firearms! We Pay Top Dollar Cash $$$ For Your Unwanted Guns! Private Collector. All Inquiries Kept Confidential-

WE WOULD USUALLY GET HUNDREDS OF HITS WITHIN THE FIRST HOUR.

Once satisfied with the number of replies and having secured more than a few burners using our own methods, RJ would coordinate with two number6, usually someone like the recently departed Fat-Dima, that were able to clean up real pretty. Next, the acquisition of a rental vehicle through the use of the same phony identification papers Boris rented space under. Finally, RJ would furnish number6 with stolen Police shields, ID cards, and forged blue-back documents that appeared like search warrants in the rare event they were stopped and searched.

For his partisanship:
RJ received a 25% graft from the profits.

With all of that in place, the trip to SLC and back would usually take about a month to five weeks. A 20,000$ investment would net me close to 180,000$ — Every once and again I would personally take the trip with number6, just to get away from Tamara and the grind.

From late '97 through the beginning part of 2001, we made between five and seven runs a year, averaging ten handguns and two assault rifles per trip. We probably brought more than 250 untraceable burners into the New York City limits.

I notified Boris.

I'd be leaving immediately and instructed him place the appropriate advertisements. I hadn't been to SLC in a while, so the first trip would be to get a feel for the environment, possibly pick up a banger or two and double back. I would obtain the majority of the parcel on my second trip, after I was able to gauge responses for the advertisement.

THE END OF MAY.

Conny and I were already on our way to SLC in a silver police-model Crown Victoria cruiser we'd rented with fraudulent ID's. In our possession were our "duty weapons," 10,000$ of my paper, and two NYC Police tins.

I swear | *If we were just a little more stupid.*
We could have been the police.

Early on, we hit a pretty nice lick. A fairly desperate collector was prepared to sell us eight of his semi-automatics for four grand.

He thought he was getting over.

A local gun show finished off my obligation to Tiger.

WE SAFELY RETURNED HOME BY THE LAST WEEK OF JUNE 2002.

That's when things got really interesting. Conny's pressing finally got the better of me. I agreed to meet with his contact, Igor "Monya" S. and at the very least listen to his plans for the next important financial crime. For the nine sticks he took for me | I at least owed Conny that.

THE MORNING OF JULY 2ND 2002.

Conny and I made our way into the Soho area of Manhattan to meet with Monya at a fashionable eatery across from the Burberry boutique.

Monya was already there to greet us.

A greasy Russian, he stood at five-feet, seven inches.

His oval face didn't do a good a job hiding his pudgy cheeks. He used the few long black hairs he had left at the forefront of his scalp to comb-over his receding hairline. Monya's scrawny lips puckered when he extended his hand for a shake. I noticed his gold Rolex Daytona and that he was dressed expensively. "Gary Gunz, I been looking forward to meeting with you for a while. I respect your talent," he squealed, in a whiny, crackled voice.

Every time he spoke, it sounded like he had something to hide.

"Thank you," I replied.

Monya stunk as if he'd been doused in an entire bottle of cologne. It carried a luxurious tang but couldn't hide the reek of garbage that lay underneath it. That's exactly what he was | Garbage.

Monya was *pareyn* of a prominent *Bratan* in the *Zeamlaanskaya* Brotherhood, a close associate of ours. They pretty much did the same thing we did, focusing primarily on financial crimes.

They had a good-lookin' hustle.

It drew the attention of Gene T. who at the time was looking to redeem himself in the eyes of our *Bratva*, you know, after snitching out your humble friend and narrator.

So Gene went to putting the screws to Monya and extorting ten percent of his skim. Monya didn't alert his *Bratan*, he just paid, out of pocket | I guess he didn't want the violence.

Regardless, he had to do something quick or risk the 3R's.

Monya called his father, a *Vor* from the old school.

With his help, he enlisted the services of a Canadian hitter to come work things out. After agreeing on a price (20,000$), Monya wired the funds and set the wheels into motion. It would have all worked out fine, if not for the small matter of the Canadian's phone being wire-tapped by the Mounties for an unrelated case.

They had Monya — *BallsDeep.*
They had his father too.

Monya and his father both copped a plea for reduced charges of aggravated assault and agreed to three calendars, to be served at the federal prison at Allenwood. That's where he and Conny began brain-trust. I knew any involvement with this zero was trouble from the instant my glimpsers peeped this ShitSack.

Still, he was an opponent of Gene's.
How does the saying go | The enemy of my enemy...

Monya ushered us quickly towards a booth near the kitchen, above the loud numbing lull of the trendy village music.
There he broke it down for me.

And I give it to you, my anxious reader.
My very last financial fraud.
It's one for the textbooks.

One I won't ever forget.

Most of the conventional rackets had already been sealed off. Shut-tight. Even crafty, highly lucrative ventures, like the currencies were already becoming dangerously obsolete.

Greedy Russians criminals demand attention.

Some mysterious force—*lets call it stupidity*—compels them to broadcast their business out on full blast. Convicted felons pushing six figure exotic vehicles and carelessly flaunting gaudy $700 Versace florals | Worthless zero's smoking skunk dope right out in the hallway of rented Trump Tower condos. Yah — Why not just call 1-800-FBI and let the receptionist leave a memo for BaconFace "Busy stealing money. Please do not disturb."

Big surprise | The federals were already savvy to the hustle, and since the advent of the Euro-dollar pickings were even slimmer.

Conny was right.

If there was ever a time for something new, it was now.

What Conny and Monya proposed was a lot like the currency fraud, it was purely fictional, and we'd keep (steal) 100% of all investor's money. It also resembled the currencies, in that we'd manufacture all the paperwork as well as invent a fabricated track record showing sizable past returns for our established clientele.

++||— Одесса Мама at its finest —

WHAT I'M SAYING TO YOU NOW IS "HEDGE FUND."

It was the key to fame, fortune, and riches, or so I was told. First, I had to figure out what exactly a hedge fund was.

. . .

HERE IS THE WIKIPEDIA DEFINITION OF HEDGE FUND;

"A hedge fund is an investment fund charging a performance fee and is typically open to only a limited range of investors. In the United States, hedge funds are open to accredited investors only. Because of this restriction they are usually exempt from any direct regulation by the SEC, NASD and other regulatory bodies.

Though the funds do not necessarily hedge their investments against adverse market moves, the term is used to distinguish them from regulated retail investment funds such as mutual funds and pension funds, and from insurance companies.

Hedge funds' activities are limited only by the terms of the contracts governing the particular fund. They can follow complex investment strategies, being long or short assets and entering into futures, swaps and other derivative contracts.

The funds, often organized as limited partnerships in the United States, typically invest on behalf of institutions and high-net-worth individuals. A common objective is to generate returns that are not closely correlated to those of the broader financial markets."

I'LL TELL YOU WHAT IT MEANS TO ME SOMEONE LIKE ME.

It's another grey area of the marketplace that's completely unregulated. As long as we didn't put our business out to the street, we'd able to do the 'ole in-out and grab a few lemons take-home.

"I'm telling you, Gunny, we need to crank this for no more than eight or nine months. That's it. We can clean up with this *here*," Monya announced. "I don't know. It seems real sketchy, this hedge fund shit. We've got no leads, no crew, no office, nothing. I'm skeptical about this whole thing, you know, after Cousin Al's dogshit went down like it did," I insisted. "You don't worry about nothing Gary. I got leads I've been holding for years. Gruntal, Pain-Webber, that old school micro. Hasn't been touched in years. And I know you been keeping all your old clients on the stash," Conny said excitedly.

"We pitch in three ways for the office. I already got my eye on a space. And about the *brigada*, we got a fresh batch of youngbloods on the come-up. They look up to you and Conny like legends in the game. It's gonna be cake to get 'em trained and pushing product," Monya stated. I paused for a moment, contemplating the prospect of a new crop of criminals ready to pledge-all to the brotherhood. "How about the Cousin? You know me and Conny still with *Pushkatzkaya*," I affirmed. "Fuck him. You see how dirty he did you. This is the rebirth, brother. We're gonna make ourselves a *new Bratva*, starting with us. He lost all loyalty from his *Bratans*. They got shafted like you did. Bobby Tiger and his *brigada* already got down with us. Besides, he ain't coming back for who knows when. Motherfuckers gotta eat. It's time to take what we came for and get to moving the fuck out this shit. It's gonna flush both of us heavy. You my dawg forever bro. No matter what you decide" Conny proclaimed, putting his arm on my shoulder.

I considered the very nature of my situation.
My finances were depleted to a derisory forty dimes and falling.

Conny was right | From the very start all the chips were stacked against me. I was a convicted felon and could never be a registered-rep. I was getting old and tired of playing the game. I felt hackneyed from endless hours on the phone, burned out and jaded. I had all this talent, wasted on stale endeavors, which yielded nothing but regret and shame. My entire life I felt like a prisoner. Like a stranger in a no-name town.

I took a deep swig from my flask then reached in my pocket and pulled out my DuPont lighter then spun it between my thumb and forefinger. Finally, I lit my Newport.

"Eight or nine months you said?" I mumbled. "That's right, Gunny. A year, max. We can start working on the paperwork now. We could be ready in two months and then we home again, baby-boy," C affirmed | He knew before I knew.

++||— He was Older|Colder —

"I'm in. Give me whatever information you have on hedge funds and I'll start making it happen," I announced.

The three of us raised our beverages.

"Loyalty," Conny avowed.

"Unconditional Love," I confirmed.

I quickly began putting it all together.

* * *

By December of that year we were in a shoddy upstairs office located in the small area between Little Italy and China Town.

On New Year's Eve, Conny and Monya composed an intense gathering. We threw a party at National restaurant fully knowing that Sammy Movefaker would probably be there.

In fact, we were counting on it.
It would be the ideal opportunity to unfold our influence.

With everyone either turning informant or ghosting-out, there was room for advancement. Bugsy was home from a two-year stint on Rikers for forgery in the 1st. He was original TF and fiercely loyal to Conny — Bugsy wasn't very brainy but prompt with his vengeance.

He and his RoadDog Kazuole were on an aggressive campaign of recruiting fresh neighborhood youngbloods. They brought about eighteen hungry freshmen ranging in age from fourteen to nineteen to our position located in the back of the main hall area.

At the table adjacent ours sat Bobby Tiger, his *brigada*, and Jerry Albania with a few of his loyalists. While I was playing business-owner|dope-fiend, The Tulips were hitting licks all over town.

We all raised our glasses in *L'chaim* and greeted the young recruits into our party.

"Welcome," Conny said diffidently.

"We receive you all tonight as young brothers" he continued.

I moved my chair over, allowing C to rise and address the arrivals. They all assumed seats at a table near ours that we specifically prepared for them.

"Who are you?" the most ambitious looking of the bunch asked defiantly — Pausing for a moment, Conny approached the youth who had inquired, he closed in until they were almost eye2eye. Conny wiped the cigarette ash from his costly denims and sneered a bit before supplying his retort.

"For all y'all that's not heard.
I'm C-Murder:
I done|done things y'all ain't never heard of.
I done slung-rocks, pushed-stocks, locked-blocks,
|| Slapped Cops ||
I've had to merk clowns, and I done|done time.
Ψ I'm a *fool-boy* Ψ
You call me "DaFool" if y'want.
Willin' to die *for mine*."

Conny lifted his pants making sure the handle of his blaster intimidated the assembly before he sat back down next to me and winked. "Now this gentleman here," Conny stated, putting his hand on my shoulder.

"This here's Gary Gunz.
By twenty-five he survived it.
Russian tyrant | Outdrink an Irish.
Bright but violent, he *invites* the sirens.
Y'all learn a little something from this man," He finished.

Conny stood again to lecture the young initiates.

I LISTENED TO HIS STORIES FOR A BRIEF MOMENT.

It was the same rhetoric I'd heard for years.

A carefully crafted indoctrination designed to impassion irrevocable allegiance | To romance its listeners into believing our life was sexy and that we were in control.

Truth | It was a fictitious demonstration of an enchanted life in which bonding your duty to the brotherhood guaranteed you greatness and certified your victory — I let out a faint chuckle before finishing my teacup of potion and excusing myself to the restroom.

Conny was finishing up his speech when I returned.

"So there you have it..."
he paused looking at me for a moment.
"Listen to this lesson that I'm stressin'
"Shake with your right: but in your left hold the Smith&Wesson."

The initiates stared in adulation.

I GLANCED AT THE PLEDGES.

I didn't recognize any of the youngbloods. Not that I could have, they all looked like anonymous blurs to me. It wasn't the combination of Georgi+Norco+Cocaine — I needed that just to keep baseline.

I 'd seen too many youngsters try to make it on the come-up. I just didn't pay attention anymore. I didn't make new alliances. I didn't want to run the risk of committing my affections to anyone new — *I knew this game too well* — If even one of these young hustlers made it past twenty-two, it would surprise me.

I remained completely detached.
It was the only way I could keep my mettle.
It was the only way I could keep *from snuffing all of it.*

Although I didn't know their faces, I recognized the glances they threw. Expressions of distrust and envy. I recognized the starvation in their eyes. The way they gawked at our Rolexes and Italian leathers.

Every single one of them looked like BennyBlanco *from the Bronx.*
++||— Ready to make his power movement —

MOVEFAKER CAME IN WITH YALLENA SOMETIME BEFORE MIDNIGHT.

He didn't notice me, alone, in a darker area of the back section. Conny saw him before I did and signaled to me.

"Wait a tick C, it'll be better when he gets comfortable," I mumbled. Conny nodded and I sat back and downed a full teacup of my potion. A few minutes after the ball dropped, I stood and cut my way through the packed auditorium toward Sammy's table.

I had to be sure this grabbed everybody's attention.
That was the point.

The music slowed to a crawl as I approached him.
Both Conny and Bugsy were close behind.
Sammy and Yallena were dressed gaudily and sat with two members of the National family, her father and older brother. They were stunned when I grabbed a chair from the table next to theirs, pulled it close to Sammy, and faced it backwards to sit comfortably.

"What's good Sammy?" I slurred, already drunk; out of sanity. "Don't answer. Just listen," I said.

Yallena, her father, and brother attempted to leave.

"Nobody goes anywhere till Gunny is finished," Bugsy commanded, flashing the chrome blaster in his pants.

"Do you know who we are?" Yallena's father barked in a heavy Russian accent. "I don't fuckin' care," Bugsy cackled.

He mushed the back of his head hard and heavy, causing a violent jerk forward.

Conny crossed his arms and laughed.

"Gary, I'm sorry about everything. I know I fucked you bad," Sammy cried. "I changed though. I'm not into any of that shit no more. I went to rehab, I been going to AA meetings. Lana's having a baby, Gunny. Please brother," Sammy pleaded. "I just came here to eat and have a good time. Please." Both he and Yallena began to cry, and as I noticed their tears, I thought briefly of Judi — *My poor Judi.*

"You changed, huh Sammy?" I queried. "I don't think you changed at all. You were never in the game, so how could you leave it?" I laughed, then leaned over to look at the table.

There was an assortment of luxurious foods scattered about.

Sammy had a plate of fish next to him.

I puckered my lips then grabbed a piece with my hands and bit into it. "Nasty," I snapped and threw it back on his plate. "You eating this shit Sammy? It's nasty as fuck. Here's some flavor," I said, sucking back all the mucus from inside my nose, a nasty bunch lined with blood and cocaine residue — I spit it onto his plate.

"Eat up then," I stated coldly.

He looked at me despicably.

I bellowed a hollow laughter.

"Eat your food then," I screamed, backhanding him hard on his left cheek. After he had finished his plate, I told him what was expected. "I don't care how, Sammy, you produce fifty stones in the next two weeks. Bugsy here is gonna see you. Don't make him Jet-Li you. I'm gonna pardon the other fifty, due to the fact that you leaving us. Make it a parting gift, you know, for the baby and all. From Uncle Gunny. I'll tell you this though, I hear about you so much as trying to sell an illegal firecracker, its GameOver. You're on your last life, Sammy." I rubbed his freshly shaven head then lightly slapped his forehead.

Bugsy guarded the table while we assembled our party and exited to the street.

Sammy never came up with the paper.

In fact | He was the NowhereMan.

I later found out, he left town the next day and didn't return until after I died. Last I heard, he married Yallena, and the National family fronted them a few hundred thousand for a limousine service in Queens.

APRIL OF '03 THE HEDGE FUND FULLY SET INTO MOTION.

Delays in properly facilitating the back-end kept us in a hold pattern for a while.

The hedge fund itself prospered insistently. Near the end February of 2004, we'd misappropriated more than two million dollars of investors' money.

I would love nothing more than to report to you that everything went according to plan, and I received my 33% share of the 2MM$.

That would just have been wonderful.

I probably would've spent most of it on prostitutes, the rest on pills and freebase. *Then* — On to the next big score.

THINGS DIDN'T GO ACCORDING TO PLAN.

Not my plan anyways.

I'd been receiving small installments of 30-50K monthly. That was the program, until we dropped the curtain. Most of it I gave away to the dopeman. What little remained was spent on said prostitutes.

In the end, it was the same story.
++||— Monya burned-off with all the money —

Of course he came up with the same bullshit. "The feds found out about the funds and froze everything. What can I do," he said.

In reality | I ate through most of my share just maintaining my lifestyle and supporting my highs. I didn't see it that way though. I wanted retribution for all the wrong that had been done me.

Somebody always has to pay.

IT WAS THE END OF FEBRUARY 2004.

I was left with roughly 100,000$, a couple Rolex watches, and a closet full of decent clothes. That's about all my years of life had brought me. I had no future — *I was miserable.*

Tamara left a few days prior.

We called it a separation, but in reality, we were never really together. The Gary she married was long gone. In his place, a broken proxy of a man. It wasn't her | It was me.

++||— *I couldn't look at myself* —
How could I possibly look at her?

433

MARCH 2004.

I met Conny at the Seagate bathhouse — *He had a new plan.*

Some kind of real estate scheme he claimed would put us back on the map. "This time it would be legit," he claimed.

Bugsy alerted me to C's real situation.

His mother was one of those fortunate few late for work in the fallen towers of September 11th. Her entire office was decimated. Only she and one other survived. She collected more than 3MM$ in insurance money and government assistance.

Conny was richer than he let on. He wasn't after money. He wanted the power and respect that came with being a boss. He felt like it was *his* time, like he deserved it.

IT WAS BECOMING INCREASINGLY CLEAR:

My time *was about* deaded.

I needed to get out of this game forever.

Maybe open a restaurant — Call it *'Gunnys'*.

"People" would come just on principle.

I TOLD CONNY I NEEDED ANOTHER TRIP TO SLC.

I even asked him to come, but he refused. He met a woman in the meantime. A pretty young girl named Judi.

++||— *They were having a baby* —

APRIL 16TH.

I filled the trunk of a beige Crown-Victoria I rented with clothes enough to keep me for a few months. On my person I carried my entire net-worth, 91,000$, and two large baggies filled with assorted tablets — *I had a different plan this time.*

This time I would triumph.

I gave Boris ample notice to place numerous advertisements for firearms. In two months, he fielded more than fifty replies.

The Plan: procure over a one hundred burners and bring them all home at once — *That would net my elusive million dollars.*

I would finally be content.

Mid-July | Posing as an out-of-town real estate speculator, I rented an apartment in an exclusive district of town square. If I'd learned anything, it was to do my business right under their nose — Where they least suspected. I used some of my cash to purchase a black Ford 1500 pickup, the bed of which I intended to fill to the brim with blasters.

Then drive home and get right back to it.

* * *

SEPTEMBER 16, 2004.

It was a day like any other day.

Another day, like the handful of days that preceded.

I woke up next to a blonde large-breasted female named Misty. She was the managing agent of the building I rented at. She enjoyed crystal-meth and pills. Our mutual love of such vices had drawn us together. She was staying with me, at my apartment.

Neither of us had slept much for weeks.

Sometime during our stay together, Misty discovered my true intentions — *It must have been the room full of guns that gave me away.*

I had business to attend to at a suburb about three hours away and had managed a few hours' sleep the night before. There was a gentleman there willing to part with a Springfield 1911 for 250$.

What a deal, I thought.

I installed the almost-full pint of vodka on my nightstand, swallowed a glob of pills, and smoked a bowl of the crystal. I put on my best denims and inserted Ace into an in-the-pants holster I bought at a local gun show. Already showered, I dabbed on some cologne and instructed Misty to ready a steak for my return, in about six or so hours.

Inside my "secret" room, I had more than thirty dimes and ninety blasters big and small.

++||— I was about ready to make the BlockHot —
In a few days | I was ready to big-action go home

Yep, a day like any other.
A day like all of my other pointlessly vacant days.

A REAL DEAL IT WAS.
The deal of my *DeathTime.*

Ψ — Ψ — Ψ

1.
2.

PART 4

Life After Death

✳✳✳

14

ONLY G-D CAN JUDGE ME

You come full circle
  Now you're home
  Without the gold — Without the chrome
  And this is where you've always been
  You had to lose so you could win
  -Elton

WE CHOSE TO COME HERE.

                    By we, I mean us human beings.
              And by here, I mean the planet Earth.

HUMANS CHOSE TO COME TO EARTH.
  Man, that one was the hardest one for me to wrap my mind around.
  I didn't want to believe it when I heard — I lived my entire life under the pretense that I never chose to be born, let alone come to Earth. I thought it a curse of some kind having to endure the burden of life here | On this filthy mudball.

A place of unfairness and cruelty.
Where I was *forced* to be an animal.

I justified all my actions based on the assumption that I was here against my will. I would often think '*I never wanted this life, so I'm gonna do whatever I gotta do, so I can get what's mine.*'

The moral implications didn't matter to me.

I was like a POW, trapped inside a cell by enemies of the state.
If I needed to jump out on a guard or two to get some extra rations, that was fine by me. They had me trapped : *What could I do?*
What the fuck did it matter matter anyways.

Then I learned some universal truths.

Out of all them, *that one*, was the hardest for me to swallow.
It went against everything I based my life on. It went against all of my learned fundamental thinking and behaviors.
++||— *Four minutes of death has a strange effect on a soul* —

WE CHOSE TO COME HERE SO WE COULD GROW SPIRITUALLY.
Think of Earth as a boot-camp for the soul. The lessons we have to learn while we're in the material plane, in physical form, are pivotal for our spiritual evolution and our ultimate destination towards higher understanding.

The ultimate goal is communion with God.

Right around now, you're probably asking yourself what a despicable zero like me could ever know about God, or even better, how you got roped into reading about a born again _____ on a mission to convert every single creature on the planet (living or dead) to _____ or face the consequence of an eternity burning in a hell where they tear out your fingernails and shove massive pineapples up your pooter.

I'm no fanatic.
I'm not even religious for that matter.
And as for knowing about God | I probably know less than most.

I know what I know | *Truth.*

The traditional hell you hear about in church or temple or wherever it is you donate your valuable time and money is falsehood.
I don't know whether it's a lie or a hoax or wishful thinking.
Reality is, I don't know much of anything at all.
If I did, I would never have ended hanging by the neck in a freezing 6X9, where I went straight to hell.

Hell is nothing.
In hell there is no you.

Only black nothing — You just cease to exist.

All your thoughts, dreams, passions, hopes, loves, experiences, your very being, the essence of *you* is no longer. You simply get recycled into the great cosmic recycle bin for your lifeforce to get reused in some other productive way.
Maybe a vindictive, punishing God would forever banish you to a place of torture. I'm here to tell you that God is neither cruel nor malicious — God is just God — Attempting to explain God is equivalent of describing the internet to an ant | It's not possible.
And trying to understand God, for me, has always been pointless.

He's a God and I'm a Gary — *I'll just leave it at that.*

Let's say for instance that God *did* put you in that horrible place, you know, if you didn't meet the criteria for going up to the altar, so you could pray for all eternity instead.

So now you're in red hell, horned devils everywhere poking you in the bunghole and burning your flesh in giant copper pots.

Well at least there is a you.

The place I'm referring to is nothing.
Total dark|blackness, where you're completely erased.

Sorry kid, you didn't make the cut | Gotta go.
Like *you* were never even *here* to begin with.

There can be no worse possible outcome

Wanna know how I know? *Cause I been there.*

Most all of us, sometimes as early as birth have been led to believe in the concept of heaven and hell.

I was told that after my death, based upon choices and actions throughout the course of my life, I would be judged by a long, white-haired, bearded God (who looked much like Charlton Hesston). He would sit up on his ornate towering throne, a mysterious God always shrouded by clouds high up in the sky. God would have a list of all things I did wrong and he would recite them to me verbatim, one at a time: Then he would dole out his punishment.

I'm gonna give you this one small piece of wisdom.

It's a real jewel.
Look at it later if you want | It's yours to keep.

GOD *really doesn't care* what we do.

SURE, HE WANTS US TO GROW SPIRITUALLY AND DRAW CLOSER TO HIM.

But the real fact of the matter is that God is perfectly content leaving us down here to it.

Many people confuse free-will with the ability to do whatever we want, whenever we want. We live in a world based on scientific constraints and physical limitations.

I pose this question to you | *What can we really do?*
Can we be in two places at once?
Can we breathe under water?

Can we teleport to the Himalayas *and shake hands with Dr. Strange?*
Just by willing it?

As much as we would like to, we can't survive without basic necessities such as food, clothing, and shelter. The simple truth of it is that we, as corporeal beings, *can't* do what we want at all.

Free will is a great concept, but it lacks credibility.

I have come to find that free will is merely the ability to make choices. To choose whether we want McDonald's or KFC. To pick whether we want to wear slacks or a dress. To decide whether we should use the premium gasoline or the cheap stuff.

Life is a series of decisions.
They all lead into one another.
Each one is a continuation of the last.

In reality, there is only one real choice to make.
Right | Wrong — God or Ignorance.

Stupid *is a choice too.*

EVERY SOUL, INSTINCTIVELY, HAS AN INCLINATION TOWARDS GOD.

We are born into this world with it.

Some will argue that there are persons who inhabit these lands who were never granted this insight. I am inclined to believe their speculation as preposterous — More so, downright ignorant.

Go ask a death-row inmate or a fox-hole soldier what they think about that. Those continually in the presence of death are able to navigate clear through the rubbish and better see with soulful, deep spiritual insight.

THERE ARE OTHERS PROCLAIMING A MONOPOLY ON GOD.

Commit yourself fully. Follow close their preachings. Volunteer in their ministries. And most importantly of all, with your greatest enthusiasm, eagerly give away the bulk of your paper money, and they will make use their exclusive direct channel to God to manifest for you magnificent blessing that you are now entitled to receive.

Under no circumstance can you ignore these very specific instructions, lest damnation to an eternity of red hell is a surety.

These convinces are quite adept at well...Con(vince)ing.

Fabricating fear and enticing our covetous materialist programming, that sounds more like *"the Carrot and the Stick"* rather than a Supreme Being on the lookout for our best interest.

I can safely state these facts to you sincerely | I know Truth.
Unfortunately|Fortunately, I had to die to find it.

It was never God's intention to judge us for anything we did, may have done, intended to do, or thought of doing.

In the end, God doesn't judge us | *We judge ourselves.*

When we die, our spiritual eyes are opened and we realize the universal truths, some of which I'm now discussing. Once our eyes are opened to Truth, it becomes easy to judge ourselves.

. . .

WHAT OUR JUDGMENT IS *REALLY* BASED ON IS OUR INTEGRITY.

Our character | Mainly how we treated others and how well we fulfilled our purpose for living.

Every single one of us has purpose to fulfill.

We each have a task to do, a mission to complete. As unique beings we are each given unique gifts and come to earth for so many countless different reasons | I don't know what yours are.

Most of the time I don't even know mine.

THE MEANING OF LIFE — I'VE SO OFTEN PONDERED IT.

I've heard many deeply philosophical definitions.

Mine is the one I took back with me from the dark|black nothing. One of our most popular beliefs is the notion that life is about learning how to love.

Love is easy.

I love eating BlueBell ice-cream.
I love looking at SciFi-movies.
I love the moon and the ocean.
I love GeorgiVodka+LortabTablets.
I love doing 1hundred*mph* on my HD SoftTail.
I love my Scorpion carbine.

I Love My Mother.
✧ ✧ ✧

Life Meaning #1: Forgiveness.

Forgiveness now that one — *That one's Fucked up.*

About the hardest thing there is to do is forgive.

It takes character.

It requires courage.

It demands selflessness.

I would like to take a small moment to share something intimate with you. In order for me to be forgiven | I must first forgive.

And I'll be GodDamned *if I want to.*

Especially when I'm justifiably hurt or wronged.

When deep within my core I *know* that you have done me an undeserved slight | The very last thing that I want to give *you* is my forgiveness.

Here's the funny thing though.

It was only when I forgave *Everybody for Everything* that I was granted the keys to the blessings I never deserved.

When I gave myself permission to pardon every single Hurt, Slight, Hardship, Unfairness, BrokenPromise — Every last little piece of DirtyNastiness that I had in some way been a part of, *either inflictor or inflicted* — It was at the exact moment that I received my reward.

A massive download of Truth.

Life Meaning #2: Truth.

Something an alcoholic|doper like myself finds very elusive.

445

I'm not talking about "the truth."
Truth in itself is what I'm referring to.

Truth with a capitol T.

You see, "the truth" is created in the truth factory.
It's manufactured to fit the narrative of the elites, the super-rich, the communists, the capitalists, the church, the mosque, the working-class, antifa, the tea party, talk radio, CNN, FOXnews | *All of them.*

They each and everyone have a truth that they believe to be well...the truth. That's not the truth that I'm getting at.

Look for it, and you'll understand what it is. Seek it out in the same manner that a prospector searches for his vein of gold | Allow *nothing* to stand in your way.

You'll recognize it when you find it.

Protect it from corruption, use it with consideration, share it wastefully and it will remain forever yours to keep.

It is purposefully kept secret.
On this plane of existence | Truth is Priceless.
Its rewards are Limitless.

We chose to come to Earth is to develop character.
The primary foundation of our character is Integrity.
Our integrity is the only thing we get to take with us when we go.
As a being who died for four solid minutes and granted a few tiny insights. I present to you my definition of integrity:

Integrity: *Allowing yourself to go through pain, whether it be emotional, physical, mental or spiritual, as a result of standing for Truth.*

Here's a simple example.

Your rent is due, but you just lost your job and have no money to pay. You hand your last twenty to the gas station attendant to fill your tank, so you can go to an interview tomorrow

He hands you back change for a hundred dollars.

What do you do?

Integrity is what we do when nobody's around, when nobody is watching. It's how we behave when all of the chips are down, and we're presented with an opportunity to be dishonest for the right reasons.

Another for instance.

Your friends are racist and insist on blaming minorities for their problems. Tonight, they decide to take their ignorance to the next level and find someone to smash on. You know that it's wrong but don't want to alienate yourself from your closest peers.

What do you do?

Do you decide to not show up and let your "friends" carry out their plans without you? Do you come out and tell your main-homeboys they need to put the brakes on their plans? Do you sprint down to the police station and sound the alarm on your main-homeboy#1? Do you succumb to peer pressure and do what you know to be wrong—not to disappoint your "friends"?

Integrity.

NELSON MANDELA — A man with integrity.

All he had to do was sign a piece of paper that denounced everything most important to him and the authorities would let him go home | *He did twenty-seven calendars instead.*

That's what all this is really about.

In the afterlife, there is no language.

Beings don't speak English, French, or Turkish. We communicate through thoughts, which are heard by all other spirits around us.

We're drawn to those that think like we do.

Nobody thought like me.

Or perhaps I was just ashamed of the way I thought.

It didn't make a shit anyways | The end result was the same. I went to lonely dark|blackness of hell. Here's the funniest|saddest part: If it's as I say. If in the end we *really* do judge ourselves—Only we can choose to put ourselves there—I guess in the end, you start thinking about the beginning, about what really happened, how you came to this particular end | I lied to live and ran from Truth.

My entire life, I was looking for an answer.

I was determined to get to that answer however I had to.

++||— Even if that meant taking yours —

I never even knew the question.

I consistently filled the emptiness inside, the large hole that I had at the center of my core, with dope, alcohol, and as much material wealth as I could stuff, in an effort to mask the fact that I was indeed sick from the inside out. Spiritually bankrupt would probably be a better description.

I woke up handcuffed to a chair.

I found myself inside the waiting room of a hospital bearing the initials of an American president who was never elected and put in a position of leadership during a pivotal and tumultuous time in our nation's history.

When I came back to life, some of my first realizations:

> Colors were more brilliant.
> People didn't look the same.
> The world smelled strange.

> *Everything was different.*

Jailers returned me to my padded hole where I sat quietly for a couple more days than a few.

> I didn't know what happened.
> I just knew I wasn't the same anymore.
> But I somehow knew everything would be alright.

Within a month I was returned to general population where I met with an attorney assigned to me by the court.

He filled in the blanks.

The woman staying at my apartment did indeed find my private chamber of firearms and cash. She notified her brother, a state trooper. He and two of his comrades decided it was time to transfer ownership of the contents of said chamber to themselves.

> Possession is 9|10th of the law.

They intended to make the transplant while I was out purchasing a new blaster. Maybe I was early—perhaps they were running late. I noticed my front door cracked and a shadowy figure slightly protrude from the entrance as I walked back from the parking garage.

Before returning home, I made the time to stop at the gun range to try out my new Springfield 4|5. I purchased a box of hollow point shells and proceeded to load the magazine.

You know, just-in-case I need to blast.

> Ace at my side, already had a killing slug in the hole.

I took the new blaster, the 1911 4|5 auto, out her box, inserted a full magazine—*racked it*— then ducked under the auto nearest my door and waited to make sure I wasn't hallucinating.

I hadn't slept for over a week. This could all have been some trippy visual byproduct of my insane mind and my inability to keep from installing dope and GeorgiVodka into my bloodstream. I waited long enough to see the stranger light a square. After finishing the remainder of my pint, I did the same.

I didn't say a word.
I just started blasting.

Both my heaters spit shells into the hallway.
The bandit ducked into my apartment and returned fire.

I ran up to the entrance only to hear two other voices coming from inside. I fired through the door, emptying both my magazines into the apartment then darted towards the staircase for some cover.

Then I heard it | Apparently one of the intruders had discovered my stash. He was now holding of my Chinese Kalashnikovs (converted to full auto) and began rapidly bursting projectiles throughout the entire area.

I ran up the stairs | I needed out of there.
I didn't know what was going on.
++||— *Everything was lost* —

By the time I made it to my pickup at the front entrance of the garage, three police cruisers in a roadblock pattern, were already waiting for me. Seven uniforms with their guns drawn guarded the exit | *They fired the second they saw my face.*

I saw the air break as two missiles whizzed by my head.
I let go of my guns and dropped to the floor.
I don't know what hit first.
Me *or the blasters.*

I was looking at attempted murder on three plainclothes. It was ShowsOver|*ThatsAWrap* for your humble friend and narrator.

God had other plans.

I don't know why he chose to give *me* his grace. I've been told not to ask such questions. The I longer I stick around and not put that shit inside me | More will be revealed.

The lawyer informed me that all of the evidence, all ninety-ish firearms and my thirty thousand cash were gone. The troopers at my apartment weren't there to crack "the mysterious case of the ugly New-Yorker with a hundred blasters." Fuck-no | They were there to steal my shit. And they wanted that type of heat about as much as wanted 25toLife — So they went right ahead and stole all my shit.

They also took (stole) the two heaters I shot at them.

They really had nothing.

Except the room and hallway full of bullet holes.

They did have that — It wasn't enough to get me much time without the actual heaters. They knew it. When they brought me to the bullpen and booked me I had twenty or so Norco pills in my pocket | Those charges would stick for sure. The dope plus the bullet holes and they had something more than a little.

Out of the entire circuit, my judge was the harshest on drug offenses — Her son, a hopeless dope fiend, had been through dozens of treatment centers and prison.

With no end to his pathetic existence in sight, he decided to snuff it | *It worked better for him* than it did for me.

I was looking at time for sure.

As fate would have it, she wasn't there for my court appearance, had some important stinky bigshit business to do.

The replacement judge was more sympathetic.

My court-appointed managed to persuade him that I was a dope fiend in need of rehab instead of prison time. The honorable Judge Nary GaveAShit said he knew just the thing for me.

I was sentenced to complete a nine-month "treatment" program, after which I would be on probation for two years with mandatory attendance at three Alcoholics Anonymous meetings per week, for the duration of those two years.

* * *

THIS WAS NEVER WHO I INTENDED TO BE.

I had such good intentions.

How many mistakes does it take before you're bad?

Does it start with a harmless little white lie and slowly progress to fraud—murder—worse? Does it matter if you do the wrong things for the right reasons?

TS Eliot famously said "Most of the evil in this world is done by people with good intentions" And what is it again that they always say about the road to hell...

IF I DIDN'T KNOW ABOUT SOMETHING.

It was my job to convince you that I did well enough to gain your trust and part you from your money | I always had to be the smartest and the best. Everything I'd once known to be true and right had collapsed. The lies, deceit, and transgressions of my life had come full circle.

I WAS RIGHT BACK AT THE BEGINNING.
All of my intelligence | My best thinking, had failed me.
I didn't know much of anything anymore.

EVERY MAJOR RELIGION HAS A RESURRECTION.

You become "Reborn" It's a rebirth of values, morals, and convictions | A rebirth of faith.

Faith: *The sincere belief that as long as I continue to walk with my feet and do the very next right thing that meets the path in front of me, everything will work out exactly the way it was supposed to.*

Although I don't subscribe to many religious theories.

I do believe in rebirth — *I'm forced to* | It happened to me. When I came back to life, the only thing I knew was that I wanted no part of my old one. Nobody would answer when I called them.

All my so-called friends had abandoned me.

Well that's not all the way true | After calling Tamara's law office more than a dozen times, she finally accepted my collect call.

She tastefully notified me that she and my 'forever brother' RJ had been fucking for years. Tamara wanted a divorce so they could wed and live happily ever after | I didn't contest.

That whole life was a fictitious hoax created for the sole purpose of disguising the truth.

There was no loyalty.
No honor — No respect | All illusions.

All I ever gained from my criminal activities, The street fame and material wealth, it was never enough. How could it be? I never knew what I wanted to begin with.

EARLIER ON.

Perhaps sometime at the very start, possibly even when I had made that very first decision to compromise my integrity. We briefly touched on the differences surrounding intelligence and wisdom.

You know the real difference between intelligence and wisdom?

Intelligence dictates that 2+2 equals 4 | *Everyone knows that.*

Wisdom — *What the fuck is a 2?*

I don't know what 2 is | *Nobody does.*

I didn't know who I was anymore.

And I had no idea who I wanted to be — *Gary Gunz* — He died hanging by the neck with a pair of shit-stained pants in a freezing cold jail cell. Suicide is often referred to as "the coward's way out." I can't say that it is or isn't. What I can attest to without hesitation is that Gary Gunz was in terrible pain and had lost all hope. He had given up and was ready to listen, only like the *dying* can be.

IT TOOK FIVE WEEKS FOR A BED TO OPEN AT THE TREATMENT FACILITY.

In total, I spent less than two months in county lockup. A small price to pay for my life of crime, attempting to smuggle over ninety firearms across state lines, and shooting at officer CrumbFace.

My luck was working overtime | *Or so I thought.*

FUNNY ANECDOTE: A priest and a Rabbi are sitting in the front row of a championship boxing match. The champion comes into the ring. *The crowd cheers.* The contender soon follows, but before the bell rings, he crosses himself, you know, that thing where he waves his hands around to make the cross symbol. The Rabbi turns to the priest and asks "What is he doing that for? What does that mean?"

The priest answers "Nothing, if he doesn't know how to fight."

I had survived the streets.
Suicide | My best efforts at snuffing it.

Even though I survived death, what I didn't know was how to live.
I needed to learn some basic character.

TWO MEN FROM THE "TREATMENT" FACILITY CAME TO PICK ME UP AT THE jail. They were pleasant, neatly dressed middle-aged fellows who introduced themselves and Chris and Mike.

My impounded pickup had been auctioned off to the highest bidder (undoubtedly a family relation of the same "lawmen" that boosted my graft). I had in my possession the sum of my earthly belongings, a pair of jeans and a camouflage t-shirt.

> For the first time in as long as I could remember,
> I walked outside without Ace | *I missed him.*

They took me to a white van and drove more than one-hundred miles to a twelve-acre plot of land in a scarcely populated area of a suburb. Both men were residents of the program and in the third and final stage of their treatment. They described some of the day-to-day activities at the center. I didn't understand much of what they said. Long years of substance abuse tend to stunt your emotional growth.

> Emotionally, I was a newborn.

THE FACILITY WAS A GRIM COMPOUND-LIKE STRUCTURE.

It spanning more than twenty-five-thousand square feet—was located near the beginning of the lot. A tall flagpole at the front of the parking area waved a banner displaying the facility's name and motto, "A Place for Change"

There were no bars or picket towers, although the type of place this was, there should have been. There was only a small parking lot at the entrance of the compound and a loading dock at the rear right corner. We pulled into the loading bay and exited the auto.

I was taken to a carefully manicured entrance area.

Two other residents performed an intake procedure that entailed signing about thirty pages of paperwork and disclaimer forms. I was then given a bowl of food from the cafeteria and rushed to a dormitory for a shower.

"REHAB" IS A SUGGESTIVE WORD.

It evokes any range of imagery or emotions — Its definitions largely dependent upon the visualization of the person who's imagining it. When people hear "rehab" they tend to picture a state-funded hospital where semi functioning, doped-up patients are detoxified off crack-cocaine, heroin, or alcohol.

Some people even imagine that rehab is a classy, sleek looking place like the Betty Ford Clinic, where patients are kept in white robes and Dr. Oz types treat them like superstars.

Where I was at fit neither stereotype.

In theory I guess it can be called a treatment center.

What it really was a 'Therapeutic Community'.

Although there are community supervisors (paid employees), a TC (Therapeutic Community) is a rehabilitation facility where a structure system has been established that allows it to be resident-operated. Older members (dope-fiends who've lived there longer) act as the counselors and dole out "treatment" (punishments) for behavioral infractions committed by any of the residents.

Perhaps it wasn't a conventional treatment facility.

But trust me: *I did not get shortchanged on my treatment.*

THE FACILITY WAS A SELF-CONTAINED UNIT.

Other than consumables like food and hygiene items, it was completely independent from the free outside world.

There were plenty of rules. *This place* — It was more like a culture. The fundamental principle is that dope and alcohol are never the real problem. The root cause of our addictions was our behavior. If we could find a way to reprogram our negative behaviors, then we could cure ourselves of all our difficulties.

It really sounded great.

I'm sure for some it was.

Immediately after a shower I was given a newcomer packet and escorted into a classroom to begin my learnings.

There were about fourteen classroom desks, the cheap kind with an arm to write on attached to the side, affixed in a circular pattern. A ramshackle teacher's desk and a swivel whiteboard were positioned at the front of the room. There were no windows, oaktag bulletins with keywords and slogans were coving them.

Two older members lectured the class.

I was asked to introduce myself to my "peers" (other dope-fiends who came in and went through the newcomer process around the same time I did) | They all welcomed me cheerily.

This wouldn't be so bad, I thought.
My thinking was flawed.
It was my best thinking that brought me there to begin with.

A TC WORKS ON THE THEORY THAT THE PATIENTS TREAT EACH OTHER.

At the very basic level you have a "pull-up".

This TC defines a pull-up as a friendly, sometimes stern, reminder of something you have said, done, or failed to do.

When you catch another resident doing something they shouldn't be, not doing something they are supposed to, or saying something inappropriate to anyone either in the facility or outside of it, it's your duty to "pull them up."

These phrases here are your six basic PullUp starter pack.

"You can't say that." "You can't do that."
"You can't express that." "Be more aware."
"You need to follow up." "Stay on top of that."

Of course you're encouraged to be creative and come up with your own. Every pull-up, whether valid or invalid, *must* be "supported."

The definition of support is simply saying "Thank you" and correcting the problem. Once a pull-up is made it becomes a "situation." There's no bickering, it's either supported or not supported — You can't take it back or talk about it afterwards, that's called "going back into a situation" and is a situation all in itself.

Every situation *must* be "relayed."

A relay is a snitch move.
A dirty cheese-eating rat snitch move.
Something that goes against every street instinct you have.

On the street
++||— Snitches get stitches —
And dirty cheese eating-rats end up in fuckin' ditches.

You report the situation to an expediter[1] who jots it down on a special paper then places a batch at the end of the day in a relay bin.

All relays are handled by coordinators.

If your name appears on a relay form at the end of the day you're called in for "operations." Operations is a room with two older members, usually a male and a female of different ethnic backgrounds, who sit you down and review the incident with you then deliver an appropriate "assessment".

The assessment is your *"treatment."*

That's a great word, "assessment."
It's really a cruel punishment.

You can't call it a punishment.
Calling it that would create a situation.
Requiring further assessment | *More punishment.*

There are plenty of other rules — I'm thinking you get the idea.

THE FIRST THIRTY DAYS — I DIDN'T GET TO SEE MUCH "TREATMENT."
There wasn't much of anything to do.

Three times a day we went from the classroom to the cafeteria for chow, then back to class. The two older members let us outside into an enclosed vestibule attached to the dorm rooms we slept in to smoke squares that were issued us by the facility (they gave me thirteen packs a month of generic brand cigarettes) four times a day.

Every morning we would go around the room stating our name, our date of entry, and a list of things for which we were grateful for.

Then we chanted the philosophy, a drawn out mission statement.

We did this EveryDay | *All day long.*

What in the fuck was a *gratitude*?
And how, for fuck's sake does one get *"grateful"*?

TWO DAYS A WEEK FOR AN HOUR.

A drug treatment counselor named Richard would come into our classroom and lecture us on dope+alcohol. He was a sincere and caring man, a rarity in that type environment.

We sat once for a personal session and spoke rather candidly. He seemed to understand me a little better than I did.

I didn't have many friends.
It was lonely.

It's not that I missed my old life.
I didn't even know what a life was.

I cried a lot those first thirty days. I cried for myself, for all the things I thought I'd lost.

I didn't know it yet.
But I had to lose so I could win.

I knew that after getting a minute glimpse of Truth I could never again live the way I had.

My problem: I knew no other way to live.

When you tell the same lie over and over and over ++||— *Again* —
For so many years you've told and retold this lie to yourself. Everything is based on lies — *You just don't know when it becomes safe to stop lying and finally tell Truth.*

AND THERE SAT I.

The sum of all of my best efforts netted me a seat in a room of dopers and left me on the-balls-of-myAss. No worldly possessions save the aforementioned camo t-shirt— *It wasn't even a nice one.*

Stripped of everything, you become forced to take a long hard look at yourself — *I had to accept myself for who and what I was, or I would never be able to grow and develop my true potential.*

Here's the thing — I lacked humility.

DICTIONARY.COM DEFINES "HUMBLE" AS:

hum•ble Pronunciation [huhm-buhl, uhm-]

—adjective

1. not proud or arrogant; modest: to be humble although successful.

2. having a feeling of insignificance, inferiority, subservience, etc.: In the presence of so many world-famous writers I felt very humble.

3. low in rank, importance, status, quality, etc.; lowly: of humble origin; a humble home.

4. courteously respectful: In my humble opinion you are wrong.

5. low in height, level, etc.; small in size: a humble member of the galaxy.

—verb (used with object)

6. to lower in condition, importance, or dignity; abase.

7. to destroy the independence, power, or will of.

8. to make meek: to humble one's heart.

Man, that sucks!

Reading that I wondered why anyone would actually *want* to be humble | Well, definition #1 isn't that bad.

Here's what humility means to me.
Humility: Being one among many, an extension of my fellow man.
Not being any better or any worse than my fellows.
The same yet different.

Humility is more often than not confused with humiliation. Some of us, unfortunately have had to learn our humility through humiliation | *Some of us,* meaning me.

Great news about a TC.
The humiliations supply room is stocked up full.
There are *never* shortages.

> A TC is designed to break you down.
> Build you back up, and then break you down again.
> Go ahead and ask me how | *Humiliation.*

I moved from A-dorm into B-dorm after thirty-one days of newcomer orientation.

B-dorm, located on the other side of the building, housed a majority of the male residents. A long narrow T-shaped hallway led into private units that housed two or three men each.

I was assigned work on a line-out sheet that was updated daily and placed in the cafeteria every night. The facility held contracts with local businesses, a few very large organizations, and sports complexes. Work consisted mostly of menial|manual labor jobs and humiliating functions that nobody else in the whole world wanted any part of | I will list some examples shortly.

THE PROSPECT OF WORK HORRIFIED ME.

My entire employment history consisted of criminal activity. I'd never worked an honest day in my life.

At the TC, there wasn't a choice — If I didn't work, they'd kick me out the facility. According to the deal I signed, failure to complete the "treatment" regimen would bring about full punitive damages, which ranged anywhere from two to twenty years in the clink. The upside was that after full terming all the stipulations including the probationary period, all charges would be expunged from my record.

LEGITIMATE JOB #1 CONSISTED OF "CLEANING OUT" A SPORTING FACILITY.

White vans would drive nine residents to the massive stadium immediately after the games, where we would walk up and down the bleachers with blowers attached to our backsides, blowing all the trash to the very bottom. Then someone would come with a big broom and trash bags to clean up the debris.

So reading this you might say to yourself:

That doesn't sound that bad — You'll be pleased to know, my wonderful reader | It was terrible.

<small>PICTURE THIS IS YOUR MIND'S EYE:</small>

Your local football stadium before a game.

Imagine to yourself how sanitized the entire place looks, from the confection to the commodes.

Now if you can, try to envision that same stadium after a game, full of empty beer cans, peanut shavings, partial eaten hot dogs, the occasional used condom, all sorts of wonderful ooze and slimy substances clinging on to the concrete, attaching to the stairs and the backside of the seats.

Somebody had to clean spotless this amazing mess.

There were nine poor wretched somebodies, me included.

We cleaned mostly bear handed as plastic gloves would just end up sticking to the stuff that was well... already sticky. And the delightful blowers that we wore. They were antiques that leaked gasoline and ran so hot that their outlines burned themselves into our backsides. Occasionally, we were required to assemble then disassemble the bleachers.

That was amazing fun.

The entire process took about nine hours. Since I was the new guy, before we left, I got to disinfect the toilet — I got to clean up all the puke and diarrhea.

<small>PROBABLY THE WORST JOB OF ALL:</small>

We would have to roll out plastic snap-together flooring inside a large bubble where the athletes trained for their games. Every spool of plastic floor weighed about four-hundred pounds. It would take all nine of us to roll out the floor and if we didn't do it perfectly it wouldn't snap together right, we'd have to roll it back up and do it again. It took more than thirty spools to cover the entire Astroturf.

This was a backbreacking|spinetingling process that usually took no less ten hours, sometimes twelve-fourteen. The nine-man crew that rolled it out would be the same unlucky nine that would have to roll it back up.

Rolling it up was trice as hard as rolling it out.

All residents going out to contract services work were issued a brown lunch bag with two stale sandwiches, a warm caffeine-free diet coke, and a rotten cookie. All the food we ate was procured as a donation from the local food bank—most of it was out-of-date stale.

There were other jobs.

Most involved either getting shit and piss on me or enormous trash bags filled with street-butter busting all over my face.

I WAS FINALLY ABLE TO REALIZE HOW HARD MOST PEOPLE HAD TO WORK.
Long, tough, grueling hours at jobs they hated, just so they could feed their families, and on the rare occasion go and snack on popcorn at the picture show.

The same people I'd taken advantage of all my life.

WE WORKED SEVEN DAYS A WEEK.
If we weren't outside working, there was always something to be

done around the facility. The facility charged twenty dollars an hour for our labor and kept all that money for the cost of our "treatment."

The treatment itself — We were only granted that wonderful pleasure after a long day of spine-tingling labor.

I didn't know how to behave very well.
I was called into operations almost every night.

Most of the trouble I got into was over women and squares. They kept all the women in C-dorm. Relationships weren't permitted amongst the men and women in the facility — They happened anyway. Sharing cigarettes wasn't allowed either. What you had was what you had — Thirteen packs a month doesn't last very long for dope-fiends needin' to get their lungs right. We weren't allowed to have any paper money — *Plenty of us did.*

THE FIRST RULE INFRACTION WOULD RESULT IN A "VERBAL."

A verbal was a lecture on why that particular conduct was wrong. If the problem persisted, it became a behavior, and the "treatment" would increase in severity.

Here are some examples of the punishments:

500-10,000 word essays due the following morning before work. Having to carry around a giant clock, which told everyone you had a problem with being late on the floor. The person wearing a massive set of keys around their neck wasn't allowed to communicate with anybody in the facility.

Wearing signs around your neck with cute little saying like:

"I'm a dope-fiend who can't shut my mouth."
"I don't know how to control myself."
"Ask me why I'm such an idiot."

"Ask me why I wet my bed."
"Ask me why I play with myself,"
et cetera.

A "full physical" was the most severe method of punishment.
They called this form of treatment a "learning experience."

Full physical means that they shave your head bald and you're made to wear a pantyhose around the top of your head and a yellow t-shirt. Your entire day is spent in the kitchen where you were instructed to "plug in" (recite the philosophy over and over).

If you stayed misbehaving in the kitchen, they'd make you do something special like: Clean a pot till further notice. Stand and face a wall from house open till house close (9AM-11PM). "Scrubs"— A barbaric form of punishment where you're made to get on your knees and scrub one floor tile with a toothbrush until further notice. It's devastating on the knees and I've seen it put people in the hospital.

95% of the facility's residents got there the same way I did.
Required by the courts to complete the program.

The other 5% were indigents who really didn't care what happened to them as long as they kept getting three hots and a cot.

Much of those required to be in treatment were looking at heavy prison time if they didn't complete the program.The community supervisor (paid employee) dangled this fact over our heads. It was his free-pass to do whatever the fuck he wanted with us.

The degradation was often too much for anyone to bear.

I saw people looking at ninety-nine calendars walk right out the front door and take their chances in prison. I probably would have left too—*if I had anywhere to go*—Or any money to get me there.

My first full physical was over cigarettes.
I asked a female for a square, she relayed it.
I got my head shaved and two weeks in the kitchen.

Once you're in the kitchen, it's tough getting out.

I got caught trading cigarettes, then got into a "contract" with a female. Contract meaning we got caught fucking in the staircase. "Contract" is TC speak for a negative agreement between one or more persons. An example: You bought dope from your dealer, you're in a contract with him. You stole underwear from one of the other residents, you're in a contract with yourself.

I did three full physicals in row.

I was already a veteran by my third month in the facility, able to pilot through bad situations, and stay out of "getting into a wreck" (out of operations). I'll tell you the one that finally broke me down.

Staring at the kitchen wall all day.

I had kidney problems, you know, from all the pills and GeorgiVodka. I complained to Danny R., the community supervisor, about the pains. He thought I was faking, trying to weasel out of another day in the kitchen. Instead of getting medical attention, he ordered me face the wall from house open—house close.

I'm glad I did.

I had what many would call a moment of clarity looking to the wall. I saw my whole life in that wall | Past, present, and future.

I had nothing and was going nowhere.

If life was a video game, I certainly wouldn't be hitting the 'save' button. And if I was paying somebody to manage my life, I would have fired that motherfucker a long ways back.

I promised myself I would never go back to that dark place again.

I wanted a future.

I committed to changing my life.
funny | How could I change what I didn't have.

I never had a life.
I had an existence.
A slave to my own demons.
I roamed the earth looking for something.
I didn't know what, but I was ready to take yours in the meantime.
One of the soulless vampire creatures:
Trapped inside their own greed.

I finally understood:
Change is possible only if I change by reason of my own desire, or the learning and change will never be permanent.

After that day I stopped misbehaving.

MY FIFTH MONTH AT THE FACILITY.

They made me a senior Expediter, and I was moved into D-dorm. Only upper-structure residents (prisoners) lived in D-dorm. The rooms were all small, single-person occupancy with their own commode — They granted a bit of privacy.

Although Expediter isn't upper-structure, I was pretty much a guarantee for Operations Manager. I stayed through every piece of *"treatment"* the TC was capable of producing.

That was the program's real slogan "Just Stay."

Willing to do anything, I stayed, hoping I would come out better at the end of it. It earned me respect among the newcomers and the older members. By that time, *I was an older member.* Truth was, I'd just become a better manipulator. That's what a place like that really teaches you.

++||— How to hide it better —

The whole logic is painfully flawed.

It's full of cynically hateful revenge tactics that dehumanize your emotions — That's how did they did me when I was a newcomer. Now I was expected to pass it back.

There was no real treatment there.
I mean c'mon | *The shit was make-believe.*

Where in the real world are you can gonna tell your drunk co-worker: "You see all that drinking you're doing? Well you can't be doing that on this floor." Or the youngblood who's about to hold you up at knife-point: "Put that knife away and stay on top of that." It may work well in a controlled environment, but in the real world — It's TomFoolery.

Sometimes "graduates", (people who completed all three phases of the TC) would come back and lecture us on how wonderful their lives were after completion. What they didn't tell you; 90% of graduates went back to doing dope the minute they walked out of there. Out of the three-hundred plus people who were there during my stay, only two that I know of are sober today.

One, if I don't count myself.

There were many abuses of the rules — Residents figured out how to manipulate the rules to work for them. I lived life as a master manipulator and I'd be GodDamned to do it again.

SIX MONTHS INTO THE PROGRAM.

I had just signed paperwork to be the new Operations Manager. I'd been through every dehumanizing piece of nastiness that the place had to offer. Now it was my duty to pass it on to the younger members. By the time most got into upper structure, they were glad to do it. It was like sweet revenge for them. That's how it worked, and I wanted no part of it.

I got everything I needed from that place, now it was time to leave the rest behind. With only two months left, I checked myself of out of the facility.

I would love nothing more than to foul-mouth the TC.
To tell all y'all what type of piece of shit it was.
How it did nothing for me.

Unfortunately, I cannot.

It gave me some good sober time, allowing me to put things into perspective. It showed me that if you sober-up a car-thief, all you have is a sober car-thief. It showed me examples of exactly who I didn't want to be.

Ultimately, it taught me some gratitude.

It was the middle of the day of my fifth month.

About two dozen of us were working a contract service job, in the parking lot of a sporting facility that I first felt gratitude.

This particular piece of unpleasantness involved changing out huge plate tiles of Astroturf. It was our job to carry the incredibly heavy plates out of the stadium, take them apart, then give them a complete overhaul before reassembling and putting them back where they belonged. It was a tedious process often requiring a fourteen-hour workday. When we unpacked our lunches, we each found a slice of cheese with our sandwiches.

I hadn't tasted cheese in more than seven months.
I didn't expect any cheese | *We never got any.*

Suddenly, an unexpected warm feeling of undeserved bliss filled my core. Elation over something that would be utterly insignificant to most meant the world to me—*Gratitude*—I made sure to never forget that feeling.

Gratitude:
Knowing that I don't have to do anything — *I get to do it.*

I came out of there knowing for the first time in my life:
If you don't stand for something:
++||— *You'll fall for anything —*

I CALLED BORIS, MY ONLY SLC CONTACT, TO PICK ME UP AT THE DOOR.
It was a violation of my stipulations, but I was prepared for it.

I knew it would all work out | *It did.*

Boris took me to a hotel, near his office, in an affluent wealthy area of town. He left me with a thousand dollars in cash and the keys to his old pickup.

I contacted my lawyer the following morning and he set an appointment with the judge to reconsider my deal. In meantime, he told me to find work, a place to live and to immediately attend AA meetings. Boris easily set me into an apartment in the same area. He was a real estate broker, that's what he did. He also fixed up a job in his office that entailed me doing a whole lot of nothing. It was a good life he had, selling real estate, it was 100% legit and made him large sacks of green money.

I got to thinking I might do the same.

I ATTENDED MY FIRST AA MEETING IN MAY OF '05.

I always thought Alcoholics Anonymous was for homeless salvation-army types who lived under bridges. I sat down in the back corner of an open discussion and listened. People like me and some not so much like me, faced the same day2day struggles I had been challenged with my entire life.

I came to that meeting hoping to stay out of prison.

I needed to stay sober but wasn't convinced that anyone there really knew how. The environment I was coming out of everybody was a liar. How was this going to be any different? In truth, I didn't have a choice. Law enforcement required me to go meetings. So I went with no expectations | Just hope.

Hope: A supreme faith that if I continue to walk with my right foot forward, 1 foot after the next | All things become possible.

That very fist AA meeting I attended: What I saw and what I heard, it was Truth.

I resolved to return the following day.

In the following weeks, everything worked out just how it was supposed to. After meeting with the judge, my lawyer was able to amend my stipulations to show that I'd completed the treatment program as prescribed by the courts.

I saw AA working for others.
I continued to attend AA meetings.

Actually, what I did was submerge myself into the program of Alcoholics Anonymous. I didn't work much at Boris's company. Instead, I attended three meeting a day for my first year. I cleaned ashtrays. I scrubbed toilets. I mopped floors. I hung around talking to every old-timer that would listen to me. I looked at how their lives had changed; how they had recovered from a hopeless state of incomprehensible demoralization. Know why it's incomprehensible?

> Because it's *my* demoralization
> And *you* can't possibly comprehend it.

One of my main problems:

I was still suffering from terminal uniqueness. My story was much worse than anyone's — *I was just too far gone.*

> I still didn't think it would work for me.

But after my soul returned back from the black|darkness of the forever lost, I was willing to try just about anything

The next day I found, a man with great convictions and a simple faith. A spiritual man who would be able to see past my transgressions and foster courage and character. I asked him to help me become more like himself and together we got right to working the twelve steps of Alcoholics Anonymous.

You wanna know why it's called "working" the steps?

It could be called "taking" the steps.

> It's called "working the steps" because it's work.
> No alcoholic|dope-fiend wants to work.
> We all want something for nothing.

That's the True nature of my illness.

I feel as though I'm entitled|deserve everything in the whole fucking universe. Why should I have to work for anything? These fools here, they must not know what the fuck I am?

> Maybe *they* have to work | I'm different.

Nope, no real alcoholic wants to work because work is hard.

It requires faith enough to know that the only things worth having are ones that are earned.

Like

—|| ⚐ ||— **WISDOM** —|| ⚐ ||—

HERE'S THE THING ABOUT WORK | AT THE END OF A JOB YOU GET PAID.

The payoff: Joy. Happiness. Serenity. Peace. Comfort in my own skin. I got all of these but only *after* having worked for each and every one of them. I got all of these *only* after having *worked my entire ass off* for each one. One at a time | 1x1. And I'm *no different* than *any of you.*

The way I see it today:
If you want the rainbow, you're gonna need to install the rain.

I used to think myself *special* — That I was too cool, too smart, too savvy, too handsome, too bright, too talented for any of that terrible stuff that *they* said would happen, too happen to *me. Shit* | I know now that I'm no different from any other pain-old, average, garden variety addict who loves to install dope in his bloodstream. And every last little bit of ugly *they* said would happen: Well it not only happened — It happened *exactly* like they said it would.

Know why I love dope+alcohol? I love the effect.

I love how the world looks when I'm fucked up on it. *Doesn't matter if it's better or worse* | Just different.

I'M A PICKLE | A PICKLE STARTED OUT LIFE AS A CUCUMBER.

Then someone threw it in a jar and added some salt water. Enough time went by for it to marinade and the cucumber morphed into a pickle. Once the process completes it can't ever go back to being a cucumber, it will always be a pickle | No matter what.

Today, I'm alright with that.
I don't even *really know* what a pickle really is.

I'm alright with that too.
I just know I'm a pickle and that's just the way it is.

I SAT DOWN WITH THAT SPIRITUAL MAN OF GREAT CONVICTION.

That same one that I mentioned earlier (in AA we call that a sponsor), after having worked the steps, and told him exactly what I wanted out of life, then how I planned to get it.

He just nodded and smiled.

I guess after more than thirty years of sobriety, you learn how to deal with bullshit like mine a little better than most.

The last Saturday of September 2005.
I picked up my one-year sobriety chip.
On my own| I couldn't have stayed sober for a day.

Shortly after my one-year birthday.
I met with my sponsor and informed him of all the things I thought I wanted out of life... they weren't really what I wanted at all. You wanna know what this fucker said to me.

"I already knew that, Gary."

Boy did I get hot. "I thought you were my main AceBoone, my mainhomeboy#1. You're supposed to be out there cuttin' it up for me.

How come you didn't tell me then?" I demanded. "Because I wanted God to tell you," he replied.

I can't fault him for being right.

I WOULD LIKE TO TAKE A MOMENT TO ADDRESS THE ISSUE OF GOD.

You want to know about *my* God, fair enough | Come holler at me. We can argue Jesus, Buddha, The Devil. We can talk about the Devine Feminine, the Source Field. You and I, we can discuss reincarnation. The wheel of Karma. We can talk about all and any holy and spiritual matters of the utmost importance.

I'll be glad to take you through what I know and I don't.

The reality is | *My* concept of God doesn't have to look anything like *yours*. What I believe God to be has absolutely no bearing on the facts that's I presented you.

Facts are facts | God is God.
One has nary a thing to do with the other.

I know exactly what you're thinking right about now—this Gary fella he's gotta be a couple slices short of pizza|pie. How can he possibly talk to me about God when he has no idea about the God that I worship. The God that I believe in is far superior, much more|better, than Gary's pathetic God. You know what, that may be very well True | *Or it might not.*

Truth is Truth.
What happened to me when I took the long-nap | Truth.
The wisdom I was granted upon my return | Truth.

A lucky few of us come into the world already knowing Truth. For the rest us, we need to discover it for ourselves. Most of my concepts have evolved the longer I've stayed sober — God in particular.

Still, I don't know much about God.
Real talk | I still *don't know much* of *anything at all.*
The whole thing doesn't make much sense to me none whatever.

THIS WORLD *will never be my home.*

The only thing that's really changed is that *anything* making sense is no longer a requirement for me to know who I am as a man, who I am as a person, who am as I being of eternal light.

⊨ Our souls never die ⊨

The only thing I'm sure of is that God can do *all things* and all this shit down here — *Everything* — is not my property.

I just get to use it for a quick little while.

Truth: God's grace and love brought me back to His world when by all rights I deserved death more than life.
Now I have a debt to pay — *More like an obligation.* I have now become obliged to practice my convictions and too never forget what it took for me to get RightHere|RightNow —|— *This Moment* —|— It's all we really have. Yesterday's gone and tomorrow might never make it.

INTEGRITY IS SOMETIMES A PAINFUL ROAD.
Pain is a part of life. If we weren't supposed to feel pain we never would have had the receptors installed — Misery *is optional.*

I don't expect it to be an easy journey.

After having lived a life of exploiting weakness and finding shortcuts. Easy is something I no longer put much value into.

Experience warns me that easy is seldom cheap. My cost for easy has been very high.

I'VE PAID FOR my EASY
— ♠ — In Spades — ♠ —

Truth be told: I don't expect anything.

I don't expect to have a warm bed tonight, or for my shoes to fit, or for my truck to start when I turn the ignition, or for my truck to even be there when I walk out my home.

Today I have no expectations | I merely have a preference. I would prefer my socks to be clean. For my house to be standing in the same place it was before I left for the store. But if none of the happens—it *wouldn't bother me* a lick—I didn't expect it to.

I'M FIXIN' TO DROP Y'ALL A LITTLE YODA WISDOM:

Expectations lead to resentment.
Which leades to jealousy.
Jealousy leads to fear.
That always leads to hate.
And hate *leads to the dark side.*

Next thing you know, I'm holding GeorgiVodka and a burner (or in Yoda's case a lightsaber) wondering what the fuck happened.

No sir | *Not me.*
Not on my watch.

My sobriety is my golden treasure.

I chase after my sobriety the same way I chased after my dope. *The same way I chased after* that next big score. If it was three in the morning and I was fresh out of YaY, the dopeman wouldn't answer, and all the liquor stores were shut—that never stopped me. I'd put on my Timmy's, started up my auto, and got to looking for my next dose. I couldn't be stopped until I found it.

That's the same way I treat my sobriety.
Like the motherfuckin Juggernaut:
++||— Nothing can stop it —

I know now for certain I never have to live that way again.
But all of that is contingent upon the maintenance of my spiritual condition — *A condition that I need to maintain on a daily basis.*

That's all we really have y'all.
—|— 1day —|—

Every time someone got hurt, I went jail, or I smelled gunsmoke. *Every single time*, Alcohol and dope were painted on the canvas. They were only a symptom of my real problem. The three pounds of dense matter that's between my ears | Thats my problem#1: ME

I've got the big house, new truck, and a great job.

I never came to AA and stayed sober for any of that.
—|— I got it though —|—
I didn't come to AA and stay sober to learn a trade.
—|— I did though —|—

I never even had to ask.

GOD DOES HAVE A SENSE OF HUMOR.
I work a job that *I swore I would never do.* I'm happier doing this work than any work I have done in my life. I'm not great at it. After much practice, I'm just OK

. . .

ANOTHER INTIMATE SECRET:

I never did anything in my entire life that I was just OK at.

I *only* did things *I knew I was excellent at.* I needed people to take notice and sing praises of my greatness.

I demanded to be noticed because *I was special* and that meant that I was better than *you* — I now realize that *the nature of my being depends upon the depth of my character and I can only find peace and happiness when I have given my best to the task at hand.*

Today | I can be OK *with being just* OK.

MY LIFE TODAY ISN'T THE LIFE I EVER HAVE IMAGINED MYSELF HAVING.

I never would have asked for such a life.

It's a beautiful one filled with friends, family, and love.

True friends, not the fair-weather type I'd been dealing with all my life. I'm able to be gentle and kind with them. With some help, I learned how to do that.

I don't have to hide who I really am anymore.

I no longer have *anything to hide.*

NOVEMBER OF '06.

That same hateful judge that I was for sure would lock me up for the rest of forever—*same judge*—let me full-term my probation early. In the state of Utah, I'm no longer a felon.

I'll tell you what's more.

New York state has been playing catch-up for years, trying to input their criminal records. By the time they got to mine, the building it was kept in burned down. God, Spirit, אלוהים, Allah, however you see your Devine Creator. Yah, That same one, went ahead and burned down a building —|— *Just for me* —|—

I look in the mirror and don't recognize the person I see.
Gary dropped his Gunz that rainy September day.
++||— I'm no longer *Gary "Gunz" Govich* —
Now, I'm just plain old Gary.

YOU WANNA KNOW WHO I AM?
I'm the guy at the supermarket buying ham and eggs.
I'm the fellow you let into your home to practice his trade.
I'm on that Harley you passed on the interstate.
I'm sitting in the front row of your local AA club.
I'm the guy smiling to greet you at Walmart.
I'm with my little boy in front of you in line at the picture show.
I helped you pick out paint color at Sherwin Williams.
I hand-made your bacon cheeseburger at Wendy's.

I'M YOU — I'll tell you something else.

As much you may not like it — YOU'RE ME.

I KNOW MY WORDS HAVE REACHED YOU IN A SAFE AND TIMELY FASHION.
Exactly the way *they were supposed to.*

Please | Take them same way you take your coffee.

We will meet someday, you and I.
No masks | No disguises — *the* **True** *we*

Of that I am certain.

Until then: May God bless you.
May God forever grant you splendor and peace.
May God keep you and always hold you in his countenance.

ThankYou.

I.

To my Mother and Father | No words of mine *can* **EVER** *Thank You.*

If not for the love and nurturing care of J|D G. this would never have happened. They believed in this project, *in me*, when the people closest made a shit on me — *They didn't even know me.*

I would like to take a moment and thank my loving wife N|S.

This 10th Anniversary edition would never have been a reality without your sacrifices. You have made me a much better me — No matter what *I will always love you.*

To my LittleMainHomeboy#1 D|J.

I used to think you were an empty cup that I was responsible for filling up. Now I just have fun watching you make it. I hope that one day you might read these words and discover something that I couldn't.

I want to especially thank M|C.

I must have sent this thing out to a baker's dozen editors. Nobody got it. Everyone wanted to twist it around, conform it to what the world considers 'the norm'. You are the only one who could take something like this and make it better. Really, *you're the only one.* You understand struggle. That's what makes you beautiful.

I am so grateful that you decided to be a part of this S|W.

Your art is compelling and powerful. The value it adds to this project is immeasurable. Most artists of your talent are lazy braggarts or too afraid for their art to actually touch people. You're the real thing, fearless and bold, I am proud to know you.

To my beautiful reader:

If I can change | We all can change together.

And that to me, it's worth more *than a billion dollars.*

Look what I done in my life
I had to count and count it again to make sure the money was right
My enemies wanna be friends with my other enemies
I don't let it get to me
They love to talk
Me I'm just done in a hype
Me I'm just Done... done... done...
——— *DONE* ———
-Drake

I would very much like to take this opportunity *to thank you* for allowing me to share with you my most valuable words.

The creation of this tenth anniversary edition brings with it a victory hard won. *We get so very few of those in our lives.* It's only for you, my beloved reader, that I agreed to raise up my sword. And it is only because you granted me your favor that success was possible.

This honor you have permitted me has substantiated the difficult choices that were required for me to bring to you my impassioned words in the exact way they were intended for you to look at them. *And the knowledge that my words have touched you* if even in small ways makes well worth the rigorously winter journey those words have made to reach their destination. That honor has not been taken for granted — I will *only* accept it with the deepest of thanks, for you have given me the ability to present to you now my everything.

It brings me gladness remarkable to give back to you that which you first gave me.

At work a few days ago, during our lunch break, the lead man at one of my worksites glanced into my truck as I jotted notes for my next work. He knocked on my window and asked: "Is this how you write books? Is that what you do? Write down whatever comes to your head and just make a book out of it?" My reply "Sure, yeah that's how I do it".

The reality—*in this life*—in this particular timeline and especially in this world full of nothing—nothing is ever as it appears. I very much wanted to tell this man the truth. It was all I could do to keep myself from exposing what it really takes to create anything of personal value. In fact, I may have, if I felt he would have understood.

Writing a book is surprisingly easy. Every one of us has a story to tell, every single soul on this planet has endured, suffered, overcame, stood, fallen down, then stood back up again. We enjoy tales of courage—the story of immovably bold bravery. All of us—myself included—absorb the words of such stories. They enter through our mind's eye and flow to our hearts, and those stories become tales of our own battle, the only real battle—*bad against good*. Whatever the outcome we are able to comprehend new meanings, gain relief from old hatreds, and acquire greater understanding of struggle and conquest. All it really takes to author a work of any kind is a little bit of stick-to-it-ness and a fair amount of patience. The writing part doesn't make a shit whether a piece is good, bad, or mediocre. It isn't even the story that matters as much as the effort.

Last night, it was about two a.m. My wife and I were having trouble sleeping, so we scoured various streaming services in search of something to keep our minds occupied. I normally don't look at the news; it mostly consists of depressing prejudiced bullshit. We searched on YouTube for interesting content, and we stumble on a Vice news report. For those of y'all that don't know what Vice News is, it's an HBO-sponsored program that airs nightly and presents "unbiased and underreported" news. The unbiased part I tend to disagree with, but the underreported part is what my wife and I are fascinated by — This particular half-hour report focused on a gentleman named David Fussell. He's a bloke who hails from London

England and has been dubbed "The Homeless Film Director"—this was something both of us had to have a look at.

David was your friendly neighborhood Englishman who ended up living on the street for several years. He wasn't a dopefiend or an alcoholic or (from what I could surmise) an evil-natured person. He was about as ordinary as Earl Grey tea and Shepard's Pie. Well, except, of course, for the exception. David Fussell had a dream that he couldn't let go of. David Fussell wanted—*needed*—to create a horror movie.

This horror movie making business had swirled around in his head for years, and he believed beyond the shadow of a doubt that his film was unique—*remarkable*—he understood that only he could be the person to see it bear fruit and was convinced that his film would bring satisfaction and add value to people's lives.

So David got to making his movie. Unfortunately, poor ole' David soon come upon the crossroads. Live long enough in this world and you'll come upon it: *How the fuck do I afford to buy groceries, pay for housing, keep the lights on, put diapers on my seed?* How do I keep a job and chase down my dream?

By design, the world we live in requires us to break our asses to make the elite, the 1percent, the ruling class whatever the handlers call themselves in this cycle even richer. So we occupy our minds with HBO and pop music. As long as the game is on telly and they bring us our steak sandwich at Applebee's we convince ourselves not to look at the truth—*the one we all know what it is*— We gotta wear ourselves down because if we take a break, maybe we'll have time to think. To understand that if we get off that hamster wheel, we're done for. Homeless—backpack-shopping cart-popup tent—*all of it.*

We're given just enough to afford to scrape by. To not stir up trouble. The few of us who decide to shut off our imaginations and study hard, get that master's degree, do the doctorate—we lock ourselves in *all the way.* Once we complete that long path, we're strapped with an enormous amount of debt from student loans and we get to begin our lives at the bottom of the pile. *Like crabs in a bucket.* Those that push—smash—bully—force their way to the top are rewarded with a luxury vehicle, one small vacation per year, and sometimes a modest retirement. Those who don't, usually sit at their terminals and at the hint of trouble hide under their desks then sneak off to take the command bus back home—*just to do it all over again*—they are usually rewarded with a slightly less luxurious vehicle, one small vacation per year, and sometimes a modest retirement.

I'm not saying there's something wrong with traveling that road. It's the path most traveled—it works for the majority of people. Most of us feel like we just don't have a choice. We've got people counting on us to make "smart" decisions. I have intimate relationships with many who traverse this path. They are invariably good-natured and wonderful souls. They provide for their families. They give up their own desires to ensure their loved ones' needs are met and create the possibility for their next generation to chase after dreams that will never be their own. It takes tremendous character to lead that type of life, an altruistic life of sacrifice.

It's a perfect design. Flawless, really. The world requires us to view this selfless concession as admirable.

There are those of us as well, that see this as insanity.

They see right through the veil. To us it's plain as peanuts—this entire fucker is rigged from the start—they can't stand to play any part in it. We are taught to consider these souls freeloaders and vagrants. Upper structure deems them "useless eaters" and tries to either set them up on the government dole or conjure a circumstance where they can turn them into dopefiends. The end result of both scenarios being the same—total control. The way it's figured, they'll either conform or die pitiful and lonely. You find these wretches compiled into makeshift campsites, defecating on the streets of San Francisco, Lost Angeles, Seattle along with other "underreported" cities and townships. The bureaucracy has created a billion-dollar industry from their existence.

We all see it, yet all we can do about it is gawk, mouths wide open at the horror and inhumanity—*how can we do anything*—we ourselves are only a few months away from being them.

Then there's the rest us: In the scant time it's taken me to relay to you this correspondence, our numbers steadily diminish. We are the ones who provoke and defy this artificial construct.

RENEGADES || We are an exceptionally uncommon creature.

For some unfathomable reason we just cannot let go of our dreams. No matter what the cost or how disastrous the consequences, we refuse to relinquish our unambiguous vision in which that thing of our own creation is made manifest into this reality.

Society advances when its outcasts recognize their autonomy. The "losers", the "loners", the "fat kid with the coke bottle glasses"—these are the people who engender sweeping change within our world. From the dawn of recorded history, there's been this drive to make something significant out of almost nothing at all; the ability to rework discarded rubbish into beautiful artwork and tools of progress. All the things we take for granted, our entire modern world, was at one time some crazed imagining that grew into concrete thought, then became courageous action. The will to overcome the adversities of failure is what's given us air-conditioning, ice cream waffles, Michael Keaton as Batman, Ram trucks, and football stadiums.

All of the great pioneers Nicola Tesla, Henry Ford, David Icke, Frank Miller, the Wright Brothers—*they were renegades*. They refused to conform.

The establishment challenged their ideas, their peers thought them fools and surely they were mocked even as they made clear steps toward realizing their destiny. The esteem we carry for such people is far greater than that which we are mandated to hold for the toilers. What an insane duality | As a society supposedly consisting of educated cultured people we challenge and suppress anything that doesn't fit into our miniature square shaped box of normalcy.

By design it's near impossible to bring forth radical beauty or innovation. Everyone and everything in this environment is positioned to deter us, every mistake along the way is scrutinized, *we are ridiculed and mocked*—the oppression clouds our vision, makes us question our efforts and ultimately presses us just hard enough to concede and fall deep into the big letdown that, "I tried to warn you," you were doomed from the start would happen.

What really used to burn me up hellfire hot, the unbreakable ones—those who *will* Never *give it in*—they finally succeed and the world, which has discouraged and challenged them from the jump, applauds these people for their extraordinary genius.

That's got to be the most incredible what-the-fuck. The same folks that told you to get your head down out the clouds "No one will ever give shitɪ about your thing. You done got yourself into a wreck again. You need to move on kid, *this whole thing here*—it's just not for you." Yeah, those same son|ofa|motherfucks they get to be first to twittering how you were always boutit|boutit.

The tight embrace, the phony smile and y'all together one more again—up in the VIP. The pathetic spectacle would first confuse me and after a short while anger me. My only escape a dizzy drunk on warm vodka straight then reach for the Glock9milly.

That's exactly how it was before—staring down 25-Life—I hung myself in a padded jail cell with a pair of shit-stained pants.

Four minutes dead and still none of this anything seems right. The Truth — I don't even know if I returned to the place I came from. I do know I'm not angry anymore. I do know for certain that we are both, you and I, together right now, we are exactly where we're supposed to be.

Back to Dave the Englishman.

I'm looking at this homeless man on my television, I instantly jump inside his skin. I'm thinking now about what this man had to give just to pay the ante. For his chance to sit at the table, he gave them everything. All his chips just to play his one hand. This was an intelligent man. He knew the rules—*it's not like they even try to hide it*. The house always wins. Dave sat down anyway—I understand the cost of his sacrifice.

Early 2006, I was deeply in love with a woman I had been married to for years. I was an apprentice of my trade. I volunteered, working with troubled youngsters. I was learning the ingredients that turn a boy into a man. For the briefest moment, I enjoyed a peacefully simple yet meaningful life | Then I started writing.

The first key I pushed felt like I released the green Hulk monster. I began mashing the keys harder and harder then faster and faster.

A solid year of up staying up till 3 a.m. restless nights and back to work, tools out, 8 a.m. roll back up at 5 p.m. tireless days and the end was almost near.

Before I continue, for you to fully understand, I am compelled to share with you a quick story. I'll be brief and to the point.

It's a simple piece that I'm titling "The Story of Debbie."

Debbie was exceptionally pretty, not Vogue Magazine pretty, but she held a simple beauty. It was the kind that most men and even woman were naturally drawn toward. She had that girl next door, fly-fly-over-states beauty that they try to capture in margarine commercials. When you talked to her, you felt a comfortable softness, more like a tender understanding that Debbie would appreciate your heart and never take your hardships for granted — She was very easy to love.

Debbie began her career at a large Fortune 500 chemical company. And there she stayed. For thirty-five years, Debbie held a job at this prestigious outfit, before retiring, having kept the same position her entire career. I would continually wonder how she was able to do that. One Sunday, right after we left the church house, I had to ask her: "Debbie, how did you survive that job for all those years?" "Well that's just it," she said. "I survived." You see, Debbie was constantly worried about "losing her job" yet outlived numerous regime changes, multiple occasions of tyrannical managers, various reorganizations, and every single layoff. It's actually a really simple formula. All you have to do is stay under the radar. Never get noticed; never stick your neck out; never take a chance of any kind; never befriend an ally or forsake an enemy. Really, just do nothing. She recalled that sometimes she had to hide under her desk to avoid being noticed. She hated her job but felt trapped inside. Towards the end, the board of directors was so amused, they actually created a special position for Debbie. She got to come to work, relax in her spacious window office, lean back in her comfy recliner, and surf the web. Everyone could walk by, wave hello to Debbie, and simper. She was considered meaningless, something of a company mascot, a charming imbecile who had somehow managed to slip between the cracks — *Rather a sad tale*, the story of Debbie.

In my humble opinion | A person without a dream is like a car with no gasoline.

Ordinarily someone like Debbie would be a short amusement for my man parts and I would get right back to it. To me though, she was no ordinary someone. Debbie was my wife. I loved Debbie in the most reckless way; I held nothing back. She had my entire heart. Dangerous business for a renegade to carelessly expose the delicate parts of their essence to a Debbie.

November 2007 Thanksgiving weekend.

A few close friends had come to our home for a traditional family meal. I'll never forget the day. Early that September my manuscript was completed, soft-edited, queried, and had already received multiple requests for submission. I was very proud of my completed work—*I knew what it was*—There are things in this world that we just know. I was dumbfounded. These words could not possibly have been mine. The process of writing that first, semi-polished copy was a powerful and transformative one. Sometimes, When I read it to myself, I didn't even know how some of those words made it onto the page. Intuitively, I understood that any alteration would diminish the influence of my words, and that was something I could never allow.

We hadn't checked our mail for about a week.

I'm that guy mailmen hate. I let my box get stuffed so full that mail carriers have to invent ingenious ways to cram it inside, it becomes a game of Tetris just for them to do their jobs.

Inside that pile of junk was a letter from one of the more well-known publishers. They had received my completed manuscript and loved the story. In fact, they wanted to purchase it for fifty-thousand American dollars. Great news huh? Debbie thought it was the best thing she'd heard since they announced the seventh installment of

Harry Potter was finally available for purchase. I didn't think it was quite as good though. The fifty large came with a thick string tied into a pretty little bow. The deal was they would get my story—and once I accepted the money, I would give up all rights. I would get to go cash the check and they could do whatever to it | Chop it up, change it, shelf it, shred it. It would be theirs and could no longer be mine and would certainly no longer be yours.

Throughout many years of my life, and many terrible circumstances, whenever it was offered—*I took their money*—I was no longer for sale. Even if we desperately needed that money, I wouldn't have tooken it. Career Criminal was something created for you my dearest reader. I couldn't contaminate it with their money

I'll save you the rest of the details and take you right to the part not but two weeks later, just a few days before Christmas where I'm packing up a bag.

So really interesting fact: Every single one of our "friends"—*save one*—sided with Debbie. "You're a fool leaving alone that money, Gary. She's a good woman. You need to take that money and go on home." — Yep that.

The only motherfucker who gave me relief was a man that hardly knew me. His wife snatched up his newborn son and left him a few weeks prior. This man understood me—*a warrior*—he wouldn't sell them his dreams no matter the cost. And after two whole years of marriage, his wife, also, was about tired of waiting on his dreams. That was the second woman that ran him off. His heart was already hardened. He had an extra room about the size of prison cell he let me stay in rent free until either I tucked away my penis and went back to Debbie or mustered up enough strength to get the fuck back up.

March the following year.

I never went "home" and I was regaining the courage to poke my head back out. If you let yourself love someone that deeply and recklessly; Give them all of it, when they make that massive shit on your heart then tread all over your dreams—*it hurts so much it's hard to breathe.* I forced myself up. Left in my possession was valuable work I had been entrusted with and now obligated to bring to you.

In 2008 self-publishing was considered a novelty and mostly done for vanity works. '08 before Iuniverse sold to digesting Authors House, they were one of the most reputable self-publishing options available to indie authors. Right now, I can POD this tenth anniversary and immediately make both print and e-book available. It's a few clicks of the mouse and a few hundred dollars || Done.

In '08, bringing Career Criminal to print was almost four-thousand dollars. The e-book would cost an additional few thousand. Hiding from the world in my main homeboy's spare bedroom, money was a little tight. I was ready to go but six-hundred dollars short. I dialed my family—For sure they would understand. "We talked to your wife, Gary. Dumbass, you need to get that money right now. The fuck is wrong with you. Take that fifty before they change their minds, write you another story and go on home to your wife. Debbie's a damn good woman. She's waiting for you." And then —click—they hung up the phone.

I got that last seed money for Career Criminal from a person that barely knew me. Imagine you that if you can. Strangers, they had nary a horse in my race. They believed in the value of my cherished words enough to provide the final component. On the second day of November 2008 I was able to complete the task and bring you—as Promised—the first available printing of Career Criminal: My Life in the Russian Mob | Until the Day I Died. Epubs and Mobis weren't really a thing until after 2010. Amazon introduced KDP and made it simple to post e-books early 2011—April 2011 the digital version was up and running.

The next few years passed slowly, and in the meantime—you know why they call it "the meantime"—because it's mean and it's time. The former life I felt was so outstanding was swapped for something far more amazing | In 2012, movie offers hit my inbox.

I specifically instructed the company I published with to not give my information to anyone. A few persistent individuals got through. Among them a young film school graduate. I could sense the passion in his words—*I got that feeling*—then we spoke on the phone and that's when I knew for sure. This youngblood would make a blockbuster someday. I trusted him with my story.

Five full years passed, and the options I entrusted to Joe were about to expire. Two days before expiration, I got a call from Joe, He was no longer a fresh-out-of-school film student. With a few solid features under his belt he was finally ready to make the movie | The exact way he intended to.

I sold the same options twice with the guarantee that he would start filming within a few months. True to his word, "Caviar" started filming almost immediately and then, my dearest reader—real funny, I know you're gonna love this one here.

What number do you think was typed out on that movie check? Fifty||motherfuckin||thousand$$$$American. That, with the original option check made sixty—*but who's counting*—Ha Fuckin Ha.

So here we are. Like I said—RightNow|RightHere—*right where we are supposed to be.*

Happy ending time:

I get the most awesome—most beautiful—black belt badass wife Model2.0 and the bonus prize—the toughest little sonofafuck any daddy could hope for. This little brickhouse is twice the stubborn I ever was. He's the gremlin that eats cyanide spits out green motorbike acid then craps out ZyklonB, wipes his diaper pants all over your mirror then demands to look at Michael Keaton as Batman.

I Love him *like my Tavor loves select fire full auto mode.*

Okay, I know I shouldn't have. Before a back broken wet-eyed Gary Govich left his fully paid-for house penniless. I was able to work up just enough fuckyou to give Debbie my final prophecy "When they make this into a movie. Imma ride my Harley back by this house at 2a.m. smoke my tire enough to set your grass blazing and rev my pipes so loud I wake up every dog and set off every last alarm in this hamlet." I know, it was childish—*but I'll be* GodDamned—I felt like a young Sylvester Stallone the precise moment he knocked Clubber Lang the fuck out the box.

The best part of all: We get to give you the book you were supposed to get in the first place. *You did that* — Not me | YOU

And now Natalie, Mel, Stevie, Sampy and of course your most humble friend and narrator are honored to present to you, polished, pressed, fully loaded || And NEVER OverEasy.

Career Criminal: The Code of The Streets

Please | *Enjoy it with our compliments.*

None of that other shit matters—Thank you most of all for that.

Small bit of poetic justice; two weeks after my righteous partner's wife ran him off —His dream || The one that he'd been chasing for over twenty years—I watched him pull the letter out his mailbox. He got every single last bit of it—BOOM—an extraordinary victory, he was glowing gold like Bruce Leroy right after ShoNuff pulled his head out the soup and Bruce said, "*I am.*"

Just this morning we're riding our Harley SoftTail motorbikes:

Leathered out — chaps, biker boots–the kind with the chain through the heel. *I'm talking about*—leather Harley vests.

—||— OutlawRenegade1000 style —||—

It was the perfect sunny day — The wind felt wonderful as it tickled my chin and nose through the vents of my matte black full-face cover. We pulled into a small dining area to have our usual lunch at a popular gourmet food truck outpost about halfway into our ride.

The area itself was far from the main road and on Sunday mornings there weren't very many patrons. I enjoyed stopping there during our rides. *I was overcome with a strong feeling of peace.* I grabbed myself "The Cousin Vinny," a tasty homemade meatball submarine, dusted off my denims and we sat down.

After our meal we indulged on some of Nicaragua's finest—Padron 4000's. He'd picked up a box straight from the Padron factory a few days prior. We put our feet up on plastic lawn chairs and looked up to discover clouds that looked like icy crystals swirling across the pure blue sky. They delivered a seamless pattern of webs that shifted and then reformed back into other stunning mysterious shapes.

I grinned at my main-homeboy#1.

We chiefed on those stogies for a full hour and didn't speak word1 to each other | It was a sweet moment *for both of us.*

In the Land of the Blind — The OneEyedMan IS KING.
Question EVERYTHING.

And I sleep —And I dream of the person I might have been. And when I'll be free again—And I speak Like a someone who's been to the highest peaks. And then back again—And I swear—That my grass is greener than anyone's—Till I believe again—Then I wake—And the dream fades away —And I face the day—And then realize—That there's got to be some hero in me—There's got to be some hero in me— *Though sometimes it's so hard to see*—There's got to be some hero in we

—*Jefferey Gaines*

✲ In Loving Memory OF Pappy ✲